The
Ultimate
ROTTWEILER

Edited by
ANDREW BRACE

Photo courtesy of the ARDK.

RINGPRESS

Designed and Published by
Ringpress Books Ltd,
PO Box 8, Lydney, Gloucestershire GL15 6YD, United Kingdom

Discounts available for bulk orders
Contact the Special Sales Manager at
the above address. Telephone 01594 563800

First Published 1995
© 1995 RINGPRESS BOOKS

ISBN 1 86054 030 9

Printed in Hong Kong

Contents

Title page photograph: Finnish and Swedish Ch. Leonpold von Urbano.
Photo: courtesy Katriina Vuorieno.

The Contributors

The Ultimate Rottweiler is written by leading experts who have an unparalleled knowledge of Rottweilers.

ANDREW BRACE (EDITOR) has been involved in dogs all his life, breeding, showing and judging. He judges Working, Hound, Utility, and Toy Groups, plus Best in Show at Championship level, and is approved to award Challenge Certificates in some fifty breeds. He has written a specialist book on judging and writes regular columns for Britain's weekly newspaper, *Dog World*, as well as the USA's *Dog News* and Australia's *Oz Dog*.

LARRY ELSDEN: Larry has been involved with breeding and showing dogs in partnership with his wife, Judy, for over forty years. They own the Chesara prefix, which is known worldwide for its top-quality Rottweilers. They have made up some twenty Rottweiler Champions. Larry judges at Championship level; he has judged Rottweilers at Crufts, as well as travelling worldwide on judging appointments. He has been a member of the British Kennel Club for over twenty-five years and has served on most of the KC committees. A former Chairman of the Rottweiler Club and the British Rottweiler Association he writes on the History of the Breed (Chapter One), and gives an in-depth analysis of the Rottweiler Breed Standards (Chapter Nine).

DOROTHEA GRUENERWALD: Dorothea has owned Rottweilers, in partnership with her husband William since 1959. She bred her first litter in 1964, using her Von Gruenerwald prefix, and has since produced twenty-eight AKC Champions. She is an AKC judge, currently licensed to judge Rottweilers, Bernese Mountain Dogs and Australian Shepherds. Dorothea has written extensively on the breed for the past thirty years in such publications as *Dog World*, the *AKC Gazette*, and *The Rottweiler Quarterly*. She also served as editor of The American Rottweiler Club's Newsletter for ten years. In this book, Dorothea gives detailed coverage of the Rottweiler in North America (Chapter Seventeen).

BARBARA BUTLER: Barbara's Upend prefix was registered in 1944, and she has made up Champions in Rottweilers, Dobermanns, Miniature Bull Terriers, Deerhounds and Sussex Spaniels. Her first Rottweiler was acquired twenty-seven years ago, and since then she has made up six British Champions and twelve overseas Champions. Barbara, an International Championship judge, has always been actively involved in the working side of the breed. She has qualified home-breds at Working Trials, and other dogs of her breeding have worked herding cattle, carting, and as gundogs. In this book she writes about the Character of the Rottweiler (Chapter Two), Caring for a Puppy (Chapter Three), and Socialisation (Chapter Four).

ALISON BIGG BVetMed MRCVS: Alison, an expert in canine nutrition, qualified from the Royal Veterinary College, London, in 1987. After a short period in research, she entered a mixed practice in Gloucestershire where she worked for seven years. She has contributed the chapter on Diet and Nutrition (Chapter Five).

ROY HUNTER: Roy started his career as a police dog handler and was eventually promoted to being in charge of all operational dogs in London. In civilian life, Roy started a dog training club, and competed in Working Trials and Obedience. He became the chief instructor for the British Rottweiler Association, specialising in these two disciplines. Roy writes on Advanced Training (Chapter Seven).

KATE PINCHES: Kate first became involved with Rottweilers in the early 1970s and registered the Cuidado prefix in 1976. The kennel has since bred six British Rottweiler Champions, plus many overseas Champions. Kate judges the breed at Championship level, and is scheduled to judge at Crufts in 1996. In this book she writes on Breeding Rottweilers (Chapter Thirteen) and Rearing a Litter (Chapter Fourteen).

LIZ DUNHILL: The Fantasa prefix is well-known in Britain and overseas, and Liz's kennel is currently the most successful in the UK, taking the Rottweiler on to a new plane in terms of quality. Her prowess as a trainer and handler are legendary. In *The Ultimate Rottweiler*, Liz writes on The Show Ring (Chapter Ten), and The Rottweiler in the UK (Chapter Sixteen).

MARY MACPHAIL: Mary has bred, trained and exhibited Rottweilers for some thirty years under the Blackforest prefix. She is a much sought after specialist judge, and has judged Rottweilers in twelve different countries.. Mary has qualified five of her dogs in Working Trials and has had two Therapy dogs. She uses her vast knowledge of working with Rottweilers to write on Basic Training (Chapter Six) and The Working Rottweiler (Chapter Eight).

DR MALCOLM B. WILLIS is Senior Lecturer in Animal Breeding and Genetics in the Faculty of Agriculture at the University of Newcastle upon Tyne. He specialises in the study of genetics in relation to dogs, and is known worldwide for his books, articles, seminars and lectures. In this book he turns his attention to the genetic make-up of the Rottweiler (Chapter Twelve).

STEVE DEAN BVetMed, DVR, MRCVS: Steve has had twenty years' experience as a veterinarian. He is actively involved in the show world, breeding and exhibiting under the Tyrian prefix, and also judging at Championship level. However, he is best-known for his popular column in Britain's weekly newspaper, *Dog World*. In *The Ultimate Rottweiler* he writes on Health Care (Chapter Nineteen) and Breed Associated Diseases (Chapter Twenty).

Other contributions have come from HELEN READ (Australia), ALISON FRANKS (New Zealand), TONY ONG (Singapore), KATRIINA VUROINEN (Finland), DENYSE TUTT (South Africa) and CYNDY ORDMAN (Zimbabwe).

GERMANY

We are indebted to the Allgermeiner Deutscher Rottweiler Klub (ARDK) for their help with **THE ULTIMATE ROTTWEILER.**

German contributions have been co-ordinated by HANS-JURGEN EBERBACH, President of the ADRK, with material supplied by: HELMUT FREIBURG Richterobmann (Supervisory judge) ADRK and WILLI HEDTKE, Hauptzuchtwart (Chief Breed Warden) ADRK, who has special responsibility for Breed Problems.

Chapter One

HISTORY OF THE ROTTWEILER

ORIGINS

While it may be an attractive thought that the Rottweiler has a long and ancient history, with stories of the Roman Legions tramping through the Alpine passes accompanied by large black-and-tan dogs who fell out from the line of march in the Black Forest area, the truth is that we owe the Rottweiler to Germany and to German breeders operating at a very much later date than Roman times. It may or may not be true that the Mastiff-type dog, of which the Rottweiler is an example, originated in the Mediterranean area and spread from there into northern Europe. It probably got there a long time before the Romans, and the big Mastiff type was known in Britain and elsewhere in northern Europe long before the legions marched north.

However, the Rottweiler certainly has one link back to the Romans and that is in its name. Breeds of dogs acquire their names for many different reasons. Some are named after their function; a very small number after a person, often someone involved in their early development; but the vast majority take their name from a place or geographical area. The Rottweiler has taken its name from the town of Rottweil in southern Germany, and it is probably true to say that the fame of the town worldwide stems from the breed of dog which bears its name.

The region where Rottweil is situated was conquered by the Romans in 74AD who then made it an important trading and administrative centre. Rome lost control of the area about 260AD. The old Roman name of Arae Flaviae disappeared to be replaced by the name Rote Will, literally Red Villa after the red bricks and tiles used in its buildings. The name then evolved into Rottweil.

Over the centuries the town continued to develop as an administrative and commercial centre, and it is to the latter activity that we owe the Rottweiler. Cattle dealers from as far away as France, Switzerland and Hungary bought and sold their stock in the Rottweil cattle market, creating a need for a dog that could not only drive and control cattle that were probably half wild, but could also protect the cattle from predators, both human and animal. The herding and guarding of cattle, sheep and other stock was an important function of the dog in a peasant economy. It has been pointed out that there is often confusion between the "sheep herd" dogs and the "shepherd" dogs. While the function of the "sheep herd" was to drive and control stock, the "shepherd" dog has as his prime purpose the duty of safeguarding the stock from marauders. The thrifty peasant farmer who developed the ancestors of the Rottweiler looked for a dog that could combine both functions.

The need for such a dog was not unique to the Rottweil area. Other parts of Europe produced big, tough, courageous dogs for the same purpose. There were and are variations of coat, colour etc., but the basic function of the dog was the same. The Bouvier des Flandres, the Maremma, the Pyrenean and the group of Swiss mountain dogs are just a few of the many types produced for this purpose which became individual breeds. What is certain is that dog breeders, as such, go back much farther in history than any of the breeds which they eventually produced. Curiously, Britain with its long list of breeds for all purposes has not developed a native breed of

The Rottweiler bears little resemblance to other herding breeds, and shows a stronger resemblance to the Mastiff-type dogs, used as fighting dogs and guards.

Photo: Carol Ann Johnson.

this type. Methods of farming (and in particular large-scale sheep farming) produced breeds of the collie type which, while lacking the guarding ability of the heavier dogs, were more suitable for the task of working sheep, while the task of acting as a guard dog was left to breeds with no herding ability.

While the ability of the Rottweiler as a herding or droving dog cannot be denied, it is an interesting fact that both physically and mentally it is a very different type to the general concept of a herding breed. Hans Korn, generally considered to be one of the great experts on the breed, wrote in 1939 that the Rottweiler showed few of the characteristics of other cattle dogs and that it appeared to be far closer to the broad-mouthed Mastiff-type dogs used as fighting dogs and as guards. Korn was of the opinion that the original cattle dog, developed over the centuries, was modified by the introduction of a broad-mouthed breed, probably the Bullenbeiser, the ancestor of the Boxer.

This theory is given support by the fact that old illustrations of the Bullenbeiser show it with a "tiger striped" coat, one of the colours permitted in the first Rottweiler Standard. It is interesting to speculate when and why this introduction took place. While not suggesting that it was as late as the beginning of this century, it is a fact that illustrations of the breed at that time show a far more hound-like head and body than we expect in the Rottweiler today. Bearing in mind that it was about that date that the Rottweiler began to make his name as a police dog, one can only wonder.

THE SWISS THEORY
A variation on the possible origin of the Rottweiler is contained in a small book which is one of my Rottweiler treasures. Entitled *German Dogs in Word and Picture* by E. Von Otto Bensheim, it was published by the German Kennel Club in 1928. Although printed in Germany it is in English with the translation credited to a C. Charke M.A. To add a further thread to an already tangled skein, the dedication is to His Highness the Maharaja Dhiraj of Patiala. The book lists some twelve breeds giving their character, uses and a Standard. It uses the most elaborate and flowery language, and at times wanders off into matters of philosophy far removed from the subject of dogs. It makes a lengthy tale of the well-known story of the police Rottweiler who made a multiple arrest and would not allow Prince Henry of Prussia to give him a congratulatory pat until his handler sat down and removed his helmet. On the origin of the Rottweiler it suggests that its ancestors were the Swiss cowherds' dogs who, having brought the cattle down from the Swiss mountains to Rottweil, remained and flourished. It gives all credit to the German breeders saying "the rich and royal feeding placed at his disposal by a kindly force of circumstances, turned the comparatively weak Swiss dairyman's dog into a mighty and husky fellow." It is not an unreasonable theory that the Swiss dogs lie behind the Rottweiler and it is certainly probable that the Bernese Mountain Dog and the Rottweiler share some common ancestry. Most knowledgeable dog breeders will agree that a long-coated Rottweiler only needs some white patches to be a Bernese.

GEOGRAPHICAL INFLUENCES
There is really little benefit to be gained in speculation as to the original ancestors of the Rottweiler. A major factor is the relatively poor communications in the region. High in the mountain valleys each locality developed the dog that suited their needs. Any dog, including the rare animal from outside the immediate area that offered any chance of improvement, would be used to a considerable extent and as a result type tended to become fixed. This inaccessible and mountainous corner of Europe produced a disproportionately large number of the breeds that we know today, almost all of them multi-purpose, guarding and herding breeds. In general these breeds have a harsh, weather-resistant coat and sturdy bodies, and most of them are above

RIGHT: The Rottweiler was bred as a strong, sound dog, used for driving cattle and for protecting them against predators, both animal and human. Photo courtesy: Mary Macphail.

BELOW: Ch. Farwest's Arizona with Ellen Minturn in the USA. The herding instinct is still strong in the Rottweiler today. Photo courtesy: Ellen Minturn.

The first Rottweilers were expected to combine draught work with their duties as droving dogs and guards. Today, carting is popular worldwide.   Photo courtesy: Pamela Wilkinson Grant.

average size. By the Middle Ages the area around Rottweil had developed a dog not too dissimilar from the one we know today, although there was a long way to go before he became what we would recognise as a Rottweiler. However it is probable that he had already acquired the name and it is likely that the name existed long before the recognisable type. In fact the name was probably applied to a group of dogs of varying sizes, colours and abilities.

THE BUTCHER'S DOG
The name Rottweiler was often qualified by the title of "butcher's dog". There are two possible reasons for this. Firstly, butchers did not in the past have their meat delivered as a carcase ready for jointing. The old time butcher went out and bought cattle on the hoof and drove them home to his own abattoir, thus creating the need for a herding and droving dog. Secondly, there was the practice of bull baiting, a practice that had a practical and legal basis as well as providing a brutal spectacle for the local population. It was actually illegal to kill a bull that had not been baited by dogs. Firstly to let everyone know that a bull was being killed, so that the meat could not be sold as prime beef, and secondly because it was believed that meat from an animal that was killed after violent exercise would be more tender. A butcher would keep dogs for this purpose and it is obvious that such dogs needed to be both powerful and courageous.

COLOUR VARIATIONS
Another indication of the diverse background of the Rottweiler is the question of colour. Today we insist that the Rottweiler comes in one standard set of colours, black and tan without any white markings. This was by no means true in the past. The first Standard for the Rottweiler, written by Albert Kull in 1883, under the heading of colour said "Preferably and most commonly black with russet or yellow markings over the eyes, at the lips and on the inner and underside of the legs as well as on the bottom. Alternatively, black stripes on an ash grey background with yellow markings, plain red with black nose, or dark wolf grey with black head and saddle, but always with yellow markings. White markings on the chest and legs occur very frequently and are admissible if they are not too extensive."

By 1913 the Standard published by the International Rottweiler Club, of which more later, gave under colour: "Black with well defined russet or orange markings on the extremities, over the eyes and on the muzzle. Also brown with yellow markings, blue, or plain red with black mask and black line down the back."

In 1914 yet another Standard was issued listing under colour: "black with russet or yellow markings, occasionally orange with lighter markings. Small white markings on chest and belly are not faults but are not desirable."

It was not until 1921 that the Allgemeiner Deutscher Rottweiler Klub (ADRK) achieved overall control of the breed and finally settled the colour question with a Standard that demanded black with clearly defined mahogany to yellow markings, although it still accepted, but considered undesirable, small white markings on chest and belly. To emphasise the abandonment of all colours except black and tan the same Standard when listing faults says "the plain red Rottweiler which used to occur, though not very often, with a black or light mask or a black line down the back, as well as Rottweilers of other colours, blue or brown, are not recognised because of suspected cross breeding and the same applies to long coated Rottweilers." While I entirely agree with the desire to standardise on black and tan it was perhaps a little early to be quite so disparaging on the question of cross breeding. Furthermore, although we have eliminated the other colours we are still able to produce white spots and long coats at all too frequent intervals despite many years of selective breeding. In passing, it is of interest that the Dobermann, who is generally believed to have the Rottweiler amongst its forebears, can still produce coats of blue and brown. One almost constant theme running through the permissible colours of the early

Minzenhof Yazz, bred in Finland by Maijaliisa Rainesto, owned by Katja Hammar and Mika Reini-Kainen. In 1921 the Allgemeiner Deutscher Rottweiler Klub stipulated that Rottweilers must be black, with clearly-defined mahogany to yellow markings.

Photo courtesy: Katriina Vuorinen.

Am. Can. Ch. Cannon River's Oil Tanker CD TT: America's top winning Rottweiler in the show ring, with a total of 22 All Breed Best in Shows, 70 Group 1's and three Rottweiler Specialty Best in Shows.
Photo: Woodward.

Standards is the demand for tan markings. These markings occur in a very wide range of breeds from the Chihuahua up to breeds like the Rottweiler.

Whatever the breed the positioning of these markings, over the eyes, muzzle, chest, feet and bottom is the same. Although usually associated with a black main body colour the markings can occur with other main colours. Even the Sussex Spaniel with a main colour of golden liver can at times produce the tan markings as a slight variation of shade but still in the usual positions. Presumably the 1914 Rottweiler Standard listing as a possible colour "orange with lighter markings" would have looked rather similar.

As far as I know, there is no particular breed, type or place of origin that can claim to be the original source of the tan markings. The fact remains that they are genetically extremely dominant and we should perhaps be thankful that those who finalised the colour of the Rottweiler chose such an attractive combination.

Any attempt to look at the origin of the Rottweiler by a study of the colour variations is not going to get us very far. The colours given cover a vast range of alternatives and could suggest the infusion of a number of different breeds or perhaps more correctly types. The picture that does emerge is that "a good horse can be any colour" and that during the days when the Rottweiler began to make his name it was his courage, intelligence and strength that mattered rather than his appearance.

It is probable that the white markings have some significance with regard to temperament. In the ADRK publication *The Rottweiler in Word and Picture,* published in 1926, it is pointed out that in the past Rottweilers came in two sizes. For work as a draught dog a large heavy dog was required. In fact, big was probably beautiful, as the larger the dog the greater the weight that it could pull. However, when it came to working cattle the large dog was at a disadvantage. It was too heavy to spend long periods running around a herd, its weight could be damaging when herding and its height meant that it bit cattle high on the shoulder, thus damaging the meat, rather than biting low down on the hock.

The dog used for cattle herding was considerably smaller and lighter, giving greater agility and endurance and restricting its bite to the lower, less valuable parts of the cattle. The two sizes were kept separate for breeding purposes and would by today's standards be considered as separate breeds, or as distinct divisions of the same breed. The same ADRK publication states that much more interest was shown in keeping to the present-day colours as far as the large strain was concerned, while with the smaller strain the important characteristic was its working ability with colour being ignored. It goes on to say that because colour was ignored there was no attempt to eliminate the white markings in the smaller strain and that Rottweilers with white markings were more intelligent and biddable. Most of us who know the modern Rottweiler would agree that dogs with small white markings continue to be excellent workers.

I can understand the desire of the tradesman with a smart delivery cart wanting an equally smart-looking dog to pull it and therefore considering colour as an important feature. I find it more difficult to accept that the white markings in the small strain continued to exist merely because no one bothered to eliminate them, and I consider that is far more likely that some other breed or type which carried white markings was deliberately introduced because working ability and intelligence were considered desirable.

POLICE DOG

During the latter half of the 19th century the reasons for the Rottweiler's existence began to disappear. The need for a dog to drive cattle ceased with the arrival of rail transport and the pony or donkey took over the task of pulling a cart. Rottweilers still had a high reputation in a limited area, but were virtually unknown in the outside world. A major study of German breeds by Ludwig Beckman published in 1894 did not even mention the Rottweiler, while a Rottweiler exhibited at a dog show in 1882 is described by someone writing in 1926 as "bearing little comparison with our present requirements".

However, by 1910 the Rottweiler was officially recognised by the German Police Dog Association as the fourth police dog breed. The other breeds recognised at this time were the German Shepherd Dog, the Dobermann and the Airedale Terrier. The 28 years between 1882 and 1910 saw the breed go from obscurity to national acclaim – a large leap for Rottweilers and, one must assume, the result of some very hard work and skilful breeding for their owners and breeders. Fortunately for the Rottweiler, the "dog fancier", a person who loved a breed for its own sake had arrived on the scene. No longer was dog breeding solely for the purpose of producing a working animal. Breeders set out to preserve their chosen breed in the form in which it had been handed down to them while at the same time they also set out to refine and improve it when they considered that this was necessary.

In attempting to ascertain what sort of stock these breeders had to work with one can only try and put together scraps of information from history and the information contained in the early Standards. Much of the useful information in the Standards is not in the description of the ideal dog but in the list of possible faults. I have already tried to point out the diversity of tasks, the variations in size and the wide range of colours. From the possible faults we can find that some animals were too long, light and Greyhound-like. Others were overweight and clumsy. Heads failed by being too large and unwieldy or by resembling a hunting dog.

One of the milestones in the development of the modern Rottweiler must be its acceptance as a working police dog in 1910. His success in this role meant that his fame spread throughout Germany and beyond. However, to have achieved this position it is obvious that the comparatively nondescript and unknown dog of the late 1800s must have changed to a considerable degree. We know that in 1905 a Rottweiler was selected as a "fine dog of unusual breed and irreproachable character" to be presented to the President of a dog show organised by the Association of the Friends of Dogs in Heidelberg. From this we can assume that the breed was recognised and more or less settled in its present form, although not well known. It is also safe to assume that the Rottweiler was already showing the exemplary character that we have grown to admire.

THE FIRST STANDARD

The first detailed description of the Rottweiler is in the Standard for the breed written by Albert Kull in 1883 and published in 1901 by the International Club for Leonberger and Rottweiler Dogs. Kull founded this club in 1899. These were the breeds originating from the German district of Swabia which was the link between the two breeds, rather than any suggestion that they were genetically connected. This first attempt at a Standard for the breed is of interest not only because much of it is still valid today but also as an indication of what the breed could look like at that time. I have already dealt with the variation in colours, but it would appear that the coat length was greater than today, being described as "unusually thick", "reasonably long" and "very abundant", although it does list "too long and soft" as a fault.

The description of the general appearance of the dog is one that we would recognise and it makes the point that bitches are always smaller than the males and longer in the back. Separate figures available give the ideal height and weight of the Rottweiler in 1883 as about 23.5 inches and 66 lbs. This means that the Rottweiler at that time was about 2 inches shorter at the shoulder and little over half the weight of the ideal dog today. Compared with the Rottweiler at the present time the dog of 1883 was a much lighter, leggier animal. While it may be a fault in translation it asks that the ears are "lying back" except when alert. Under the heading of tail the Standard states "the dog is often born with a stumpy tail and this is always preferred". Bearing in mind the difficulties that many countries today are having with the requirement for a docked tail, I can only wish that this hereditary characteristic had not been lost. The requirements for character in 1883 echo the ideal temperament of today. "Courage, endurance and good nature" are emphasised. The good nature, friendship and companionship with people, which endears the breed to us today, existed a hundred years ago and must reflect the long and close relationship of the Rottweiler with the human family. This virtually paradoxical gentleness comes almost as a surprise when one remembers the rough and tough nature of the dog's original tasks.

While Albert Kull must be given the credit for being the first person to codify the description of the Rottweiler, the hard work of actual breeding is usually considered to be the work of Albert Graf who was one of those who chose the Rottweiler that was presented to the President of the Heidelberg show in 1905. He was prepared to commence "systematic breeding" of the Rottweiler. The phrase used is interesting, implying as it does that there had been little system in the past.

The Germans are organised and they like to work within a clear set of rules. An American or British dog book will contain suggestions as to how to breed dogs, whereas the German equivalent will contain regulations on the breeding of dogs. This is not said with any critical intention. Many of the great dogs of the world have their origin in Germany and one cannot criticise a system which can produce these results. With regard to control, the Germans have always had one major advantage. Unlike the British system where registration of all breeds is in the hands of the Kennel Club, in Germany registration is handled by the breed club. In other words, if you do not conform to the breed club's requirements your dog is not registered and you are left outside the system, unable to sell or show your stock as pedigree animals.

BREED CLUBS

The International Rottweiler and Leonberger Club had a short life and its major claim to fame must be as the publisher of the first Standard. In January 1907 the first club devoted solely to Rottweilers was founded in Heidelberg with Albert Graf as secretary and Karl Knauf as chairman. This was the Deutsche Rottweiler Club. Albert Graf could start his systematic breeding and the first Rottweiler registered was his Rusz von Brukenbuckel who went on to become a champion. Less than four months after the formation of DRK, a second club was formed with the title of the South German Rottweiler Club. This club had little success and is chiefly remembered for issuing a Standard asking for a pincer bite.

Order and control had not yet been achieved and a situation developed that will be well known to anyone who has been involved with a new breed. A third breed club was formed, the International Rottweiler Club. This club absorbed the South German Rottweiler Club. The breed now had two clubs, both working to establish the Rottweiler, both with similar Standards although there were differences of opinion about size and undercoat. Both clubs maintained breed books.

Policemen played a major part in the progress of the Rottweiler at this time. Their influence and interest can be seen in the way that the breed developed both physically and mentally. The use of Rottweilers by the police was also a major reason for the rapid spread and popularity of the breed throughout Germany and beyond. The German Rottweiler Club became affiliated to the German Police Dog Association, while the International Rottweiler Club had the police Commissioner of Frankfurt as its chairman from 1912 to 1915.

The two clubs continued to exist side by side until 1921. To a certain extent they were complementary to each other, although each tended to have a different aim. The argument was basically between type and temperament or between the show ring and working ability – an argument which is still familiar today, although we have all come to realise that to have a good-looking dog is not enough, the dog must also be intelligent and of good temperament. The German Rottweiler Club went for working ability as opposed to looks and many of the early

These German-bred Rottweilers typify the sound temperament that all breeders should strive to produce.
Photo courtesy ADRK.

police dogs came from their breed book. If you look at the photographs of these dogs you will see lightly built dogs, hound-like heads with little stop and long narrow muzzles, large ears, long sloping croups and tucked up loins.

The International Rottweiler Club concentrated on producing a dog that would win in the show ring. They wanted a dog that would consistently breed true to type, uniform in appearance and with a stronger and more clearly defined head. Their first great sire was Leo von Canstatt. He and his great grandson, Lord von der Teck, were the first sires to be used repeatedly with the aim of establishing strong bloodlines which would continue into the future. Lord sired some sixty-three litters, giving us stock with a broad dry head, shorter muzzle and an improved top and under line. He was mated to his full sister, Minna von der Teck, and produced Arco Torfwerk, sire of one hundred litters.

Then as now, the Germans believed in making the maximum use of an outstanding stud dog. These dogs produced a long line of winners and can be considered as the principal foundation stock of the modern Rottweiler. I have often wondered why, in view of the success of the mating between Lord and Minna, the Germans have always been opposed to what we in Britain and the USA call line breeding. While few of us would use the very close mating of brother and sister, many breeders have produced excellent specimens using the so-called "classic" mating of grandfather/granddaughter.

There was an unsuccessful attempt in 1913 to amalgamate the two clubs. However in 1921 it was agreed that the two clubs would merge and the Allgemeiner Deutscher Rottweiler Klub came into being. A compromise Standard was agreed and the affairs of Rottweilers have been in the hands of the ADRK since that date. This successful merger of the two opposing ideals of work and show ring have continued to the present day, although there have been some disagreements along the way.

After the amalgamation which created the ADRK the emphasis tended to be on the show ring. Breeding was almost entirely limited to stud dogs who were beauty champions from the old IRK stud books. From the point of view of the appearance of the dog this trend did nothing but good. Whether or not this concentration on beauty had an adverse effect on the temperament and working ability of the Rottweiler is a matter for debate. Certainly the Rottweiler today and over the last forty years has shown little sign of losing his high intelligence and working ability.

The later German policy of requiring that only dogs who had passed the appropriate working tests could be allowed to win in the show ring, or to be used for breeding, has helped to maintain the breed's working ability. The Rottweiler was used successfully by the German Army during the 1939-45 war, and post-war has attracted worldwide acclaim as a police dog. Perhaps the greatest proof that it has retained its desirable character, a combination of tough courage and gentle good humour, is its enormous success throughout the world as a family companion and pet.

WORLDWIDE POPULARITY

Geographically, the Rottweiler has shifted away from his birthplace. In 1905 there was only one Rottweiler bitch to be found in the town of Rottweil. In 1965 the greatest number of German breed supporters was to be found in the Rhineland with the area of the breed's origin still showing relatively small numbers. However, the breed had by then achieved worldwide fame, with its supporters running into thousands, especially in the USA and Britain.

While it may be of interest to humans to know that they are descended from kings and queens, or more likely from a long line of peasants, the value of knowing the ancestors of a breed of dog is really only in the information that it gives us about the dog as it is today, or, if we are trying to preserve the qualities of a breed, then history can tell us what those qualities should be, or at least what were considered desirable in the past.

Of course, like any human, any dog, at any time had two parents and this chain goes back to the beginning of time, depending on your own theories as to how the world evolved. A generation in dogs is only some two years and five generations or ten years, let alone a thousand or two, can make a considerable difference to both the appearance, the character and the working ability of a breed, even though hereditary aspects will continue to appear for a very long time.

In the Rottweiler we have a dog whose ancestors for many centuries worked as droving, draught and guard dogs. The breed lived close to man and developed a high standard of intelligence and a friendly, adaptable nature. Not much more than a hundred years ago, there were wide variations in size, colour and conformation. At that time the German breeders started to control and refine the breed and produced the dog that we know today. So, even if the big black and tan dog did not climb the Alpine passes with the Romans, we can be sure that breeders during the last hundred years or so have produced a dog who would have been quite capable of doing so!

Chapter Two

THE ROTTWEILER CHARACTER

DEVELOPMENT OF THE BREED

The Rottweiler, history tells us, was originally used as herder for cattle – and to protect the drover and the cash! In other words, the Rottweiler was a 'drover's dog', a distinct breed in many parts of the world. These dogs may not necessarily have looked the same or shared the same type, but their character would have been similar. They would have had to herd cattle, often out of sight or sound of the drover, and so they would have needed to rely on their knowledge, and to think for themselves. This certainly helped to produce a reliable animal who could do basic work without assistance. Once the cattle were sold, the cash would be tied round the dog's neck, and so the next task was to protect the money from thieves, while the drover, no doubt, enjoyed refreshment at the local hostelry. This meant the dog had to be a good guard, hence the development of this instinct, although the primary job was herding.

As a herder, the Rottweiler would have had to develop an "eye" when challenged by an awkward cow or bull, in order to stand his ground and subdue the animal. This is in exactly the same way as a Collie subdues a ram or ewe, and it is often seen in Sheepdog Trials. I have had Rottweilers who, when walking in a field of cattle, would not allow the beasts to approach nearer than about ten feet. The dog would simply stand and look at the beasts, and they would not come any nearer. That is "giving them the eye". I am glad to see this instinct still survives in many of the breed, as can be seen by the reaction of males, in particular, when they are stared at by ignorant visitors to shows when the dogs are benched (which is common practice at Championship shows in the UK). Staring is regarded as a direct challenge to the dog.

When I had cattle, I found that my Rottweilers would round up and drive home any animals who managed to get out of their field. I have bred a lot of Rottweilers who have worked cattle on local farms – one bitch regularly fetched in the cows twice a day, and between times she accompanied the hunters out at exercise! So the herding instinct still survives.

Later on in history, Rottweilers were used as draught dogs, particularly in Belgium, and were capable of pulling large loads. This work possibly added patience and tolerance to the character of the breed, and this is a trait which is retained today. If fairly treated and respected, the Rottweiler will, in turn, give loyalty and service.

LOVE AND DEVOTION

It is the Rottweiler's outstanding character and temperament that have made it so universally popular, so it is very surprising how few specialist books highlight this aspect of the breed – and so potential owners cannot appreciate what an exceptional dog they are planning to purchase.

My first Rottweiler was a large lady, Chesara Dark Brocade, known as Emma, and she epitomised the Rottweiler's loving temperament. She would nurture and love any small animal, particularly pups. When she was about ten months old, I had a miniature Bull Terrier who was due to whelp. This resulted in a Caesarean section, one pure-white puppy, and a bitch with no

Ch. Pottersdale Fatal Free at Jacraila. The Rottweiler character combines calm self-assurance, with boldness and fearlessness.

Photo: Carol Ann Johnson.

Ch. Crown Prince of Gallah, owned by Mr and Mrs Auty. The Rottweiler has an innate sense of superiority, and as a result, they seldom fight.

Photo courtesy: Mr and Mrs Auty.

milk who couldn't care less. I started to hand-rear this tiny puppy, and when she was only twenty-four hours old, I noticed Emma was dripping milk from her teats. I put the pup into Emma's bed – and I had no more worries for the next seven weeks! I have never seen a pup who was so well-loved, and so well cared for.

Emma's next effort was to help with two ten-week old Fox cubs. Although she did not feed them, she cleaned and loved them – even though she was puzzled at uncanine behaviour. Some four years later, Emma whelped her second litter of six pups, and two days later my Boston Terrier bitch had five pups, again by Caesarean. The Boston did not come round properly from the anaesthetic for two days, and during this time Emma left her own pups every two hours to feed and clean the Boston's litter! It was wonderful to see this very large Rottweiler settle in with the tiny Bostons, only leaving when they were full and cleansed – this is the wonderful character of the Rottweiler. There is an interesting sequel to this story. The Bostons did not see Emma from the time their dam took over at two days old until they were six weeks of age. Then, Emma walked across the lawn near the pups. They caught her scent and ran after her as fast as possible. I had no idea that the scent imprint could be so strong.

THE GUARDING INSTINCT
That was one side of Emma's character; she was also a super hunter of rabbits – which she ate with relish – a companion of children, and a superb guard. On one occasion I had a visit from a representative from a firm of dog food manufacturers. He came in and was sitting at a table, about eighteen feet from Emma's bed. I noticed that she would not take her eyes from him – then he moved very suddenly, and in a flash Emma was by his side, fixing him with her eye. He froze and so did I. I was so surprised. He left almost at once! Emma had never done such a thing before and did not do it again. There was obviously something very odd about the man. That is another side of the Rottweiler character – and who would worry with such an animal in the house? Emma 'gave him the eye', rather as she would to cattle – but she certainly meant business.

INHERITED FACTORS
Part of the character of the Rottweiler is inherited, which is why the importance of choosing dogs bred with care cannot be over-emphasised. Unfortunately, some breeders do not seem to mind using breeding stock with very bad characteristics, such as nervousness, and this trait seems to come through with great persistence. In a certain area some decades or so ago, a very well bred dog, too nervous for the show ring, was acquired by a quite unscrupulous person who used him on every available bitch. Inevitably, some pups were sold to equally commercially-minded people, who bred their bitches at every season. Most of these animals' owners knew little, and cared less, about pedigrees, except to supply a copy to new owners with the puppy farmer's dream – a Kennel Club 'litter-recorded form'. These were in force in the UK at the time, but now, thankfully, they are no longer in use. (This type of registration allowed one puppy to be named from a litter and the rest were 'litter-recorded' at a cost of £1 per head, and included a registration form for each puppy, given to the new owner.)

In the course of time, half-brothers and sisters from the original nervous dog were mated. The results were bad. Training classes were getting six to twelve-month-old pups already biting their families – and these were real fear-biters, who would do their best to remove the hand of anybody trying to touch them. Most of these dogs had to be destroyed. This story shows how important it is to buy from stock bred for the correct character of the Rottweiler.

DOMINANCE
The three main Breed Standards – the German, the British and the American – conjure up a picture of the ideal Rottweiler character. All three Standards emphasise the blend of calm self-

assurance with boldness and fearlessness. The Rottweiler should not be either nervous or aggressive, but should have natural guarding instincts. I particularly like the British description: "calm gaze should indicate good humour".

The Rottweiler is a very dominant dog. We know the breed is vastly superior to all other dogs – and the Rottweiler does too! Therefore, these dogs will very seldom fight. A Rottweiler will give the 'eye' to other males, and then let them go about their business. If a fight does take place, it is usually because man has interfered, or even put one dog on a lead. In almost thirty years of exercising Rottweilers loose, I have never known one to start a fight with a strange dog.

Being such a dominant breed, they know they are vastly superior to all other beings, and so they will live happily with small animals in the household and large animals outside. I find males love to be in the puppy pen with their babies, and they are extremely careful when moving around. As the pups get older, they will assist the dam in correcting the pups, which is so important in their future lives. I have found the most macho of males living in the house will go all soft and gooey over a young small breed puppy, allowing any liberties to be taken – even to the extent of having his favourite bone pushed out of his mouth!

I have found the only time my male Rottweilers will not tolerate another male Rottweiler is on their own property. Outside the gate, everything is fine. At shows and other events, a male will ignore males, but will always have an eye for the girls! My own dogs will tolerate males of other breeds coming on their ground, such as Deerhounds, Bull Terriers and Collies, as well as the small breeds. Being such a superior breed, the Rottweiler does not see any other breed males as a threat in any way – least of all to their bitches! This tolerant attitude makes for a very calm animal under most circumstances, hence the 'calm gaze' indicating good humour.

COURAGE AND ABUSE

The Rottweiler is also an animal of great courage and will not be deterred by pain or fear when the instinct to retaliate is aroused. A great protector of family and property, many stories have been told of great courage at all times, even when wounded. However, this degree of courage has created problems for the Rottweiler.

Criminals have made use of the breed, and with completely incorrect handling, the Rottweiler can become a lethal weapon or, indeed, can be trained as such. A mixture of abuse and poor training can effectively ruin the Rottweiler character. I heard of a case recently where two dogs, father and son, lived in a yard with a bitch. When the bitch was on heat the dogs, naturally enough, were continually having fights; whereupon the owner hooked the younger dog to a chain and beat him with a stick. The younger dog was eventually sold, thankfully to someone who had considerable experience with dogs. At this stage, the dog was four years old; he had never been on a lead or had any training, and had lived in a yard since birth. However, he had a good pedigree, and with skill and understanding on the part of the new owner the true character of the dog emerged. He now lives a very happy life, with plenty of exercise, love and food. This also illustrates the importance of the breeding behind the dog. If this dog had been bred from nervous animals without self-assurance, I do not believe he could have emerged as a pet, companion and guard – and now he has the self-assured calm gaze of the breed.

Some five years ago, I met a lady who owned a Rottweiler bitch that was ten months of age. The lady was complaining that her bitch did not show an interest in guarding – as she owned a small Post Office on the outskirts of a town she felt she needed a guard. I pointed out that ten months was quite early for a Rottweiler to begin to guard. I thought that with maturity and growing confidence, she would soon realise that she could guard. Some four weeks later, the lady noticed a man trying to look into the Post Office window and then he entered the shop. Immediately, the Rottweiler bitch, who slept on a bed behind the counter, shot out and attacked the man, who quickly ran out. The owner rang the Police, who were able to pick up the man, only

Understanding the Rottweiler character is the key to forming a successful partnership.

The Rottweiler is a great protector of home and family.

Photo: Carol Ann Johnson.

to find he was armed! How did the young bitch know? She could have smelt fear on the man – people give off pheronomes when frightened, which the dog can recognise. Or perhaps the little bitch smelt the firearms. Whatever stimulated her, it was a tremendous reaction from such a young bitch. Needless to say, the owner was delighted, and now really feels safe with her bitch as guard. Despite her youth at the time of the incident, it would be very unusual for a Rottweiler not to attempt to guard in such a situation.

PRESERVING CHARACTER

The Rottweiler is, I think, treated with respect in most countries, even if required to fulfil rather differing roles. In the West Indies, on islands such as Jamaica, the Rottweiler is kept mainly for guarding purposes, with showing as a secondary role. This is not necessarily to the detriment of the breed, provided the correct character is bred for, and some care is taken to preserve type. In the UK the situation is entirely reversed, and the majority of Rottweilers are bred solely for show, and as long as they will pose on the end of a lead and be gaited round the ring, the owners are happy – provided their dog wins! In such a situation it says a lot for the breed to find that the correct character and temperament do survive in the great majority of animals. In such an ancient breed, where character has been strengthened and developed for countless generations, it will stand quite a lot of wrong breeding, as evolution is a slow process.

However, I find the situation very worrying, and I am convinced that the best way to preserve temperament would be to have a compulsory working test before any working breed animal could become a Champion. With Rottweilers, the type of Obedience practised at clubs and shows is not really suitable to assess the breed. The ability to obey stereotyped orders does not show the true character of the breed. Working Trials and Working Tests do allow some degree of freedom for the dog to think independently, particularly in the higher stakes.

SENSITIVITY

All Rottweilers love to work and to please their handlers/owners. They will give everything to please, but this is not a breed to be bullied. If you try to force a Rottweiler to do a certain exercise, you will meet with a stubborn refusal. Rottweilers need a particular style of handling to get the best from them, and this is why the breed has not been universally accepted as a police dog. Generally, breeds used for work are very dependent on their handlers and will do as ordered. We have all seen the German Shepherd Dog who will obey without question. A Rottweiler is much too independent to do this. However, those who understand the Rottweiler character have forged extremely successful partnerships.

The Rottweiler is such a versatile breed, it does not really matter what they do, as long as they can enjoy and achieve. I know of one Rottweiler male who has used his herding instinct to keep an eye on his young human family. If one of the children strays too far away, the dog rounds them up and gets them back to their parents. This developed without any training, and is evidence of the soundness of the true Rottweiler character. The breed is also very popular with the British Army, where the dogs have a strenuous working life, and live with their handlers and family.

The late, much-missed Jack Cooper had a really good working male, and when he knew he was dying he decided that the dog should continue to work. This Rottweiler was no fireside pet; he lived for Working Trials, and was still young, so Jack arranged for the Army to have him. The dog was swift to adapt to his new life, and, in the opinion of the Army dog section, he has to be one of the best workers they have had. To me, this shows the character of the Rottweiler – to leave a master he had known from birth and to settle so well. Did he know his master had only a short time to live and wanted him to take on a new boss? Who knows? I think this is just another episode showing Rottweilers are psychic to a degree, which is all part of their unique character.

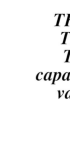

THE ALL-ROUND TEMPERAMENT
The Rottweiler is capable of adapting to a variety of different lifestyles:

Backpacking is becoming an increasingly popular pastime. These Rottweilers have no problem trekking all day and carrying their saddlebags.
Photo courtesy: Mary Macphail.

Skating in Norway – and the Rottweillers keep their footing as well as their owners! Note the undocked tails.
Photo courtesy: Mary Macphail.

Skateboarding in the USA.
Photo courtesy: Carol Woodward.

Carting with a difference!
Photo courtesy: Barbara Butler.

NERVOUSNESS

The American Breed Standard has an additional part to the section on character and temperament, and this is an instruction to judges to excuse any shy Rottweiler from the ring. It goes on to give a clear definition, so judges cannot be accused of bias and opinion! It states: "Shyness – a dog shall be judged fundamentally shy if, refusing to stand for examination, it shys away from the judge. A dog that in the opinion of the judge menaces him/her or exhibits any signs that it may not safely be approached or examined by the judge in the normal manner shall be excused from the ring. A dog that in the opinion of the judge attacks any person in the ring shall be disqualified."

In the UK I have seen nervousness displayed in the show ring, and I feel the American stipulation to disqualify such dogs should be adopted universally. There is no trait in a dog worse than nervousness: it can lead to aggression, and a fear-biter is the most dangerous of all. The English Kennel Club does deal with any dog showing aggression, biting, or attacking the judges: the dog may be banned from exhibition and also from being bred from. Personally, I think this is essential. It is not sufficient to ban a dog from the show ring when nervousness/shyness is an inherited trait. It is completely out of character, particularly when the dog is in a non-threatening situation.

I am not saying that Rottweilers should never bite. If a dog's family or family's property is threatened, then the Rottweiler must protect to the best of its ability.

THE ALL-ROUND TEMPERAMENT

The great thing about the Rottweiler character and temperament is the ability to live in any kind of situation with the family, looking after them and protecting them under any circumstance. One of the very best males I ever bred was Champion Upend Gallant Gairbert. In my opinion, he had a perfect Rottweiler character and temperament. A very kind dog, he was a real goer. He was very full of himself, and as a young dog he needed a firm hand, but he never attempted to bite in the whole of his long life of twelve and a half years. Gairbert could protect very effectively under all circumstances. He would never allow strangers to come too near me, and if people got at all unpleasant he simply stood on his hind legs and snarled into the person's face, without even putting a foot on them, which was very effective indeed. He was sensible and safe with all livestock, and adored children. He was perfect with pups, and helped to rear a tiny Lancashire Heeler and a Sussex Spaniel, among others.

Gairbert was very territorial and knew exactly the boundaries of our property and, as he could clear six-foot weld mesh in his time, it was just as well. When over the boundary, he immediately stopped guarding, as on the day when he roared at some strangers walking in the field next to ours. He leapt the six-foot fence and landed at their feet. The group froze; he greeted them, and went off to the river to hunt! I will never forget the looks on their faces!

Another example of this was when Gairbert met some friends, who had come to visit us, about fifty yards up the road. They made a fuss of him and they walked together to our house. The front gate was closed, so the friends opened the gate to let Gairbert in. He entered, turned around and told these people in no uncertain manner that there was no way they could come through the gate! This highlights the Rottweiler character of knowing the boundaries, and only guarding on their property, which is a tremendous asset.

In the UK, recent legislation (The Dangerous Dogs Act, 1991) has meant that we are breeding for a quieter character, less liable to be provoked into the odd nip. We must watch out that we do not lose the essential characteristics, and must always remember that Rottweiler breeding is working dog breeding. All mating should be worked out with this in mind, as should judging in the show ring. The structure and soundness should enable the animal to work, and, as said before, any signs of diversion from the correct temperament must be penalised.

Von Gallingen's Painted Lady CDX: High in Trial at her first two AKC Agility Trials. Owned by Michael Dembeck. Rottweilers need to use their working ability if they are to be truly content.

Photo courtesy: Catherine Thompson.

All Rottweilers are individuals, with their own special personality.

Photo: Carol Ann Johnson.

INDIVIDUAL CHARACTER

Just as no two dogs look alike, so characters are never quite the same, although being correct for the breed. Over the years I have trained three dogs and one bitch for Working Trials. While the basic training is similar, the differing character and temperament of each animal means you have to adapt your method to suit the individual concerned, and there is always one exercise a particular dog does not seem to grasp and something different must be tried in order to make the dog understand what is required. With each of my dogs it was a different exercise. This makes training interesting, and does bring out the differing individual characteristics, which otherwise might not be noticed. One thing they all had in common was that they all loved to work. If the show people would give time to working training, they would find that they had happier, much more alert dogs to show. Dogs who are stimulated in this way have something to live for, and they look forward to working sessions with joy. I have seen this transformation take place, and it is truly remarkable. All working dogs need to use their ability if they are to be really content with life.

FAMILY LIFE

The Rottweiler character is superb, but it must never be forgotten that they are big and powerful dogs, some as heavy as their owners or even heavier, and they must be taught correct behaviour to live as family dogs. My grandchildren have all been reared with Rottweilers; one family acquired a nine-week-old bitch puppy when their eldest child was three years old, and the baby was at the crawling stage. They all grew up together, and the puppy seemed to know not to nip. The family consists of three girls now, and the Rottweiler, aged nine, still looks after them.

My other son has one boy, now aged three and a half. When he was born, two Rottweilers lived as family – a dog of ten years old and a sister to the other family bitch. With correct introductions, there were no problems with the Rottweilers. Unfortunately, the male suffered from a tumour and had to be put down when the baby was a year old. He was replaced with a large male puppy a few months later. This large dog, now almost two years old and known as Willy, has really grown up with Ralph and they are great pals, playing happily together, alongside guinea pigs, rabbits and hens. The old bitch is also involved and enjoys the games.

To me, this is how the breed should behave, but these dogs have been reared and trained correctly, as well as having the basic good character of the breed. However, rescued Rottweilers, who have been ill-treated, beaten and abused, can still adapt and settle in new homes, which makes you realise how important it is to preserve the true Rottweiler character. It is a great responsibility for all people who breed litters to see that this happens, whether they breed one litter or many.

THE ADAPTABLE ROTTWEILER

The Rottweiler has had many varying jobs in the past, but looking at construction, the breed is very different to other herding breeds such as Rough and Smooth Collies and German Shepherd Dogs. Old English Sheepdogs are similar in build, but very different in head. The Rottweiler has a broad head and very powerful jaws – much more like the old guarding breeds of Mastiff type. Although agile, the Rottweiler is not built for fast turns and short bursts of high speed, so it is very interesting to see how powerfully the herding qualities have come through down the generations to combine with the guarding instinct, giving us the character we have in the Rottweiler today.

I think the Rottweiler is one of the best, if not the best, breed as an all-rounder. Ideally, the Rottweiler should be a family dog, living with all ages of people, but not treated as a person, rather as a character in his own right. This is a dog who will adapt to almost any type of living conditions and situation. Becoming a member of a family does not prevent a Rottweiler being

The perfect family dog, as long as parents train both dogs and children to respect each other.

Photo courtesy: Pamela Wilkinson Grant.

BELOW: Am. Ch. Bergenhof's Gunther V Nelson CD, TD, owned by John Harrison. The Rottweiler is a dog who will never let you down.

Photo courtesy: Dorothea Gruenerwald.

trained to undertake other activities. In fact, it will make for a more complete life, as this is a breed that needs to use its brains and to achieve. The Rottweiler is equally happy as a working dog, with the police or army, or as a general farm-worker. The breed can also be used as gun dogs, using the tremendous sense of smell and retrieving with a soft mouth. But let an aggressive poacher appear, and the dog's bite will be far from soft! My own dogs have frequently found and retrieved wounded pheasants after a day out by the local shoot, and these are birds missed by the gun-dogs working with the local shooting party. Maybe the Rottweiler should also be classed as a hunt, point and retrieve breed and not just as herders and guards! The Rottweiler will certainly hunt and will quarter a field naturally, without basic training, in search of rabbits or hares or anything else! A tireless trot covers the ground with no apparent effort, and an excellent nose will locate any animal.

I used to take my dogs hunting at a grass airfield, when it was not in use. One bitch, Nicky, would always go across the long grass and find a tame hedgehog, which promptly rolled into a ball. In spite of the prickles, she would carry him on to the short grass and put him down at my feet. He got so used to being collected every day he was not at all scared. He would unroll and run back home! This happened regularly, and he seemed to enjoy the whole exercise and was never hurt in any way. I think Nicky looked on him as a friend – although as far as all the other creatures were concerned, she was there to hunt. This subtly typifies the Rottweiler personality, and once you have owned one, you will be content with no other breed. The Rottweiler is a powerful, impressive animal who can adapt to almost any task. This is a dog who will never let you down, and will protect you and yours. Just make sure the breeding is right, and the great character of the breed will show itself in a wide variety of ways.

Kassmax Master Maccocca, pictured at six months of age. The male will grow into a big, powerful dog, and will have a more dominant character than a bitch.
Photo: Carol Ann Johnson.

Jacraila's Femme Fatale, pictured at seven months of age. If you are new to Rottweilers, you are better off choosing a bitch.
Photo: Carol Ann Johnson.

Chapter Three

CARING FOR YOUR PUPPY

MAKING THE DECISION

Taking on a dog of any breed is a big responsiblility. Taking on a Rottweiler, who will grow into a big, powerful animal, is a far greater responsibility. Before taking this step, it is essential to consider all the pros and cons of dog ownership, and in particular, to decide whether a Rottweiler is the right breed for you and your family.

This is a breed that requires space, sufficient finance to feed and care for a large dog, and the commitment to train and socialise the dog to become a civilised, well adapted member of the community. As already discussed (Chapter Two: The Rottweiler Character), this is a breed with strong guarding instincts, and these must be channelled so they are an asset and not a liability. The Rottweiler is potentially a loyal, devoted member of the family, living with children and with other animals, but you cannot expect this to happen without supervision, discipline, and training. However, if you are prepared to take the right steps, you will be rewarded with a canine companion that will be second to none.

DOG OR BITCH?

Having decided on a Rottweiler, the next decision is the sex of your puppy. If you already have a dog, or dogs, then the problem is easier, for if you have a male the choice would usually be a bitch. Rottweiler males are usually quite friendly with small males – except small Terriers or Yorkies (which are small Terriers!) – but if you are not experienced, then it is advisable to choose a bitch. Sometimes bitches will not live happily together, but they will usually take to a puppy bitch and become friends. No dogs like to be on their own, and almost every adult who is alone will welcome a pup of either sex! However, if you already have a Rottweiler male then go for a bitch. It is possible to keep Rottweiler males together if you are an experienced trainer and handler, but if trouble arises it could be impossible to restore peace on a permanent basis.

If you are new to Rottweilers, then in almost every case, you will be better off with a bitch. A bitch is smaller and not quite so bouncy as a male, but both sexes are equally loving with children. Pups can be trained and treated rather like children. If your kids are out of hand and disobedient, then most breeders will not sell you a puppy, on the assumption that if you cannot train your kids then the same would apply to your puppy! Both children and puppies should be treated with love and firmness.

FINDING A BREEDER

Do buy your puppy from a reliable breeder. Your nearest Rottweiler Club secretary will probably be able to help you; telephone numbers of club secretaries can be obtained from your national Kennel Club. Visit the kennels and see the breeding stock before making a decision. All good breeders will welcome you and will answer any questions. In order to assess temperament, it is important to meet the adult dogs, and this will give some indication of the type of Rottweiler the

The puppies should look bright and alert. This is a sure sign of good rearing.
Photo courtesy: Carol Woodward.

The breeder will know the puppies as individuals and will advise on which puppy will be most suitable to your lifestyle.

Photo courtesy: Carol Woodward.

The Rottweiler puppy should look like a miniature version of the adult.

Photo: Carol Ann Johnson.

kennel produces. Do not reserve a puppy and then buy from somewhere else without telling the breeder from whom you ordered a puppy. This is both rude and unfair. Nobody minds if you buy elsewhere, if notified – otherwise a pup may be kept for you. It is common practice to pay a deposit as a guarantee of good faith, once the pups are a week or so old. This is the time to ask about hip scores of parents, whether they have passed a temperament (character) assessment, and if they are show winners and/or work in any capacity such as Obedience, Working Trials, herding, etc.

ASSESSING THE LITTER
When you visit to see the litter, if they are under seven or eight weeks old, you may not be allowed to touch them. No breeder will risk infection, which is so easy to carry despite obvious precautions. By the time the pups are eight weeks, and old enough to leave the breeder, they may have had primary inoculations. They should be fully wormed and they will be on four meals per day.

You may be able to pick a puppy, but many experienced breeders prefer to allocate the pups to the most suitable homes for temperament. The very lively and extrovert pups will go to the more experienced buyers, while the older couple will be more suited with a quieter pup.

Viewing the litter as a whole, at six to eight weeks, the pups should look chunky and thick-set, possibly with heavyish coats, which means they will have the correct double coat when adult. There should not be any feathering on the ears or down the backs of the legs. In fact, Rottweiler puppies look rather like little bears! There will be a small difference in size; the dogs may be larger than the bitches and there may be variation within the sexes. Do not worry about this, as I have often seen the smallest in a litter finish off the largest when fully mature. The average weight at eight weeks is about 14 lbs to 15 lbs.

The litter should look fit and healthy, and should be clean. The kennels should be fresh and clean with free access to outside runs so that the puppies have begun to house-train themselves. The run will most likely be made of flags or concrete, but there should be access to grass when the weather is dry. Pups do not really play properly or groom themselves on any form of concrete. The pups should have bright, clean eyes and a clean, moist nose. However, if they have just awakened in a heated room, the nose may be dry and warm.

A SHOW PROSPECT
If you wish to get a puppy with show potential then ask the breeder for one showing promise of a good specimen. Do not expect to buy a show puppy just like that; most people will only sell a puppy as 'promising'. Puppies can change a good deal, and good animals can be ruined by poor rearing and management, as so very much depends on feeding and exercise. Growing puppies can be affected by too much or too little of the correct food, too many additions to the diet, and by too much or too little exercise.

When choosing a puppy, the best plan is to have a mental picture of your ideal Rottweiler, and then try to find a puppy to match. A pup at about eight weeks is a miniature of the adult. Look for dark eyes, a short back and well-laid shoulders with correct length of upper arms. The puppy should have plenty of bone, straight legs, and the bend of stifle required in an adult. Watch the puppies move: this is the best guide to their conformation. The only things you cannot assess are feet – all pups have neat feet as babies – and the length of neck, which may not develop until seven or eight months. However, if you buy from an experienced breeder and the breeding is good, you just may get a future Champion!

PREPARATIONS
When you visit the breeder prior to collecting your puppy, you will be told how the litter has been

Am. Ch. Pomac's Lex P Vanlare CD HIV, pictured at three months age. A breeder will know which puppies have show potential.

Photo courtesy: Dorothea Gruenerwald.

Puppies need a lot of sleep, so it is important to provide comfortable sleeping quarters where your puppy can rest undisturbed.

Photo courtesy: Pamela Wilkinson Grant.

fed, so you will be able to get a supply of the same food. The breeder will probably give you enough for the first two or three days, but it is as well to be prepared. It is important not to introduce any dietary changes during the settling-in period when the puppy will be prone to stomach upset. This applies particularly if your puppy has been given milk, as even a change of type or brand can cause loose bowels. I have found that goat's milk can cause problems, unless the puppy has been reared on it. Evaporated milk seems to suit most puppies. Avoid the numerous supplements which are advertised. These can do more harm than good, and if you are feeding a well-balanced diet, they are simply not necessary.

SLEEPING QUARTERS
It is also important to have a place for the puppy to sleep which is warm, draught-free and quiet. Like babies, pups need to play, feed and rest, and at eight weeks puppies sleep a lot. Too many pups arriving at their new homes do not get enough rest. This affects growth, and the puppy will look leggy and lighter in body than normal. So where shall your Rottweiler sleep? I think the best arrangement is to purchase a fairly large crate, about 36 ins long, 26 ins wide, and 38 ins high. When the pup first comes home, you can put a small cardboard box lined with bedding in one half of the crate with newspaper all over the base. This means that if the puppy needs to relieve itself during the night, or at other times, the paper will be used. No puppy likes to mess the sleeping quarters and so the crate is a good training aid.

The crate needs to be positioned out of draughts and placed in a family room such as the kitchen. I put a rug over the sleeping end to prevent draughts. The puppy will soon regard the crate as a home, and will go into it when tired, and also use it to store favourite toys. It is possible to get water containers to hook on to the inside of the crate, or non-spill bowls which can be used in the crate. However, if water is available at all times outside the crate, it is rarely necessary to supply water in the crate, with the exception of periods of very hot weather. Most pups tend to play with the container – with inevitable results – and so this is best avoided if possible.

COLLECTING YOUR PUPPY
Now you are ready for your pup. If you have made prior arrangements with the breeder, you can ask if your puppy can be given half of a very mild travel-sickness tablet the night before collection. This nearly always prevents any car-sickness. I have a theory, based on experience, that if a pup is never allowed to be car-sick, there will never be a problem with this. I believe that puppies react like children, in that once they have been sick and felt ill, they will expect to feel ill every time they get into the car – so you get a chain-reaction!

When you collect your puppy, make sure the breeder gives you a diet sheet, a copy of your dog's pedigree, Kennel Club registration document and a receipt for the purchase price. In the UK it is common practice to insure puppies for the first six of weeks when ownership is transferred. However, this is not the case in North America and elsewhere. The reason for providing insurance is that all puppies are very vulnerable during the settling-in period. They are exposed to a lot of stress as they get used to new people and new surroundings, and this makes them a target for any 'germs' that may be around. It is a good idea to take a helper with you in the car, so that the puppy can sit comfortably on a lap and be reassured during the journey home.

ARRIVING HOME
As soon as you get home let your puppy out into the garden to relieve itself. When the pup obliges, praise, and then you are ready to go into the house, and give the pup a chance to explore. At this stage your Rottweiler will be on four meals a day, so follow the diet sheet for a few days, before making any changes. Your puppy will need to be with somebody most of the time for the first week or so, and by the end of that period you should have a house-trained pup! I reckon that

An indoor crate is an invaluable item of equipment, and most puppies soon learn to regard it as their special den.

Photo: Carol Ann Johnson.

Leaving home: Breeder Liz Dunhill (left) provides the puppy with the diet it is used to, which will aid the settling-in process.

Photo: Carol Ann Johnson.

most pups can be clean in a week, except for the occasional 'mistake' in the night.

The best plan is to go with your puppy into the garden on every occasion – do not just let the puppy out in the hope of achieving the desired result. The aim is for the pup to understand what is required. Your Rottweiler should go out first thing in the morning, immediately on waking, and after every meal. Stay with the pup, and give lots of praise when your pup performs. When you are in the house, keep an eye on the pup during active play periods. At the slightest sign of looking for a spot to squat, pick the pup up, go outside, and give the usual praise when your pup obliges. When the puppy squats, it is helpful to use a training word or command that will be associated with the action. It does not matter what you say, "Be a good dog", or whatever you like, using the same words every time. Soon the puppy will catch on and will perform on command – a very useful piece of training, whether you have a show, working or pet dog. By the end of the first week, your Rottweiler should be clean in the house.

Never leave your puppy loose in the house when you go out. In this situation a pup will become very stressed, not knowing if you will ever return, and becoming extremely lonely. If you have to go out, leave your puppy in the crate, preferably with some toys. If a puppy is left to roam you are likely to get damaged furniture, chewed carpets, etc. It is useless to punish when you return, as the puppy will have no idea why you are cross. If you correct a puppy, this needs to be done within two seconds, otherwise, as far as the pup is concerned, the punishment is being inflicted for nothing. This is a very important point. If you do not observe this rule, it can ruin your relationship with the puppy. As time passes, your dog will learn to mistrust you, which will inhibit any progress with training.

FEEDING

Your puppy will need regular feeding times, and if the meal is not cleared up within ten minutes, remove it and discard what is left. At the next feed give a little less, until the pup is cleaning the bowl. It is a good idea to buy a feeding bowl especially for your puppy, and let the pup eat undisturbed. Rottweiler pups vary: some will gulp their food down in seconds, others will chew each mouthful. So your puppy must have time to feed at its own pace. Be careful not to over-feed – some pups to tend to be very greedy.

It is best to stick to the amounts given by the breeder on the diet sheet provided. For the first few days I have found it is advisable to give smaller feeds. The pup is likely to be off food to begin with, because of the new environment and lack of competition from littermates. So give your puppy a chance to settle, and then increase the food to the correct amount. Never be tempted to hand-feed, or give tasty tidbits to tempt the appetite. Rottweiler pups are very clever and will soon have you pandering to every whim! Feed only at meal times, stick to the correct diet, and do not leave discarded food lying around. Arrange the meals so the last feed at night is meat and meal rather than milk – a drink of milk at bedtime will hinder house-training.

All breeders have their own ideas about diet. Personally, I advocate the traditional diet of wholemeal biscuit and raw meat, or better still, raw green tripe, with a little bone meal, plus eggs and milk. Many breeders have had great success rearing puppies on complete diets, but you need to know exactly what goes into the feed. I feel there is a danger that some complete diets can push a puppy's development on too fast. Big breeds must have time to grow and to develop at their own pace.

I wean my pups from the age of three weeks on raw meat. This is natural food and never upsets the digestion. Wholemeal puppy biscuit (kibble) is added to the meat as they get older. I do not recommend feeding vegetables; dogs are not good converters of vegetable matter. In the wild they would eat the stomach contents of their prey, which is already partly digested. Hence the desire of pups to eat cow and horse droppings to get some 'vegetables'. Obviously, all pups are different, and so you will need to judge the right amount to feed. You want a nice firm, well-

covered pup – not one covered in layers of fat. I find a good routine is to feed meat or tripe for breakfast, puppy meal (wholemeal) with a little meat for dinner, milk (if the pup is used to having it) with a few pieces of dry puppy meal in the afternoon, and at bedtime the last meal should be soaked puppy meal and meat, with the bonemeal mixed in. At about twelve weeks your puppy may be ready to drop to three meals per day. I find pups will indicate when four meals are too much by not being so keen on either breakfast or tea. In this case, cut out a feed and divide the day into three mealtimes, still giving breakfast and a good meal before being let out last thing at night – pups sleep better with a full tummy!

During this time you will be increasing the quantities of food gradually as the puppy grows. The best way to test if your puppy is the correct weight is to run your fingers down the sides and over the ribs. If you can feel the ribs easily, but your fingers do not feel dips between the rib bones, then the pup should be about the right weight. When, and if, you ever change the diet, do so over a period of a week or more. Start by using the usual food plus a little of the new, and then gradually increase the new and reduce the old until the change is complete. It is not a good idea to change diets, and it is not necessary to provide variety in the diet. Pups and adults will happily eat the same diet forever! So if it suits, stick to it. Changes should only be made if the pup is not developing as you would wish.

At six months of age most pups are ready to drop to two meals per day. If you feel your puppy needs to continue on three feeds, keep to this regime for a little longer. It may be that your dog tends to be a bit lean, but soon you will find that two meals a day are sufficient – although most Rottweilers would prefer more! Continue with the bonemeal supplement; your dog needs to grow and develop, building bone and muscle for quite a while yet. Rottweiler males are not near maturity until about three years old. This does not mean they are still getting taller, but are passing from the human equivalent of the twenties to the forties!

INOCULATIONS

Inoculation schedules vary from area to area, but your puppy will probably need to start the programme within a week or so of going to a new home. Before this time you must not allow the puppy to move off the premises, or to come into contact with any other dogs, except those owned by you. Your puppy needs to be protected against distemper, infectious canine hepatitis, leptospirosis, parvovirus, coronavirus and rabies in the countries where applicable. Some breeders give young puppies injections against parvovirus only. In which case, the puppy will need a repeat at twelve weeks and again at four to five months. As Rottweilers are susceptible to parvovirus, this is very important.

It is best to keep your puppy away from other unknown dogs until ten days after the inoculation course has been completed. Before this time you can take your puppy out in the car, and carry it – but not in public places. In spite of the protection available, there are quite often outbreaks of distemper and parvovirus, mainly from areas with a population of stray or roaming dogs and unwanted pups. Let your puppy have full run of the garden for play and exercise during this period. Thereafter, inoculations are limited to an annual booster.

FACING PAGE

TOP: Give the puppy a chance to explore its new home.   *Photo: Carol Ann Johnson.*

LEFT: Watch out for potential hazards, like this garden pond, as puppies are extremely inquisitive.
                                        Photo: Carol Ann Johnson.

TOP: At mealtimes, your puppy will probably miss the competition from its littermates.

Photo: Carol Ann Johnson.

LEFT: Play is an important part of development, and so it is important to provide a variety of suitable toys.

Photo: Carol Ann Johnson.

PLAY

Toys and play are very important for developing puppies. Give your Rottweiler several different toys, and it will soon be apparent which is the favourite! A good selection of toys is available at most pet shops, but do not forget, Rottweiler pups have very sharp teeth and strong jaws, so make sure your puppy cannot chew the toys into bite-size pieces which could be swallowed. A hard, solid rubber ball, medium-to-large in size, is impossible to swallow. The pup can chase and chew it, and later be encouraged to retrieve it. Squeaky toys attract pups, but they are usually made of soft plastic which can be chewed.

My pups always love large squeaky rubber 'hedgehogs' and these do last well – but the squeak usually comes out if chewed too much. My old dog, now almost eleven years of age, has had four of these toys during his lifetime. He always goes to bed with it, fetches it on command, as well as using it as a retrieve or search article.

Hard, nylon bones are popular, and the best ones last and last – it seems impossible for a dog to chew lumps off, although the edges tend to get rather ragged! A fresh marrow bone, given perhaps once a week, is very important, This will help to remove the baby teeth at around three to four months, and will keep the adult teeth clean and healthy. Keeping the teeth free from tartar also prevents bad breath. My old dog has beautiful clean teeth, although they have worn down a little. He still has all his teeth, and no bad ones. He has always had a knuckle-bone a week, and he does eat most of it – given time! All adults love to gnaw at bones. The cut end is full of nutritious bone-marrow, and a pup will spend hours licking this out. All dogs and puppies should be supervised when given a bone, and puppies must be trained to give up the bone on request.

An old sock stuffed with rags or other old socks makes an ideal article for puppy retrievers. Take this when you go for walks and encourage the puppy to bring it to your hand. Refuse to pick the sock up when you have thrown it for the pup and most will soon learn to hold the article until you take it from the mouth. This gives your dog basic training in retrieving. If you plan to work your Rottweiler in Obedience or in Working Trials, you should, hopefully, avoid those embarrassing moments when your dog refuses to let you have whatever he is holding!

Puppies are usually possessive with their special toys, bones, food, etc. It is essential that you, the boss, are able to take anything from your puppy. When the pup is feeding, use a command, such as "Leave", pick up the bowl, praise, and then put the bowl down again. You can start this training after a couple of weeks, once the pup has settled. The same rule applies to bones and toys. You must be able to take them away, and then return the item to the puppy after praise. It is no use starting this training with a large seven- or eight-month pup.

Start when your Rottweiler is young and small. This training is essential in establishing control over your dog, and it may even prove vital if your dog picks up something dangerous, such as poisoned bait. I once sold a Rottweiler puppy to a couple who already owned a middle-aged Labrador Retriever and I explained the importance of this part of the training programme. What did they do? They took the bone from the puppy as recommended – and then gave it to the Labrador! After this happened a couple of times, the Rottweiler pup refused to let the bone out of his sight or his mouth! Can you blame him – he had the intelligence of his breed!

When you play with your puppy, particularly if you have a male, you, the boss, must always, *and I mean always*, be the winner. If it is a ball game, you must always finish up with the ball – and do not let the dog have the ball to enjoy on his own for a while. This applies to all you do with your Rottweiler: you must always be the pack leader. Never play wrestling games with a male puppy. One day he will be too strong for you and will try to take over as boss. This does not apply so much to a bitch, but this type of game is best avoided.

There are many things which can give your Rottweiler the idea that he can be pack leader, and so it is wise to counteract this with a number of 'house rules'. Never feed your dog just before you and your family have a meal. The dog must learn to wait until you have finished. In the wild the pack leader always eats first! Never let your dog occupy your armchair, or sleep on your bed. Subconsciously, all these things tell the dog he is the best, and wild instincts are nearer the surface than you may realise. This applies to all breeds, but Rottweilers are big and powerful, confident that they are the best – so follow these guidelines, and you will enjoy the best of your animals.

EARLY LESSONS
Most puppies learn their names in a few days. The next most important word to teach is "No". Whenever the puppy does something wrong growl a "No" in the same way the dam would have done: short, sharp and immediate. This lesson is a very, very important part of caring for your puppy, and can avert a dangerous situation if your pup is about to chew or bite into something harmful. If your Rottweiler is being naughty, or having a chew at a chair-leg, then a very sharp "No" will stop this, but do not leave it at that. Divert the puppy's attention to a toy that can be chewed. A dog must know what is allowed, and what is against the rules. Try to anticipate your puppy's next move and say "No" just as a crime is about to be committed! This is often very effective.

Rottweiler puppies do tend to 'mouth'. This is a sign of affection and a call for attention. Make sure your puppy understands that any pressure, or indeed, any mouthing is not allowed. If your Rottweiler does start to mouth, show you are displeased by giving a firm "No", and leave the dog alone in the room for a minute or two. Most dogs hate this, and will soon get the idea.

WORMING
Your puppy should be clear of worms when collected from the breeder, but this cannot be guaranteed. However carefully the litter has been reared, there may be some infestation, as worms can develop in a matter of ten days. I would suggest that you dose your puppy every four weeks for the first six months. Ask your vet to recommend a suitable treatment.

Continue worming every eight weeks after the dog is six months of age – more frequently if you see signs of infestation. It is unusual for tapeworms to be present in a puppy. These used to be picked up from rabbits and from sheep, but with modern drugs, sheep should be clear. If your dog does become infested with tapeworm, your vet will advise on treatment.

GROOMING
A daily or twice-weekly grooming session is a good idea. Use a soft brush and a metal dog comb, which has a fine and a coarse end. A comb through will remove dead hair and enable you to spot any signs of trouble, such as fleas, cuts, scratches, etc. If your puppy is scratching a lot, give a thorough examination. It could be a stray flea, and Rottweilers very often suffer from a flea allergy, which makes them very itchy. If the scratching is ignored, it can result in eczema. I have found that a lone flea may get on to the puppy or adult, bite and then leave, but the bitten spot will itch. The best treatment in this case is an injection of cortisone just under the bite. The itching ceases and the bite will very quickly heal without problems.

While grooming, check the teeth. Do this right from the start, and you will not have any problems. As you open the mouth, say "teeth", and your puppy will know what you are going to do. Puppies start teething at three and a half to four months of age. You will notice the gums becoming red or swollen. During this period, be very gentle when looking at the teeth, as the mouth will be very sore. If you hurt your puppy you may have a problem showing the teeth later on if you intend to exhibit.

The first teeth that are lost are the incisors – the small teeth in the front of the jaws. You need to keep an eye on the puppy's mouth to check that the teeth come through correctly and are not causing problems. The canine teeth can sometimes take longer to become loose. The canines are the four big teeth, two in each jaw, each end of the incisors. Don't worry, they will eventually come out, often well after the incisors. The premolars, the small teeth behind the canines, are often the last to appear. The molars, the large back teeth, usually come through after the front ones. Your Rottweiler may be seven to eight months old before teething is complete, and so the weekly bone can be a great help to your dog and to his teeth!

Check the ears, particularly if your puppy has been scratching them or shaking his head a lot. Sometimes there are problems with ear mites, which cause itching. Ask your vet for advice on treatment.

The nails should also be checked. Your puppy's breeder will have clipped the nails, but some puppies grow them very fast and so they may need attention. As the puppy grows and gets heavier, and if access is allowed to hard or rough surfaces, then the nails should wear down naturally.

The very worst surfaces for feet are the two 'C's, concrete and carpets – closely followed by slippery bare tiles! In such conditions, the puppy will walk on the large back pad and will not flex the toes. Gradually, the feet become flat and the nails turn up, and these in turn do not get worn down. If this happens, make sure the puppy spends time each day on gravel and other hard surfaces. Like all characteristics, feet have to be bred for, and really good, tight feet are never a problem. The nails point downwards and get worn to the correct length. I never have to use nail-clippers on my young pups after about ten weeks of age. They are mostly on grass with hard paths, which are a mix of slabs and gravel.

If you need to trim your puppy's nails, get a small pair of nail-clippers, with thin sharp blades. This type cut, without exerting pressure on the nail. Nail-clippers with thick blades cause pain by exerting pressure before they cut. Take off the tip of the nail where it curves slightly downwards. If it still looks too long, take a few sideways snips. In this way you do not risk cutting the quick, which will hurt the puppy and cause bleeding.

EXERCISE

Exercise is of the utmost importance. The Rottweiler is a big, heavy puppy, and the bones, and particularly the joints, are very vulnerable during puppyhood. The gristle in the joints will not harden, probably, until the pup is getting on for twelve months of age. Your Rottweiler must have exercise to develop muscle tone and for correct growth. I think the secret is to let your dog choose when and for how long to be active.

I have found the ideal way of giving the correct exercise is to have two pups of the same age, maybe from the same litter, growing up together. They are housed in a large kennel with access to a large paddock. The two dogs play when they wish, and rest whenever they feel tired. As they are similar in weight, they are unlikely to damage each other in play. No puppy should be allowed to play with a heavier dog. It is very easy for the smaller pup to get a bump in play, and then you may have weeks of nursing to repair the damage. Rottweilers do play rough, and they are heavy for their age. A lone puppy needs to be played with for a while each day, and to have plenty of toys. A large cardboard box is fun, even if you have to pick up the pieces at the end of the day!

I do not exercise my puppies on a lead until they are at least seven months of age. I am convinced that this type of exercise is potentially very harmful for two reasons:

1. The dog has to walk at your speed, which may well be very uncomfortable for him.
2. The dog cannot stop and rest when tired, and will probably be walked too far anyway.

Watch Rottweiler pups at play. This is the best form of exercise, using a lot of energy. But when the puppies are tired, they will flop down and have a snooze!

If you are able to take your Rottweiler out in a place which allows free-running exercise, you must build it up gradually. Obviously, you must wait until the inoculation programme is complete, but you can start by training in the garden so that your puppy is used to coming when called. When your puppy is coming towards you, call the name, saying "Come", and when the pup arrives, give lots of praise and fuss. Never call when the puppy is going away from you. This will teach the dog – and it will be learned very quickly – that it is alright to head off in the opposite direction when you call!

By about four months or so you will, no doubt, want your Rottweiler to wear a collar and lead sometimes, if only for safety reasons. Buy a light, leather collar and let the puppy wear it for a short time for a few days, and then all day. When the pup is used to the collar, attach a lead and let it trail. The puppy will soon get used to the feel. Then, just pick up the lead, call your puppy, who will, hopefully, go with you.

Do not let your puppy jump in and out of the car when it is stationary, to start with. This should wait until the pup is about four months old, or perhaps a little sooner, depending on the puppy. Generally, I would always help a Rottweiler puppy in and out of the car until five months of age. A heavy dog will put a lot of strain on the shoulders and front legs. It is also advisable to prevent your puppy going up and down stairs until six months or so.

Once your Rottweiler is going with you on the lead, give some lead training in the garden or park. Talk to your dog, encouraging a nice walk by your side, on a loose lead. Do not allow your puppy to pull, and use a simple command to keep him by your side. I always use "Come in", and I rely on my tone of voice to keep the dog in check. A dog will pay more attention to tone than to the actual words! Your Rottweiler should be under good control by ten months of age or so, but this must be constantly reinforced if your Rottweiler shows any inclination to pull ahead.

By this time your puppy will be ready for a little road-walking. Work up from half a mile to about two miles by the time your dog is twelve months of age, plus free-running places where this is permitted. Never forget you have a large dog, who has a natural feeling of superiority. With correct care and firm handling, you will have a true friend and protector for you and your family – and long may you enjoy that very special companionship.

Chapter Four

SOCIALISATION

THE FIRST EIGHT WEEKS

This is a very important part, if not *the* most important, in rearing and training your Rottweiler to become a balanced, sensible animal, who will accept everything that life can throw at him! Socialising begins almost at birth. The breeder should, very gently, handle the puppies every day, so they will accept it as a normal part of life. At about fourteen days old, as the eyes open, care must be taken not to startle the pups by sudden movement before their eyes begin to focus. At this stage, I always have a radio playing during the day, which helps the puppies get used to different voices and sounds, as well as music, so they are not likely to be frightened later.

During this period the puppies will be handled more and more as weaning takes place. I always call my pups when offering food, even if they are, as is usual, all round my feet! This is the beginning of training and it works very well. At about five weeks old the pups are allowed out of their puppy-run into the garden for about ten minutes, where they get used to differing scenery and sounds, and they may meet the odd toad or, in my garden, pigeon. They are let out before a feed is due, and so they are eager to return to the puppy-run when called for a meal. At this stage their mother is with them, and sometimes Dad or Grandad, or other dogs, so they start mixing as well as being corrected by their elders, should they do something naughty. This is a very important part of growing up.

My small grandson, from the age of two, has played with pups as soon as they are on their feet – under supervision, I might add. He will take them for walks round their puppy-run when they are tiny (the run is about 15 yards by 10 yards) and later play with them in the garden, so they start to learn how to behave with children.

By six weeks the puppies spend a lot of time in the garden and start to explore the shrubbery and flower-beds (which does not improve the flowers), and they learn to dig holes. By now they are used to quite a lot of different situations and have been into the house for short periods. Unless the pups are involved in something very interesting, they will come when called. Most importantly, they are only called when I am sure they *will* come, otherwise they will very soon learn that when you call, they can ignore you. You have made them disobey, and this can become a habit.

At seven weeks the pups have their first experience of the car, when their first injections are due. I give them half a travel-sickness tablet the night before the journey, to make sure none of them are sick. I never actually take the puppies into the surgery; the vet does the inoculations while they are in the car. So, they enjoy their first outing because they have not felt sick, and they have seen a new person. The injections they ignore completely. This is a good foundation for future car travel, and, being all together, they are happy.

CHANGING HOME

Between seven and eight weeks the pups will be leaving for their new homes, and the purchasers

Vahvan-Tassun Chiquitax, bred by Sinni Ellonen in Finland, photographed and owned by Monica Anderson-Anttila. When a puppy leaves its mother and littermates, it is the start of a major new learning experience.

must be advised on socialising their pup (preferably in writing as well as verbally). They should also be advised to keep in touch and to let you know of any problems that arise. The puppies will now spend longer periods in the house, and will have to accept a wide range of different noises and new experiences, and get used to meeting new people. Check any signs of nipping at the earliest stage; this can be a habit with Rottweiler pups.

Give the puppy time to get used to the vacuum cleaner, which can appear to be quite a fearsome object. Do not push it towards the pup, let the puppy come to it, which will happen, given time. Machines like dishwashers and washing-machines are generally ignored, most likely because they do not move. In most cases, your puppy will quickly adapt to life in a busy household. If there are children, the pup will love to play, but never allow children to hit or pull the puppy about. The dog's only defence is to bite, and if a puppy has been hurt, you cannot really be surprised or impose blame for this reaction.

At this stage your Rottweiler should be socialising with family pets – cats, rabbits, mice, birds, or whatever. The puppy must learn to accept whatever kind of pet is kept in the family. These should be introduced, perhaps singly, and all interaction should be supervised. In this way there is no opportunity for trouble to arise.

I heard of a Rottweiler male who spent a lot of time sitting by his owner's pool of Koi Carp, watching every movement. When the fish out-grew the pool they went to stay elsewhere, while a bigger pool was dug. In due course the fish returned home, much to the joy of the Rottweiler, who resumed what could be called his friendship with the fish. One day his owner was horrified to see him with a large and expensive Koi Carp in his mouth. She immediately thought the worst of the dog, but when he brought her the fish it was not injured in any way and had a lot of small gravel stuck to it. Apparently, the fish had jumped out of the pool, and the dog was doing his best to help it. It did not suffer any ill effects, and the Rottweiler resumed his vigil by the pool. Curiously, the Koi did not struggle while it was held by the dog, which could well have resulted in serious injury.

It cannot be stressed too strongly how important it is to teach your puppy to give up anything on request, including food, bones or toys. Play with your dog as much as you like, *but you must always win any game*. The Rottweiler is a very macho breed, and so you must never give the impression that your dog can be the boss. This is an extremely important part of socialisation and begins with the young puppy. Whatever you are using as a play article must, at the end of the game, finish up in your possession. Stop play while your puppy is still keen to continue, and keep the article. Give different toys for your puppy to play with, alone or with other dogs. A lady who bought a male Rottweiler from me socialised him so well that when he had a bone, she only had to ask and he would drop his bone into her lap!

A dog fouling outside its own premises is today considered very anti-social, so as part of socialisation I would include training the dog to use its own particular spot in the yard or garden, and ensure this is always used. A small area of concrete slabs is ideal, and this can be hosed and disinfected as required. Training can start when you first acquire your puppy, and can be worked in with house-training (see Chapter Three: Caring for Your Puppy).

When taking your puppy into the garden, carry the pup to the place you have already prepared; when you get the desired result, give lots of praise and fuss every time the visit is successful. For the first week or so it is helpful to have some wire netting around the area, by which time the pup will go with you to the right spot and very quickly learn to use it.

Do not clean the slabs too well at first; your puppy will learn more quickly if he can smell it is the right place. It is essential to go out with the pup for a few weeks to make certain the correct place is always used, until it becomes a habit. It is well worth the effort in the long run. You will have a very clean garden, and you can take your dog to the slabs before going on an outing. However, accidents do happen, so make sure you always go out equipped, so you can clean up

THE ADAPTABLE ROTTWEILER
With sympathetic handling, a Rottweiler can be trained to be trustworthy with all animals – no matter how big or how small.

LEFT: Breckley Rough Diamond helps to feed the goats.
Photo courtesy: Mary Macphail.

BELOW: The new puppy has to learn to live with all members of the family – even if they include Vietnamese Pot-bellied Pigs!
Photo courtesy: Barbara Butler.

ABOVE: This ten-month-old Rottweiler has learnt to respect smaller animals.
Photo courtesy: Barbara Butler.

RIGHT: Living with a pony poses no problems for these two Rottweilers.
Photo courtesy: Mary Macphail.

Happy Family: Two Rottweilers and a cat live in harmony.
Photo courtesy: Kimberly Barton.

The most important lesson of all – learning to live with the
small human members of the family. All interactions with
Rottweilers and small children should be closely supervised.
Photo courtesy: Barbara Butler.

after your dog, if necessary. Obviously a male will lift his leg while out; it is his way of marking his territory, but town dogs should stop being anti-social and only do this in suitable places. It is quite possible to teach your male to go on command – or when you allow him. All Working Trial and Obedience dogs are so trained.

You cannot take your puppy out until the inoculation course has been completed. However, you can carry the pup where there is traffic, in order to get used to traffic. Although outings will be restricted, your Rottweiler will be getting used to family life.

Let the pup join in family activities as far as possible, so long as there is no danger of getting over-tired or over-exercised.

SOCIALISATION AND TRAINING CLASSES

Once inoculations have been completed, your puppy can go out and about. If you have a puppy socialising class in your area, do go to it. This will give your Rottweiler the chance to meet and become familiar with many other pups and people. These classes are ideal, but unfortunately they are not always available. The classes will teach your puppy to mix with all types of dogs, and it is particularly important to get used to being with small breeds. Your Rottweiler must realise that a dominant nature is not the solution to all situations and relationships.

If you can find a good training class nearby, then go to it. Make sure the trainer is reputable and understands Rottweilers. If you are lucky, you may have a Rottweiler club/class within reach, and these are generally first-class. Most clubs will not take pups until they are six months old, and by this age you should have got your Rottweiler walking happily on a lead without pulling, and sitting on command. Unless you wish to do competitive Obedience, it is better to attend a class specifically for pets. The tuition will be similar, but there will be much less pressure on you and your dog, and nobody will worry too much if your Rottweiler does not sit straight. Here your dog will meet and learn to accept all the larger breeds. This involves meeting other dogs face to face, and walking past without taking any notice. Your dog will learn a Down-stay, which is one of the most useful exercises. When you are out, perhaps in a large field, if your Rottweiler does not come when you call, you can give the "Down" command, followed by the "Stay", and then walk up and put your dog on his lead.

In addition to going to classes, take your Rottweiler to places where there are loose dogs, such as in a park, and your dog will learn to be reliable with them in this situation. Do not interfere: let them sniff round each other and you will find they will then go their separate ways. Rottweilers always think they are the best, so they do not waste time on what they consider to be inferior dogs.

BROADENING HORIZONS

Once your puppy is trained to walk on a collar and lead, then further socialising can go ahead. A very good place to get a puppy used to traffic is a car park. You can stand with your puppy and let the cars go past you. They are not moving fast, and so will not be so menacing as on the road. If it is not too busy, walk your puppy round the strange cars, and let strangers approach you and make friends with your pup. I feel it is much better to have an animal that is slightly apprehensive of motor vehicles in general rather than one who will happily walk close to moving cars.

My own dogs are exercised on narrow country roads, and are trained to get out of the road on to the grass at the side, or up the bank, if a car comes by. In fact, when they hear a vehicle approaching, they just sit and wait until the road is clear. They are certainly not frightened of the vehicles, and if they are in town, they are perfectly happy walking on the pavements.

Rottweilers do need to be socialised towards moving objects, like prams, bicycles, children on roller-skates – even wheelbarrows. Puppies are attracted to moving objects, and if not taught otherwise, they are quite likely to attack them as they get older. As with most things, the dog should be introduced to moving objects at an early stage so that seeing such things is a part of life, and therefore accepted as part of the pattern of living.

I heard of a family who took a rescue dog from a welfare kennel, and on the fairly long drive home they stopped in a rest area to exercise the dog. Immediately the dog was let out of the car, on a lead, he attacked one of the car-wheels, despite efforts to pull him off, and he actually ripped the tyre. Who knows why the dog reacted in this way? It was very distressing for the potential new owners, who returned the dog to the welfare kennel. Dogs from welfare are normally well assessed for potential character faults, but you would hardly expect to test for wheel and tyre-wrecking. I think all medium-to-large breeds are fascinated by wheels and similar moving objects. It is so natural and instinctive to chase anything moving and most dogs don't have much opportunity to use these instincts, unless they are country dogs with access to hunting wild rabbits, or other small animals.

Local agricultural shows are excellent socialising places. There are lots of people, children, dogs and farm animals, also noisy farm machinery. Here you can go near the machines safely, unlike when they are actually working. Walk your Rottweiler along the cattle stalls, and if you see an undue interest in the animals, give a very sharp "No", and, if needed, a tap on the backside with the lead end, so the dog quickly learns not to pay too much attention to the stock. Command your dog to come in close and sit by you. I always use "Come in" when I want a dog to sit close by my side, with the emphasis on the "in".

This method can be used successfully in a variety of situations; for instance, if your dog goes forward to investigate something which is better ignored. I have found that, used properly, this method is successful after one or two occasions. Then the dog will "Come in" at once, rather than receive a smack on the backside, which he never actually connects with you. But, as always, you must be one step ahead, and anticipate what your dog is likely to do.

At agricultural shows you may well find ferrets, birds of prey, working Terriers, and even a pack of foxhounds. These animals and birds are nearly always very good-mannered; they are under control and will usually ignore your Rottweiler. Equally, your Rottweiler must learn to ignore them! Introduce your dog to all these forms of livestock. Obviously, any dog will look and be interested, but the aim is to instil the lesson that your dog must stay by you and not go and investigate.

I took Theo (Champion Upend Gallant Theodoric) to our local agricultural show when he was ten months of age. He was absolutely fascinated by everything, and he behaved very well. He has always loved babies, and every pram and pushchair needed to be investigated. He would give the occupant a wet kiss, and then (his main objective), he would carefully remove the doll or teddy-bear and try to go off with it. He just loved cuddly toys, and still does at eleven years old!

At this show he met all the various animals, but was not too interested, although he found the goats quite extraordinary. I imagine he thought they were a new type of sheep! I spent some time looking at the stands, and one was displaying sheepskin products, including gloves. When we were some distance away from the stand, I glanced down at Theo who was proudly carrying a sheepskin glove! All in all, that day was perfect for socialising, and Theo learned a lot. Although Rottweilers have excellent memories, it is a good idea to reinforce the lessons learned by going to a similar event. Our Country Fairs were much bigger events, and there was even more useful experience to be gained there, such as clay pigeon shooting. If you are attempting to introduce your Rottweiler to this type of experience, start at a distance and gradually move closer. You will have to decide how close to go, as it is very noisy, but your dog should get used to gunfire as part of the socialisation process. Some similar noises are fairly common, and if your dog knows they are harmless, there is no reason for a bad reaction. Personally, I do not think many gun-shy dogs are frightened – I think the noise actually hurts their ears. This idea is based on my own observations.

Cats are often a source of trouble. It is easy for your dog to accept the family cat, but, given the opportunity, stray cats are seen as fair game. So you must be very firm, and teach your dog to ignore cats. Chasing is a natural instinct – how else does a wolf live?

It is always difficult to train against inborn traits. The best plan is, if possible, to take your dog into the country on a lead, and insist that all the farm stock be ignored. If you have observed a tendency to chase, do not let the dog off the lead; it is far better to be safe than sorry until you are completely confident. Livestock markets can be useful for teaching control, but these are not places where the unruly dog will be welcome. Never forget, farm animals of all kinds are the capital of the farmer from which he has to make a living.

If your home is in the country, then you will need to take your dog into town for socialisation. This will give you the opportunity to walk about among people, and hopefully meet children.

Shops used to be very good for socialisation, but now most of them ban dogs. Shopping areas are ideal places for a young dog, with lots of fresh faces and plenty of activity.

HOLIDAYS

Do take your Rottweiler on holiday, if at all possible, and please do not put a young dog into boarding kennels. These are busy places and, with the best will in the world, the staff cannot give a youngster the attention that is needed, and this may well undo some of your good socialising. Your dog will be lonely, and not knowing that you are coming back in due course, will probably bark or howl in his misery, and may well be reprimanded for this. Your dog may be very clean, but if insufficient opportunities to go outside result in soiling the kennel, this could end up with the dog being dirty on returning home. Generally, Rottweilers are a very clean breed, if given the chance. Puppies of five to six weeks do not dirty inside their kennels during the day when they have continual access to the outdoors. As your dog gets older, if you can find a suitable boarding kennel, then do, but try to find a kennel that is used to Rottweilers, with staff who understand the breed. If you take your Rottweiler on holiday, try to spend time by the sea and get your dog used to water. Most dogs love it, particularly at places where the tide comes in over flat sand, so it is shallow. Most dogs love galloping and playing in fairly shallow water. Unfortunately, there are now many restrictions with regard to taking dogs on beaches, but in the winter months these are often lifted.

SUMMARY

The aim of every Rottweiler owner should be to have a well-trained, well-socialised dog, who will adapt happily to a variety of different experiences and situations.

If you already have a well-socialised adult and then have a new puppy, things will be easy indeed. The puppy will follow and copy the adult, and will gradually learn good behaviour and how to behave in various circumstances. It will just be a case of guiding the puppy along the right lines and making sure there is no risk of over-exercising while still young. Beware if your adult has even one bad trait. Inevitably, this will be the first thing your new puppy will learn, and this could even encourage your adult to transgress in other ways. Pups can be very persuasive, and any young-at-heart adult can be led into a bit of fun and general bad behaviour!

If you have a puppy on its own, you are responsible for the whole process of socialisation. This may seem time-consuming, but you will not regret a minute of the time spent or the effort involved when you see your dog developing into a well-mannered individual, who you can take everywhere with you.

Chapter Five

DIET AND NUTRITION

One thing my wife and I've said over and over – we will not feed Rover at table, even though he begs and nuzzles up against our legs and toward us is forever turning those looks of hunger, hurt and yearning... We have agreed and that is why we only do it on the sly.

Richard Armour "On the Sly"

INTRODUCTION

Nutrition has never been the sole domain of the medical practitioner or of the veterinary surgeon. It is relatively recently that the medical profession has developed clinical nutrition to the point that there are professors in the subject, and that veterinary surgeons in companion animal practice have realised that they have an expertise to offer in this area of pet health care. This is curious because even the earliest medical and veterinary texts refer to the importance of correct diet, and for many years veterinary surgeons working with production animals such as cattle, pigs and sheep have been deluged with information about the most appropriate nutrition for those species.

Traditionally, of course, the breeder, neighbours, friends, relatives, the pet shop owner and even the local supermarket have been a main source of advice on feeding for many pet owners. Over the past fifteen years there has been a great increase in public awareness about the relationships between diet and disease, thanks mainly to media interest in the subject (which has at times bordered on hysteria), but also to marketing tactics by major manufacturing companies. Few people will not have heard about the alleged health benefits of "high fibre", "low fat", "low cholesterol", "high polyunsaturates", "low saturates" and "oat bran" diets. While there are usually some data to support the use of these types of diets in certain situations, frequently the benefits are overstated, if they exist at all.

Breeders have always actively debated the "best way" to feed dogs. Most Rottweiler owners are aware of the importance of good bone development and the role of nutrition in achieving optimal skeletal characteristics. However, as a veterinary surgeon in practice, I was constantly amazed and bewildered at the menus given to new puppy owners by breeders. These all too frequently consisted of complex home-made recipes, usually based on large amounts of fresh meat, goat's milk, and a vast array of mineral supplements. These diets were often very imbalanced and could easily result in skeletal and other growth abnormalities.

Domesticated dogs usually have little opportunity to select their own diet, so it is important to realise that they are solely dependent upon their owners to provide all the nourishment that they need. In this chapter, I aim to explain what those needs are, in the process dispel a few myths, and hopefully give some guidance as to how to select the most appropriate diet for your dog.

ESSENTIAL NUTRITION

Dogs have a common ancestry with, and are still often classified as, carnivores, although from a nutritional point of view they are actually omnivores. This means that dogs can obtain all the essential nutrients that they need from dietary sources consisting of either animal or plant material. As far as we know, dogs can survive on food derived solely from plants – that is, they can be fed a "vegetarian diet". The same is not true for domesticated cats, which are still obligate carnivores, and whose nutritional needs cannot be met by an exclusively vegetarian diet.

ENERGY
All living cells require energy, and the more active they are the more energy they burn up. Individual dogs have their own energy needs, which can vary, even between dogs of the same breed, age, sex and activity level. Breeders will recognise the scenario in which some littermates develop differently, one tending towards obesity, another on the lean side, even when they are fed exactly the same amount of food. For adult maintenance a Rottweiler will need an energy intake of approximately 30 kcal/lb body weight (or 65 kcal/kg body weight). If you know the energy density of the food that you are giving, you can work out how much your dog needs; but you must remember that this is only an approximation, and you will need to adjust the amount you feed to suit each individual dog. This is best achieved by regular weighing of your dog and then maintaining an "optimum" body weight.

    If you are feeding a commercially prepared food, you should be aware that the feeding guide recommended by the manufacturer is also based on average energy needs, and therefore you may need to increase or decrease the amount you give to meet your own individual dog's requirements. In some countries (such as those within the European Community) legislation may not allow the energy content to appear on the label of a prepared pet food; however, reputable manufacturing companies can and will provide this information upon request.

    When considering different foods it is important to compare the "metabolisable energy", which is the amount of energy in the food that is *available* to a dog. Some companies will provide you with figures for the "gross energy", which is not as useful because some of that energy (sometimes a substantial amount) will not be digested, absorbed and utilised.

    There are many circumstances in which your dog's energy requirement may change from basic adult maintenance energy requirement (MER):

WORK
Light	1.1 - 1.5 x MER
Heavy	2 - 4 x MER
Inactivity	0.8 x MER

PREGNANCY
First 6 weeks	1 x MER
Last 3 weeks	1.1 - 1.3 x MER
Peak lactation	2 - 4 x MER
Growth	1.2 - 2 x MER

ENVIRONMENT
Cold	1.25 - 1.75 x MER
Heat	Up to 2.5 x MER

    Light to moderate activity (work) barely increases energy needs, and it is only when dogs are doing heavy work, such as pulling sleds, that energy requirements are significantly increased. Note that there is no increased energy requirement during pregnancy, except in the last three weeks, and the main need for high energy intake is during the lactation period. If a bitch is getting

Vonvernon Deacon Blue of Treflonyre
in action.
Diet is dictated by a dog's energy levels
and must be adjusted accordingly.
Photos courtesy: R. Evans

sufficient energy, she should not lose weight or condition during pregnancy and lactation. Because the energy requirement is so great during lactation (up to 4 x MER), it can sometimes be impossible to meet this need by feeding conventional adult maintenance diets, because the bitch cannot physically eat enough food. As a result she will lose weight and condition. Switching to a high-energy diet is usually necessary to avoid this.

As dogs get older their energy needs usually decrease. This is due in large part to being less active caused by getting less exercise, e.g. if their owner is elderly, or enforced by locomotor problems such as arthritis, but there are also changes in the metabolism of older animals that reduce the amount of energy that they need. The aim should be to maintain body weight throughout old age, and regular exercise can play an important part in this. If there is any tendency to decrease or increase weight this should be countered by increasing or decreasing energy intake accordingly. If the body weight changes by more than ten per cent from usual, veterinary attention should be sought, in case there is a medical problem causing the weight change.

Changes in environmental conditions and all forms of stress (including showing), which particularly affects dogs with a nervous temperament, can increase energy needs. Some dogs when kennelled for long periods lose weight due to a stress-related increase in energy requirements which cannot easily be met by a maintenance diet. A high-energy food containing at least 1900 kcal of metabolisable energy/lb dry matter (4.2 kcal/gram) may be needed in order to maintain body weight under these circumstances. Excessive energy intake, on the other hand, results in obesity which can have very serious effects on health.

Orthopaedic problems such as rupture of the cruciate ligaments is more likely to occur in overweight dogs. Dogs frequently develop heart disease in old age, and obesity puts significant extra demands on the cardiovascular system, with potentially serious consequences. Obesity is also a predisposing cause of non-insulin dependent diabetes mellitus, and has many other detrimental effects on health, including reducing resistance to infection and increasing anaesthetic and surgical risks. Once obesity is present, activity tends to decrease and it becomes even more necessary to decrease energy intake; otherwise more body weight is gained and the situation is made worse.

Rottweiler puppies are prone to the development of juvenile obesity if, in an attempt to have a large adult dog, they are allowed to grow too rapidly. These overweight puppies are more prone to the development of skeletal problems such as hip dysplasia and osteochondritis. They also then have a lifelong predisposition to adult obesity with the multitude of risks this brings. Dogs, especially bitches, are also more likely to develop diabetes mellitus if they are overweight.

Prevention of obesity in the Rottweiler is essential to avoid such conditions as described above, but this can be difficult when "fashion" dictates a heavy-framed animal.

Energy is only available from the fat, carbohydrate and protein in a dog's diet. A gram of fat provides 2 1/4 times as much energy as a gram of carbohydrate or protein and so high energy requirements are best met by feeding a relatively high fat diet. Dogs rarely develop the cardiovascular conditions, such as atherosclerosis and coronary artery disease, that have been associated with high fat intake in humans.

Owners may think that protein is the source of energy needed for exercise and performance, but this is not true. Protein is a relatively poor source of energy because a large amount of the energy theoretically available from it is lost in "meal-induced heat". Meal-induced heat is the metabolic heat "wasted" in the digestion, absorption and utilisation of the protein. Fat and carbohydrates are better sources of energy for performance.

For obese or obese-prone dogs a low energy intake is indicated, and there are now specially prepared diets that have a very low energy density; those which are most effective have a high fibre content. Your veterinary surgeon will advise you about the most appropriate type of diet if you have such a problem dog. Incidentally, if you do have an overweight dog it is important to seek veterinary advice in case it is associated with some other medical condition.

CHOOSING A DIET

The first important consideration to make when selecting a maintenance diet, is that it should meet the energy requirements of your dog. In some situations, specially formulated high-energy, or low-energy diets will be needed to achieve this. Other nutrients that must be provided in the diet include essential amino acids (from dietary protein), essential fatty acids (from dietary fat), minerals and vitamins. Carbohydrates are not an essential dietary component for dogs, because they can synthesise sufficient glucose from other sources.

Do not fall into the trap of thinking that if a diet is good for a human it must be good for a dog. There are many differences between a human's nutritional needs and those of the dog. The amount of nutrients that a dog needs will vary according to its stage of life, environment and activity level. For the rest of this section life-cycle feeding will be discussed.

FEEDING FOR GROWTH

Growing animals have tissues that are actively developing and growing in size, and so it isn't surprising that they have a relatively higher requirement for energy, protein, vitamins and minerals than their adult counterparts (based on the daily intake of these nutrients per kg body weight).

Birth weight usually doubles in seven to ten days and puppies should gain 1-2 grams/day/lb (2-4 grams/day/kg) of anticipated adult weight. An important key to the successful rearing of neonates is to reduce the puppies' energy loss by maintaining their environmental temperature, as well as by ensuring sufficient energy intake. Bitch's milk is of particular importance to the puppy during the first few hours of life, as this early milk (called colostrum) provides some passive immunity to the puppy because of the maternal antibodies it contains. These will help to protect the puppy until it can produce its own immune response to challenge from infectious agents.

Survival rate is greatly decreased in puppies that do not get colostrum from their mother. Orphaned puppies are best fed a proprietary milk replacer, according to the manufacturer's recommendations, unless a foster mother can be found. Your veterinary surgeon will be able to help if you find yourself in such a situation.

Obesity must be avoided during puppyhood, as so-called "juvenile obesity" will increase the number of fat cells in the body, and so predispose the animal to obesity for the rest of its life. Overeating is most likely to occur when puppies are fed free choice (ad lib) throughout the day, particularly if there is competition between littermates. A better method is to feed a puppy a daily ration based on its body weight divided into two to four meals per day – the number decreasing as it gets older. Any food remaining after twenty minutes should be removed.

Proper growth and development is dependent upon a sufficient intake of essential nutrients, and if you consider how rapidly a puppy grows, usually achieving half its adult weight by four months of age, it is not surprising that nutritional deficiencies, excesses or imbalances can have disastrous results, especially in the larger breeds of dog. Deficiency diseases are rarely seen in veterinary practice nowadays, mainly because proprietary pet foods contain more than sufficient amounts of the essential nutrients. When a deficiency disease is diagnosed it is usually associated with an unbalanced home-made diet. A classical example of this is dogs fed on an all-meat diet. Meat is very low in calcium but high in phosphorus, and demineralisation of bones occurs on this type of diet. This leads to very thin bones that fracture easily, frequently resulting in folding fractures caused simply by weight-bearing. In growing puppies it is particularly important to provide minerals, but in the correct proportions to each other. The calcium:phosphorus ratio

should ideally be 1.2-1.4:1, and certainly within the wider range of 1-2:1. If there is more phosphorus than calcium in the diet (i.e. an inverse calcium:phosphorus ratio), normal bone development may be affected. Care also has to be taken to avoid feeding too much mineral. A diet for growing puppies should not contain more than two per cent calcium. Excessive calcium intake actually causes stunting of growth, and an intake of 3.3 per cent calcium has been shown to result in serious skeletal deformities, including deformities of the carpus, osteochondritis dissecans (OCD), wobbler syndrome and hip dysplasia. These are common diseases, and while other factors such as genetic inheritance may also be involved, excessive mineral intake should be considered a risk factor in all cases.

If a diet already contains sufficient calcium, it is dangerously easy to increase the calcium content to well over three per cent if you give mineral supplements as well. Some commercially available treats and snacks are very high in salt, protein and calories. They can significantly upset a carefully balanced diet, and it is advisable to ask your veterinary surgeon's opinion of the various treats available and to use them only very occasionally.

A growing puppy is best fed a proprietary pet food that has been specifically formulated to meet its nutritional needs. Those that are available as both tinned and dry are especially suitable to rear even the youngest of puppies. Home-made diets may theoretically be adequate, but it is difficult to ensure that all the nutrients are provided in an available form. The only way to be sure about the adequacy of a diet is to have it analysed for its nutritional content *and* to put it through controlled feeding trials.

Supplements should only be used with rations that are known to be deficient, in order to provide whatever is missing from the diet. With a complete balanced diet *nothing* should be missing. If you use supplements with an already balanced diet, you could create an imbalance, and/or provide excessive amounts of nutrients, particularly minerals.

FEEDING FOR PREGNANCY AND LACTATION

There is no need to increase the amount of food being fed to a bitch during early and mid-pregnancy, but there will be an increased demand for energy (i.e. carbohydrates and fats collectively), protein, minerals and vitamins during the *last* three weeks. A bitch's nutritional requirements will be maximum during lactation, particularly if she has a large litter to feed. Avoid giving calcium supplementation during pregnancy, as a high intake can frustrate calcium availability during milk production, and can increase the chances of "eclampsia" (also called "milk fever" or "puerperal tetany") occurring.

During pregnancy a bitch should maintain her body weight and condition. If she loses weight her energy intake needs to be increased. A specifically formulated growth-type diet is recommended to meet her nutritional needs at this time. If a bitch is on a diet formulated for this stage of her life, and she develops eclampsia, or has had previous episodes of the disease, your

FACING PAGE
TOP: Cuidado Street Life Of Schlosswig.
The Rottweiler is a large, impressive-looking dog. The aim is to be well-muscled, like this dog.
Rottweilers should never be allowed to become overweight.
Photo: Carol Ann Johnson.

LEFT: Puppy growth and development is dependent upon a sufficient intake of essential nutrients.
Photo: Carol Ann Johnson.

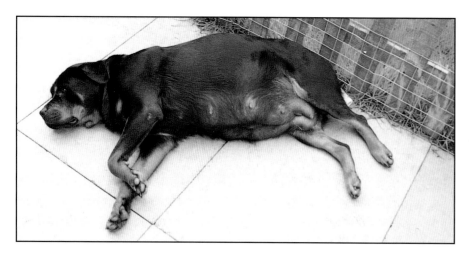

This bitch is seven and a half weeks in whelp. There is an increased demand for energy (carbohydrates and fats), protein, minerals and vitamins during the last three weeks of pregnancy.

A bitch's nutritional needs will be at their maximum when she is feeding her litter. These puppies are six days old.

Photo: Kimberley Barton.

Until weaning starts, the mother must provide for all the puppies' nutritional needs.

Photo: Kimberley Barton.

veterinary surgeon may advise calcium supplementation. If given during pregnancy, this is only advisable during the very last few days of pregnancy when milk let-down is occurring, and preferably is given only during lactation (i.e. *after* whelping).

FEEDING FOR MAINTENANCE AND OLD AGE

The objective of good nutrition is to provide all the energy and essential nutrients that a dog needs in sufficient amounts to avoid deficiency, and at the same time to limit their supply so as not to cause over-nutrition or toxicity. Some nutrients are known to play a role in disease processes, and it is prudent to avoid unnecessarily high intakes of these whenever possible. The veterinary surgeons at Hill's Science and Technology Centre in Topeka, Kansas, are specialists in canine clinical nutrition and they are particularly concerned about the potential health risks associated with too high an intake of the following nutrients during a dog's adult life:

Protein
Sodium (salt)
Phosphorus

These nutrients are thought to have an important and serious impact once disease is present, particularly in heart and kidney diseases. Kidney failure and heart failure are very common in older dogs and it is believed to be important to avoid feeding diets high in these nutrients to such an "at risk" group of dogs. Furthermore, these nutrients may be detrimental to dogs even before there is any evidence of disease. It is known that salt, for example, can be retained in dogs with subclinical heart disease, before there is any outward evidence of illness. Salt retention is an important contributing factor in the development of fluid retention (congestion), swelling of the limbs (oedema) and dropsy (ascites).

A leading veterinary cardiologist in the USA has claimed that 40 per cent of dogs over five years of age, and 80 per cent of dogs over ten years have some change in the heart – either endocardiosis and myocardial fibrosis (or both). Both of these lesions may reduce heart function. Phosphorus retention is an important consequence of advancing kidney disease which encourages mineral deposition in the soft tissues of the body, including the kidneys themselves, a condition known as "nephrocalcinosis". Such deposits damage the kidneys even more, and hasten the onset of kidney failure.

As a dog ages there are two major factors that determine its nutritional needs:
1. The dog's changing nutritional requirements due to the effects of age on organ function and metabolism
2. The increased likelihood of the presence of subclinical diseases, many of which have a protracted course during which nutrient intake may influence progression of the condition.

Many Rottweiler owners are aware of a condition called gastric dilatation and torsion, commonly known as "bloat". This life-threatening condition was previously thought to be due to the ingestion of a high fat or carbohydrate meal. Current thinking is that bloat is due to aerophagia (the intake of large amounts of air with a meal), common in deep-chested individuals, and the predisposing factors may be:

Genetic make-up
Competitive feeding
Strenuous exercise around meal times
Excitement at feeding time.
The last three factors encourage rapid eating.

Special highly digestible diets are available from veterinary surgeons to feed to at-risk individuals. Energy requirements usually decrease with increasing age, and food intake should be adjusted accordingly. Also the dietary intake of some nutrients needs to be minimised – in particular, protein, phosphorus, sodium and total energy intake. Dietary intake of other nutrients may need to be increased to meet the needs of some older dogs, notably essential fatty acids, some vitamins, some specific amino acids and zinc. Unlike humans, calcium and phosphorus do not need to be supplemented in ageing dogs – indeed to do so may prove detrimental.

INTERPRETATION OF LABELLING ON PET FOODS

Labelling laws differ from one country to the next. For example, pet foods sold in the USA must carry a Guaranteed Analysis, which states a maximum or a minimum amount for the various nutrients in the food. Pet foods sold in Europe must carry a Typical (as fed) Analysis, which is a declaration of the average amount of nutrients found from analysis of the product.

"COMPLETE" VERSUS "COMPLEMENTARY"

In the UK a pet food must declare whether it is "Complete" or "Complementary". A "Complete" pet food must provide all the nutrients required to satisfy the needs of the group of pet animals for which it is recommended. At the time of writing there is no obligation for a manufacturer to submit such a diet to feeding trials to ensure that it is adequate.

In the USA some manufacturers submit their pet foods to the feeding trials approved by the Association of American Feed Control Officials (AAFCO) to ensure that they meet the nutritional requirements of the National Research Council (e.g. the Hill's Pet Nutrition range of Science Diet products). A "Complementary" pet food needs to be fed with some other foodstuff in order to meet the needs of the animal. Anyone feeding a complementary food as a substantial part of a dog's ration is obliged to find out what it should be fed with, in order to balance the ration. Failure to do so could result in serious deficiency or imbalance of nutrients.

DRY MATTER

The water content of pet foods varies greatly, particularly in canned products. In the USA there is a legal maximum limit (78 per cent) which cannot be exceeded, but no such limit is in force in Europe and some European canned petfoods contain as much as 86 per cent water. Legislation now makes it compulsory for the water content to be declared on the label and this is important, because to compare one pet food with another, one should consider the percentage of a nutrient in the dry matter of food.

For example, two pet foods may declare the protein content to be 10 per cent in the Typical Analysis printed on the label. If one product contains 75 per cent water it has 25 per cent dry matter, so the protein content is actually $10/25 \times 100 = 40$ per cent. If the other product contains 85 per cent water, the protein content is $10/15 \times 100 = 66.6$ per cent. This type of calculation (called Dry Weight Analysis) becomes even more important when comparing canned with dry products, as the water-content of dry food is usually only 7.5-12 per cent.

You can only effectively compare pet foods if you know:

1. The food's energy density
2. The dry weight analysis of the individual nutrients.

COST

The only valid way to compare the cost of one food against another is to compare the daily feeding costs to meet all the needs of your dog. A high energy, nutritionally concentrated type of diet might cost more to buy per kilogram of food, but it could be cheaper to feed on a cost per day basis. Conversely, a poor quality, poorly digestible diet may be cheaper per kilogram to buy, but actually cost more per day to feed, because you need to feed much more food to meet the dog's requirements. The only valid reason for feeding a food is that it meets the nutritional requirements of your dog. To do that, you need to read between the marketing strategies of the manufacturers and select a diet that you know provides your dog with what it needs.

HOME-MADE DIETS

What about home-made recipes? Well, theoretically it is possible to make a home-made diet that will meet all the nutritional requirements of a dog, and all foodstuffs have some nutritional value, *but* not all published recipes may actually achieve what they claim. The reason is that there is no strict quality control of ingredients, and the bioavailability of nutrients may vary from one ingredient source to another. If you feed a correctly balanced home-made diet, they are often time-consuming to prepare, usually need the addition of a vitamin/mineral supplement, and if prepared accurately can be expensive. Variations in raw ingredients will cause fluctuations in nutritional value. The only way to be absolutely sure that a home-made diet has the nutritional profile that you want is to mix *all the* food ingredients plus supplements, treats, snacks, scraps etc. in a large pot, homogenise them and have a sample analysed chemically (this costs well over £100 (US$160) for a partial analysis). Compare this analytical content with the published levels for nutrient requirements. You may feel that feeding an existing home-made recipe passed on to you, or developed over a number of years is adequate. But how do you know? What is the phosphorus level of the diet that you are feeding? An undesirably high level of intake may take a long time before it results in obvious problems.

Sometimes the condition of your dog(s) will give you an idea that all is not well with the diet you are feeding. One of the most common questions asked by breeders at dog shows is "Can you recommend a diet that will keep weight on my dogs?" Unless there is a medical problem (and in such cases you should always seek veterinary attention first), the only reason dogs usually have difficulty maintaining their weight is simply that they have an inadequate energy intake. This does not mean that they are not eating well – they could be eating like a horse, but if the food is relatively low in energy content, and if it is poorly digestible, your dog may be unable to eat sufficient food to meet its energy needs. Large bulky faeces are an indicator of low digestibility. A poor-looking, dull, dry or scurfy coat, poor skin and other external signs of unthriftiness may also be an indicator of poor nutrition. How many "poor-doers" and dogs with recurrent infections are on a diet with a marginal nutritional level of adequacy?

SUMMARY

The importance of nutrition has been known for many years and yet, sadly, it is still surrounded by too many old wives' tales, myths and unsubstantiated claims. The emergence of clinical nutrition as a subject in its own right has set the stage for the future. Hopefully, in the future we shall hear about the benefits and dangers of different feeding practices from scientists who can base their statements on fact, not merely opinion. Already we know that a dog that is ill has different nutritional requirements from a healthy dog. In some cases dietary management can even offer an alternative way to manage clinical cases. For example, we currently have the ability to dissolve struvite stones in the urinary bladder simply by manipulating dietary intake instead of having to resort to surgery.

But please note, dietary management is not "alternative medicine". Proper nutrition is key to everything that a living animal has to do, be it work or repairing tissues after an injury. It is not an option; it is a crucial part of looking after an animal properly. If you own a dog then you should at least ensure that the food you give supplies all his/her needs, and avoids the excessive intake of energy or nutrients that may play a role in diseases which your pet could develop.

Chapter Six

BASIC TRAINING

"You will receive back from the dog only what you put into him. Dogs that are loved love in return. Dogs that are educated develop their minds. Dogs that are communicated with learn to communicate with their owners. Dogs that are respected achieve self-respect and confidence."
PATRICIA GAIL BURNHAM

INTRODUCTION

The majority of people do not have a dog merely to look at, like a painting hanging on a wall, to be admired by owner and visitors alike. Appearance, of course, plays some part in initial selection, but, most importantly, it should always be remembered that most dogs are sold as pets to fulfil the role of family companion, bringing pleasure to young and old alike, throughout the lives of each. What an idyllic picture this conjures up! And it is a scenario that, happily, is often seen, to the contentment of man and dog alike. When this is not so, the result is likely to be needless destruction of the dog or passing the dog from home to home, causing stress and exacerbating any problems which may have arisen in transit.

It would be false optimism to say that with proper guidance every dog and every owner would live together happily ever after, because account has to be taken of the abilities and circumstances of the owner, the temperament and breed of dog, and the compatibility of the two. This is where a realistic appraisal of the type of dog wanted should be made well before purchase, and a breeder chosen with great care.

The word 'training' can strike a chill note when new owners are told that they must *train* their puppy, conjuring up visions of rigid, regimentalised sessions – a heavy-handed approach which must be carried out come rain, come shine. There is little, if any, indication of the enjoyment which results from these interactions, as well as the pride in having a happy, well-adjusted and obedient dog, which is a pleasure to live with and take about.

The term 'upbringing', on the other hand, is infinitely more appropriate and less daunting. While it does indeed include training, it encompasses the on-going process of socialisation with all that that implies: accustoming the puppy to the complex world he will have to live in – the noises, smells and sights, as well as meeting other people and animals. The dog must have sufficient confidence to take all these experiences in his stride.

AN ORDERED LIFE

A dog thrives when living to an established routine. This means regular meals at set times of the day, allocation of sleeping quarters and toys, and consistency in the commands given, e.g. "Sit", "Come" (to me), etc. Uniformity of approach in all things, including diet, should be the norm. All this starts before the puppy leaves the breeder, when the owner buys the bed (or crate), the first collar and lead, food/water bowls, toys, decides where the puppy will sleep, and what commands will be given, which the entire family must use. Saying "Sit" one day, and "Sit down", "Lie down", "Drop", "Flat", or "Platz" the next, will only result in a thoroughly confused animal.

WHAT IS BASIC TRAINING?
Basic training is showing in a sympathetic, easily understood way, what is required from the dog (or not required) to fit the role of family companion. I am not concerned here with more advanced training for work, or for competitive purposes. Without this background of basic training, a Rottweiler, or any dog for that matter, is not a satisfactory companion and is likely to be a liability to himself and to others. (It is impossible to separate early training and socialisation, and so I have included my own comments on socialisation, which add emphasis to the material covered in the previous chapter.)

GENERAL POINTS
An important point to emphasise at the outset is that many different training methods exist, and there is no one way to teach something. Indeed, good trainers change their methods over a period of time, looking for more effective ways to help their dogs to learn what is required. However, it can be stated with certainty that a harsh, unsympathetic and boring regime is counter-productive. While the dog may learn in time, the learning process will not be enjoyed, and this will be revealed by the dog's demeanour.

Puppies are keen and eager to learn, but since their span of concentration is much shorter than that of an adult dog, training periods must be kept short (five minutes once or twice a day), with lots of encouragement and reward (praise and tidbits). With older dogs, too, sessions should be short, ten minutes or so, finishing on a positive note, with the dog having obeyed a command and carried out an exercise correctly. Then follows playtime, providing an enjoyable finale for dog and owner. Should training continue for too long, the dog becomes bored and effective learning stops. This can – and often does – result in the owner losing patience and becoming exasperated, adversely affecting the relationship between the owner and dog.

Following on from this, another golden rule: training should never take place when the dog is unwell or tired, nor, obviously, straight after a meal, nor, most importantly, when the owner is out of sorts or weary. Some dogs take much longer to learn a command/exercise than others. This is due, among other things, not only to the individual dog's intelligence and willingness to learn, but also to the ability and experience of the trainer, the consistency, frequency and duration of training, and the method of training suiting the dog.

LEARNING AND BEHAVIOUR
Dog training has been divided into two different areas (Volhard and Fisher, 1983): teaching your dog something he would not do on his own, and inhibiting him from indulging in activities not to our liking, which he would do on his own! Training affects a dog in several ways:

1. Establishes a level of communication and understanding between dog and owner.
2. Teaches the dog to 'work' for the master.
3. Gives the dog something to do.
4. Provides a tool to circumvent problem behaviour, e.g. Sit-stay to stop jumping up.
5. Gives self-confidence.
6. Teaches a dog to learn.

Bringing up your Rottweiler in the most effective way to enable you to enjoy a happy relationship, demands some time and effort on your part, as well as an understanding of breed traits and the developmental stages through which all dogs pass. These are termed 'critical

DEVELOPMENTAL STAGES
All dogs go through a series of developmental stages, and it is what happens to them during these phases which will affect future behaviour.

IN THE NEST (0-49 days): The puppies develop from tiny, helpless beings into independent individuals. This is the time they should learn about their immediate environment.

HUMAN SOCIALISATION PERIOD (7-12 weeks): The ideal time for a puppy to go to its new home.
Photo: Carol Ann Johnson.

periods' and they are the same for all breeds, although the effect varies between breeds and individuals.

Ideas still vary on what is the right age to start training a puppy, but opinion now is that it should start at the age of seven to eight weeks when the puppy goes to its new home. There are several reasons for this. This is when the puppy is young, and most eager to learn, so does so easily and quickly. A puppy will learn anyway, whether taught or not, and it is up to the owner to ensure that the puppy learns the right things, rather than acquiring unintentional bad habits. Also, of course, Rottweilers and other large breeds are much easier to manage physically when they are small.

DESIRED BEHAVIOUR IN THE COMPANION DOG

There are no 'instant dogs'. A good rapport between owner and dog is established only when the latter conforms to a generally acceptable pattern of behaviour whereby the dog should:

1. Come when called.
2. Be clean in the house.
3. Not pull on the lead when taken out.
4. Stay in one place when told to do so.
5. Have no anti-social habits, such as barking, chewing, jumping up, etc.
6. Give up objects, such as bones and toys, on command.
7. Not be aggressive over food.

This is the minimum standard to be realised and, once achieved, should ensure a mutually satisfying lifelong relationship.

UNDERSTANDING YOUR ROTTWEILER

Before explaining in detail how to attain the goals of behaviour mentioned above, I shall outline the developmental stages which all dogs go through, and which affect behaviour. There is much ignorance among the general public on the subject of canine mentality, and this leads to errors in training, 'in reading' the dog, and in dealing with him under everyday living conditions. Being aware of what behaviour is likely to occur during the various stages forewarns the owner.

IN THE NEST (0-49 DAYS)

During this period the puppy develops from a blind/deaf little animal to one which has developed adult brainwaves, the senses of sight, sound and smell, learned to behave like a dog through interacting with both the mother and the littermates and, it is fervently to be hoped, been introduced by the breeder to the environment around the home. This includes meeting strangers of all shapes and sizes, being introduced to a variety of noises, in fact anything which will broaden the puppy's horizons – all carried out sensibly, safely and non-traumatically.

HUMAN SOCIALISATION PERIOD (7-12 WEEKS)

Seven to eight weeks is the ideal time for a puppy to go to its new home, when socialisation (introduction in a kindly and careful way to all the sights, sounds and smells of the complex world in which we live) *must* begin, if it has not already been started. If this does not happen, then the pup, when adult, may behave in an unpredictable way, being fearful or aggressive. Puppies which go to their new homes before the age of seven weeks tend to be noisier and prone to fighting. The cessation of interactions with the rest of the litter, allied to the attendant learning of body posture language and different vocalisations, means that the puppy will not reach full potential, although training can improve this.

"FEAR" PERIOD (8-12 weeks): A puppy is very sensitive to new experiences at this time. *Vahvvan-Tassun Chiquitax, owned and photographed by Monica Anderson-Anttila.*

SENIORITY CLASSIFICATION PERIOD (12-16 weeks): This is when the puppy works out the social hierarchy of the family.

Photo: Carol Ann Johnson.

FLIGHT INSTINCT PERIOD (4-8 months): This phase corresponds with physical adolescence. Seven-month-old litter sisters: (left to right) Jacraila's Fatal Finesse at Herronrock, Jacraila's Femme Fatale and Jacraila's Fatal Attraction.

Photo: Carol Ann Johnson.

YOUNG ADULTHOOD AND MATURITY (1-4 years): Dominant animals may test again for leadership.

Photo: Carol Ann Johnson.

Conversely, puppies which are not placed with their new owners by seven to eight weeks need to have at least fifteen minutes' individual time with a human – contact away from dam and littermates. This enables the puppy to deal with the environment alone and to gain confidence. If this is not done, the dog will always be a pack animal. This is the time when attachment to a human (or humans), termed 'bonding', occurs, peaking at eight weeks of age.

"FEAR" PERIOD (8-12 WEEKS)
A puppy is particularly sensitive to new experiences at this time, when anything perceived as traumatic may have a lasting impact and may be generalised. No elective surgery, e.g. hernia repair, should be undertaken and, bearing in mind that touch masks learning, visits to the veterinarian for necessary inoculations should be made as pleasant as possible by giving your puppy a hug and a tidbit.

Fear reactions, even towards something familiar, may be manifested by the dog at other times. Deal with these by ignoring them, and directing the puppy's attention to something pleasant. Do not pet or reassure your puppy, as this may be interpreted as approval of his fearful behaviour.

SENIORITY CLASSIFICATION PERIOD (12-16 WEEKS)
This is the time of 'cutting the apron strings' when the puppy wants to explore the world out there – a stage in the process of maturation. This is when the puppy also figures out the social hierarchy (order of importance) of the family. This starts by testing humans by biting/nipping, and it is imperative that this is checked immediately. Take your puppy by the neck and give a quick shake with the form command "Stop" or "Ahhhh". Discipline is instant and over.

Most dogs are not interested in becoming pack leader, but Rottweiler males develop strong characters, so any attempts to become 'top gun' should be recognised and checked immediately. Rough games involving shows of strength like wrestling, tugs-of-war, or allowing the puppy to grab and pull on the end of the lead must be avoided.

FLIGHT INSTINCT PERIOD (4-8 MONTHS)
Corresponding to physical adolescence, the duration of this phase may vary from several days to several months. The puppy explores surroundings and stops coming when called. Training, which should already have been started, will take care of this problem. Teething now takes place, resulting in the chewing of objects. This is where a crate (or indoor kennel) proves invaluable (crate training will be discussed under the heading Practical Training). Ensure your puppy has toys to chew on, such as hard rubber bones or rings (but *not* balls which can be swallowed) and ensure that interesting objects like gloves, shoes, etc. are not left within reach.

YOUNG ADULTHOOD AND MATURITY (1-4 YEARS)
The larger the breed, the later it matures (2-4 years in the case of Rottweilers). Dominant animals may test again for leadership, and there is an increase in the level of aggression. Continuing training, which should be kindly but firm, should take care of this. Maturity may also mean that two dogs which have hitherto got along well, no longer do so.

PRACTICAL TRAINING
Allow your puppy a couple of days or so to settle into your home and to become familiar with the surroundings. Remember that leaving both dam and siblings is a major upheaval, and so the puppy should be introduced to a new regime as easily as possible.

CRATE TRAINING
An indoor crate (or kennel, as it is sometimes called) is invaluable for owner and puppy alike,

and while the initial outlay may not be cheap, it is worth every penny. Crates are useful for house-training, for providing somewhere for the puppy to rest and sleep (a personal 'den'), and, most importantly, to ensure that the puppy is unable to chew carpets, furniture or other valuable objects while the owner is not around to supervise.

Crate training can begin immediately your Rottweiler puppy arrives. Buy a crate which is large enough for an adult, and put it in a draught-free space. Cover the floor of the crate with paper, and on top of this place a blanket or fleece-type covering. Do not expect a puppy to go immediately to the crate and accept it. Few, if any, puppies will have been accustomed to this sort of sleeping/rest accommodation by the breeder, and it is therefore essential to give your puppy time to get used to it.

Start by letting the puppy investigate. If you detect a reluctance to go inside, put the puppy in for a brief moment, and then let him out again. Then put the puppy in, close the door but open it immediately. Give lots of praise and a tidbit. Gradually build up the time the puppy is inside, and in the case of puppies which are apprehensive – some are – put food beside the crate and then inside. Eventually the puppy will regard the crate as 'home', happily going in and out at will.

A word of warning: *never* use the crate as a punishment cell or leave the puppy in it for long periods. During the day an hour (or longer if the puppy is sleeping) is sufficient, and five to six hours at night. Your puppy should be put in his crate for rest after playing, after a meal (following a visit to the toilet area), and when you are out of a room containing 'chewable' items. Another advantage of a folding crate is that it can be taken from room to room, so the puppy can be introduced to noises and experiences such as vacuuming, television, etc.

HOUSE-TRAINING
Some puppies become clean in the house more quickly than others, but much depends on the owner's vigilance and dedication to the task. Because of their limited bladder capacity, puppies need to urinate and defecate more often than adults, so the owner should take the puppy to a designated toilet area in the garden (always the same place) at specific times, namely when the puppy wakes up after a sleep, after eating and drinking, after playing, and if observed sniffing the ground and circling. Give a command such as "Be quick" or "Quickly" etc. at this spot, and praise lavishly when the puppy obliges. Most puppies catch on very quickly!

If a puppy makes a mess in the house, never scold unless the pup is caught in the act, when a stern "Ahhh" should be given, followed by the owner taking the pup outside to the toilet area. Puppies have short memories and they cannot associate a previous 'pool' or 'mess' with a scolding, unless actually caught in the act. Rubbing a puppy's nose in mess is an action which belongs to the Stone Age. *Don't do it!*

Since dogs in general dislike soiling their sleeping quarters, a crate is a most useful aid in accelerating house-training. It may well be a few weeks before a puppy is able to be clean overnight, so it is very necessary to have a blanket or fleece at one end of the crate and paper at the other. Some people reject the idea of having a crate for a puppy, feeling it is cruel to confine them. I strongly disagree with this viewpoint and say in support of the crate: Watch how the puppy happily goes in and out once habituated to it. However, for those owners who do not wish to have one, the puppy should be taken outside after the situations outlined above. The room with the puppy's bed, e.g. the kitchen or utility room, should be covered in newspapers. The area which these cover should be gradually reduced until papers are only put by the back door, and then these are eventually discarded.

GENERAL TRAINING
Bearing in mind that a young puppy's concentration is easily disturbed by 'interesting' sights/sounds/smells, the owner should ensure that training takes place in a controlled

TRAINING EXERCISES
Demonstrated by Jenny Dennis and Wannonas Winter Masquerade at Hartsmoor. When training a youngster remember to work in a distraction-free environment, and keep the training sessions short, positive and happy.

LEAD TRAINING: When your puppy has become used to trailing the lead along on the ground, you can then work at holding the puppy on lead and attracting its attention.   Photo: Carol Ann Johnson.

LEAD TRAINING: Encourage the puppy to walk on your left handside, using the command "Heel".
Photo: Carol Ann Johnson.

COMING WHEN CALLED: Start this exercise as soon as your puppy arrives home. Make sure you always sound happy and enthusiastic, so that your puppy wants to come to you.

Photo: Carol Ann Johnson.

environment, free from distractions, such as other people or animals moving about. As the puppy's training progresses, distractions in the form of noises, people, etc. should be introduced.

It is in the early months that a puppy is inquisitive and most ready to learn. During this formative period, the owner must put in time to bring out all the latent possibilities, and all interactions should be sympathetic and kind – for harsh methods belong only to the age of the dinosaur!

COLLAR AND LEAD TRAINING

Sometimes the breeder will have put little collars on the puppies, but if not, this should be done soon after your puppy arrives home. Initially, the pup will object, scratching and pawing it, so it may be necessary to use a form of distraction. However, it should be a fairly painless process! In the case of dogs which wear a collar all the time (and I think this is advisable), it should be made of leather, with a buckle, not a check chain or any other similar type, as these may become caught up and cause the puppy or adult to choke to death. *This has happened.*

After the puppy has become familiar with the collar, the next step is to attach a lead to it. Allow the puppy to trail the lead along the ground. This should be done when you are present, and on home territory only. When this is accepted, take up the end of the lead, encouraging the puppy to follow, but without any jerks or steady pulls on the lead. Finally, changes in direction should be introduced by coaxing and by the use of tidbits, followed by a guiding hand on the lead.

Having a dog which pulls on the lead is extremely tiring and annoying; teaching the puppy to heel naturally progresses from directional control. Still in a distraction-free environment, place the puppy on your left side, walk in a large circle, using the command "Heel". Always use the same command. Should the puppy pull ahead or sideways, stand still and guide the pup back to you, with the command "Heel', giving a tidbit when the pup responds. Rough pulls and jerks are quite unnecessary. Start with a few steps, gradually increase the distance, and you will achieve results.

COMING WHEN CALLED

A vital exercise to teach, this should be started as soon as the puppy arrives home. At this stage the pup will not have any notions of independence and will be very ready to come for a fuss. Use a word like "Come" in a light, happy tone of voice and reward with lots of praise and a tidbit when the puppy obliges.

Teaching this exercise should start indoors, gradually progressing to a distraction-free area which is secure, e.g. the garden at home. There will come a time when the puppy starts to explore and will ignore the command. This is the time to introduce a long line (36 feet or thereabouts). Attach it to the collar, leave it trailing, and then give the command "Come". This should be accompanied by a quick jerk on the line, and then lavish praise and a tidbit when the puppy comes. Introduce distractions, and then take your puppy to different areas and situations. Do not be in a hurry to take the line off. Practice and more practice is the way to achieve reliability – a dog which does not come when called is a distinct liability.

Always make a fuss when your puppy comes to you – even if the pup is carrying a 'forbidden' object! When your puppy is taken out for a walk and is off-lead, make a practice of calling the pup to you, praising and then giving a release command. If you only call when it is time to put the puppy on the lead, this may lead to a reluctance to come to you.

It should never be forgotten that a dog is a pack animal, so while one dog may be obedient, two dogs together may react in a very different manner. The greatest care must therefore be taken if more than one dog is let off the lead at a time. It must never be taken for granted that they will both respond in a disciplined way. First of all, test them together in an ordered environment, then introduce controlled distractions.

THE SIT: Start by teaching this lesson using a tidbit. The next step is for the puppy to associate the command "Sit" with the correct response. If your puppy does not sit, apply gentle pressure to the back to reinforce the command.
Photo: Carol Ann Johnson.

STAYING IN ONE PLACE:
The secret is to build up this exercise gradually, so the puppy does not get into the habit of breaking the Stay.
Photo: Carol Ann Johnson.

LYING DOWN: Start with the puppy in the Sit and lower a tidbit to ground level in front of the puppy. Give the command "Down" as the puppy goes into the correct position.

Photo:
Carol Ann Johnson.

THE SIT

Teaching your puppy to sit is an easy exercise. The pup already knows how – it is simply a matter of learning to do it on command. Tidbits are again an invaluable aid to learning. Hold one in your hand a little in front of the puppy's nose, just above eye-level, and give the command "Sit". Looking up at the tidbit causes the puppy to sit, at which point the tidbit should be given, along with praise.

However, it takes time for a puppy to associate the command "Sit" with the action required. So when your puppy does not sit, gently (repeat, gently) apply pressure to the back, just above the tail, and then give the tidbit when the pup is sitting.

Practise this exercise every day for about a week with four to six repetitions each time. Your goal is to have the puppy sit on command without being touched. Eventually, give a tidbit only every second or third time. Rottweilers are real 'foodies', but occasionally tidbits do not work. If this is the case, stand your puppy by your left side, put your right hand in front of the pup's chest, then gently slide your left hand down the back, 'tucking' the pup into the Sit position by applying pressure equally behind the stifles and against the chest.

LYING DOWN

As with the Sit, the puppy knows how to lie down, and it is for you to teach it as a 'correct' response to the command. There are several methods of achieving this, but the one I prefer has the puppy sitting by your left side. Hold the puppy by the collar in your left hand and have a tidbit in your right hand, which you show. Lower the tidbit to the ground in front of the puppy, simultaneously exerting a gentle downwards pressure on the collar and giving the command "Down", or you can use "Drop", or "Flat" if you prefer. Give the tidbit and praise when the puppy is in the correct position.

Practise this as for the Sit (above) until the puppy will lie down immediately on command, without any pressure on the collar. Thereafter, practise only once or twice in a training period to keep it fresh in your puppy's mind.

STAYING IN ONE PLACE

This is an invaluable exercise, and time should be taken to ensure the puppy remains steady in one position for a very short time before attempting longer stays. Some owners tend to rush things, resulting in the puppy becoming unreliable. This can be a difficult problem to cure, so take matters slowly.

Yet again, there are various ways of going about teaching the exercise. This is the method I prefer. An easy way of starting is by having the puppy sit by a door or gate for about fifteen seconds, then allowing the pup to go through on a command such as "OK" or "Right". I am not an advocate of making dogs wait in front of their food bowl before being allowed to eat. Instead, make the puppy stay before getting in a car, at the kerbside when taken out, and before being petted, etc.

Some puppies find this exercise irksome; even so, they must not be allowed to get up from the sit or lying position until the owner has given a release command such as "OK". If the puppy moves, put back into the sit or down as before. Do not expect a young puppy to sit for more than a minute at a time.

Trying to teach this exercise first thing in the morning, after the puppy has been sleeping or in the crate for a period, is not recommended as the pup will be feeling very energetic and disinclined to stay still! Initially, have the puppy stay in one place, either sitting or lying, for not more than a minute, increasing the time very gradually. Always give a release command. With a lively, bouncy puppy, a lead may be used to prevent running off. If the pup moves, go back to him, *never* call the puppy to you.

SOCIAL TRAINING

It is much easier to prevent bad behaviour from developing than stopping it once it has become established. Living companionably with a dog depends on teaching some social skills which make the animal a pleasure to have around.

Undesirable behaviours include jumping up on people, chasing other animals and moving objects, being aggressive towards people and or dogs, possessiveness over food and other objects, begging for food from the table, chewing household objects, barking, digging, and so on. Training for desired behaviour – sit, lie down, coming when called, staying, ignoring distractions, etc. – goes hand in hand with training to prevent bad behaviour from developing, and the two start together.

SOLICITING FOOD

Dogs which whine, drool or paw at their owners in an attempt to be given tidbits from the table are a pest. Unless you are the kind of person who actually enjoys dispensing goodies at mealtimes, do not allow the habit to start. When you are eating, put the puppy away in the crate or, if you do not possess one, in another room.

JUMPING UP

I do not use the command "Down" to get the dog to lie down, as I use it in the jumping up situation. With large breeds, like Rottweilers, unexpected leaping up, particularly with small children, can mean dirty paw-marks or tears in clothing at best and, at worst, injury can result.

Whenever your puppy jumps up – and this is often when greeting you – go down to floor level. Tell your puppy to sit, then quietly and calmly praise and pet for just a few seconds. Accustom your Rottweiler from the outset to 'earn' petting by sitting.

If you have a dog which has been allowed to develop this habit, you need to adopt a consistent approach. If your Rottweiler jumps up when you come in, ignore him for a short while. Then ask your dog to sit. Crouch down (do not loom over), and pet for a few brief seconds. When other people, known or unknown to the dog, come to the house, put your dog in the down position, and instruct the caller to ignore the dog. Do not allow them to make a fuss of the dog for about quarter of an hour or so, and then only briefly. To cure this behaviour it will be necessary to practise frequently until the dog is completely reliable. Never respond to jumping up except by ignoring your dog.

CAR TRAVEL

A large number of dog-owning households have a car, and most dogs enjoy outings with the family. Unfortunately, some dogs are prone, initially at any rate, to car-sickness which is uncomfortable for the dog and unpleasant for the owner. A careful introduction to the pleasures of motoring should be initiated once the puppy has settled in.

Let your puppy sit in a stationary vehicle with you. Give a tidbit while you are there. Then, drive a few yards down the drive or the road – always when the dog has an empty stomach. Increase the distance slowly. At the end of a short journey, take the puppy for a short stroll and/or have a play, so that the dog will perceive getting into the car as a pleasurable event. Sometimes having another dog in the car can help a puppy to settle down.

The puppy must not make an association between the car and being sick. This is manifested by the dog drooling immediately on getting in the car – regardless of whether it is moving or not – followed by bouts of sickness once the car moves away. That is why an acclimatisation period of sitting in the stationary car with the owner, being given a tidbit and being fed in the car is so important for those dogs which are sensitive to the motion of the car. Make sure the car is cool, though not with a gale blowing through wide open windows! Even with all these precautions, some dogs may persist in drooling, feeling uncomfortable and being sick, so a travel-sickness remedy should be obtained, after taking veterinary advice.

I think it is unkind to allow the condition to persist without trying medication, for, sooner or later, usually sooner, the owner gives up and leaves the dog at home, because "the dog hates the car" or "the dog is a bad traveller". It may take time to resolve the problem but it is worth the effort. Having your Rottweiler in the car with you is reassuring and companionable.

Occasionally, a dog becomes very excited in the car, leaping from side to side at passing objects. Here the solution is to confine the dog to a cage, because it is positively dangerous for the driver to have a dog behave in this way.

PROBLEM BEHAVIOUR

Some problem behaviours, e.g. chewing, barking, digging, are triggered off quite unintentionally by owners. Although I have not found Rottweilers to be great diggers, they can certainly make great in-roads on interesting objects when chewing, so it is very necessary to understand the reasons for such behaviour.

CHEWING

It is natural for puppies to chew, and positively necessary for them to do so while teething. You should therefore ensure that desirable objects, such as shoes, gloves, scarves etc., are kept out of reach and that the puppy is provided with toys of the hard rubber variety (not balls which can become stuck in the throat, with fatal results) and strong canvas strips with a knot tied in the middle (discarded jeans are very suitable). Do not give toys which can be destroyed or eaten (rawhide chews), or pieces of wood which can splinter. However, food such as apples and carrots can provide an interesting change – as long as you do not give them too often!

Even though teething has finished, owners sometimes say that their puppy or adult is very destructive, chewing furniture, curtains – in fact anything that comes the dog's way. There may be several reasons for this, and with a Rottweiler boredom comes high on the list. For a highly intelligent dog, being left alone without stimulation for hours on end causes loneliness and stress as well.

Try to spend more time with your dog, exercising and training, ensuring that the dog is not left alone for too long. When your Rottweiler is left alone for short periods, use a crate to ensure nothing can be chewed – and, of course, leave the radio switched on!

What is now termed 'separation anxiety' can cause problems when the dog is left alone in the house. When leaving or returning, do not make a great fuss of the dog, as this excites. Instead, accustom your dog to accept the comings and goings of the household as normal events to pass virtually unnoticed. Do this by behaving in a totally calm and relaxed manner towards your dog.

BARKING

Barking can be caused by the same circumstances as chewing: the dog is left too long alone and is lonely, bored or anxious. As in the case of chewing, spend more time with your dog, increase exercise, as well as keeping on with training sessions, and play games together – but this does not include 'rough-housing'. Playing games gives an interest and increases the bond between dog and owner.

BITING

All puppies have needle-sharp teeth and enjoy using them! It is up to you to train your puppy not to bite or mouth; this can be accomplished, but it is not an overnight undertaking. First of all, it is necessary for the owner to convey to the puppy when bites hurt. This is done by uttering a 'yelp', like "Ouch". Put a hand in the puppy's mouth and when it is bitten too hard, cry "Ouch".

Continue with this response, which should eventually elicit no pressure at all, when the puppy mouths.

However, until this desired state of affairs comes about, if a bite hurts and the cry of "Ouch" causes no response, then take the puppy by the jowls or scruff of the neck, saying "Ahhh" (or whatever word you choose, but it must always be the same word) and stare into the dog's eyes. It is important to 'forgive' your Rottweiler puppy, after ignoring for a few minutes: get your dog to sit beside you for a petting.

The final stage, to prevent any mouthing at all, is accomplished by telling the puppy to stop ("Ahhh", "Stop", or whatever word you have chosen), so that ultimately a command given in a quiet tone is sufficient.

AGGRESSION

TOWARDS OTHER DOGS: Rottweilers, especially males, can be aggressive towards other dogs. This behaviour must be corrected as soon as it is manifested. While an indulgent owner may smile when a young puppy squares up to an adult dog, it is far from amusing when this continues into adulthood, by which time the youngster will be strong and determined. The owner must be prepared to be very firm with a puppy to ensure that aggression toward other dogs does not become established.

Puppy training classes are now an established part of the dog training scene, and it is the socialisation between the puppies which takes place there that provides an invaluable experience in canine interaction under controlled circumstances.

It is undoubtedly much easier to prevent aggression in puppies than to overcome it in adults, and a few words on dealing with this problem in the older Rottweiler may be useful. Attending a training class with a lunging, roaring dog does nothing to resolve the situation. This needs to be dealt with initially on a one-to-one basis with an *experienced* trainer, where the dog is handled away from other dogs.

This should be continued until the trainer considers the dog may be introduced very gradually to the class situation. A check collar, fitting high up on the neck, should be worn. The owner must be vigilant at all times, giving commands in a quiet voice, giving the dog an alternative exercise to do, e.g. sit, when interest is shown in another dog. Use a short but loose lead, and ensure the dog is under control and that no escalation of interest occurs. It must be stressed that preventing aggression in puppies is much easier than trying to cure it in adults. It is a most unpleasant, inconvenient and potentially dangerous piece of behaviour.

Normal canine interactions on neutral territory should not be interfered with. A ritualistic series of behaviour patterns will ensue and if owners interfere, a fight will usually result. Male-to-male aggression is different from bitch-to-bitch aggression, as bitches do not pay attention to submissive gestures, and so fights may have to be broken up.

AGGRESSION TOWARDS PEOPLE: Dogs which show aggression towards people, resulting in biting incidents of varying severity, make headline news. Apart from the suffering caused, in the majority of cases the dog is euthanased. Society has become very intolerant of canine misdemeanours, many of which should never have happened. Situations develop in seconds, and it is the inability of the owner to foresee a problem, either by not understanding the dog's body language or underestimating the stupidity and ignorance of others, that is to blame.

Occasions when biting may occur are:
1. The dog is frightened, teased, or roughly handled by strangers or children.

2. The dog's possessions – food or toys – are threatened.
3. The dog is guarding sleeping quarters, house or car.
4. The dog is unwell or hurt.
5. The dog is protecting the family.

Dogs need to be protected from well-meaning but rough strangers, from children who have not been taught how to approach or pat dogs, and from some situations which they may not have experienced before. This is where giving the puppy/adult as much worldly experience as possible pays dividends – sights, sounds, smells and people (individuals and crowds).

RELATING TO CHILDREN

A partnership of child and dog can be mutually enjoyable, but it is vital that children are taught how to approach and handle dogs. It is quite unfair to expect dogs to put up with being teased by having their ears pulled or poked, objects stuck in their eyes, their tail grabbed or objects thrown at them. It is up to the parents to ensure that the puppy or adult is not tormented; otherwise do not have a dog until the children are older.

In the case of very young children, a dog which is not familiar with their shrill cries and sudden movements may find them alarming, so if this situation arises it must be under supervision. If a new baby comes into the household, the dog's normal routine should be disrupted as little as possible. The dog should be introduced to the new arrival when it is not crying or screaming, and allowed to be around when the baby is bathed and fed. When the dog has accepted the baby, an outing should be arranged with the dog, and the mother pushing the baby in a pram. Prior to this, the dog should be introduced to the empty pram, and walked up and down with it, on home territory. However well a dog gets on with your own children, you should not allow the dog to be present when their friends come to play, as rough play among them may be misinterpreted. No child under the age of sixteen should be permitted to take out a large, strong dog, or indeed a dog of any breed, because situations sometimes arise which may cause problems – stray, aggressive dogs, events which could cause the dog to become frightened, or other children trying to tease the dog.

POSSESSIVENESS OVER FOOD

Feeding time is always a high point in a dog's day, and should be regarded as such by the whole family. There should never be any attempt to tease or provoke the dog at mealtimes, and children can be especially trying over this. On the other hand, a puppy or adult should not be shut away while eating. It is a good idea to put the food bowl in a room, like the kitchen, where there is constant activity, but the dog should be ignored while feeding – not 'bumped into' or spoken to.

It helps if you put additional small pieces of food in the bowl from time to time, as this acts as a reassurance that passers-by are not threatening the food source, but are adding to them.

Should a dog or puppy become aggressive while eating, then you can hand-feed, a morsel at a time, or hold the bowl while the dog is eating, or drop one morsel into the bowl at a time. Again, improvement in this respect is not instantaneous; you have to persevere.

POSSESSIVENESS OVER TOYS

I think toys are essential for both a puppy and an adult dog. However, when you play together, make sure you teach your dog to give up the toy on command. I do not favour a rough, confrontational approach here, when the puppy initially (and inevitably) refuses to let go. I offer an inviting tidbit, and give this when the object is relinquished. Eventually such rewards, apart from praise, can be phased out. It is important that the owner *always* takes the toy away once the command to leave has been given.

TRAINING CLASSES

There are many dog training classes, and there is now wide recognition of the value of socialisation classes for puppies from the age of around sixteen weeks (when inoculation schedules are complete). However, before enrolling with a club it is essential that you visit one or more, without your dog, to see what is on offer. Do not go along hoping for the best; you could be very disappointed. This is what you should expect from a well-run club:

1. A pleasant manner from the instructor towards owners and dogs.
2. No rough handling of dogs by instructors or helpers – and that includes no taking difficult dogs away from owner and class, out of sight, for training.
3. A structured approach whereby courses are run for a specific period, e.g. eight weeks, with a graduation certificate on completion, after which the puppy or adult can move up to the next class.

Training clubs are not places where your dog is trained; rather they are to show *you* how to train. The best classes give out homework sheets at the end of each session which detail the exercises to be practised in the week, before the next class. It is useless to take a dog to a class, yet do nothing during the intervening week between one class and the next.

I shall conclude this chapter by mentioning briefly two areas of behaviour which are often imperfectly understood by owners: dominance and stress – the first causing concern to the owner and the second anxiety to the dog.

DOMINANCE

It has already been mentioned that dogs are pack animals, which means that in the family situation the owner must occupy the position of pack leader. This does not mean adopting a confrontational approach towards the dog, since having a knowledge of the developmental stages through which a puppy passes, it is easy to bring your dog up to regard the owner (and family) as occupying superior positions in the hierarchy. A dog does not become dominant overnight. It is a slow process and the pointers are there to see at the outset.

A dog of strong character which is allowed to sleep on chairs or beds, refusing to get off, which is allowed to go through doors or gates ahead of the owner, to be possessive with food or toys, to demand and receive attention from the family whenever demanded, will consider himself to be the pack leader, as all these privileges belong to the holder of that rank.

The discerning owner should be able to form an accurate assessment of whether a puppy is likely to have a strong character or not, and so bear in mind the question of dominance from the puppy's early days. If the puppy wants to go through a doorway, gently restrain by placing a hand on the chest or by holding the collar, depending on how forceful the puppy is, at the same time giving the command "Back". Do not allow the puppy to climb on to chairs, and make sure your puppy earns a petting by responding to the sit command. Should your puppy become possessive over food, and puppies can go through a phase like this, follow the advice given earlier. As far as possessiveness over objects is concerned, you should initiate a game, encourage the puppy to come to you and take away the toy at the end of the game, giving a tidbit and praise.

Some dominant dogs dislike being stared at by owners or by strangers, regarding it as a challenge. The dog must be taught that this does not represent a threat. This can be done by breaking up the situation by smiling, giving a tidbit, and then having a play session.

STRESS

In dog training terms, this refers to a dog or puppy being 'distressed'. Every puppy is an individual with a different psychological make-up, ranging from the tough, potentially dominant one to the more gentle and submissive little creature. While every youngster needs to be trained in manners and 'social graces', the approach of the owner/trainer must vary. What is suitable for a bouncy, extrovert puppy will not work for a quieter and more submissive one. The first requires a quiet 'cooling down', and the other type wants encouragement to boost self-confidence.

Throughout training the emphasis must be on kindly, inducive methods. There must be firmness, of course, but this should be allied to understanding and empathy with the puppy. If rough, inappropriate techniques are used, either with youngsters or adults, then a condition of stress arises which may be so severe that the animal is unable to function. Learning cannot take place in a state of fear, so fear must never be induced by training. Stress can also occur if training continues for too long a period at one time.

Stress is revealed in various ways: by decreased activity, when the dog pants excessively or becomes sleepy and lethargic, or by increased activity, jumping and leaping around. Pushed beyond reasonable limits, the dog may develop a neurosis.

A good family companion is not born, but made by the caring and conscientious owner who takes the time to:
1. Train with kindness.
2. Relate with sympathy.
3. Cement the bond between man and dog through fun and understanding.

SUMMARY
When training a puppy:

1. Never train when your dog is tired or unwell, or just after a meal.
2. Never train when you are feeling tired or out of sorts.
3. Always be gentle in handling, as puppies have delicate bones and joints.
4. Whenever your puppy comes to you, make a big fuss, and always appear to be pleased.
5. Use food and praise as incentives and rewards – these motivate and accelerate the learning process.
6. Keep training periods short (five to ten minutes at the most).
7. Give one command only, and ensure that your puppy/dog obeys first time – e.g. "Sit" followed by an immediate response, *not* "Sit, Sit, Sit!"
8. End training on a 'high' note, when the puppy has completed an exercise correctly. Then have a play session. Make training fun.
9. Always use the same command for the same exercise.
10.Always use a pleasant tone of voice, and do not shout – dogs have acute hearing!
11. Once the puppy has completed an exercise correctly, leave it like that for the current session. Do not repeat, as this can make the puppy wonder what has not been done correctly.
12. Training should be carried out on a regular basis: a few minutes a day, six days a week, in the early stages.

The secret to successful training lies in the handler being consistent, insistent and persistent.

Photo: Carol Ann Johnson.

Chapter Seven

ADVANCED TRAINING

There is a saying: "A handler always ends up with the dog he deserves." This, of course, is not always true and instructors at dog training clubs all over the world will confirm this fact. We have hard-working, listening pupils who have a dog far below the handler's capacity. We frequently observe lazy, inattentive pupils with slow reflexes who have super dogs that we know will never reach their potential while they have such a handicap on the other end of the leash. How often have instructors wished they had the right to change over some dogs and owners?

What is true, however, is that we get the service we demand. This applies to being served in a shop by inattentive shop assistants, getting a fair day's work for a fair day's pay from our employees, and of course getting the correct response from our canine friend.

THE THREE "TENTS"
The secret lies in 'the three tents'. These three 'tents' signify that handlers should be: Consis<u>tent,</u> Insis<u>tent,</u> and Persis<u>tent</u> in their training *and* attitude.

CONSISTENT: If we are not consistent, then the dog will not know where it stands, will be confused, and will 'try it on' from time to time. If we *are* consistent, the dog will know exactly where it stands, and will not jump up sometimes, be rewarded for begging at the table sometimes, lie on the sofa sometimes, move forward when told to 'Stand' sometimes. So, consistency in what we require – and the standard that we require is probably the most important factor in dog training.

INSISTENT: Linked to being consistent is the need to be insistent. We must insist that the dog does what we require, even if it means replacing the dog in position thirty times to get the correct Stand-Stay, even it is means gently placing a piece of doweling behind the canine teeth one hundred times to get the dog to retrieve. We must persevere. It is no good giving up and allowing infringements to creep in. It is no good lowering our standards in order to save ourselves the trouble of frequently 'putting the dog right'.

PERSISTENT: We *must* be persistent. We must keep going until the dog does something in the right direction, and then we can build on that. We must ensure that the dog not only obeys us, but obeys us at a high standard, both in speed and in accuracy. This high standard must be maintained always, not just when the dog feels like it! This does not mean that we have to make the dog's life a misery. We can make training, and the correct response, an enjoyable thing to do.

SENSITIVITY
The Rottweiler will respond better to love and affection than to bullying and browbeating. Although a tough dog, this breed is also quite sensitive – sensitive to attitudes and sensitive to

verbal abuse. The Rottweiler is a working breed, and needs to be worked in order to keep both mind and body occupied. Going for a walk every day, even a ten-mile walk, is not sufficient. The dog's mind must be occupied, must be developed – the dog needs to reach its full potential.

These needs can be satisfied by training. This does not necessarily mean competitive Obedience training, although this will provide a basis for future training. We can now move on from this and give the dog tasks to keep the mind occupied and the brain stimulated.

AGILITY

I introduced Agility into the Metropolitan Police Dog Trials way back in the early seventies, two years before civilian dog clubs started using it as a competition. All the obstacles now in use, apart from the Pause Box or Table, I conceived as part of the original concept.

In any type of training I advocate gradual progress: small bites of the cherry, creating strong foundations. *You cannot build a skyscraper on the foundations of a bungalow!*

THE HURDLES

Applying our principles of gradual progress, if we can get a dog to jump a bar held six inches off the ground, then it is not unreasonable to attempt a seven inch jump. Continue to increase in one inch units, and only do three jumps in one day. Rottweilers, although large, heavy dogs, should have muscles in proportion to their bulk, and should not be carrying fat. All the requirements in Agility, and in the 'Agility' group of exercises in Working Trials are well within the capability of a Rottweiler.

A clear jump should be approached at a walking pace with the dog on a leash. The leash should be held short, in the left hand, with plenty of slack between left hand and right hand. The handler should jump over the bar and continue walking. Most dogs will jump over the bar too, so, as this happens, let go of the leash with your left hand so that the dog does not get a jerk. If the dog does jump with you, and most do, then go around in a circle and jump from the same direction again. Do not use a command at this stage.

If the dog does not readily jump over the bar with the handler, then other methods must be tried. One way is for handler and dog to stand facing each other on either side of the bar, with the leash over the bar between dog and handler. Position the dog about two and a half feet from the bar. Call the dog, and give a slight jerk towards you and slightly upwards on the leash. Make sure that it is a jerk and not a pull. You can further entice your dog with a toy or a tidbit. If the dog jumps to you, then reward with lots of praise. Give lots of fuss and cuddles, give a tidbit, or throw the toy for a game.

If your Rottweiler still does not jump, then try yet another method. Stand with the dog beside you, facing the jump. Tease with a favourite toy, and then toss that over the jump, making sure that the dog cannot run *around* the jump by using your leash to prevent it. However, the dog must *not* get a jerk on the leash when landing. So, as before, use a long leash, but hold it short until the dog is committed to jump. Then let out the whole length of the leash, or let go of it when the dog is in the air – but only if you have complete control of your dog!

One of these methods *will* work (albeit more slowly for some dogs than others) if you remember 'the three tents'. Please Persist, please Insist, please be Consistent. Keep yourself 'light'; we want our Rottweiler to enjoy the exercise and to look forward to the next training session. To this end, do not overdo it. Little and often should be your maxim. We want our dog to say 'When can I do that again?', not 'Oh no! Not another training session!'

Once the dog is accepting the action of jumping, and only then, you can introduce the command. Personally, I use "Up" rather than the word "Over" as used by most Agility people. The reason for this is that you can put more emphasis into the 'U' sound than the 'O'. I reserve the word 'Over' for the contact-point obstacles, as there is no need then to be as 'explosive'.

The reason for not using the command before the dog accepts the exercise (and this applies in every aspect of training including the simple 'Sit') is that the dog may resent and refuse the exercise in the beginning. If the exercise is associated with a 'word' then the dog may continue to refuse the exercise, even though eventually performing the exercise using the first method attempted, or even if we have adopted a different approach that is acceptable to him.

THE TUNNEL

It is difficult, with the conventional apparatus, to use the principle of starting off with a short tunnel and gradually getting it longer. Many clubs use the principle of 'concertinaing' the tunnel to make it short, and then gradually lengthening it. The disadvantage of this method is that as it is shortened, the central hole is made smaller, and also the 'floor' is all rucked up and uneven, making it less palatable to the dog.

One option is to go to the expense of getting a child's 'play tunnel', and starting training on this, as it is only about six feet long. Another method (and one which conforms with the 'gradual method') is to make an 'open tunnel' with two tables laid on their sides, with a gap between them, or to use several chairs laid so their backs are facing each other. The gap between these two tables (or a single table and the wall) can start off at three feet, and then you gradually get them closer together. The dog should be held at one end. The handler goes to the other end and calls the dog. There will be no problem with this. Now, gradually get the tables etc. nearer together until the dog is going through a gap of two feet.

When the dog is happy with this, start to cover the 'tunnel' with a tablecloth or a sheet of cardboard or hardboard. To start with, approximately two feet of the six-foot long tunnel are covered. The dog now goes through what has become familiar ground, to the covered portion. Simple! Next, cover half of the tunnel, then two-thirds, then the whole length. The dog is now going through a tunnel. Now you can try with the whole length of the conventional tunnel, keeping it straight at first. Another way of inducing the Rottweiler to go through the tunnel is to get the dog to follow the handler. Someone holds the dog, and the handler crawls *backwards* into the tunnel, away from the dog. When the handler has gone backwards far enough for his head to be three foot into the tunnel, the end of the leash is passed in. If the dog does not respond to enticement – a tidbit or toys – then give a *tiny* jerk on the leash. Any response is rewarded. The handler backs up along the tunnel, and the dog follows (or overtakes!). One repetition of this is often enough (much to the relief of the handler!).

The next step is for the handler to go to the opposite end from the held dog, put his head into the tunnel, and call the dog. Next, call the dog through, without the handler putting his head in. Finally, the handler should crouch down five yards from the far end of the tunnel, call the dog, and as the dog emerges, run away. If any of these stages do not work, go back a stage. When the dog is happy going through the tunnel, the command "Through" or "Tunnel" is introduced. The handler can then stand beside the dog at the approach to the tunnel, give the command "Through", and run alongside encouraging the dog. As the dog comes out, the handler runs on. Running when the dog emerges is important for motivation, and, although it is not important at this stage, it increases speed.

If you become interested in Agility, a number of books have been written on the subject (see Appendix I), and there are a growing number of Agility Clubs. Agility is a good way of occupying a dog's mind, and keeping both you and your dog fit. I hope I've given you a taster here.

NOSEWORK

Another way of exercising a Rottweiler's active mind is to make use of their superb olfactory organ – to utilise their superb nose. All dogs can track, use wind scent, and discriminate between

Jacraila's Blitzkreig in tracking harness: The Rottweiler has a superb sense of smell. Photo courtesy: Jacraila.

Jacraila's Blitzkreig in action. In training, it does not take the Rottweiler long to associate the interesting smell on the ground with a reward at the end of the track. Photo courtesy: Jacraila.

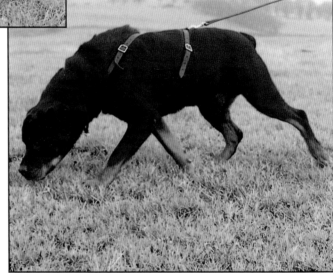

different odours. The Rottweiler is one of those breeds that learn very quickly how to use their nose in the way the handler desires.

TRACKING

There is only scope here for a brief introduction to tracking, but there are books available on the subject (see Appendix I). The easiest way to get a dog to track *where you want* is to use food. In the case of the Rottweiler, we are already 'halfway there', as the Rottweiler is, to use an American expression, 'a chow hound'. *Hunter's Concise Anglo-American Dictionary* definition: Chow Hound – "a dog with a voracious appetite".

Try to find a field with lush green grass, about three inches high, for your first attempts. A slightly damp morning, with no wind, is also desirable. As we cannot control the weather, we must take what we can. If there is any wind, you *must* have this *behind* you when initially working the dog. This is important.

Push a pole into the ground, and have someone else hold your dog for you. Walking heel to toe, go out about three yards from the pole. Back up to the pole, still taking tiny steps. Now go out two yards and back, then one yard and back. This is called a 'scent-pad'. It makes the scent on the first three yards of the track a lot stronger, gradually diminishing to that of the remainder of the track. This gives the dog an easy start. What the dog is tracking is the smell which we have left by disturbing the environment, crushing the grass, compacting the soil and crushing the micro-organisms. The track layer's individual scent has very little to do with the track.

Now that you have laid your scent-pad, tease the dog with a tug-article, and allow the dog to smell the tidbits that you have in your hand. With your helper holding your dog to the righthand side of the pole, you walk away from him in a straight line, taking normal paces, but letting your foot brush the surface of the grass as you walk.

The use of tidbits is not a haphazard affair; they *must* be placed so that the dog has to go further each time to locate the next one. Although distances are not critical, a simple way of ensuring this increase in distance is to use a system. The first track you are going to lay is only ten yards (or paces) long – yes, just ten yards. The first figure in ten is one, so you are going to place a tidbit on the ground, in your footprints at *one* pace. Now you need to increase in units of one, so the next 'food drop' is after two more paces, the next after three and the last after the final four paces. Add these figures together and you will have the ten paces of the track. At the end of the track, turn round, face the dog, drawing attention to the tug-article, and place this on the ground. Put three food drops with it – these should all be quite small. Walk back along the track to your dog. As you do so, pretend to put the food down on the ground with exaggerated gestures from your mouth to the ground.

Go around the pole to your right. As you approach it, take the dog's leash in your left hand, about two feet from the collar. Indicate the ground with the back of your right hand, and by gestures encourage your dog to go forward. Allow the dog to eat each morsel, one by one, and at the end of the track have a tug-game on that spot. It may be that this first time, when you try to get the dog to track *for you*, you will need to 'show him the ground' for the whole length of the track.

Your Rottweiler will quickly realise that there is a relationship between the 'peculiar smell' on the ground, and the provision of food and the fun at the end, and will then start to track your footprints enthusiastically. Now is the time to put a command in. The word "zoo" is softer sounding than the word "track" that some people use, but any word that does not confuse the dog with your other commands is fine.

Now you can start to lengthen the track. From now onwards, do three tracks a day. Start by doing ten yards, then twenty and then thirty yards. Keep the food drops in relationship with the first number of the length, i.e. a twenty-yard track will have food at two yards, then 2+2 which is four, then 4+2 = 6, then 6+2 which is at the end of the track, with the play article. The thirty-yard track will have food in units of three; a sixty-yard track will be in units of six, etc. It will be seen that if there are three pieces with the end article in every case, then there are only six pieces of food needed for every track irrespective of the length.

The second day of actual tracking, you will need to do a twenty-yard track, then thirty and then a forty-yard track. The next day, the sequence is thirty, forty and fifty yards. On this, the third day, double-lay (walk back along) the thirty-yard track. The forty-yard track will be 'single-laid'. After you have placed the end article and the toy, jump clear of the track and return to your dog in a half circle. Once you have built up to one hundred yards in a straight line, you can start putting corners into the track.

SEARCHING

Searching for articles or for humans is fun, and it can be useful. You may lose your car ignition keys one day, and your dog can help you if you have taught what is required. Whether you are searching for articles or for people, the principle is the same. You must work *into* the wind, which is the opposite to teaching tracking.

Start by throwing a favourite toy into some long grass or vegetation, and let your dog go and retrieve it. Do the same again, but this time pause before sending the dog. Repeat, but this time turn your dog around before sending out to retrieve. Do not turn in a complete circle, or else the dog will be facing the location where you threw the item. Turn either less than a complete circle or a little more. Running into the long grass your Rottweiler will have to start to use his nose. You will see when the dog has located it, and you must give lots of verbal encouragement. When the dog brings it back, do not ask for a 'Sit' or a 'Present', but just enthuse!

Then take the toy and toss it in the air, so the dog can catch it or pick it up without having to 'look for it' by scenting. Do this a few times successfully before you introduce a command. Use whatever command you want. Next, you can throw something into the same area when the dog is out of sight. Then bring the dog to the scene, set up in the same position as before and give the command. If you have made this game exciting enough, your dog will rush to find the article.

You may well want your dog to find articles belonging to other people. As you may not always be in the position to use what we call 'scent discrimination', it is better to train your dog to find anything bearing any human scent. Get a friend to throw the article you have been using into the grass, and command the dog to get it. Give lots of praise, and throw the toy for the dog to chase.

After you have done this a few times, ask your friend for an article – an empty matchbox, a piece of leather, a scrap of cloth, their ignition keys, purse etc., anything at all that has his or her scent on it. Now *you* throw this for the dog, repeating with other items provided by your friend. The last step in this sequence is that your friend throws his or her items for your dog. These items have none of your scent on at all. At the previous stage your friend's articles had mainly his/her smell on them and also a little of yours. At the stage before that, as your friend threw your article, he/she contaminated your scent by handling the article as it was thrown. In these four stages we have changed the dog's interest from articles bearing only your scent to having an interest in other people's articles as well.

Once you have aroused your dog's interest in other people's articles, you must only rarely use your own scent, unless you want your dog to be exclusively interested in you. Find out who your real friends are by asking them to carry some conkers, some sparking plugs, and some three-inch-by-one-inch pieces of leather cut from an old lead, etc. in their pockets for a few days before they give them to you in a plastic bag! Gradually enlarge and vary the site where your dog is to search.

SEARCHING FOR PEOPLE

Searching for people involves the same process on a larger scale. Instead of picking up the person and returning him to you, you must teach your dog to 'Speak' at the person. This is easily achieved by asking a friend to tease your dog with a toy until the dog barks, and then the toy is thrown. The next step is for the person to run away twenty yards with the dog's toy, while you hold your dog back. Release your dog who will run and bark for the toy to be thrown. Now get the person to run twenty yards again, but this time to disappear around a corner. Send your dog, and when the toy is retrieved toss it back to your helper. The helper must encourage the dog to speak again, and throw the toy once more.

Continue in the same manner changing locations, getting the person to run further before going out of sight, getting the dog to bark longer before the article is thrown. You will also need to enlist the help of other friends, so that your dog does not bark for just one person. Remember there is no aggression: the dog is only barking for the toy to be thrown.

Get the dog used to two locations near each other. Let the dog see the helper start to run towards one, and then turn the dog away. The helper should then take a roundabout route to the other familiar location, and hide. The dog should be sent in the direction where he saw the helper go.

The dog will search this area, and then appear puzzled. Immediately, by gestures and moving in that direction, entice the dog to the second spot. When the dog barks there, give huge amounts of praise.

Work out for yourself how you can enlarge on this, how you can transfer the dog barking for the helper to throw the toy, to barking for you to arrive at the scene, and for *you* to reward him.

SCENT DISCRIMINATION

If we equate a dog's sense of smell with our sense of sight we may be able to appreciate the wonderful abilities of the canines. As humans we cannot envisage the potential uses of the olfactory organs. Dogs have been employed to find leaks in gas pipes buried deep in the ground; they have located the eggs of the Gipsy Moth that was decimating forests in the USA; they have found copper ore in the mountains of Australia; they have been used for many, many years by the Dutch Police to identify suspects from the scent of implements found at the scene of a crime (other countries are now doing the same, and being given the credit for the idea).

We can use this ability as a game, or more seriously, in competitions. In competitions the dog has to identify a cloth bearing the handler's scent from other cloths, some of which are neutral, and some of which bear other people's scent. Later, in the higher classes, the dog has to identify a cloth bearing the judge's scent from among others, including two 'decoys' with another person's scent. Do not let people tell you this is difficult. It is like you being asked to pick out a Royal Blue sweater from a selection of sweaters of all colours, including two that are navy-blue.

Not everyone has perfect eyesight, and not every dog can be expected to be perfect either. But what we are asking of the dog is so basic that unless the dog is genetically unsound or has been involved in an accident affecting the olfactory organs, this task should be entirely straightforward.

To use this ability as a game, or party trick, we can ask one of a group of children to write their name on a clothes peg. This is then placed, without being contaminated by being touched by other people, among a scattering of other pegs. Tell the child to write their name on the palm of their hand and allow the dog to 'read it'. As the dog 'reads it' he will be 'taking scent' of the child, and also of the ink used! The dog should then be sent among the assortment of pegs, and should come back with the right one. If the dog fails to do this, ask the child to pick up their own peg again (without touching any others), and turn it over so the name can be seen by the dog! While doing this, the child will be reinforcing their scent on the peg.

TRAINING
Select an area of your garden and place half a dozen items randomly. I use old shoes, a mop head, old bolts, knotted rope, old skate wheels, bent-up spoons, lumps of wood and metal, an old torch, a discarded wallet, pieces of plastic – anything that a dog can pick up without risk, e.g. nothing sharp and nothing made of glass. I now have about sixty items in a four-foot square frame (to stop them spreading all over the garden).

You should start off, as I did, with about six items in the frame or area. Leave them out, exposed to the elements, for a few days. When that is done, go out with your dog, take out any easily retrievable article and bring it back with the dog to about three yards from the other items. Rub this article hard with both your hands. Show the dog the article, then throw it to one side of the others. Then let the dog bring it to you. I have said 'bring it to you', rather than 'retrieve'. Get away from formality which is in itself de-motivatory. Give lots of praise, and reward any way that you know the dog likes, for bringing it back. Now throw it again, this time in among the other items. Let the dog go straightaway to bring it back. Does this sound familiar? Look again at 'Searching for Articles'. Now throw it again, and this time pause before you let the dog go, and 'give your scent'. This means hold the open palm of your hand about two inches from the dog's nose for roughly three seconds. There is no need to practically suffocate the dog as you see some of our 'top obedience' handlers doing.

If the dog brings back the wrong article, just ignore the fact. Take it (do not replace it among the other items), give your scent once more, and send the dog in again. If necessary, put more of your (hand) scent on the article first. The dog will quickly learn by your praise or absence of praise what is required. Do not attempt to influence the decision-making process when your dog is sniffing among the articles, or the dog will always rely on you when feeling unsure. Rottweilers enjoy using their sense of smell and will catch on to this quickly.

When your dog is competent in bringing back the article after seeing it thrown in, you can develop this to retrieving 'cold'. This means that you handle an article and replace it while the dog is out of sight. You then give your scent and command the dog to retrieve. The command you give is a matter of personal choice. I use the same command every time I want the dog to go out and bring something back to me. That is, the same command for retrieving, for scent (mine or someone else's), for searching for articles – anything at all. My command is "Fetch", but I really prefer the less harsh sound of "Hold". Unfortunately, I have been saying "Fetch" for over thirty-six years and cannot change now! Any word will do, as long as it does not conflict with other commands, and thus confuse the dog.

Once your dog is really good at getting your article every time, get other people to hold things and throw them back. You then let the dog sniff their hand, and retrieve the article that the hand has held. Simple – if done gradually, and no negatives are ever used.

FUN AND GAMES

The last item in advanced training is 'Fun and Games'. These can be individual tasks, or Team Games. Everything you get your dog to do for you is enhancing your control *in a nice manner*, which is very important with our particular breed! It is also utilising the dog's brain as well as the body, which is also important for Rottweilers.

It does not matter if the tasks are as simple as giving a paw, rolling over, and roll begging, or as complicated as walking backwards, jumping through a hoop, opening or closing doors for you, or taking a handkerchief out of your pocket. Team games can be relay races of various sorts, croquet, dominoes, spelling dumb-bells or spelling heelwork, noughts and crosses (using dogs in the squares for the nought or cross), and various party games. Square dancing with dogs is another activity I am encouraging, and which is becoming quite popular.

All the above activities not only enhance your control by getting a dog to obey a command, they are also getting dogs to work under control, in close proximity to each other. Apart from any very fast games, these pastimes tend to overcome aggression as they have dogs working together while being occupied both physically and mentally.

Chapter Eight

THE WORKING ROTTWEILER

To those who make dogs a study, unending revelations are constantly being afforded as to the possibilities of the canine nature. The sagacity of the dog, his faithfulness and devotion to duty, his strong affections and intense hatreds, and his sense of humour – all these qualities are seen and appreciated by the trainer, and wise is the man who makes use of them and adapts them to his own requirements.

Colonel E. H. Richardson, 1910

WORKING HERITAGE

In 1926 the German Rottweiler Club (ADRK) issued a booklet, *The Rottweiler in Word and Picture*, the purpose of the publication being to make more people aware of the Rottweiler and to earn new friends for the Club. The aim of the ADRK was firmly stated: "The breeding of Rottweilers is and shall be the breeding of working dogs," and this aim remains as true today as it was then, although the Rottweiler has changed his occupation several times.

While the history of the breed is not documented, most cynologists share the view of the German, Richard Strebel, that it is one of the breeds originating from the Roman Empire, when strong, sound dogs were needed to drive herds of cattle and to protect them, and also to guard army camps, the dogs crossing the Alps with the armies, and breeding with the native dogs of other regions. Increasingly, the Rottweiler was used by farmers and butchers as a drover's dog, companion and guard, receiving in the Middle Ages the name of Rottweil Butcher's Dog, after the town of Rottweil (Korn 1939). Apart from these tasks, dogs were also used to pull carts belonging not only to butchers but also to bakers, milkmen and other traders. Eventually, with the coming of the railways, driving cattle across country was forbidden by law and donkeys replaced Rottweilers as draught animals, so two of the breed's occupations were lost. This was reflected by a corresponding decrease in numbers, with only one bitch to be found in Rottweil in 1905.

However, the breed was not to sink into obscurity, for in 1901 interest was shown in using dogs for police service, and in 1909 the first Rottweiler, Flock v Hamburg (Reg No 49) was taken on as a police dog by the Hamburg Force. Shortly afterwards, another policeman bought privately another Rottweiler, Max v d Strahlenburg. These two dogs acquitted themselves with great credit as police dogs and in working trials, which led to the breed being acknowledged as suitable for police work, joining three others then recognised, the German Shepherd Dog, the Airedale Terrier and the Dobermann. In 1911 a bitch, Ruth v d Freiheit, was imported from Germany for service with the Copenhagen Police, to be followed later by the dog Bello v Neufen.

This then is the working background of the Rottweiler, a heritage of strong nerves, aptitude for work and soundness of mind and body, qualities that the German Rottweiler Club is dedicated to perpetuate. Currently this is through a system of restricting breeding to those dogs and bitches which pass the official Test of Suitability for Breeding, involving assessments of conformation and character and freedom from inherited problems such as hip dysplasia and entropion. The Club issues two types of pedigrees: 'White' for a litter which has one or both parents with a working qualification; 'Pink' for a litter where both parents and grandparents have working qualifications or both parents have passed the Korung. This is essentially a 'selection' by which the best dogs and bitches are identified and listed by the Club.

BREED CHARACTERISTICS

The official (Federation Cynologique Internationale – FCI) standard of the breed lists the qualities of character which are considered to be necessary in the breed, with brief comments:

1. IN DAILY LIFE

TRAIT	REQUIREMENT	COMMENT
Self-confidence	High	Should be self-assured and out-going
Fearlessness	High	Ability to face situations with equanimity and not be intimidated by dangerous or potentially dangerous situations
Temperament	Medium	Liveliness ('vivacity'), force of character
Stamina	High	Vigour, power of endurance (resistance to fatigue)
Mobility and Activity	Medium	Ease/freedom of movement, nimbleness and quickness in movement
Alertness	High	Watchful and vigilant
Tractability	Medium-High	Controllability, willingness to please
Mistrust	Low-Medium	Suspiciousness

2. AS A COMPANION, GUARD AND WORKING DOG
All qualities mentioned in 1 (above) with the addition of:

Courage (fearlessness)	High-Very high	Bravery – boldness
Fighting instinct	High-Very high	The urge to 'fight' – to react without fear to threatening situations
Instinct for protecting	High-Very high	Readiness to defend owner/self
Hardness	High-Very high	Resistance to pressure (mental or physical) – a dog which quickly forgets unpleasant or painful experiences
Retrieving ability	Medium-High	Interest in and willingness to retrieve objects

3. GUARDING CHARACTERISTICS

Watchfulness	Medium	Vigilance
Threshold of excitability	Medium-High	Reaction threshold
Scenting ability	Medium	For people/objects
Tracking	High	For people/objects

The great emphasis placed on these characteristics by the German Rottweiler Club implemented through its Breed Warden and Test of Suitability for Breeding systems, adds up to a very special dog, one whose self-confidence, fearlessness and hardness, allied to low mistrust, mean that it is able to work independently away from the handler in a variety of situations – tracking, searching and protection work. Other qualities, such as high intelligence, loyalty to the family and ability to form strong bonds with owner and family, make the Rottweiler a dog for the connoisseur who is able to appreciate what this breed has to offer in terms of companionship, working potential and, yes, sheer joy to own.

RESPONSIBLE OWNERSHIP
Dogs that are bred to work need to be occupied, either by 'official' work with police or other services, or by being trained for voluntary work (search and rescue, therapy visits) or some form of activity, whether competitive or not (Working Trials, Obedience, Agility, Carting or Herding Tests). If left unoccupied, a Rottweiler becomes bored, a state that is likely to generate undesirable behaviour. One of the problems that beset a handsome, intelligent working breed is that they can appeal to unsuitable people – unsuitable because they can neither appreciate the sort of dog they have, nor do they know how to rear and train the dog to reach its full potential. Such people merely want a status symbol, a dog with a macho image.

The Rottweiler deserves more than this, but, unfortunately, where there is a demand, someone will step in to supply it, regardless of the fitness of the would-be purchaser. It is a fate that befalls other highly intelligent breeds of working dogs which are high in the popularity stakes. This leads to breeding for a more submissive animal, with less vitality and hardness, to make the breed more manageable for the average pet owner. In other words, breeding a dog that is quite content to lead a sedentary life. Schanzle (1967) considers that "the qualities of the Rottweiler enable him to be used either as a watch dog, as a guard and companion dog, or as a herding dog. But it is to be noted that he finds only limited application as a watch dog or herding dog. His strength clearly lies in the role of companion dog."

SERVICE DOGS

THE AUSTRIAN ARMY DOG SCHOOL
When considering Rottweilers working in this domain, the first example that springs to mind is the Austrian Army Dog School, which I was fortunate to be able to visit some years ago. To the best of my knowledge, the School employs the largest number of Rottweilers under one command anywhere in the world.

The School is situated some twenty-five miles from Vienna and thirty-five miles from the

Hungarian border, forming part of a large army training camp. It stands in several acres which include two large grassed areas for training and various buildings as well as the kennels. There is a large, concrete hut with a centre passageway and windows without glass. The dogs are taught to enter this and then quarter the hut. Another concrete construction has kennel accommodation on the ground floor and some rooms below ground level for searching. The entrance to one of these is partly filled with small coal-nuts, which the dogs have to scrabble over to gain access.

A long wooden hut provides multi-purpose accommodation: food store (meat, cereals, vitamins, etc.), staff rooms, bath area for dogs, whelping room and accommodation for sick dogs. Another training field has various concrete and breeze-block obstacles, which handlers and dogs have to climb through. The kennels are constructed from wood, and each run is filled with a fine gravel – there is no concrete to be seen here. Runs and buildings were scrupulously clean, and hygiene is maintained by the most effective cleaning process: a high-pressure steam hose capable of reaching a temperature of 140 Centigrade is used. Each kennel and run is hosed for thirty minutes twice a week. Morning and evening the kennels are cleaned in the routine manner.

All the dog handlers are civilians; the minimum recruiting age is twenty-five and retirement from the Service is at sixty-five. The selection process for the handler operates at two levels: personal and familial, for, as all army dogs live as family, it is crucial to the success of the man-dog team that the home environment is suitable. This was a matter of some curiosity to me, as current thinking (in Britain) is that a service dog, civilian or military, operates at maximum efficiency when kennelled outside, all other variables being equal. When I questioned the Head of the School, he gave reasons for this policy. The first is the advantages conferred on the animal by human contact of all types, in all circumstances; secondly the dog is with his handler and therefore under his effective control at all times; and thirdly, in consequence, there are no negative influences at work. However, a kennel is provided for occasions when the handler has to be away from home.

The responsibilities of the Head of the School are formidable: there must be an efficient field force of some 300 fully-trained dogs available at any one time. Their duties include patrolling border areas, guarding radar installations and other sensitive places, and being available in the event of any terrorist activities. At the present time there are 250 trained Rottweilers on strength. The only other breed used is the German Shepherd Dog, but numbers are kept to a minimum owing to the considerable problems posed by the high incidence of hip dysplasia and nervousness in the breed.

Basic training lasts three months, the age of entry being about one year. At the time of my visit, nine youngsters, eight Rottweilers and one Shepherd, were four weeks into their course, during which time both dog and handler live at the school. We were given a demonstration of basic control – heelwork on and off lead, recalls and so on. All dogs were worked on a leather slip collar and all wore wire muzzles. Much emphasis, indeed insistence, is placed on kindness during training, which seemed totally inducive. *Spiked collars are never used*, and the handlers must give physical praise and encouragement to their charges. This was very pleasing to see, as was the complete absence of rough handling, and the quiet tone of voice used when commands were given.

After the novice dogs had left the training field, two senior handlers/instructors with their trained Rottweilers, each six years old, gave a demonstration. As with the novices, basic obedience was shown, but, of course, it was carried out with precision. I was absolutely fascinated to see several steps of backwards heelwork being performed on command – the purpose of this exercise was to be revealed later. Agility exercises were then carried out, first through three hoops set on stakes at varying heights above the ground, then three brush hurdles, again graduated in height, then a scale jump with sloping boards on either side, and finally up steps on to a platform and down steps the other side. The last obstacle was particularly interesting, as every provision was incorporated into the design to maintain the dog's confidence during the learning stage: rubber-faced steps to prevent slipping, a lower platform on which the handler could walk to be near and give support – physical or psychological – if required, and a wire-mesh barrier on the opposite side of the platform to prevent the dog falling off. This was removable so that when the dog was confident and proficient, it could be taken away.

A display of criminal work followed, utilising the services of a very well-protected criminal, with a long chase, attack on dog and handler, and use of a gun, etc. The dog was keen, a clean and hard biter, who quickly came out on the command "Aus". After the criminal work, the dog was required to do a recall past the stationary criminal without going in to bite.

The second trained dog also gave a demonstration of criminal work, this time in the building with glassless windows. A criminal, standing in a window, fired several shots. The dog was ordered in, and he leapt through the opening and held the prisoner until the arrival of his handler. An escort through the building and out of the door took place, and here the use of the reverse heelwork became evident. In the escort, the criminal is followed by the handler, with the dog at heel off-lead. Going through a door presents the prisoner with the opportunity to escape – by smartly closing the door on his escorts. To prevent this, the criminal is ordered to lean against the opened door, facing inwards, with his hands above his head. Handler and dog then go out, both walking slowly backwards. Then the criminal is called out. This dog also gave a display of manwork while wearing a muzzle, the object being to give the handler encouragement. The style of attack was quite different, with the dog leaping high in the air at the head, shoulders and throat of the criminal. Seconds after these two bouts of criminal work were completed, I was able to touch this dog on the head, respectfully, of course, and he accepted my attentions with total indifference and absolute dignity.

The trained dogs wore a bright yellow harness as well as a collar. This was for the purpose of identifying them as trained and operational service dogs which were not to be shot at during, for example, a rabies outbreak, when a destruction policy concerning wandering dogs could be in force. On the harness was a large tag giving the registered service number of the dog.

The School breeds its own Rottweilers, for there is a continuing and increasing demand. To maintain the working ability of the strain demands that the closest attention is paid to mental resilience as well as physical functionalism, so both dogs and bitches used for breeding are fully trained military dogs. Rottweilers who fail to achieve working status are not used. Civilian-owned bitches may be mated to military dogs, but before a bitch is accepted, she is given a thorough character assessment by the Head of the School. If she fails, then a mating will not be permitted.

Two weeks prior to whelping, bitches come to the School, remaining there for five weeks after whelping, when they return to their handlers. One litter, ten days old, was there when I visited, housed in cosy indoor quarters. There was a whelping box for the pups, with a raised roof, and by the side was another box for the dam when she wished to have a few minutes away from her family. All pups in a litter are raised; a Federal law makes it illegal to put down puppies unless they are diseased. Equally, retired Army dogs are never destroyed, they live out their time naturally.

Potential recruits to the working dog force receive a radiographic examination of hips, shoulders, elbows and pasterns at the age of six months and ten months; and at six months and at twelve to fifteen months working potential and character qualities are tested. These two types of examination eliminate about one-third of the dogs. Those which are rejected are given to families as pets, without papers. At the six months test, borderline cases may be kept on and then re-assessed at the second test. When trained and on station, dog and handler are visited by the Chief Trainer and a veterinary surgeon twice a year and both dog and handler re-tested. Records are computerised and the result of each six-monthly test is fed in.

*Cnary von Dorow CD:
Paws Across Texas
Therapy Dog, bred by
Nancy Estes, owned by
Kinda Herrscher and
Nancy Estes.
The Rottweiler's
out-going character
makes it ideal as a
therapy dog.*

*Photo courtesy:
Dorothea Gruenerwald.*

*Lottie the Rottie: A
rescued dog, who
suffered appalling ill
treatment as a puppy,
now works as a therapy
dog and fundraiser for
charity. She has
collected over £4,000
for different charities
and was recently
awarded a national
award, sponsored by
Spillers, Bonio, for her
fundraising efforts.*

Photo: Positive Image.

Food is given once a day, meat and vitamins, followed by toasted bread. No biscuit is given, nor is water, only black tea – this also applies to the puppies. Apart from the ten-day-old litter mentioned above, there were several puppies of eight weeks and a couple of three months at the School. They were very well developed with stupendous bone and were very extrovert. At the time there were about sixty other dogs in kennels, and my overwhelming impression of these was their activity. They were not large Rottweilers, as it is felt – and I absolutely agree with this – that the medium-sized dog is the most viable working proposition. All the dogs were fit and hard, and extremely workmanlike in conformation. To my amazement, and that of the rest of the party, a fourteen-year-old Rottweiler dog was brought out. He looked about eight and still worked, though not as rigorously as the younger dogs. How I wish that were the rule and not the exception, for it seems we have our dogs so short a time and then they must leave us when they are wise in our ways and we in theirs, too.

POLICE AND CUSTOMS
Germany, as the country of origin of the breed, not surprisingly has Rottweilers working with both Police and Customs. In Russia the Army has its own kennels ('Red Star'), and Rottweilers are bred for use in guarding military installations. The United States employs Rottweilers as Police dogs for patrol work and drug/explosive detection, especially drug detection. There have been a few of the breed working with the Police in the United Kingdom, but, generally, the German Shepherd Dog is preferred as it is more readily available, more easily trained, matures faster and costs less to feed.

GUIDE DOGS
Rottweilers have been used as Guide Dogs for the Blind, although not in large numbers as they are quite heavy, strong dogs and of less submissive a temperament then the breeds usually selected for this task.

THERAPY DOGS
There are also countless Rottweilers worldwide who do sterling work in a voluntary capacity. As therapy dogs, they visit homes for the elderly, schools and hospitals, where their weekly visits are eagerly awaited. The temperament of therapy dogs is always closely assessed.

DOGS FOR THE DISABLED
A fairly new role for dogs – and it is not known how many Rottweilers have completed training for this role – is that of Assistance Dogs for the Disabled, whereby a carefully trained dog acts as an extra pair of hands for a disabled person.

RESCUE DOGS
At the time of writing, there are between ten and fifteen Rottweilers qualified as Mountain/Forest Rescue Dogs in Norway. Three levels of competence are recognised in this country:

A. (Top level): Dog must have normal hips and elbows and have passed all requisite tests. Qualified to go out on rescue duties.
B. (Second level): Dog has not yet reached so high a standard as those in 'A' above and are not called out unless an 'A' dog is not available.
C. (Basic level): The first step on the ladder. At this stage dogs are only just beginning their training and are not called out to work.

A breakdown of the breeds used in Mountain/Forest Rescue work is as follows:

German Shorthaired Pointers: 60 per cent
Retrievers and some other gundog breeds: 15per cent
Rottweilers and Riesenschnauzers: 10-15 per cent
Others: 5-10 per cent.

FILMS

Rottweilers have been and still are used in films. Unfortunately, they are often represented as snarling beasts, which does nothing for the image of the breed. I once provided a bitch to accompany a six-foot blonde model wearing the latest mini fashions, and others have been used in advertising all sorts of products. The same bitch also appeared as a sort of ghostly presence in the film *Parker* some years ago, and we had lots of fun in doing this, but, generally, it seems that Rottweilers have been presented too often merely as a set of teeth.

CHARACTER TESTS

The importance of character in the working and daily functioning of a dog should never be underestimated, and different types of Temperament/Character/Mental Tests are used. In Germany, for example, Rottweilers must pass the Companion Dog Test (Begleithundprufung – BH) before they are entered for the Test of Suitability for Breeding, and before they can be entered for Schutzhund Trials. These trials consist of three sections, Tracking, Obedience and Protection, and are designed to test that the constellation of traits which are required in a working dog (i.e. in guarding/protection breeds, such as the Rottweiler, GSD, Dobermann, etc.) are present in a high degree, so identifying animals which are suitable for breeding, as well as possessing qualities of type and physical soundness.

In the UK individual breed clubs hold voluntary assessments for their members, most of these devised to ascertain whether the dog is able to cope with the everyday occurrences (sights, sounds, people) of the complex world we live in. The Kennel Club recently introduced a Canine Good Citizen Test for all breeds and cross-breeds. These tests highlight the importance of good temperament and can do nothing but good for dogs in general. A concern, however, is that those people who conduct such tests should not only have an in-depth knowledge of canine behaviour, but also must possess the ability to interact sympathetically and communicate effectively with people. This is by no means always the case!

In the USA the American Kennel Club has held Canine Good Citizen Tests for several years and the American Rottweiler Club has formulated a test for Rottweilers. Sweden and Denmark hold 'Mental' Tests that dogs must pass if they are to be awarded a Challenge Certificate in the show ring. If they have not taken or passed this test, they can only be declared as being of 'Champion quality'. To become a Champion, a dog must also have qualified in an area of work: tracking, searching, retrieving, or have a Mountain/Forest Rescue qualification from Norway.

There is also a 'Mental' Test used in Denmark which is very similar to the Swedish test. The dogs go through a thirteen-point programme, taking about one hour per dog. The dogs are never hit or threatened in any way. They are taken through a course with the handler, being on-lead for some sections and off-lead for others, and the handler is not permitted to give any verbal assistance during a test in which the dog is put under pressure. The test should be conducted in a quiet forest area without any livestock or traffic (motor cycles, etc.). The assessment includes:

1 Willingness to contact – this is where the dog is introduced to the Test Leader and to the crowd of people who are his 'pack'. The dog's acceptance, by not displaying any fear or shyness, is checked.
2 Willingness to play – the handler plays with the dog, and the degree of playfulness with the owner and Test Leader is noted.

3. Curiosity – two marshalls, 20 metres away and 15 metres apart, each make a noise using mechanical means such as milk bottle with pebbles inside; the dog is assessed for attentiveness and if it searches for each marshall.

4. Hunting – a piece of cloth is moved through eight or so staggered poles to simulate a rabbit; the dog is tested on its keenness to catch the rabbit.

5. Attachment to Pack Leader – this test checks the dog's attachment to its owner through a set of stationary dummies with large eyes; the speed the dog takes and the intensity and concentration are noted.

6. Surprise – for this test a dummy is raised up at speed in front of both dog and owner at about three metres; dog's reaction is noted.

7. Noise – a bundle of chain is dropped on to a piece of tin as the dog and owner are passing close by; the dog's reaction is noted.

8. Social Fighting Behaviour – a marshall dresses up in a large cloak with dark glasses and a hat. He comes out of the forest some 25 metres away from dog and handler, moving in a set pattern; the dog's reactions are noted.

9. Threat Behaviour – a small sledge, with a half-size dummy, comes out of the forest some 20 metres away; the dog's dominance level is noted.

10. Defence – two marshalls dress up in white gowns with their heads covered, leaving large eye openings. They come out of the forest, some 20 metres away and 15 metres apart, at a slow steady pace; the dog's reaction is checked..

11. Gunshot test – the dog is tested to see whether it is gun-shy.

12. Activity – the dog's level of activity in completing all tests is assessed.

13. Nervous System – the dog's concentration level when carrying out the tests is assessed, and any conflict situations that arise are noted.

The 'Mental' Test is a demanding one for dog, handler and tester alike. The first needs to exhibit in full measure the traits required of a working dog, the second should have a good rapport with an understanding of his dog, and the tester needs to be extremely experienced and knowledgeable about dogs in general and working dogs in particular. Before being allowed to enter for these tests, in both Sweden and Denmark, the dog must be given training, as the test is complex to administer and to interpret.

The American Temperament Test Society holds tests for all breeds and includes tests on behaviour towards strangers, reaction to acoustic stimuli, reaction to visual stimulus, foot test (unusual surface), self-protectiveness/aggressive reaction.

Most Rottweiler Clubs in the UK use a test which assesses a dog's reaction to: a friendly approach, unusual approach (NOT threatening), moving/unusual obstacles, being left alone, being off-lead, loud noises, traffic, a group of people, other dogs.

WORKING EVENTS/TRIALS

For those owners who wish to do something with their dogs, apart from entering them at conformation shows, there are various kinds of working events which provide opportunities for cultivating their dog's working abilities and having a great deal of enjoyment while doing so.

Countries affiliated to the Federation Cynologique (FCI) take part in Schutzhund Trials. Other working tests are held, but not all are recognised for breeding or performance purposes, nor are they competitive, in that only a 'pass' or a 'fail' grade is given.

AD (Ausdauerprufung): An endurance test with handler on bicycle. A distance of 5.5 miles must be covered in just one and a half hours.

WD (Wachhundprufung): Basic obedience and guarding of objects.

RH (Rettungshundprufung): Rescue Dog Test – requires controllability and stability in the dog. An endurance test, tracking, with fire used as a distraction, and obedience, again with distractions, gunfire, loud noises (falling objects, masonry, metal drum, etc), noisy crowd, walking over obstacles like a raised platform, a long down stay.

BH (Begleithundprufung): Companion Dog Test. Obedience exercises on and off-lead, gunfire, crowd of people, carried out at training area. In a town, dog encounters pedestrian and vehicular traffic, is tied up and left on his own while another dog and handler pass by, does a recall (off lead) in a quiet street.

SCHUTZHUND I (minimum age for entry 14 months)	SCHUTZHUND II (minimum age for entry 16 months)	SCHUTZHUND III (minimum age for entry 18 months)
A. Tracking Handler lays track 400/500 paces long, minimum twenty minutes old. Two articles on track. Three right-angle turns. Dog on thirty-foot tracking line.	**A. Tracking** Stranger's track 600/700 paces long, minimum thirty minutes old. Two articles. Two ring-angle turns. Dog on thirty-foot tracking line.	**A. Tracking** Stranger's track 1200/1400 paces long, minimum fifty minutes old. Three articles. Four right-angle turns. Dog can track free or be on three-foot tracking line.
B. Obedience Heel on-leash. Heel off-leash. Sit-stay (handler in sight). Down and recall. Retrieve handler's article. Retrieve over jump 39 inches (handler's article). Send-away. Long down (handler in sight with distraction – another handler and dog working obedience).	**B. Obedience** Heel off-leash. Sit-stay (handler in sight). Down and recall. Retrieve two-pound dumbbell on flat. Retrieve one-and-a-half pound dumbbell over 39-inch jump. Retrieve over six-foot wall. Send-away. Long down (handler in sight with distraction – another handler and dog working obedience).	**B. Obedience** Heel off-leash. Sit-stay (handler in sight). Stand-stay. Retrieve four-pound dumbbell on flat. Retrieve one-and-a-half pound dumbbell over 39-inch jump. Retrieve over six-foot wall. Send-away. Long down (handler in sight with distraction – another handler and dog working obedience).
C. Protection Hold at bay and bark. Attack on handler (by 'criminal'). Pursuit and hold at bay (Courage test).	**C. Protection** Search for criminal. Finding and barking. Attack on handler. Pursuit and hold at bay. (Test of courage, fighting instinct and hardness).	**C. Protection** Search for criminal. Finding and barking. Attack on handler. Pursuit and hold at bay. (Test of courage, fighting instinct and hardness).

Note: More work is required from the dog in the SchH III tests and more pressure is put on him.

Schutzhund training has become an increasingly popular sport in the USA, and Rottweilers respond well to this particular discipline.

Photo courtesy: Pamela Wilkinson Grant.

Jagen Blue Jola CDEX, IDEX, WDEX, TD, PD with handler Tony Crompton. Schutzhund requires a great deal of intensive training, as the Rottweiler must show courage and aggression in protection work, but this must always be under the direction of the handler.

Photo courtesy: Tony Crompton.

TRACKING DOG TEST
(Fahrtenhundprufung)
(Minimum age for entry 16 months)
The dog must have qualified SchH I first.

Track
1500 paces.
Stranger's track.
Three hours old.
Six angles.
Four articles.
Three cross-tracks.
Dog on thirty-foot line or tracks free.

General note: Gradings of Excellent, Very Good, Good, Satisfactory, Unsatisfactory are given according to the marks obtained.

The sport of Schutzhund has a large following in the USA and was introduced to Britain within the last few years. It should be noted that Schutzhund Trials are not recognised by either the American Kennel Club or the English Kennel Club.

The AKC runs Obedience Trials, Tracking Trials, Agility Competitions and Herding Trials (for specified breeds only).

OBEDIENCE TRIALS

Novice	Open	Utility
(To qualify CD)	Class A: Have CD title but not CDX.	Class A: For dogs qualified CDX but not UD.
Minimum age six months.	Class B: Have CDX title.	Class B: For dogs qualified UD.
Must not have qualified CD.		
Heel on-leash and Figure 8.		
Stand for examination	Heel free and	Signal Exercise
Heel free.	Figure 8.	Scent Discrimination Article 1 (metal).
Recall.	Drop on recall.	
Long sit (handler in sight one minute).	Retrieve on flat.	Scent Discrimination Article 2 (leather).
	Retrieve over high jump.	
Long down (handler in sight three minutes).	Broad jump.	Directed Retrieve.
	Long sit.	Moving Stand and Examination.
	Long down	Directed Jumping.

Note: The height and length of the jumps is according to the height at the withers for Rottweilers.

Tracking Two levels:
TRACKING (TD)
Before being able to enter the Trial, the dog and handler must attend a pre-trial 'certification',

after which a licensed Tracking Judge attests to the fact that the team is capable of passing a tracking test.

Stranger's track: 500 yards in length, several turns, two of which should be right angles. One article on track. Age of track – not less than half an hour nor more than two hours. No time limit for working track as long as dog is actually working.

TRACKING DOG EXCELLENT (TDX)

Stranger's track over varying terrain. Crossing road, two cross-tracks. Three articles. Track not less than three hours old, with more than five turns.

In the UK there are five stakes in Working Trials.

COMPANION DOG	UTILITY DOG (Qualification UD)	WORKING DOG (Qualification WD)	TRACKING DOG (Qualification TD)	PATROL DOG (Qualification PD)
I. Control Heel on-lead. Heel off-lead. Recall to handler. Sendaway. **II. Stays** Sit two minutes. Down ten minutes.	**I. Control** Heel Free. Sendaway. Retrieve dumb-bell. Down ten minutes. Steadiness to gunshot.	**I. Control** Heel Free. Sendaway. Retrieve dumb-bell. Down ten minutes. Steadiness to gunshot.	**I. Control** Heel Free. Sendaway and directional control Speak on command. Down ten minutes. Steadiness to gunshot.	**I. Control** As tracking dog. **II. Agility** Clear jump three-foot. Long jump nine-foot. Scale jump six-foot.
III. Agility Clear jump. Long jump. Scale (with stay and recall). *Note: The height and length of these jumps is according to height of dog at withers.*	**II. Agility** Clear jump. Long jump. Scale (with stay and recall). *Note: The height and length of these jumps is according to height of dog at withers.*	**II. Agility** Clear jump three-foot. Long jump nine-foot. Scale jump six-foot	**II Agility** Clear jump three-foot. Long jump nine-foot. Scale jump six-foot	**III. Nosework** Search four articles. Track two articles. Not less than two hours old. Half-a-mile long.
IV. Nosework Retrieve dumb-bell. Elementary search for three articles.	**III. Nosework** Search four articles. Track not less than half-an-hour old – two articles. Half-a-mile long.	**III. Nosework** Search four articles. Track not less than one-and-a-half hours old. Two articles. Half-a-mile long.	**III. Nosework** Search four articles. Track two articles. Not less than three hours old.	**IV. Patrol** Quartering the ground. Test of courage Recall from 'criminal'. Pursuit and detention of 'criminal'

THE WORKING ROTTWEILER
The Rottweiler responds well to the stimulus of training, and this large breed is surprisingly agile when tackling obstacles.

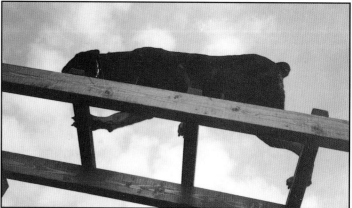

LEFT: Misty Black Mountain CDEX, UDEX tackles the A-frame, while retrieving a dumb-bell.
Photo courtesy: Tony Crompton.

ABOVE: A Rottweiler will perform the most difficult task if it has complete trust in its handler.
Photo courtesy: Mary Macphail.

RIGHT: This obstacle, nick-named 'Ben Nevis' poses no problems for the well-trained Rottweiler.
Photo courtesy: Violet Slade.

BELOW: This obstacle requires a tremendous sense of balance.
Photo courtesy Violet Slade.

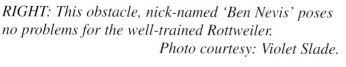

Working Trials are scheduled at two levels – Open and Championship, and dogs work their way up from CD to the higher Stakes. Before being able to enter Championship UD, WD, TD or PD, a dog must qualify in the Open equivalent of these Stakes by gaining a Certificate of Merit. Qualification in UD Championship Stakes and higher ones with the grading of Excellent depends on the marks gained.

Obedience Classes (UK) may be scheduled at all-breed Open and Championship shows and at breed shows at which entry is restricted to one breed. There are six classes: Pre-Beginners, Beginners, Novice, Class A, Class B, Class C, and dogs work their way up the classes. Standards of precision are extremely high in this type of event, and although some Rottweilers have done well, they are more suited to Working Trials.

Agility Classes (Elementary, Starters, Novice, Intermediate, Seniors, Advanced) have a variety of obstacles and layouts. Rottweilers do compete and, although very competent jumpers, cannot match breeds such as the Border Collies for speed.

CARTING

The Kennel Union of South Africa runs Carting Competitions, and a dog which wins three KUSA Carting Certificates, each from a different judge, qualifies as a Carting Champion. There are two classes, Novice in which all work is done on the lead, and Senior where all work is done off-lead. The exercises are: Basic control; Heel work; Recall; Stay (a group exercise); Harnessing and Hitching; Basic commands; Manoeuvring; Control in the presence of a distraction.

BASIC COMMANDS

Dog performs the following exercises – haul forward at normal pace, fast pace, slow pace, stop (stand still), back-up and stay.

MANOEUVRING

In the Novice Class this will be at the judge's discretion. In the Senior class the cart will be loaded with a load provided by the judge, according to the size of the dog.

The course to be followed by the handler and dog includes: circular patterns, at least three turns of 90 degrees, two of which shall be in different directions, broad curves, narrow areas, removable obstacles (gate, branch or similar).

The 'back-up' should be performed during the manoeuvring course, the purpose being to show that the harnessed dog is able to back-up on command should he inadvertently be led by his handler into a tight corner where turning is impossible.

A distraction is introduced at a point to be determined by the judge. This should not occur at a point where a basic command is given or to be given. No deviation either towards or away from the disturbance is permitted although a short stop, a prolonged stare or short bark are permissible.

Many carts pulled by one, two or even six Rottweilers feature in parades and displays in the USA. In the UK it is against the law to take a dog pulling a cart on to a public highway – legislation arising from the practice in the 19th Century of using dogs for draught purposes and running them until their paws were raw or they were totally exhausted.

HERDING TESTS AND TRIALS

Despite the Rottweiler's background as a cattle herding and droving dog, it was not until June 1994 that the American Kennel Club added the breed's name to the list of those allowed to compete in its official Herding Tests and Trials, although a few Rottweilers had been entered in events run by all-breed herding clubs.

There are two types of events run under the auspices of the AKC: Herding Tests and Herding Trials. The former is the easier of the two, having fewer elements and with the judge permitted to give competitors suggestions on how to complete the course. A dog may qualify for a title after successfully completing two tests under two different judges. Herding trials are more difficult, having more elements, and to qualify a dog must compete at three trials under three different judges.

The qualifications which may be awarded are:

HERDING TESTS
HT Herding Tested Dog
PT Pre-Trial Tested Dog

HERDING TRIALS
HS Herding Started Certificate
HI Herding Intermediate
HX Herding Excellent
H Ch Champion (dog must have gained HX and then gained points in Advanced Classes)

The courses increase in difficulty as the dog moves up the scale. Rottweilers have shown much aptitude for this work, and it is difficult to discern who enjoys it most, dog or handler!

The stock to be used for all-breed herding tests are sheep/goats, or ducks/geese/turkeys or cattle. The suitability and quality of the livestock used is extremely important, and the club running the event must ensure that the very explicit rules laid down by the AKC are followed, including the experience and welfare of the stock.

A Herding Standard for the Rottweiler was formulated and appeared first in the June 1990 Newsletter of the Canadian Rottweiler Club. It reads as follows:

HERDING STANDARD FOR THE ROTTWEILER

INTRODUCTION

The Rottweiler was developed as a multi-faceted herding and guard dog that should work all kinds of livestock under various conditions, i.e. town or country. He is intensely concerned with gathering and controlling and can be very protective of 'his' stock.

The Rottweiler is only one of several herding breeds developed in the same general area in Germany from the same or similar base stock. The others are still used in their original function and have not become known in the Americas.

TRAINABILITY

The Rottweiler is highly trainable when he can see a purpose to his actions. If bonded to his handler the desire to please is excellent. Young males especially should be started young on ducks to gain confidence and to condition them to working off the stock. Adolescent males can be difficult to start. Because of their assertive character and youthful lack of confidence, they often feel the need to exert too much force and dominance. This usually results in their total loss of control of the stock which in turn causes an even more forceful dominant reaction and eventual total frustration.

Keeping the dog off the stock initially with a long pole seems to be the most successful method, as a line increases force and frustration. Once the dog realises that he has more control working off the stock the battle is won. His great desire for control and his good natural balance will keep him working back where he is most effective.

The female Rottweiler is normally much easier to start as an adult, being more receptive to discipline and less inclined to excessive force. A large number of females are not forceful enough

The Rottweiler was originally used to pull carts.
These two Rottweilers are pictured in the USA.
Photo courtesy: Steve and Charlotte Johnson.

to work cattle initially and should be started on ducks or sheep. Training to gather is easy since herding instinct is very high and the Rottweiler gathers naturally. There is seldom a need to punish for gripping or biting as the Rottweiler is unusually inhibited in using mouth on stock and should never be encouraged to do so. When necessary he will nip with the front teeth only, not using the canines.

If possible, the Rottweiler is best started as a puppy on ducks and then graduated to sheep and trained in much the same fashion as a Border Collie. They can then be moved to cattle. Some may never be able to work cattle.

The more confidence a Rottweiler has the less forceful he becomes, unless it is needed, and the easier he is to train.

WORKING STYLE
1. The Rottweiler should show a natural gathering style with a strong desire to control.
2. The Rottweiler generally shows a loose-eye and has a great amount of force while working well off the stock. They make much use of their ability to intimidate.
3. The Rottweiler will often carry the head on an even plane with the back or carry the head up

ABOVE: Ch. Farwest's Arizona PT,
JHD herding sheep in the USA, with
handler Ellen Minturn.
        Photo courtesy: Ellen Minturn.

FACING PAGE: The Rottweiler can be
trained to herd sheep, cattle – and even
geese!
        Photos courtesy: The Kentish Express
                and Beckett Newspapers.

but have the neck and shoulders lowered. Some females will lower the entire front end slightly when using eye. Males will also do this when working far off the stock in an open field. This is rarely seen in males when working in indoor arenas.

4. The Rottweiler has a reasonably good natural balance.

5. The Rottweiler force-barks when necessary and when he is working cattle uses a very intimidating charge. There is a natural change in forcefulness when herding sheep. When working cattle he may use his body and shoulders and for this reason should never be used on horned stock.

6. The Rottweiler, when working cattle, will search out the dominant animal and challenge it. Upon proving his control over that animal he will settle back and tend to his work.

7. The Rottweiler has little power from behind for driving cattle and therefore is best utilised as a control along the sides to turn stock, and to gather strays.

8. If worked on the same stock for any length of time, the Rottweiler tends to develop a bond with the stock and will become quite affectionate with them as long as they do as he says.

9. The Rottweiler shows a gathering/fetching style when working sheep and learns directions easily. He drives sheep with ease.

ENDURANCE
The Rottweiler is a natural trotter and, if built correctly, can trot for long distances. Hot weather bothers these dogs, particularly the males. His great force and control over sheep allows him to expend minimal amounts of energy when working this type of stock. When working cattle (especially strange cattle) the Rottweiler will often seek out the dominant animal and establish his own dominance thereby allowing himself to relax as he works later. Since he does not use mouth he expends great amounts of energy in his intimidating charges and periodic tackles to control unruly cattle. It is therefore necessary for him to establish his control at the start.

UNDESIRABLE TRAITS
1. Biting without strong provocation.

2. A dog that cannot be taught to work off the stock, but continues to use excessive force.

3. Extremely hard dogs that do not learn to avoid being kicked or dogs that viciously attack stock after being kicked.

4. A dog that lacks the desire to control and dominate (since a large part of the Rottweiler's working ability comes from this desire).

These Herding events are well supported, increasingly so, by Rottweiler owners in the USA, and it is to be hoped that other countries will introduce them in the not too far distant future.

CONCLUSION
Whether employed with the Police, Army or other official agency, trained for competitive events or kept as a much-loved family companion, the Rottweiler can fulfil everything that can be desired in a dog. I can do no better than quote from a book by Hans Korn, a Rottweiler expert, writing in 1939:

"It is upon the preservation of his good character that the Rottweiler must depend if he is to retain his circle of faithful adherents. His place is where mere external, elegant or grotesque exaggeration of form do not set the standard, but when a dog with particularly well-marked qualities of character is desired and esteemed. This is not only, nor in the first place, a question of the use of the Rottweiler as a working dog, but also and above all the question of the dog as a domestic pet in the home, in business and in the workplace – the watch-dog, companion and guard dog."

Chapter Nine

THE BREED STANDARDS

SELECTIVE BREEDING

First came the dog, then came the Standard. All breeds existed in something similar to their present form for many years before their characteristics were codified into a written Standard. Every breed has been developed by selective breeding because someone, somewhere, wanted a dog with particular abilities and qualities. Throughout the long association between dog and man, man has developed dogs that fitted his particular need. As a result we have dogs designed to act as guards, as aids to hunting, as herding dogs, as draught dogs and even as nothing more than cuddly pets. The list of tasks that man has asked of the dog is endless and even today we are still developing and modifying the dog to serve our special needs.

Although the description was not written down, the person anxious to have a dog to serve a specific purpose knew what was wanted. To the hunter of wild boar it was probably sufficient to look for "a big dog with a powerful bite". Even when reduced to writing, some British Standards seem to have made little progress beyond this stage. Fortunately, the majority of Standards have, from their beginning, set out in fair detail a full description of the dog.

For thousands of years, man has deliberately selected for breeding those animals which embodied the characteristics which he required. The result is the multiplicity of breeds which we know today. Many of the variations reflect the power, wealth, and position in society of those who developed them. The nobility could afford to own a number of types, each highly specialised for a particular task. They hunted with the ancestors of the Borzoi or Deerhound, guarded their gates with the heavy Mastiff type, while their children played with a small, pretty, Toy dog. The peasant farmer, however, could not afford to house and feed a number of different types for different purposes: a multi-purpose dog was needed, one who could herd livestock, guard both stock and homestead, help with hunting and even act as a draught dog. Finally, as the dog needed to live as part of the family and be a companion to the children, it needed a calm friendly nature. The dog that eventually became the Rottweiler is probably the world's finest example of the multi-purpose dog.

The concept of an ideal dog carried in the mind of the breeder worked perfectly well for many hundreds of years. It had a number of advantages, among them the ability to modify and change the dog to conform with the wishes and personal preferences of the breeder. It was no one's affair but his own as to what size, weight or colour a man's dog was when the only criterion was the dog's ability to carry out its desired task. However, some breeders were better than others and a successful producer of the right type of dog would find that his stock was in demand, with the result that a particular and recognisable type would begin to develop. Selective breeding enabled such breeders to perpetuate their particular type, and individual and recognisable breeds began to appear.

Gradually the role of the dog in society began to change. There was a gradual decline in the need to keep a dog as a working animal. However, the dog that had worked at the side of people for thousands of years had been firmly established as a friend and companion. Humans no longer demanded that an animal should earn its keep and were prepared to keep dogs solely for the pleasure they brought. The interest in dog ownership meant that many owners, while having no need for the abilities inherent in the different breed types, felt that their qualities were worth preserving. At the same time human competitiveness meant that owners began to compare their dogs with those of their fellow owners – and the dog show was born.

DRAWING UP A STANDARD

The preservation of breed types and the interest in dog shows lead to the formation of clubs to serve the interest of particular breeds. At this stage it became necessary to codify the description of the breed, resulting in the Standard as we now know it. Bearing in mind that all dog breeders are convinced that *their* type is the most desirable, there must have been many bitter battles before a common standard acceptable to all was agreed.

Because all breed types were developed with a particular task in mind, it is important to remember that all the different characteristics of a breed are there for a purpose. A few characteristics may be there for cosmetic or aesthetic reasons, but the vast majority are necessary to enable the dog to carry out the job for which it was developed. "Is the dog able to carry out its original purpose?" must always be one of the questions asked by a judge or breeder when interpreting the Standard or considering a dog.

To the modern breeder, exhibitor and judge, a Breed Standard describes an ideal specimen of a particular breed; a perfect dog to which the breeder and exhibitor aspires and against which the judge compares the dogs exhibited before him. It is a "blueprint", a written description or word picture aiming to create in the mind of the reader an image of the Rottweiler as we would like to see him. Because the dog is a living creature it is not possible to reduce this description to a precise list of requirements together with exact measurements, drawings and specifications. Breeders and judges are therefore required to interpret the Standard, and as a result there will be variations as to the amount of weight which different persons will place on the various faults and virtues.

There is nothing wrong with this. If all judges thought the same way the same dog would win all the time and there would soon be no more dog shows. Even more important, this variation of interpretation means that the overall quality is maintained, and no single aspect of the breed is given undue emphasis. However, variation in the individual interpretation of the Standard does not give the right to make major changes in the breed. Some breeders who consistently fail to produce stock which conforms to the Standard will attempt to alter the interpretation of the Standard, or even suggest that the Standard should be changed.

To a certain extent, the British and American attitude to the Standard is that it is written on "tablets of stone" and that it should not be altered. It is considered to describe the ideal specimen of the breed, and if the dogs being produced do not fit the Standard then the dogs must be changed, not the Standard. The Germans, however, tend to use their Standard as a regulator in that if a fault becomes common in the breed then the Standard will be amended to correct the fault. At times this approach gives the impression that a feature which, in the past, has been considered desirable, has suddenly ceased to be so or has had its importance diminished. There are advantages and disadvantages to both approaches, and in Britain and in the USA we are always aware that we owe the Rottweiler to Germany, and that their opinions must always be given careful consideration.

Those who write Standards have to be aware of the dangers of stating that a certain feature is desirable if excessive attention to the feature could act to the detriment of the dog. Terms such as "narrow skull" or "long back" can result in breeders exaggerating these aspects to the point where the dog suffers physical deformity. In my opinion, the Rottweiler does not suffer from a

Standard containing this kind of exaggeration. Certainly, when the original British Standard was produced, the final draft was checked by a veterinary surgeon who had a long experience of dogs and dog breeding and he gave it a clean bill of health. Almost thirty years of breeding to this Standard has confirmed that there are no aspects of the Standard which could, if exaggerated, act to the detriment of the dog.

In the show ring, the interpretation of the Standard as the description of the ideal dog has resulted in breeders attempting to clean up and improve the appearance of the breed. This desire should not be seized on by those who dislike the show ring as evidence that "show breeders" ruin a breed. In fact, show breeders are usually extremely conscientious in their wish to preserve the breed in the form in which it has been handed down to them.

As a result, while maintaining the overall picture of the dog, they have succeeded in improving such aspects as ear placement and size, topline, bone quality and the overall clarity of outline. Colour, which is purely cosmetic, has received considerable attention and is in general, clear, rich and well defined. If you compare photographs of Rottweilers taken in the early 1900s with the dogs of today there can be no doubt that the dog of today is the better looking animal. One area where there has been considerable pressure to modify or change the Standard has been on the question of character or temperament. The modern dog has to live in the community, and there has been a demand from the public and from some judges and exhibitors that the Rottweiler temperament should be changed, probably to make it a softer, more easy-going dog. The desire to reduce all breeds to the common level of soft, cuddly, loveable and submissive household pets has already destroyed the true character of many breeds, and it would be a tragedy if this was allowed to happen to the Rottweiler.

Furthermore, a study of any of the Standards will show that the existing requirements are for a dog who is calm and good-natured. Much of the Rottweiler's appeal is in his tough, courageous spirit and his willingness to defend his owner and his property – a dog that lives up to its other German name of "dark guardian of the family". Where the fault lies when a Rottweiler transgresses is in the failure of breeders to breed to the Standard as far as temperament is concerned, sometimes ignoring temperament faults in favour of physical attributes. Equally, you cannot blame the Standard when a dog is deliberately misused or wrongly trained.

In the USA and Germany, the Rottweiler Standard is controlled and published by the relevant breed clubs. To most of us this is the correct approach. The Standard is in the hands of those who know and understand the breed. In Britain the Kennel Club claims the copyright of the Standard. The original British Standard was produced by people who owned and were knowledgeable about the Rottweiler. In the late 1980s a Kennel Club committee was given the task of standardising both the layout and the terminology of all the British Standards and in carrying out this perfectly sensible task some of the warmth and feeling which comes from close association with a breed was lost. In the following pages I propose to discuss all three Standards, the German, the American and the British. They all describe the same dog, with minor variations, but differ in the amount of detailed description and in their phraseology. The ADRK Standard has to be accepted as the prime source for anyone studying the breed. It is the basis on which both the American and British Standards were originally written and both countries set out to produce what was in fact the German Standard written in English. While it is true that a judge with a knowledge of any one of the Standards is capable of judging the breed anywhere in the world, national Kennel Clubs require that judges officiating in their country judge in accordance with the national Standard. This does not normally produce a problem, except on the question of disqualifying faults which will be discussed in the relevant section. Judges should also be aware that some countries who have in the past used the British Standard, e.g. Australia, now use the Federation Cynologique Internationale (FCI) Standard, which is, under the country of origin rule, the German, Allgemeiner Deutscher Rottweiler Klub (ADRK) Standard. Whatever your own country of origin, the study of all three of the Standards can only improve your overall knowledge of the breed. There were a number of German Standards produced during the formative years of the breed. Some of the requirements contained in these Standards are contrary to what is considered desirable today. These Standards are discussed in the chapter on the origin of the Rottweiler, on the grounds that they are a part of the development of the breed.

I propose to discuss the Breed Standards by quoting the relevant section from each, followed by my comments. To do this it has been necessary to rearrange the order in some cases, but all parts of the Standards are included.

GENERAL APPEARANCE

ADRK: The Rottweiler is a medium-large, robust dog, neither gross nor slight nor spindly. In correct proportion he is compact and powerfully built indicating great strength, manoeuvrability and endurance.

AKC: The ideal Rottweiler is a medium large, robust and powerful dog with clearly defined rust markings. His compact and substantial build denotes great strength, ability and endurance. Dogs are characteristically more massive throughout with larger frame and heavier bone than bitches. Bitches are distinctly feminine but without weakness of substance or structure.

UK: Above average size, stalwart dog. Correctly proportioned, compact and powerful form, permitting great strength, manoeuvrability and endurance.

All the Standards give actual desirable sizes as a separate section. The terms "medium-large" or "above average size" are intended to give a quick indication of size by comparison with say a Labrador or Boxer which could be described as medium or average size. These terms should not be considered as expressing a desire for size for its own sake. A big dog is not necessarily beautiful. Excessive size can lead to a clumsy, cloddy dog without the power of endurance and manoeuvrability which is also required.

The term "stalwart" used in the UK Standard is defined in the dictionary as "strong, sturdy, dependable and courageous", which I consider to be a perfect description of the Rottweiler. Many people like to use the word "balanced" when discussing the proportions of the ideal Rottweiler. Whatever phrase you use, it is virtually an instinctive feeling that the dog is right or wrong. 'Correctly proportioned' must be used with the demand in all three Standards that the dog must be "compact and powerful". "Compact" is defined as "neatly fitted into a confined space" and "solid, firm". "Compact" should not be interpreted as square even though a square dog can look very attractive.

The AKC Standard is to be commended for putting in writing something which all experienced Rottweiler breeders should be aware of but sometimes neglect to implement. This is the distinct difference in size, and to a certain extent appearance, between dogs and bitches. Males should be larger overall, heavier-boned and more masculine in appearance. Bitches should look feminine and be lighter in bone and finer in head. It should be possible to tell the sex of a Rottweiler when standing in front of the dog. A large bitch can still show these feminine characteristics. Femininity is not just a question of being small and petite. A "doggy" bitch is just as undesirable as a "bitchy" dog.

PROPORTIONS AND SIZE

ADRK: The length of the body measured from the point of the prosternum (breast bone) to the rear edge of the pelvic edge (ischial protuberance) should not exceed the height at the

*Correct proportions:
The length of the body
should be slightly
greater than the height
at the withers.*

highest point of the withers by more than 15 per cent.
Height of males 61 to 68 cms. Ideal size 65 to 66 cms.
Height of bitches 56 to 63 cms. Ideal size 60 to 61 cms.
Weight of males about 50 kilos. Weight of bitches about 42 kilos.

AKC: Dogs 24 to 27 inches. Bitches 22 to 25 inches with preferred size being mid range of each sex. Correct proportion is of primary importance, as long as size is within the standard's range. The length of body from prosternum to the rearmost projection of the rump, is slightly longer than the height of the dog at the withers, the most desirable proportion of the height to length being 9 to 10. The Rottweiler is neither coarse nor shelly. Depth of chest is approximately fifty percent of the height of the dog. His bone and muscle mass must be sufficient to balance his frame giving a compact and powerful appearance.

UK: Dogs height at shoulder between 63 to 69 cms (25 to 27 inches)
Bitches between 58 to 63 1/2 cms (23 to 25 inches). Height should always be considered in relation to general appearance.

There is a one centimetre difference between the maximum heights for dogs in the German, British and American Standards. This is not significant. Personally, while I am happy that there should be a clear difference in size between dogs and bitches I prefer the smaller difference given in the UK Standard to the major size variation contained in the ADRK Standard and to a lesser degree in the AKC one.

The body proportions are important. I find the simplest explanation of these proportions to be the AKC Standard, also used in the UK one but in the section under Body, which gives the ratio of height to length as 9 to 10. Applied to actual size this ratio means that a dog which stands 27 inches at the withers should have a body length of 30 inches. Many people, and I agree with them, consider that a slightly greater length in proportion to height is acceptable in bitches.

The depth of chest in relation to height plays a major part in the overall appearance of the Rottweiler. A dog of 27 inches at the shoulder whose depth of brisket is only, say, 11 inches is obviously wrong, as is the dog measuring 25 inches whose depth of brisket is 15 inches.

The ADRK comments on weight should be noted. An overweight dog loses manoeuvrability and is incapable of carrying out the original purpose of the breed. The cult of excessively large dogs by some breeders is wrong and should be penalized by judges.

CHARACTER AND TEMPERAMENT

ADRK: He is descended from friendly and peaceful stock and by nature loves children, is affectionate, obedient, trainable and enjoys working. His rough appearance belies his ancestry. His demeanour is self reliant, with strong nerves and fearless character. He is keenly alert to and aware of his surroundings.

AKC: The Rottweiler is basically a calm, confident and courageous dog with a self assured aloofness that does not lend itself to immediate and indiscriminate friendships. A Rottweiler is self-confident and responds quietly and with a wait-and-see attitude to influences in his environment. He has an inherent desire to protect home and family, and is an intelligent dog of extreme hardness and adaptability with a strong willingness to work, making him especially suited as a companion, guardian and general all-purpose dog. The behaviour of the Rottweiler in the show ring should be controlled, willing and adaptable, trained to submit to examination of mouth, testicles, etc. An aloof or reserved dog should not be penalized, as this reflects the accepted character of the breed. An aggressive or belligerent attitude towards other dogs should not be faulted. A judge shall excuse from the ring any shy Rottweiler. A dog shall be judged fundamentally shy if, refusing to stand for examination, it shrinks away from the judge. A dog that in the opinion of the judge menaces or threatens him/her or exhibits any sign that it may not be safely approached or examined by the judge in the normal manner, shall be excused from the ring. Any dog that in the opinion of the judge attacks any person in the ring shall be disqualified.

UK: Appearance displays boldness and courage. Self-assured and fearless. Calm gaze should indicate good humour. Good nature, not nervous, aggressive or vicious: courageous, biddable, with natural guarding instincts.

The sections of the Standards dealing with the character and temperament of the Rottweiler are without doubt the most important parts of the three documents. Regrettably they are also the requirements which are neglected by far too many breeders. One only has to read the physical description of the Rottweiler to realise the vital importance of having the correct temperament. Failure to appreciate this has done far greater harm to the breed than any failure to achieve the ideal physical appearance. For this reason this book contains a separate chapter on the character of the Rottweiler.

All three Standards reflect the admiration which devotees of the Rottweiler feel for the breed. The AKC Standard in particular goes to great lengths in its attempt to describe the desirable temperament. Reading it one cannot resist the feeling that American Rottweilers of the correct temperament must trot around wearing little gold halos around their heads. I gain the impression that the parts of the AKC Standard dealing with behaviour in the show ring have been written in a very worthwhile attempt to correct character faults that are appearing in the breed. While I agree that it is part of a judge's duty to take action against dogs of bad temperament, I feel that these aspects should be covered by an instruction to judges rather than as part of the Standard.

I would also criticise the emphasis in the AKC Standard on the requirements for "aloofness" and "hardness" without the compensating requirements mentioned in the other two Standards of friendliness, good humour, good nature and affection. The UK Standard contains the phrase "calm gaze should indicate good humour". My wife, Judy, whose experience as a judge and breeder of Rottweilers probably puts her in the top ten in the world, has always said that the Rottweiler who looks you straight in the eye with a calm, honest, friendly but alert gaze immediately scores a number of winning points when she is judging.

The attitude towards other dogs given in the AKC Standard is important. *It is necessary to differentiate between the Rottweiler's attitude to humans and to other dogs.* Towards humans he is certainly good-natured and biddable and has natural protective instincts. Towards other dogs the Rottweiler is convinced that he is the greatest thing on four legs and is prepared to prove it with any other animal that questions his dominance, while at the same time showing great gentleness and tolerance to those who are smaller and weaker. In his relationship with all other beings the Rottweiler has a great sense of his own dignity and expects to be treated with the respect that he deserves.

HEAD
ADRK
Skul: Medium long, the backskull broad between the ears, the forehead line seen from the side only moderately arched. The occiput is well developed without protruding excessively.
Skin: The skin on the head is tight fitting but allowance is made for some wrinkling when dog is alert.
Nose: The bridge of the muzzle is straight, broad at the base and slightly tapering. Nose is large, rather broad than round, always black with proportionately large nostrils.
Muzzle: Must never be long or short in comparison to the backskull.
Lips: Black close lying with the corners closed, gums should be dark.
Jaw: Strong. Broad upper and lower jaw.
Cheeks: Pronounced cheek bones (zygomatic arch).
Dentition: Complete (42 teeth), bite is strong with the upper incisors closing like scissors over those of the underjaw.
Eyes: Medium large, almond shaped, of dark brown colour with tightly fitting lids.
Ears: Medium large, pendant, triangular, set well apart and high. When brought forward, well placed ears will broaden the appearance of the backskull.

AKC
Head of medium length, broad between the ears: forehead line seen in profile is moderately arched: zygomatic arch and stop well developed with strong broad upper and lower jaws. The desired ratio of backskull to muzzle is 3 to 2. Forehead is preferred dry, however, some wrinkling may occur when the dog is alert.
Expression is noble, alert and self assured.
Eyes: Of medium size, almond shaped with well fitting lids, moderately deep set neither protruding nor receding. The desired colour is a uniform dark brown.
Ears: Of medium length, pendant, triangular in shape: when carried alertly the ears are level with the top of the skull and appear to broaden it. Ears are to be set well apart, hanging forward with the inner edge lying tightly against the head and terminating at approximately mid cheek.
Muzzle: Bridge is straight, broad at base with slight tapering towards tip. The end of the muzzle is broad with well developed chin. Nose is broad rather than round and always black. Lips, always black: corners closed, inner mouth pigment is preferred dark.
Bite and dentition: Teeth 42 in number (20 upper, 22 lower), strong, correctly placed, meeting in a scissors bite, lower incisors touching inside of upper incisors.

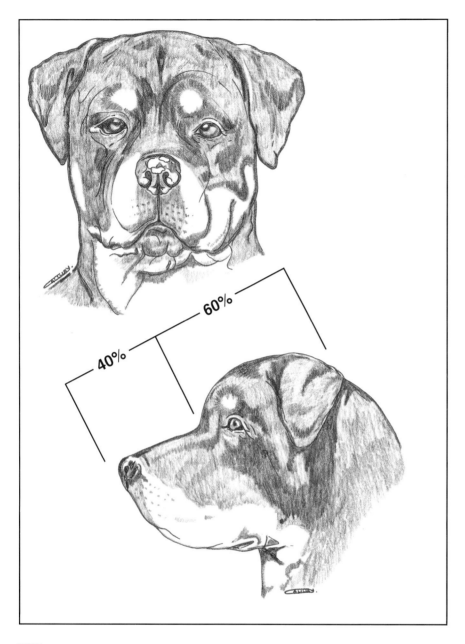

THE HEAD

The correct head, viewed from the front.

The correct head in profile.

UK

Head and skull. Head medium length, skull broad between ears. Forehead moderately arched as seen from side. Occipital bone well developed but not conspicuous. Cheeks well boned and muscled but not prominent. Skin on head not loose, although it may form a moderate wrinkle when attentive. Muzzle fairly deep with topline level and length of muzzle in relation to distance from well defined stop to occiput, to be as 2 is to 3. Nose is well developed with proportionately large nostrils, always black.

Eyes: Medium size, almond shaped, dark brown in colour, light eye undesirable, eyelids close fitting.

Ears: Pendant, small in proportion rather than large, set high and wide apart, lying flat and close to cheek.

Mouth: Teeth strong, complete dentition with scissor bite i.e. upper teeth closely overlapping the lower teeth and set square to the jaws. Flews black and firm, falling gradually away towards corners of mouth, which do not protrude excessively.

It would be a great pity if judges concentrated on the quality of the Rottweiler's head to the detriment of its other features. However, a Rottweiler with a poor head is a very nondescript animal, while a good head completes an attractive picture. There is considerable variation in incorrect Rottweiler head types. There are over-large, round heads, usually with too much wrinkle and with a relatively short muzzle stuck in the middle of it, the teddy-bear type; while others are of the long muzzled, narrow skulled type more like Labradors.

The emphasis on a well-developed zygomatic arch reflects the strength and biting power of the Rottweiler but over-development of this feature will give a heavy coarse Bull Mastiff type of head. While the stop, which is where the muzzle joins the skull, should be well defined, it should not be so pronounced as to give a beetle-browed effect. A pronounced zygomatic arch with too little stop will resemble a Staffordshire Bull Terrier type head.

The comparative measurements for the length of muzzle and the distance from stop to occiput can be confusing, especially as the AKC and UK Standards reverse the measurements, although the final answer is the same. Reduced to simple measurements this requirement means that if the distance from the tip of the nose to the stop is two inches then the distance from stop to occiput

INCORRECT: This Rottweiler has excess loose skin at the neck, and appears 'wet'.

INCORRECT: A snipey-looking Rottweiler, showing lack of muzzle depth and lack of stop.

INCORRECT: The skull is too high and rounded, giving a domed appearance.

THE EYES

CORRECT:
Almond-shaped,
with close-fitting
lids.

INCORRECT: These eyes are too
pale in colour, sometimes referred to
as 'yellow' or 'bird of prey' eyes.

INCORRECT:
These eyes are different in size.

INCORRECT:
The eyes are set too close.

INCORRECT:
The opposite problem –
the eyes are set too wide apart.

INCORRECT:
The eyes are round.

INCORRECT:
The eye-lids are without hair.

THE EARS

CORRECT: The ears should be small in proportion to the rest of the head, lying flat and close to the cheek.

*INCORRECT:
These ears are too long.*

INCORRECT: The ears are high-set, sometimes known as a 'terrier set'.

*INCORRECT:
The ears are set too low.*

*INCORRECT:
The ears break at the outer edges.*

*INCORRECT:
Rose-shaped ears.*

should be three inches, both figures increasing in proportion. The requirement for an almond-shaped eye with close-fitting eyelid is a good example of the original purpose of the Rottweiler influencing the modern Standard. The close-fitting eyelids helped to protect the eyes of a dog moving in a cloud of dust behind a herd of cattle. Loose eyelids which expose the eye to dust and infection are also extremely unattractive. Equally an excessively deep-set eye buried deep in folds of flesh can be indicative of entropion.

I am not happy with the changes in both the ADRK and AKC Standards demanding ears that are medium-large or medium size. Previously all Standards demanded a small ear and I consider that this is the most attractive, provided that it is correctly shaped and positioned. The correct small ear is admittedly more difficult to achieve, and it is to be hoped that the demand for a large ear is to correct the tendency for small ears to "fly" rather than an attempt to change the ideal standard to fit poorer quality dogs. As with many breeds of German origin the question of teeth becomes a major issue. The question of disqualifying faults, including dentition faults, is dealt with later in this chapter but there are aspects of teeth which need consideration. I have no argument with the desirability of a scissor bite but there are arguments for accepting that a pincer bite (i.e. meeting edge to edge), if not the ideal, should at least be acceptable. In the wild, predatory animals such as wolves, wild dogs and jackals have a pincer bite which is the most suitable for tearing the flesh of their prey and is also necessary as a means of grooming their coats. In the past the pincer bite was considered as acceptable, although not desirable, and it may be that we are demanding something which may be desirable in humans but not in dogs. It is also possible that the demand for a scissor bite leads eventually to an overshot bite, which is certainly inefficient as far as the dog is concerned.

NECK
ADRK: Powerful, moderately long, well muscled, slightly arched, dry without dewlap or throatiness.

AKC: Powerful, well muscled, moderately long, slightly arched and without loose skin.

UK: Of fair length, strong, round and very muscular. Slightly arched, free from throatiness.

Both "moderate" and "fair length" are indeterminate descriptions for anyone trying to visualise the ideal Rottweiler. Powerful is the key word. Look to the balance of the whole dog and remember that it originally needed sufficient strength in the neck and shoulders to first of all grip and then throw down an animal far larger than itself. This does not mean that you should accept a "bull neck", which is often found with an upright shoulder blade.

BODY
ADRK
Back: Straight, strong, tight. Loin is short, strong and deep.
Croup: Broad, medium long, gently sloping, neither flat nor steep.
Chest: Roomy, broad and deep (approximately 50% of the height of the dog at the withers) with a well developed forechest and well arched ribs.
Abdomen: Flanks not drawn up.
Tail: Docked short so that one or two tail vertebrae remain.

AKC
Topline: The back is firm and level extending in a straight line from behind the withers to the croup. The back remains horizontal to the ground while the dog is moving or standing.

THE BODY

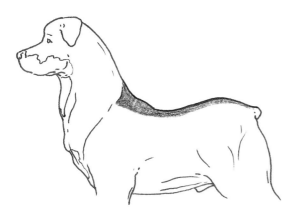

INCORRECT:
The topline is soft, resulting in a swayback.

INCORRECT: This dog lacks rear
angulation, and is high in rear.

INCORRECT:
A roach back.

Body: The chest is roomy, broad and deep, reaching to elbow with well pronounced forechest and well sprung oval ribs. Back is straight and strong. Loin is short, deep and well muscled. Croup is broad, of medium length and only slightly sloping. Underline of a mature Rottweiler has a slight tuck up. Males must have two normal testicles properly descended into the scrotum.
Tail: Tail docked short, close to body, leaving one or two tail vertebrae. The set of the tail is more important than length. Properly set, it gives an impression of elongation of topline: carried slightly above horizontal when the dog is excited or moving.

UK: Body: Chest roomy, broad and deep with well sprung ribs. Depth of brisket will not be more, and not much less than 50% of shoulder height. Back straight, strong and not too long, ratio of shoulder height to length of body should be as 9 is to 10. Loins short, strong and deep, flanks not tucked up.
Croup: Of proportionate length and broad, very slightly sloping.
Tail: Normally carried horizontally, but slightly above horizontal when dog is alert. Customarily docked at the first joint, it is strong and not set too low.

The relative proportions of the body have already been dealt with under the heading of

"Proportions and Size". The strong sturdy body of the Rottweiler is one of his many attractive features. The requirement in the AKC Standard for the back to remain horizontal to the ground while the dog is moving or standing should be noted. Once you have seen a Rottweiler move like this you will understand why this is considered a very desirable requirement.

The ribs should extend well back giving a short loin. The short loin enhances the almost level underline which should be virtually parallel with the topline. A tucked up flank destroys the short coupled appearance which is desirable.

I am not happy with the current ADRK requirements as to the croup, preferring the AKC and UK requirement for "slightly" or "very slightly" sloping. In my opinion the ADRK use of "medium long" and "gently sloping" runs the risk of creating Rottweilers with a low tail set and of losing that elongation of the topline so rightly called for in the AKC Standard.

FOREQUARTERS
ADRK
Forequarters: Overall, seen from the front, the forelegs are straight and not set close together. Seen from the side, the lower leg is straight. The shoulder angulation should approximate 45 degrees.
Shoulder: Well placed.
Upper arm: Lying correctly on the body.
Forearm: Strongly developed and muscular.
Pastern: Somewhat springy, strong and not steep.
Feet: Round, well closed and well knuckled, pads hard, nails short, black and strong.

AKC
Forequarters: Shoulder blade is long and well laid back. Upper arm equal in length to shoulder blade, set so elbows are well under body. Distance from withers to elbow and elbow to ground is equal. Legs are strongly developed with straight, heavy bone, not set

THE FOREQUARTERS

CORRECT:
The legs and feet are straight, and not set too close together.

INCORRECT:
The pasterns are bending in, known as a 'fiddle' front.

INCORRECT:
The feet are toeing in.

INCORRECT:
The front is
too narrow,
and the feet
are toeing out.

INCORRECT:
The front is
too wide.

THE FEET

CORRECT:
Compact, tight,
'cat' foot.

CORRECT:
The pastern is
slightly sloping.

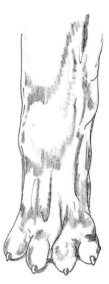

INCORRECT:
The foot is
splayed.

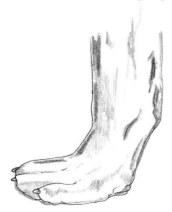

INCORRECT: The
pastern is 'soft', and
the foot is flat.

close together. Pasterns are strong, springy and almost perpendicular to the ground. Feet are round, compact with well arched toes, turning neither in nor out. Pads are thick and hard. Nails short, strong and black. Dewclaws may be removed.

UK
Forequarters: Shoulders well laid back, long and sloping, elbows well let down but not loose. Legs straight, muscular, with plenty of bone and substance. Pasterns sloping slightly forward. Feet: Strong, round and compact with toes well arched. Pads very hard, toe nails short, dark and strong.

The AKC Standard probably gives the best description of the shoulder requirements if read with ADRK requirement of an angle of 45 degrees. The term "well laid back" applied to the shoulder in the AKC and UK Standards is merely asking for the angle of 45 degrees without giving an actual measurement. The same angle can also be described as a 90 degree angle between the scapula or shoulder blade and the humerus or upper arm. An over-muscled shoulder, often described as "loaded in shoulder", will produce a bad front movement giving no room for the dog to extend itself so that it paddles along with its elbows flying.

The straight, heavy bone of the front legs is a Rottweiler feature, as are the compact tight "cat-like" feet. The slightly sloping pastern – and the emphasis must be on "slightly" – acts as a shock absorber when jumping or moving. Fewer and fewer breeders are removing the front dewclaws. Only the AKC Standard mentions them and even then removal is optional. The operation is very simple if carried out at a few days old and doing so certainly results in a cleaner front leg and also obviates damage in adult life by the claw being caught or torn.

HINDQUARTERS
ADRK
Hindquarters: Overall, as seen from the rear, the rear legs are straight and not set close together. In a natural stance the articulation between the upper thigh and the lower thigh forms an obtuse angle.
Upper thigh: Moderately long, broad and very muscular.
Lower thigh: Long powerful and heavily muscled, sinewy with strong tendons, well angulated, not steep.
Feet: Somewhat longer than the front feet, nevertheless tight knuckled, with strong toes, no dewclaws.

AKC
Hindquarters: Angulation of hindquarters balances that of forequarters. Upper thigh is fairly long, very broad and well muscled. Stifle joint is well turned. Lower thigh is long, broad and powerful, with extensive muscling leading into a strong hock joint. Rear pasterns are nearly perpendicular to the ground. Viewed from the rear, hind legs are straight, strong and wide enough apart to fit with a properly built body.
Feet: Are somewhat longer than the front feet, turning neither in nor out, equally compact with well arched toes. Pads are thick and hard. Nails short, strong and black. Dewclaws must be removed.

UK
Hindquarters: Upper thigh not too short, broad and strongly muscled. Lower thigh well muscled at top, strong and sinewy below. Stifles fairly well bent. Hocks well angulated without exaggeration, metatarsals not completely vertical. Strength and soundness of hock highly desirable.

HINDQUARTERS

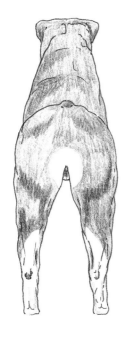

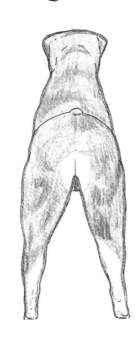

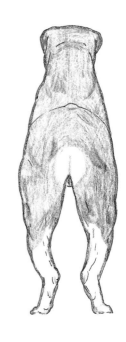

CORRECT: The legs are straight, and not set too close together.

INCORRECT: The legs are set too wide apart.

INCORRECT: Hocking in and/or toeing out.

INCORRECT: Too narrow at the hocks.

INCORRECT: Hocking out, and/or toeing in.

Feet: Strong, round and compact with toes well arched. Hind feet somewhat longer than front. Pads very hard, toenails, short, dark and strong. Rear dewclaws removed.

The upper thigh comprises the muscle groups surrounding the femur or thigh bone. The lower thigh is the muscle region between stifle and hock joint. The stifle or knee joint requires to be fairly well bent. The hind angulation of a Rottweiler, like so much of the breed conformation, is sensible and not exaggerated. The ideal is somewhere between the hind angulation of the German Shepherd Dog and the straighter stifle of the Mastiff. Handlers sometimes create a false impression of over-angulation by placing the dog with the hind legs stretched out behind. When correctly posed the toes of the hind feet should virtually touch a vertical line dropped from the haunch although the dog may stand naturally with one foot slightly forward and one just to the rear of this line. A straight stifle would spoil its stride and take away that powerful rear-end drive that looks so impressive. The broad, well muscled thighs of the Rottweiler are one of the breed's special features and the muscles should be clearly visible especially on the upper thigh.

The AKC statement that the "angulation of hindquarters balances that of forequarters" means that the femur lies roughly parallel to the scapula or shoulder blade, while the tibia lies in the same plane as the humerus. Failure to meet the AKC requirement that the pasterns are nearly perpendicular is all too common. Nothing looks worse than a Rottweiler which is down on its pasterns. This is often linked with a dog that has excessively long hind feet. While it is technically true that the hind feet are longer than the front I suggest that you ignore this aspect and aim for a tight compact hind foot.

Hind dewclaws are not required in any of the Standards. The ADRK Standard implies that they should never have been there while the AKC and UK ask for their removal. I would suggest that the ADRK requirement is the correct one. There is some evidence to suggest that a dog who has had hind dewclaws, even if they have been removed, tends to be cow hocked. It is perfectly possible to greatly reduce the incidence of hind dewclaws by selective breeding and I would suggest that you do not breed from stock that carries them .

MOVEMENT
ADRK
Movement: The Rottweiler is a trotter. The back remains firm and relatively motionless. The gait is harmonious, positive, powerful and free, with long strides.

AKC
Gait: The Rottweiler is a trotter. His movement should be balanced, harmonious, sure, powerful and unhindered, with strong forereach and a powerful rear drive. The motion is effortless, efficient and ground covering. Front and rear legs are thrown neither in nor out, as the imprint of hind feet should touch that of fore feet. In a trot the forequarters and hindquarters are mutually coordinated, while the back remains level, firm and relatively motionless. As speed increases the legs will converge under body towards a centre line.

UK
Gait/movement: Conveys an impression of supple strength, endurance and purpose. While back remains firm and stable there is a powerful hindthrust and good stride. First and foremost, movement should be harmonious, positive and unrestricted.

The Rottweiler's function as a droving dog, spending long hours behind a herd of cattle, is the reason for the demand that he should be a "trotter". For this reason he is normally moved at this

MOVEMENT

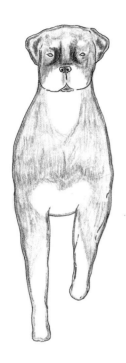

CORRECT:
Foreword
movement is
balanced and
harmonious
with strong
forereach.

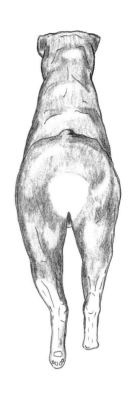

CORRECT:
Powerful rear
drive.

CORRECT:
When the
Rottweiler
trots, the back
remains level.

speed in the show ring and exhibitors should resist demands by some judges that the dog should be moved at a walk. Frankly, the Rottweiler does not walk well. His movement degenerates into an untidy rolling waddle. There is an interesting theory that the correct slow movement for a herding dog is the amble, that is, when the front and hind legs on the same side move in unison with one another as a pair. It has been argued that the amble can be increased to the gallop and back to the amble again with less strain than reaching the gallop from the trot. For a herding dog constantly changing speed and direction the amble would appear to be the most economical answer. However, it is also admitted that the amble places a heavy strain on the spinal vertebrae. The amble is also unattractive to look at and I am sure that we are wise to condemn the amble and stick to the trot as the normal gait for the Rottweiler. The AKC are wise to point out that, as speed of movement increases, the legs will converge under the body towards a centre line. While judges expect that the dog's legs will move in a straight line when coming towards them or moving away, this is only possible and reasonable at a steady trot. Increase the speed, the laws of mechanics take over and the legs will move inwards. This does not mean that it is acceptable for the dog to single track, be out at elbows, toe in or out, or cross the front legs when moving; neither should it move wide in front.

COAT
ADRK
Coat quality: Consisting of outer coat and undercoat. The outer coat is medium long, coarse, thick and straight. The undercoat must not show through the outer coat. On the back of the rear legs the hair is somewhat longer.

AKC
Coat: Outer coat is straight, coarse, dense, of medium length and lying flat. Undercoat should be present on neck and thighs but the amount is influenced by climatic conditions. Undercoat should not show through outer coat. The coat is shortest on head, ears and legs, longest on breeching. The Rottweiler is to be exhibited in the natural condition with no trimming.

UK
Coat consists of top coat and undercoat. Top coat is of medium length, coarse and flat. Undercoat, essential on the neck and thighs, should not show through top coat. Hair maybe a little longer on the back of the forelegs and breechings. Long or excessively wavy coat highly undesirable.

The Rottweiler coat is a true working dog coat, designed to keep him both warm and dry by virtue of the double layer of top and undercoat. The top coat should be weather-proof and water-resistant. It should feel harsh to the touch. A thin, sleek "Dobermann"-type coat is a serious fault, as is a soft, wavy, curly or long coat. The coat should lie flat, although it may show a very slight wave at certain stages of growth. The undercoat may be black, grey or fawn, the first two being the more common. The black undercoat, which is often soft and woolly, is sometimes difficult to see because of the black top coat. While all the Standards demand that the undercoat should not show through the top coat, this is unavoidable at some stages of moulting. The grey or fawn undercoat tends to grow thicker than the black undercoat and will become visible when the top coat (guard hairs) have become thin. Most judges accept this temporary visibility and in fact consider that it gives conclusive proof of the presence of the undercoat. The AKC wisely point out that under hot climatic conditions the Rottweiler will reduce its amount of undercoat or virtually lose it altogether. There is slight a disagreement between the UK Standard and the AKC and ADRK versions on the subject of long hair on the legs. The UK states that it may be a little longer on both the forelegs and breechings, while the others limit the longer hair to the breechings only. Personally I prefer the ADRK and AKC requirements and have never found the length of hair on the forelegs to be significant if the rest of the coat is correct.

COLOUR
ADRK
Colour: Black with sharply defined dark reddish-brown markings on the cheeks, muzzle, under the neck, on the chest and legs and also over the eyes and under the tail.

In some European countries the Rottweiler's tail is not docked. In most cases, the tail resembles the Labrador Retriever's thick 'otter' tail.

occur on areas other than the chest, the most common being one or more white feet. Fortunately such markings are rare but must be considered a serious fault.

All Standards are in agreement that the tan should be dark rather than light. The AKC Standard may be offering a slightly lighter tan with the use of the word "rust". While the mahogany tan is probably the most attractive, this colour can have a tendency to sootiness. The very pale sandy tan is undesirable and often goes with excessively large areas of tan.

FAULTS
ADRK: Faults.

Lightly boned, poorly muscled, insufficient leggy appearance.

Head: Houndy, too narrow, weak, too short, too long or too coarse, shallow forehead (faulty or insufficient stop).

Foreface: Long or pointed muzzle, ram's or split nose, convex or concave bridge of the muzzle, light or spotted nose.

Lips: Open pink coloured or flecked lips, or lips with open corners.

Jaw: Narrow underjaw.

Cheeks: Over-prominent cheeks.

Bite: Level bite.

Ears: Too low set, heavy, long, leather too thin, pulled back in such a manner as to stick up, and ears that are not properly carried.

Eyes: Light in colour, protruding i.e. lids not fitting tightly, too deep set, too big or too round eyes.

Neck: Too long, thin, poorly muscled neck, dewlap or throaty.

Body: Too long, too short, narrow.

Chest: Flat-ribbed rib cage, round rib cage, shallow rib cage.

Back: Too long, weak or sway backed, roach backed.

Croup: Steep croup, too short, too flat or too long.

Tail: Too high set or too low set.

Forequarters: Narrow set or crooked forelegs. Straight shoulder, faulty or deficient elbow

placement, too long, too short or too straight upper arm; weak or straight pasterns; spread toes, too flat or too arched toes, stunted toes, light nails.

Hindquarters: Poorly muscled thighs, sickle-hocked or cow-hocked or bow-legged, too little or too much angulation. Dewclaws.

Skin: Wrinkled skin on head.

Coat condition: Soft, too short, too long, curly coat, lacking undercoat.

Colour: Incorrect colour, poorly defined, too extensive markings.

AKC Faults.

Size and proportion: Lack of proportion, undersized, oversized, reversal of sex characteristics (bitchy dogs, doggy bitches).

Eyes: Yellow (bird of prey) eyes, eyes of different colour or size, hairless eye rim.

Ears: Improper carriage (creased, folded or held away from cheek/head).

Muzzle: Total lack of mouth pigment (pink mouth).

Bite and dentition: Level bite; any missing tooth.

Coat: Wavy coat. Open, excessively short or curly coat; total lack of undercoat; any trimming that alters the length of the natural coat.

Colour: Straw-coloured, excessive, insufficient or sooty markings; rust marking other than described above; white marking any place on dog (a few rust or white hairs do not constitute a marking).

Summary: The foregoing is a description of the ideal rottweiler. Any structural fault that detracts from the above described working dog must be penalized to the extent of the deviation.

DISQUALIFYING FAULTS
ADRK:
Overall: Obvious reversal of sex characteristics (bitchy dogs and the reverse).

Demeanour. Anxious, shy, cowardly, gun shy, vicious, excessively suspicious (distrustful), nervous.

Eyes. Entropion, ectropion, yellow eyes, two eyes of different colour.

Dentition. Overshot, undershot, dogs with missing pre-molars or molars.

Testicles. Unilateral cryptorchid or cryptorchid males. Both testicles must be well developed and properly descended into the scrotum.

Coat. Exceptionally long and curly coated dogs.

Colour. Dogs that do not have the typical black ground colour in combination with correctly placed brown markings; white marks.

AKC
Eyes: Entropion. Ectropion.

Bite and dentition. Overshot, undershot (when incisors do not touch or mesh); wry mouth, two or more missing teeth.

Body. Unilateral cryptorchid or cryptorchid males.

Coat. Long coat.

Colour. Any base colour other than black; absence of all markings.

Temperament. A dog that, in the opinion of the judge, attacks any person in the ring.

The British Kennel Club covers the question of faults by having a blanket statement in all Standards that "Any departure from the foregoing points should be considered a fault and the seriousness with which the fault should be regarded should be in exact proportion to its degree."

While neatly avoiding the task of listing and grading faults, this approach is of little help to those wishing to learn about a breed. The UK approach also completely rules out any question of a fault being of such importance that the dog must be disqualified, as it would be for a particular fault under the ADRK and AKC rules.

The British argument on faults is that the judge must be allowed to weigh all faults against virtues and make a decision based on his assessment of the overall dog. I would, however, be surprised if a British judge gave a significant placing to a dog showing any one of most of the faults requiring disqualification under the ADRK or AKC Standards. However, I would not be happy if I was expected to disqualify a dog with one missing pre-molar as required under the ADRK rules, and I consider the AKC approach to be the more reasonable one.

The British Kennel Club does require a judge to report any dog that he or she considers to be vicious and the judge is allowed to dismiss it from the ring. The decision as to whether the dog should be permanently banned from the show ring and also from breeding, rests with the Kennel Club. Because such a report may result in a permanent ban, many judges are loath to report such cases unless the dog actually injures the judge or some other person. In my opinion, there may be a case for inserting aspects of bad temperament as a disqualifying fault in the UK Standard. However, any application of the disqualifying faults rule with regard to temperament must be carefully considered in conjunction with the requirements in all the Standards as to character and temperament. It would be very wrong to interpret as having a bad temperament, the actions of a dog who was displaying the requirements of "fearless character", or "boldness and courage". Both the ADRK and the AKC Standards go to considerable lengths to clarify this point.

The list of faults other than disqualifying ones is a very useful aid to understanding the details of the Standards. A feature which may not be understood when the ideal is described, may become clear by looking at the undesirable alternatives.

CONCLUSION

It is now some forty years since the Rottweiler began the rise to international fame. When American and British breeders produced their first national Standards they set out to do nothing more and nothing less than reproduce the German Standards in English. Looking at the current AKC and UK versions, it is obvious that there has been a slight but definite drift away from the original. Some of this is the result of a variety of translations and interpretations of the meaning of the original German. The ADRK would be doing a great service to Rottweilers if they produced an authorised English translation of their Standard which, subject to minor amendments to comply with individual national rules, could be used by all countries. This matter is becoming more urgent now that some other English-speaking countries have adopted the FCI/ADRK Standard.

These, then, are the Rottweiler Standards in use in Germany, America and Britain plus all the other countries which use one of these as their own Standard. Judges and breeders will vary in the emphasis that they place on particular aspects. Obviously those aspects which could affect the dog's health and ability to lead a normal life are more important than those which are largely cosmetic. However, you must, when making decisions based on the Standard, whether breeding or judging, take all the breed's features into account.

Line drawings by Carole Lilley.

Chapter Ten

THE SHOW RING

I find the breeding and showing of pedigree dogs the most rewarding hobby imaginable. It is, in fact, one of the largest participant sports, with people from all walks of life, of different ages, colours and creeds, congregating almost every weekend, in order to compete with their dogs, and to win honours in the breed – perhaps even achieving the goal of campaigning a Champion.

To the uninitiated, we dog show people must appear totally insane. We tolerate the most extreme weather conditions, travel for miles, often through the night, to reach the show venue (which is usually a field, or an exhibition hall in winter) in order to exhibit our dogs. We usually remain at the show from 9 a.m. until it closes at about 6 p.m. – then we drive all the way home again! It does sound crazy, so why do we do it?

HANDLING
The British dog show scene is dominated by owner/breeder/handlers or owner/handlers. Rottweilers do not have a 'professional handler' system, which is common practice in the USA. This system is essential in a country that is so vast. The majority of breeders cannot campaign their dogs personally, and so they use the services of professional handlers. In the UK, the more seasoned handlers will handle for other people who are unable to show their dogs, for whatever reason, and the Junior Handlers are always willing to offer their services. From a personal point of view, I only handle dogs that I either own or have bred, for the simple reason that I like to help anyone who buys a dog from me, and if I were to handle professionally (for money) then I would be competing with my own breeding.

As a breeder, my main objective is to make up/finish as many Champions as possible. Nothing gives me more pleasure than to sell a show-potential puppy to a first-time show owner, teach them all of the necessary skills, and nurture them through their first show. If you are a first-time dog show owner I always think the best ploy is to have your dog shown at the very first show by an accomplished handler. The reasons for this are twofold: firstly, you will be incredibly nervous, which does not impart confidence to the new puppy – and a bad experience at this stage could put the dog off showing for life; secondly, you are able to watch your new baby go through his paces and see the full potential – once you see how lovely your Rottweiler looked with a good handler, this can only give you the incentive to do your best. If, at the end of the day, you really feel that your Rottweiler has potential, but showing is not for you (or you cannot campaign your dog for practical reasons), then you will need to find a professional handler. You may well find that there are plenty of exhibitors desperate to get their hands on your dog, for if an up-and-coming handler is without a good dog to show, your dog may give just the break that is needed to gain recognition as a serious handler. When a dog becomes a top winner, the glory is shared with the handler, which can only be viewed as an asset to a handler's career.

I think the best example of this was the partnership of Pat Bryant and Ch. Rudi Anton Bali. Rudi was owned by the Woodward family, originally bought purely as a family pet. Pat Bryant,

BIS Select Am. Can. Ch. Goldeiche Ara von Brader: First in the Working Group, on the way to going Best in Show. The American show ring is dominated by professional handlers.

Downey Dog Photography.

Pictured (left to right): Majeika Pin Up Girl, Majeika The New Boss, and Heldenhauss Black Magic of Warrimead. In the UK Championship shows are benched.

Photo: Carol Ann Johnson.

A puppy class prepares for the judge's inspection at an English Championship show.

Photo: Carol Ann Johnson.

himself an accomplished handler/breeder of Panelma Rottweiler fame, happened to be at a show – and Pat, as everyone knows, loves a challenge, especially when it comes in the guise of a large, powerful male Rottweiler needing his unique style, particularly suited to arrogant males on a 'mission'. The rest, of course, is history – Pat made Rudi and Rudi made Pat. This incredible team notched up a total of twenty-eight Challenge Certificates, and the ultimate dream of winning Best in Show at a General All Breeds Championship Show. Rudi was the first Rottweiler ever to achieve this accolade. This record stood for ten years until at Leeds 1993 Ch. Svedala the Scandinavian took Best in Show for his owner, Trina Flowers. 'Louis' was not only Trina's first Rottweiler, but her first show dog, which proves the point that in the UK if you have a good Rottweiler it will win through, no matter who you are!

The next amateur owner/handler to achieve dizzy heights was Stewart Wright who, with his young dog, Ch. Carillana Sergeant Pepper, went through to Reserve Best in Show at South Wales Championship Show in 1994. The third Best in Show was at Richmond Championship Show in 1994, which I have to admit was the pinnacle of my career, when my own Ch. Fantasa Ultra Violet, went all the way. These are the things that make every exhibitor's world go round – but everyone has to start somewhere. The most accomplished handler was once a raw novice; successful showing is within everyone's grasp – if you have the determination to succeed.

GETTING STARTED

First of all, you have to acquire your show potential puppy. The way I started in the breed was purely by being a pet buyer and I certainly do not recommend my course of action! At the time, I already owned a rescued crossbreed Shepherd (who would not guard the skin off a rice pudding!) and having previously owned a pedigree German Shepherd Dog, I knew I wanted to stay within the 'guarding breed' type. It was while I was out for a walk that I saw a large, powerful, black-and-tan beast, and I decided to find out what breed it was. This was some fourteen years ago when Rottweilers were very rare; no one knew what they were!

Doing my research (which was asking the owner of such a fine specimen exactly what breed it was), I decided to find a breeder of Rottweilers. Like most people, I did not know about showing or the right people to buy from – I thought a dog is a dog is a dog. I was fortunate to find a vet who had bred a pet litter. He told me that although the sire was a show winner, the puppies were pet quality. This seemed fine, so I bought a well-adjusted, well-reared puppy from honest, well-meaning people – but he was not a show dog. However, I was more than satisfied; I had a lovely pet. I then met several Rottweiler owners who invited me to their homes to see their dogs (it appeared that I had been invited to become a member of the very exclusive Rottweiler owners club!). The more I discovered, the more I needed to know; so the next step was to go to a dog show. The thing which stuck in my mind was the difference between the show dogs and my own pride and joy! Yes, I had bought a pet-quality dog but there was no harm in showing him, was there? My first attempts at showing my dog were disastrous. Because there were so few Rottweilers around, the people at the training class were very unsure of how the breed should be presented. I tried to do my best, but to no avail. I had a long training lead which constantly became tangled around both my legs and the dog's. My poor dog, Max, didn't know whether he was coming or going! The judge gave me some sound advice: "Learn how to handle!" I was determined to continue with this new sport, so I decided to use Max as a training exercise – and if I won, it was a bonus! I took myself off to Championship Shows and watched the handlers perform in the ring. I then met up with another Rottweiler owner who lived locally; we struck up a good friendship and decided to travel to the shows together. I will always remember this period as the days of *no pressure!* Ruby Adey and I treated the business of showing as pure enjoyment. There was just me and my pet dog hanging loose – not caring whether I won or lost.

My, how times have changed! The classes were not very big in those days; I remember five in a class and invariably only two in the Open class. I watched the handlers very closely, and I must admit that there was great variation in technique. The Rottweilers were far more dog-aggressive; the males were constantly 'sparring' up to each other. This was used to advantage by the male handlers, to 'get the dog on his toes'. The other methods used all involved baiting with liver. Some handlers stood at the side of the dog, holding the food in front of the dog's head. The method which I preferred was standing in front of the dog and the dog looking up at the handler, who was constantly feeding it with the liver. I watched very closely and tried to emulate these techniques at home, in front of a mirror. At least this method enabled me to have a judge's eye view of my dog, as I was unable to assess his stance otherwise. With a great deal of practice and a lot of tips from other handlers, I didn't do such a bad job!

I also handled dogs for other people, which gave me more experience, and I thoroughly enjoyed myself. I also utilised this time of 'frivolity' to do my homework on the breed. I watched every class and marked up not only the results but, most importantly, those dogs which impressed my novice eye the most. I would then look at the breeding: the sire, the dam and the breeder. Eventually a common pattern began to emerge; I had actually started to *get my eye on a type!*

Eventually, I had found the bloodlines which produced the Rottweiler which was most to my liking. It was as simple as that! Now the hard part – how was I to acquire such a fine specimen? The best course of action is to go to dog shows and approach the breeder of your choice, providing they are not busy. If they are (which is usual) look up their name and telephone number in the catalogue and phone them at home. A breeder is definitely more amenable when relaxed and in the comfort of their own home, free from the stress of a dog show.

Any good breeder will have bookings for their puppies, so it may be necessary to book well in advance, which may involve waiting for that 'special pup'. However, it is important to remember that no breeder can guarantee show success; they can only offer show potential. A good tip is to find out if the breeder sells all of the litter at the same price, or if the pups are graded into 'show potential' and 'pet quality'. In my opinion, a puppy at eight weeks of age will be a miniature of what it should be as an adult; I can only speak of my own bloodlines, but I can definitely tell the pets from the 'show potential' at eight weeks. With any puppy, no matter how good, much depends on caring, nurturing, training and loving your Rottweiler.

EARLY TRAINING

Once you have bought your show-potential puppy, you are ready to begin! The puppy must be allowed to grow up and must not be over-trained; I hardly ever train young babies. I stack them on a table from six weeks old – this is not done as a training method, but as a means of assessment. The pup is also getting used to being handled and baited while I analyse structure and conformation. The best rule is: Never teach your pup to sit for food – food means Stand.

All Rottweiler handlers use a 'bum bag' filled with cooked liver, or when at home, cheese. My dogs soon learn that when the bag appears they are in for a good time. Training can be quite informal – I train my dogs in the kitchen. In addition to the training session, I also carry dog treats around in my coat pocket. So, if I put my hand into the pocket and the dogs hear the rattle of food, I have a sea of black-and-tans standing in front of me, all jostling for pole position in the hope of being the first to get a treat! The young pup watches the adults and learns that when all four feet are on the ground, a treat is given. I also teach the dogs to 'catch'. I have six Rottweilers all being attentive; I say the dog's name, and that dog catches the food when it is thrown. This not only keeps the dogs on their toes, it helps when in the ring. If, for example, a dog is getting a little bored and not using his ears, a 'catch' will immediately result in the dog becoming more alert and using his ears. The way to a Rottweiler's heart is definitely through his stomach! This game has an added advantage if you keep a number of dogs, as I do; the dogs must be taught to respect one another, and the catching game teaches them to wait their turn.

STAGE ONE: Walk the puppy into position, and keeping the pup distracted with bait in your hand, place the rear.

SHOW TRAINING A PUPPY
Jenny Dennis demonstrates puppy training with ten-week-old Wannonas Winter Masquerade at Hartsmoor.
Photos by Carol Ann Johnson.

STAGE TWO: Set up the front left leg first. Then set the front right leg. If the puppy sits down, keep lifting her up by the tummy and steady her. Use the command "Stand" at the same time.

STAGE THREE: The puppy is topped and tailed.

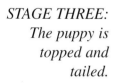

BUILDING A RAPPORT

Training must always be fun. I never use any harsh words when show training my Rottweilers; if they are not happy they will never work for you. The first thing you must do is build up a rapport with your puppy; a pup has to feel that you adore him above all else (I have ten Rottweilers and they all think that they are the only dog in my life!). Rottweilers are definitely not good kennel dogs; they need lots of human contact, which means being in the home and being part of the family. My own description of the Rottweiler is that he is not just happy being with you, he needs to be under your skin! Anyone who owns a Rottweiler will know exactly what I mean.

The first stages of training begin with teaching your dog to bait – this means getting the dog to take food gently out of your hand. Do not allow the dog to pick up food which has fallen out of your hand, or you will soon have a Rottweiler with nose pressed to the floor, searching for tidbits! If you do drop any food, pick it up quickly and give it to your dog. A show dog must learn to follow your right hand wherever it goes. Your left hand will be used to move the dog's legs. Sticking to a few basic rules not only makes handling easy, but it also avoids confusing the puppy. Frequently a show dog is bought by a couple, so a decision must be made from the very beginning as to which person is going to be the handler; it is no good changing handlers mid-stream; you will only confuse the puppy. A Rottweiler is not a toy or a robot, so treat your dog as the sensitive soul that he is. However, do not go to the opposite extreme and think that you must wrap your Rottweiler in cotton-wool.

ACCEPTABLE BEHAVIOUR

Puppies arriving at their new home, leaving their litter, only know the law of the jungle. This means that if a puppy wants something, it has to fight its siblings for it. When the puppies go to their new homes, they will probably object to having things taken from them, and they may resent being picked up and restrained. If this happens and your puppy growls at you or tries to snap, this behaviour must be quickly nipped in the bud. The best technique I have found is to shake the puppy, flip him on to his back and growl in his face. The puppy is so shocked, he becomes rigid and lies perfectly still. Once the puppy has recovered composure, the result is usually a contrite and humbler individual.

There are a few basic rules with a Rottweiler: your dog must *never* growl at you for any reason, and your dog must *never* be allowed to 'object' guard. This means that anything you give to your dog belongs to you, and if you want to take it back, this must be achieved without complaint. As far as the dog is concerned, you are 'lord and master'. Remember, good behaviour must always be rewarded; practise taking toys from your dogs – the reward for good behaviour is getting the toy back! If your dog objects by growling, this demands immediate correction. Your puppy soon learns what is acceptable behaviour – and what is not!

If your puppy is locked up in a kennel all day, the result will be a bored, increasingly independent, anti-social dog. If you treat your Rottweiler like a wild animal, this is exactly what you will get, and being a guarding breed, your Rottweiler will soon learn to over-guard and dislike people. I do not need to inform you of the outcome of such a situation. Responsible breeding and responsible ownership is the key to a well-behaved, well-balanced dog, and everyone who takes on a Rottweiler should be aware of those responsibilities.

GROOMING YOUR SHOW DOG

I have to say that I am very 'Americanised' in my attitude to both handling and presentation. I am very often shouted down by the older British fraternity, saying: "There is no need to bath a dog before every show; you spoil his coat", or "He is a working dog not a Poodle!" Well, old habits die hard with some people, and progress is a dirty word!

TRAINING THE JUNIOR
Liz Dunhill shows how to pose her bitch, Fantasa Cream Cracker.
Photos by Carol Ann Johnson.

STAGE ONE: Hold the bait and the lead up high, so that the dog cranes her neck skywards. Then, lean your upper body over the dog's head. This will put her off-balance, and she will have to walk backwards. This will result in setting the back feet parallel.

STAGE TWO: If the legs have to be moved, the same principles apply as for stacking, except the dog is distracted with bait, which helps to keep her happy. Always feed the dog with the right hand and move the legs with the left, so that the youngster does not become confused. She will expect to be fed with one hand only.

The young Rottweiler should be stroked continually to calm and reassure her, and, through the touch of your hand, she will get used to being handled and will learn to pick up the signal for which is the next part of her body to be moved.

STAGE THREE: This is probably the most difficult stage for a novice to grasp, as when the food is put into the dog's mouth with the right hand, the left hand must reach down and place the hocks.

The secret is to keep the right hand perfectly still. It is often an automatic reaction to move the 'baiting' hand, as you reach down with the left hand. This, of course, makes the dog walk forward and the handler is left wrestling with the rear end. A good way to practise is to place the bait at the dog's mouth and walk around the dog, without the dog moving one inch!

STAGE FOUR: Once the hocks are set, come back up the dog, stacking her. Then move to the front.

*STAGE FIVE:
Now lift the
forelegs and
place them in
position.*

*STAGE SIX:
Stand away from
the dog, with your
hands in the
pouch, attracting
her attention.*

*Photo: John
Hartley.*

I have never disputed the working heritage of the Rottweiler, but in this instance we are talking *show* dog, not *working* dog. If someone chooses not to prepare their dog before a show, then that is their prerogative. I am a professional, and I feel that it is totally disrespectful to the judge to present your dog for examination with a dirty coat!

My dogs are my companions as well as show dogs; they charge across the fields every morning, they are up to their necks in water and mud, and they love it! But come the weekend, two days before a show, they are bathed and groomed, their whiskers are trimmed along with their breeching, nails are clipped, and they are groomed until they shine. The night before the show they are groomed once more, and conditioned with mink-oil spray.

Rottweilers must be bathed at least two days before the show, as it takes a day for the coat to settle. Once bathed, the dog must be allowed to shake, and then I generally put the dog in a cage on dry bedding. After about an hour, take a very fine flea comb and take out all of the dead hair. The following evening, comb again, spray all over with mink-oil, then brush it into the coat.

The breeching has to be tidied (which is another skill to be learned). Never attempt to trim breeching until you know how to do it. The best course of action is to ask your puppy's breeder to give a demonstration. The whiskers and the nails also need to be trimmed. Again, if you do not know how to trim nails, ask your breeder or your vet. If you cut the quick, the pup will never forgive you and will probably have an aversion to having his feet touched, never mind nails trimmed! I have seen many an owner have a full-scale battle on their hands because of a slip made with the clippers when the dog was a puppy.

THE 'RED COAT'
This continues to be a subject of much debate and inevitably causes controversy whenever it is aired. However, it is a subject which should not be ignored. All black and tan dogs carry the ST ST gene – consequently the Rottweiler will carry 'red' in the coat. If the pup is not groomed adequately, dead coat remains and this takes on a red-rust appearance. The dead undercoat appears to stick and will not come out. The coat looks woolly and fluffy, as the puppy coat is attempting to shed. The only way to cure this problem is to bathe the dog and use the fine flea comb to loosen the dead coat and remove it. This will take a great deal of time, as the coat must be groomed every day. This problem does not affect all Rottweilers, and once the dead coat is removed, the new coat grows in normally, the 'red coat' never appearing again. There is no genetic reason for this phenomenon; it is thought to be either seasonal or nutritional. Beta carotene, which is present in some dog foods, has been a proven culprit in this red coat syndrome.

When I first mentioned this in an article, the whole idea was laughed at by some experienced breeders of many years' standing who 'pooh-poohed' the idea as ridiculous, but checking with a geneticist and talking to breeders of Bernese Mountain Dogs and Labrador Retrievers, I find they all have the same problem. I do not want to give the impression that this anomaly occurs in all black-coated breeds, or in all Rotts for that matter – for it does not. However, if it occurs in one dog, that is enough. Breeders owe it to their breed to be completely honest, and not to shy away from problems that develop in their own line. There are lots of breeders who will be completely open about their much-loved breed, and so if you are buying a puppy, you should be unafraid to ask pertinent questions about the line, and to check hip scores, etc.

THE SHOW KIT
Now that you have acquired your show-quality dog, you need to start training and to acquire your show equipment. I usually train a puppy on a half-check collar. This helps to enforce the lessons, but it means that a struggling puppy does not end up choking itself. I then progress to the nylon show collar. Check-chains are still used by some people, but they are becoming obsolete as a means of dog control. I dislike using check-chains for several reasons.

SHOWING THE BITE
Photos: Carol Ann Johnson.

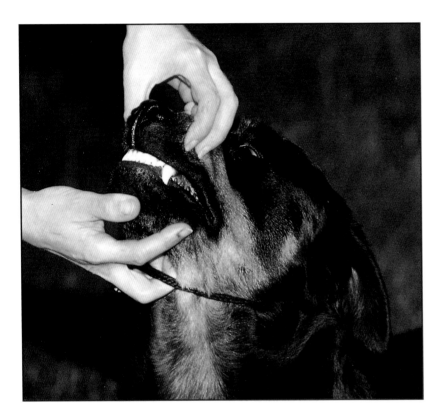

STAGE ONE: Place your left hand over the muzzle, with the thumb on one side and fingers on the other. Hold the skin just under the lower jaw with the right hand, give the command "Teeth", and gently pull the upper and lower lips back, exposing the front teeth. It is important to keep the nostrils clear, and to allow the dog to see what is going on.

STAGE TWO: Showing the side teeth. Do not obscure the teeth with your fingers, as some judges like to check a dog has full dentition.

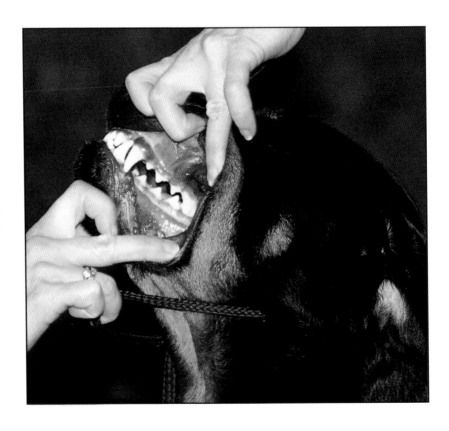

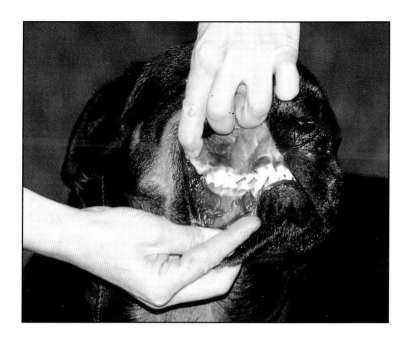

*STAGE THREE:
Showing the other
side of the mouth. Liz
usually drops her lead
and stands on it to
allow her to use both
hands.*

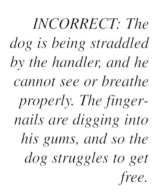

*INCORRECT: The
dog is being straddled
by the handler, and he
cannot see or breathe
properly. The finger-
nails are digging into
his gums, and so the
dog struggles to get
free.*

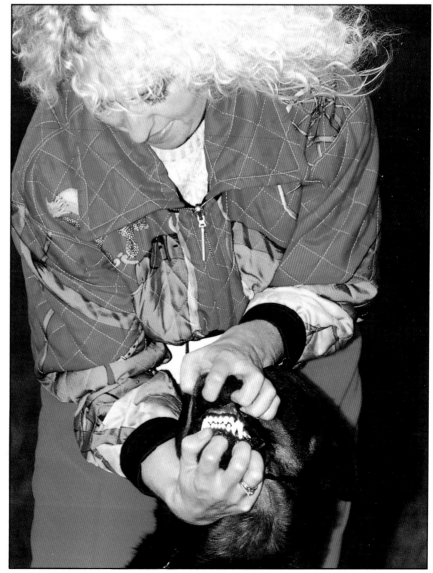

Firstly, they chop the dog's coat around the neck, leaving an unsightly moth-eaten patch. Secondly, I don't believe in bullying pups and jerking them with a chain, which jingles in their ears! This can give the dog a total aversion to moving on the lead in the show ring. I have seen many youngsters cowering away, frightened of the lead. Thirdly, chains tend to be of a length which drops over the shoulders. If a dog decides to go for another dog (heaven forbid!), then it takes more effort to pull the dog back, and you have little control if the chain is at the base of the neck. The dog simply won't feel a thing! Whereas if the dog is wearing a nylon collar, it is positioned high under the throat, giving total control to the handler. The dog that pulls will choke, and it does not take a Rottweiler long to desist from this type of unwanted behaviour. The collar always must be black, so that it cannot be seen. You should always check the collar regularly to ensure that it is not frayed or worn, as you don't want it to snap at an inopportune moment!

For a puppy, buy a fine leather lead, with a small clip, so that the puppy is not constantly bashed around the face by something heavy. Nothing looks more ridiculous than a little pup with a lead that looks bigger than him! As the Rott grows, buy a slightly thicker, short leather lead, which can be held comfortably in your hand.

LIST FOR THE SHOW BAG
1. A sturdy leather collar and benching chain. (This is needed in the UK, where all Championship Shows are benched.)
2. A rug or towel for the dog to lie on when waiting to compete.
3. A water bowl and a bottle of water. (In the summer I give my dogs honey and water. This helps prevent dehydration and provides a glucose drink for energy.)
4. A show collar and lead.
5. Water spray (to use for cooling the dogs in the ring in the summer).
6. Mink-oil spray (to give a finish to the coat).
7. A fine-toothed comb or flea comb.
8. A soft horse body-brush and a stiff horse body-brush (horse brushes are better than dog brushes!).
9. Towel and damp chamois leather or sponge (for cleaning the dog's face).
10. An aerosol spray for feet (which prevents slipping).
11. Round-ended scissors for trimming whiskers, and long, sharp scissors for trimming the breeching.
12. A long comb for the breeching (used as a scissor aid when trimming).
13. Nail-clippers and blood stop (in case you make a mistake!).
14. A bait pouch and liver (cooked, of course).
15. A ring-clip (always pack a spare, as I always forget mine!).
16. A heat-proof coat (to deflect the sun away from the dog).

CLOTHING
Everyone has their own ideas and styles of dress for the show ring, but two rules must always be adhered to. Clothes must be smart, but also practical. Do not wear anything which flaps in the dog's face or hinders movement. If you don't feel comfortable, then you will never do a good job! Shoes must be flat and slip-resistant. I always wear bright red or pink, as I feel better wearing bright clothes. It also makes you stand out in a crowd!

TIPS PEOPLE NEVER TELL YOU!
WINTER: Always take waterproof jacket and trousers and boots. Lots of judges will stay out in the rain to judge (myself included). I invested in a pair of leather, waterproof ankle-boots, which keep my feet dry and still look smart.

AMERICAN STYLE
The American style of handling is demonstrated by Liz Dunhill with Ch. Fantasa Ultra Violet.

Photos by Carol Ann Johnson.

STAGE ONE: Walk the dog into position with the collar in your left hand. The short lead is dropped down the right side of the dog, out of sight. Guide the dog's head and ease into position with your right hand.

STAGE TWO: Make sure that the nylon collar is placed correctly, i.e. right under the chin, so that no 'ruff' appears.

STAGE THREE:
Holding the collar in your left hand, transfer the dog's body weight on to the left foreleg. Pick up the right leg by the elbow, away from the body, and set the leg down under the shoulder. You can see the short lead dropped down on the dog's offside.

STAGE FOUR:
Repeat stage three, this time with the left leg. Hold the collar in the right hand, pulling the dog's weight on to the right leg. Pick up the elbow, and set down to match the other leg.

STAGE FIVE: Hold the collar in the right hand, keeping the dog's head in position, and steady the dog with the left hand. Do not allow the dog to lean against your legs.

STAGE SIX: Move the rear leg by grasping it by the hock, and work the joint with finger and thumb, setting the rear pastern down straight.

STAGE SEVEN: Repeat the same procedure with the right hock. This photo shows the positioning of the fingers around the hock joint; it also shows how far the foot is lifted from the ground.

STAGE EIGHT: Place the foot down in the correct position.

STAGE NINE: The finished position, with the collar now in the left hand and the dog looking forward. If the dog loses attention, use bait to maintain the position and to achieve expression.

ENGLISH STYLE
Liz Dunhill demonstrates the English style of handling with Ch. Fantasa Ultra Violet. The aim is to have the Rottweiller free-standing on a loose lead, using bait to keep the attention.

CONTINENTAL STYLE
The Rottweiler is encouraged to show itself off either by being attracted by a second person, or by sparring up to another dog.

Buy a rain hat which will not come off in the wind. Take a flask and sandwiches, as show food can be quite expensive. Do not be tempted to go to the bar and drink alcohol before you have shown you dog. You are there to do a good job of handling dogs, and you do not want to impair your performance. You can always go and celebrate or cheer yourself up *after* judging! Make sure you have plenty of bedding in your car so that the dogs will be comfortable when travelling. It is a good idea to invest in a crate, which gives the dogs a safe and secure place to travel in.

SUMMER: Fill a plastic bottle with water and put in it the freezer. By the time you get to the show, the water will be half-melted, and so you can give your dog iced-water all day long. In the car, cover dog-crates in a space blanket (to reflect the sun). Sun shades should be fitted to the car windows. *Never leave your dog in a car when the sun is shining – the dog could die within minutes.* Wear cool, loose clothing which looks smart. Skimpy shorts are OK outside the ring, but not in the ring! Cover yourself in sun-block, especially the tops of the arms and the backs of the legs. It is surprising how many people become badly burnt at shows. Dogs also suffer from heatstroke: I always sit the dog in *my* shadow. Keep a constant supply of honey and water at hand, and a water-spray to use on the belly of the dog. Do not use it on the dog's back, as this only magnifies the sun.

IN THE RING: Do not keep your Rottweiler showing throughout the entire class; the dog will only become bored. Never go first in line if you are a novice, always go to the middle (unless you are in numerical order). *Always* watch classes before your own to determine which ring patterns the judge is using, and watch the people in front of you. Stay calm and never rush.

If the judge asks the class to gait around the ring together, and the class is full, give yourself plenty of room. Wait for the dog in front to get halfway around the ring before you set off. Never overtake the dog in front – this is classed as bad manners. Hang back on the judge's blind side, which will give you plenty of room to put your dog at full stretch on the judge's viewing side. Always keep your eye on the judge to see if he is looking at your dog. Do not forget to look at your dog; a lot of people are so busy staring at the judge that they fail to see that their dog is not standing correctly. If you find yourself blocked into a corner by some rude exhibitor, either ask the steward to move the dogs around, or go and move to the end of the line. You have paid a lot of money to show your dog, and it is your right to have the same advantage as anyone else.

Beware the bad handler who will try and run his dog right up behind yours, attempting to put your dog off-stride and unsettle him. Turn around and tell the exhibitor to stop, or ask the steward to move you to another place. Many new exhibitors are unaware of their rights. However, never fall into the trap of being rude – politeness costs nothing. Bad behaviour should never be seen in the show ring. Always congratulate the winner, even if you do not feel that the win is warranted. Save your anger or frustration for the journey home.

These are all pearls of wisdom, and I can truly say that most exhibitors have lost their temper at some time or another, so if it happens to you, you will not be the first, nor will you be the last! Even if your behaviour is beyond reproach 99.9 per cent of the time, if you are successful, people will only remember the one time you acted badly! That is dog-showing: whenever you have a bunch of humans competing with one another you will always discover the worst side of someone!

The plus side is that there are more good people than bad. I have shown dogs for many years and I can honestly say that *all* of my friends are dog people, and I would not be without them.

Chapter Eleven

THE JUDGE'S VIEW

NORTH AMERICA
By Dorothea Gruenerwald

According to the January 1994 American Kennel Club's Judges Directory, there are 2558 accredited conformation judges of all breeds. Of this number 131 are approved to judge Rottweilers, either at the Breed or Group level; and of these there are only fifteen breeder-judges, with more working towards their licence every year. One could argue that with the seemingly undiminished popularity of the breed and the constant addition of all-breed and Specialty clubs to the annual show scene, the number of breeder-judges is quite low. This may change in the near future.

Most of our current breeder-judges have been active in the breed for many years, a few acquiring their first Rottweiler in the mid-1940s. All have many years of experience as breeders and as exhibitors dating back to the early 1960s. This background translates into a more specific, though sometimes subjective, approach to judging the breed. We also have a rather sizeable number of judges licensed for Rottweilers, who by virtue of having been successful handlers prior to their judging careers, are very capable of finding the right dogs.

Although I have been a licensed AKC judge for only four years and consider myself one of the junior breeder-judges, my background includes over twenty-five years of active participation in the breed. I was an owner-handler, finishing six of my dogs. I served as President of the American Rottweiler Club for two terms, 1975 to 1977, and as Editor of the club newsletter, ARK, for over ten years. As the breeder of twenty-eight champions (1964 to 1985), and desiring to be still involved with my chosen breed, I began working towards my judging licence. Lacking the overall judging experience of other breeder-judges in terms of actual ring participation, my personal comments are based on a shorter time-frame.

Becoming an AKC licensed judge for any breed at this point in time is a lengthy process. The AKC is constantly changing their stipulated requirements, seeking to improve the selection of judges with the implied intent of improving the quality of new judges.

An aspiring judge applying to AKC for the first time must meet the following minimum prerequisites: (1) have ten years' documented experience in the sport; (2) have owned or exhibited several dogs of the initial breed(s) requested; (3) have bred or raised at least four litters in any one breed; (4) have produced two champions out of a minimum of four litters; (5) have five stewarding assignments at AKC Member or Licensed Shows; (6) have judged six Sanctioned matches, Sweepstakes or Futurities; (7) must meet the occupational eligibility requirements under AKC Rules; (8) must pass a comprehensive 'open book' examination demonstrating understanding of AKC Rules, Policies and Judging Procedures; (9) must pass a test on the Standard of each breed requested; (10) must be interviewed; (11) must provide two references. To satisfy these and additional requirements requires time, effort, and money on the

THE AMERICAN TYPE: Am. Ch. Helkirk Weissenberg's Chance: Number One Rottweiler bitch for 1994.
Photo courtesy: Dorothea Gruenerwald.

part of the would-be judge. It is unnecessary to further detail all the convoluted arrangements whereby an applicant is finally approved to judge initially on a Provisional basis, and, after a specified number of assignments, to become a Regular Judge.

The American Kennel Club publishes *Guidelines for Dog Show Judges* which details, in general terms, the required judging procedures. All judges must physically examine each dog, i.e. must open the dog's mouth (or have the handler do so) to check dentition and bite and must check that every male has two normally descended testicles. He/she must go over the dog to determine soundness of back, hocks and coat condition. Some judges do an extensive 'hands on' examination, while others do as little as possible with a Rottweiler! For example, one well-known judge *gently* holds the left ear of an Open Class male while doing her routine examination, as if to reassure him. Actually, she is really controlling that dog until she has moved back from his head area. The judge is required to individually gait each dog to determine soundness, always using the same ring pattern to ensure impartiality.

The interpretation of the Standard is the sole responsibility of the judge. A judge can adjudicate only those dogs which are presented in the conformation ring on a particular day. The responsibility for the dog entered is the breeder's, the owner's, and finally, the exhibitor's. It is the breeder who sets type, movement and soundness by what is selected and incorporated into his or her breeding programme.

The owner must maintain the dog in show condition and develop the dog's potential. Finally, it is imperative that the handler understand the virtues and faults of the particular dog being presented to the judge. For example, knowing how to maximise the dog's good qualities, e.g. his beautiful masculine head, and minimise his 'roller coaster' topline.

In my opinion, breeders and exhibitors in the larger urban areas of the USA have numerous advantages over those living in less populated areas. There are more AKC events to attend, larger entries of Rottweilers in competition, more established breeders, more Specialties and generally more quality dogs. Rottweiler breeders actively involved with local or regional clubs or who are members of the Parent Club appear to be conscientious in their desire to improve the breed. They are becoming more knowledgeable about structure and movement and in selecting breeding stock which will complement and correct deficiencies in their bloodlines. Increasingly, more attention is given to type and structure.

TYPE VERSUS SOUNDNESS

Many years ago, at one of the early American Rottweiler Club National Specialties, a breeder turned to me and whispered "Wow, look at that dog! I wonder if the sucker can move?", and when the dog moved, a dejected "Darn!". She is now a respected breeder-judge!

Books on judging invariably address the subject of Type versus Soundness. Which is more important and why? Mongrels have no type, but can be sound. A Rottweiler does not look like a Greyhound, therefore it has a type different from a Greyhound, but both must be sound to perform the tasks for which they were bred. It is generally accepted that breeder-judges address both type *and* soundness, not sacrificing one for the other. Most evaluate the dogs on their good qualities, not on their faults. Most are very demanding and unforgiving when it comes to light eyes, any missing teeth, faulty bites, unstable temperament, or a poor head.

As all exhibitors learn sooner or later, judging is a subjective process. It is the search for the 'ideal dog' in the opinion of the judge on the day of the event. One judge's emphasis often differs from that of another judge. One can be strictly a head-hunter, another a tooth counter, another looks only for sound movement, or a good topline. This is what makes judging interesting!

The following comparative discussion covers both positive and negative comments on portions of our Standard.

HEADS

Heads have greatly improved. Rottweiler judges are seeing more dogs and bitches with good, strong heads and not the 'houndy' heads (long, narrow muzzles with long ears) as observed in the past. There are still dogs with rather plain or 'common' heads, lacking fill under the eyes, insufficient stop, and incorrect ratio of muzzle to backskull.

High on the list of needed improvement are round eyes. Regrettably, there are very few almond-shaped eyes to be seen. Even a dark round eye is incorrect. Eye colour is more uniform than in the past; however, some judges feel there still are too many dogs with light eye colour. Many years ago I judged a fun match where I saw hazel-coloured eyes on a handsome male. Obviously, I could not give him much consideration because of his very unusual eye colour. I still have not seen a 'bird of prey' eye and hope the next Standard revision eliminates this antiquated phrase. Judges are finding dogs with hairless eye-rims (the previous Standard referred to a 'hairless eye-lid' which was incorrect). Open for discussion is whether this disconcerting problem can be due to an allergy or a genetic defect. Most breeder-judges will acknowledge this fault in making final placements, but there are other more important faults to consider. While it is distracting, and the cause for this condition is unknown, in my opinion round eyes are certainly much more offensive.

Since most AKC judges are not practising veterinarians, they are very reluctant to pass judgement on entropion or ectropion specified as Disqualifications. A year ago an AKC judge, who was also a practising veterinarian, disqualified a Rottweiler for entropion. Faced with the probability that a dog has either entropion or ectropion, a judge without benefit of a veterinarian degree would most likely mentally eliminate that particular dog from further consideration, but would not disqualify it.

Ear shape and size seem to have become more uniform, but judges are still seeing ears that are rather long and improperly carried.

The emphasis on bites and dentition in the last revised Standard has motivated breeders to be more circumspect and careful in their planned breedings. Judges are not seeing as many overshot or undershot bites; now there are level bites. Occasionally, a judge will find a missing premolar on a puppy, but this can be X-rayed by the owner to determine whether there is a tooth beneath the gum which has not yet erupted (two missing premolars even on a puppy is a Disqualification).

FOREQUARTERS

Fronts continue to be a real problem. At the top of the list is straight, upright shoulders attached to short upper arms which causes a stilted, awkward movement and lack of reach. This structural deficiency is quite prevalent. Lack of forechest; shallow chests (not reaching to the elbow); out at the elbows; weak pasterns with feet turning east-west and splayed; and flat feet are still seen. Inexperienced breeders who lack knowledge of these genetic weaknesses, who lack the ability to objectively evaluate their breeding stock, and who lack knowledge of bloodlines, i.e. faulty matings of sires and dams with the same 'poor fronts', continue to perpetuate these problems.

TOPLINE/BODY

The Rottweiler with a strong topline, moving or standing, will usually win his/her class, all things being equal. This is because there are too many 'roller coaster' toplines and soft backs which continue to plague the breed. Many Rottweilers are physically out of condition when presented in the conformation ring. (Walking and swimming are great exercise activities for both dog and owner.) Bloodlines noted for strong toplines are still in the gene pool; breeders just need to be more aware of them. A dog with a long back (measuring more than ten long to nine high) is incorrect. The correct profile should be that of a nearly square dog.

Established Rottweiler breeders-exhibitors objected to the inclusion of "Underline of a mature Rottweiler has a slight tuck-up." The strength and shortness of loin is enhanced by the Rottweiler's nearly level underline (which is almost parallel to the topline). A moderate 'tuck-up' is evident and permissible on puppies, but a level underline should appear on adults. Fortunately, judges are not seeing so many mature dogs with a "slight tuck-up" in the show ring today.

HINDQUARTERS
Croups have also improved, but many still fall off too much, resulting in an incorrect tail-set which affects the level topline called for in the Standard. Rears have greatly improved, but rear 'duck feet' are appearing. This is not cow-hocked with the hocks turning in. The hocks are straight, just the feet turn out.

COAT
Specific mention of "any trimming that alters the length of the natural coat" was deemed necessary at the time due to the extensive altering of several long-coated dogs in the show ring. This situation can present a problem for judges, who have the option of disqualifying the dog on the basis of trimming (stripping or clipping) a presumed long coat, or mentally eliminating the dog from further consideration, thereby avoiding a confrontational situation with the exhibitor.

COLOUR
Markings have improved generally; however, there are still dogs being presented with excessively large triangular markings across the chest area. It has been observed that often these markings appear as a much lighter rust-mahogany colour overall. Conversely, there are many dogs lacking noticeable chest and facial markings.

Many long-time Rottweiler breeders-exhibitors objected to the addition of the colour tan in describing "The undercoat is gray, tan or black." Only in certain areas of the USA are dogs with a 'tan' or 'reddish brown' undercoat exhibited (and bred), so it seemed a matter of re-writing the Standard to fit the conditions. The German Standard calls for a grey or black undercoat.

TEMPERAMENT
Temperaments have improved greatly. Dogs are more under control, with fewer fights inside and outside the ring. "Shyness and Viciousness" which were merely mentioned in the 1979 Standard were made more explicit under "Temperament" in the 1990 Standard, at the insistence of AKC. Shyness is not to be tolerated and calls for a dog to be excused. "A judge shall excuse any shy Rottweiler, ...refusing to stand for examination, ...shrinks from the judge...menaces or threatens him/her...may not be safely approached." Every judge has the implicit authority to excuse any dog that growls or 'talks'. Since there is a big difference between a Rottweiler growl and a spoiled dog who loves to intimidate and has not been trained to refrain from 'talking' in the show ring, I believe most breeder-judges are a bit more lenient and less likely to excuse a dog that 'talks' than non-breeder-judges. But each judge has to carefully read the dog he is about to examine.

Viciousness became an instant disqualification: "A dog that in the opinion of the judge attacks any person in the ring shall be disqualified."

GENERAL OBSERVATIONS
Quality and uniformity of type has greatly improved over the past twenty years. The use of professional or semi-professional handlers has resulted in better presentation in the ring. The dog with an 'attitude', a ring-wise presence, shown on a loose lead, carries a great deal of weight in

making it to the first place position. These qualities are not mentioned in our Standard, but they do count in today's competition. Despite the negative press and the continuing breed-specific laws against all dogs, and in particular, the Rottweiler, I believe our breed will prevail as a sound working dog. The sincere breeders, past, present, and future, and our breeder-judges as protectors and teachers, will assure that place. A fundamental understanding of anatomy as it relates to the Rottweiler Standard should be one of the first lessons learned, but usually is the very last. By that time, a great deal of catching up in terms of correcting structure is necessary.

THE UNITED KINGDOM
By Andrew Brace

JUDGING QUALIFICATIONS
In Britain, the Kennel club does not give rules and regulations regarding an individual's qualifications to judge. It is a matter of acquiring experience in a breed, achieving success in the show ring and in a breeding programme, and generally serving an apprenticeship in the breed. The Kennel Club has a list of approved Championship judges, which is based on levels of previous judging experience. In most cases, the would-be judge will serve an apprenticeship of around five years, during which time they should be reasonably successful at Championship Shows, and their home-bred litters should display soundness and type. During this pre-judging period, the aspiring judge should learn as much as possible about the breed, reading books and attending seminars, and also studying the Breed Standard in great detail, working on a personal interpretation of it. It is a useful exercise to watch leading judges at work in the ring, studying their methods and working out why certain selections have been made.

Ring stewarding is a useful way to start a judging career, as this gives experience of organising a ring. The next step is to start judging at Matches and Exemption Shows, and then gradually work towards bigger shows. It is essential to keep accurate records of all judging appointments, and when a judge officiates at Championship level, this is required by the Kennel Club.

THE CHANGING SCENE
As regards the Rottweiler in the UK, I believe that the true stalwarts of the breed have done an excellent job with improving quality and maintaining type. During the great boom of the eighties, when a litter of Rottweiler meant big money to anyone who could get hold of a bitch who vaguely looked like the breed, inevitably, grossly inferior specimens found their way into the show ring. To the puppy farmer and the unscrupulous backyard breeder, the Rottweiler was manna from heaven. Then came the flood of wildly exaggerated media coverage of "Rottweiler attacks". The few which actually did involve the breed were invariably the result of totally unsuitable dogs and bitches being bred together to produce puppies with unstable temperaments, sold into unsuitable homes. With the bad Press, the bottom dropped out of the market. This was initially viewed as tragic for the breed, but, in retrospect, I feel it was in some ways the saving of the British Rottweiler, as once again the breed returned to the guardianship of those who loved, understood, and respected it.

Consequently, untypical and inferior dogs fell by the wayside, and the quality of the breed in Britain is now such that many overseas judges are of the opinion that the British Rottweilers are the best in the world – their overall type being relative to their geographical location – midway between Europe and America.

Some breed people have bemoaned lack of substance, as they see it. Personally, I feel many people confuse height with substance. The British Breed Standard has a minimum shoulder height for bitches of 23 inches, males 25 inches. It is much more important that the Rottweiler should have adequate bulk for its size, than height for its own sake, and balance has to be one of the most important aspects of any breed when it is being judged. In the British show ring you will find dogs and bitches who are correctly proportioned; perhaps some may have a touch more length than the ideal, but generally the 'off-square' outline can be found in numbers. Well-balanced, dry heads are easily found. Expressions tend to be quite good, and mouths, on the whole, are well above average. One of the most important considerations of the breed, namely temperament, is generally excellent, and I can honestly say I have never had problems with a Rottweiler in a British show ring. In fact, I have been bitten by far more Chihuahuas than I have by Rotts, Shepherds or Dobes.

Movement is a problem. The breed has a predisposition towards hip and cruciate ligament problems, and some dogs do display great weakness in the rear. The tendency to encourage over-angulation (one of the component parts of "smartness" in the eyes of some judges) may be a contributing factor to poor movement. In my opinion, a dog which has a tendency to straightness of stifle will always move with more power than a dog who is excessively angulated in the rear.

Colour and markings, while being very low on my list of personal breed priorities, sometimes are less than perfect, and many dogs win well on their overall virtue, while being over-tanned on the hindquarters. Looking at the problem in a global sense, I feel it should be watched but it should never become out of proportion. Overall I think British breeders deserve every congratulation for the job they have done with the breed, and nowadays, the Rott is always a serious contender at Group level – it was not long ago that few judges knew what they were!

A JUDGING EXERCISE

All Rottweilers must be judged by the Breed Standard which has been adopted in the country where the breed is being judged. This is the guide that all judges must follow, regardless of whether the type of Rottweiler varies from country to country. The three major Breed Standards (British, German and American) vary slightly (see Chapter Nine: the Breed Standards), and obviously, all judges form their own interpretation of the Standard.

As an academic exercise, three Championship judges: Dorothea Gruenerwald (USA), Andrew Brace (UK), and Helmut Freiburg (Germany) were asked to assess six Rottweilers – three dogs and three bitches – from a series of photographs, showing head, profile, forequarters, and hindquarters. The dogs were not named, the judges were merely told their ages.

Clearly, it is impossible to make an accurate evaluation of a dog from photographs alone, as the essential areas of temperament and movement cannot be brought into the balance. However, it is of interest to see what is in the judge's mind when a critique is being drawn up.

Andrew Brace (UK) gives his viewpoint, saying: "As a judge of many breeds, I believe that judges tend to have different priorities, which are dictated by the breed they are judging. Personally, I would place greater emphasis on accurate and powerful movement in a Working breed, bred for a specific function, than I would in a Toy breed, whose main task in life is to look beautiful and amuse its owner. Thus, movement is a major consideration when I judge the breed – ask any of my exhausted exhibitors! So, for the purpose of this exercise, I must assume that all the featured dogs have steady temperaments and that they move accurately, though the conformation, in some cases, suggest that there may be shortcomings in gait."

Helmut Freiburg, Richterobmann, is the superior judge of the ADRK, and is responsible for all German judges. His general comments regarding judging the six Rottweilers by photographs are as follows: "I have assumed that all the Rottweilers are of the correct size, as it is not possible to assess this. Neither is it possible to check the bite for completeness or correct placement. The temperament of the Rottweilers and their ability to move is also, obviously, unknown to me. I can say nothing about the feet of the dogs, as they are standing on grass. However, I confirm that the photographs are of excellent quality."

ROTTWEILER A
Bitch (3 years old)

HEAD STUDY

Dorothea Gruenerwald (USA): *"This shows a strong, somewhat masculine head with too much 'wetness'. The eyes are medium-brown and round. The ears could lie closer to the head, and the markings could be darker. However, the skull is well-developed."*

Andrew Brace (UK): *"The head could certainly be drier, and this bitch's round, very open eyes give her a rather goggled and gormless expression, which is quite untypical."*

Helmut Freiburg (Germany): *"This bitch has a strong head, with a strong, short foreface. She has dark lips and pink gums. The eyes are light-brown. The ears are medium-sized, correctly set, and are carried very well. The skin on the head is not tight enough."*

PROFILE

Dorothea Gruenerwald (USA): *"This bitch shows nice boning, and has a good length of neck. This view shows a Roman nose, and the flews are slightly open. She could have more angulation, both front and rear, and her topline could be stronger. She appears to lack sufficient forechest. The left rear foot toes out."*

Andrew Brace (UK): *"This is a problem bitch. She has a certain 'neatness' about her, which is not necessarily a word you would wish to use in connection with Rottweilers. She looks extremely compact and quite square. She seems rather upright in shoulder and her topline tends to sheer off toward the rear, giving rather an exaggerated backline, with the merest suspicion of a roach. In body, she seems narrow for a three year old bitch."*

Helmut Freiburg (Germany): *"She has a very good neck, and a straight back. She has the correct coat and clearly defined light brown markings. She is of medium size with very good bone."*

FOREQUARTERS

Dorothea Gruenerwald (USA): *"Alert looking; with straight front legs, set well apart."*

Andrew Brace (UK): *"This forehand shot would confirm that the bitch lacks development of forechest."*

Helmut Freiburg (Germany): *"The chest has good depth, and there is very good width between the shoulders, which are set close to the chest. The front end shows straight angulation."*

HINDQUARTERS

Dorothea Gruenerwald (USA): *"Strong rear. The view reveals that she lacks maturity for her age. I would have to place her in third place of the three bitches."*

Andrew Brace (UK): *"I have a feeling that this bitch has the most delightful temperament – the rear shot, which shows her licking her lips (at the handler's bait?), suggests she is quite a character, so all is not lost. Every Rottweiler has at least one redeeming feature!"*

Helmut Freiburg (Germany): *"A well-muscled back-end, and she is standing close behind. Straight rear angulation."*

ROTTWEILER B
Bitch (4 years old)

HEAD STUDY

Dorothea Gruenerwald (USA): *"This bitch has a typical, feminine head with a pleasing expression. She has light-brown, almond-shaped eyes. Her ears are somewhat large. However, her markings are good, and her skull is well-developed. Her muzzle should be broader."*

Andrew Brace (UK): *"This is the ultimate show girl! In her picture she poses like a model, and many is the judge who will fall for her. But how good a Rottweiler is she in reality? While immediately being drawn to her clean lines, her intense quality and her poise, there are aspects that worry me. From this picture, the muzzle lacks strength and development, giving her head a rather 'beaky' kind of look. The eye colour also seems rather light."*

Helmut Freiburg (Germany): *"Very good head, with short foreface. The cheek bone is not fully filled in. The eyes are brown to light-brown. The ears are medium-sized, correctly set and carried."*

PROFILE

Dorothea Gruenerwald (USA): *"Good boning with a strong topline. This bitch has a nice length of neck. Very good front and rear angulation. The rear angulation may appear somewhat over-angulated for a Rottweiler, but this is becoming the trend in the US, probably attempting to correct the straight stifles usually seen in many of our dogs."*

Andrew Brace (UK): *"The profile shows that she is far too long in the muzzle for the head to be balanced and, thus, typical. Her length of body worries me: she seems to be rather short in ribcage and long in loin, where a lightness makes her appear rather weak and hollow. This detracts from the look of overall strength and power which a Rott – even a bitch – should convey."*

Helmut Freiburg (Germany): *"This bitch has a strong neck, and a solid back. She has the correct coat with clearly defined brown markings. She is of medium size with very good bone."*

FOREQUARTERS

Dorothea Gruenerwald (USA): *"Strong front, with a good depth of chest; good markingS."*

Andrew Brace (UK): *"She is nicely marked, obviously in wonderful condition and seems to have a certain 'showmanship' which will, I am sure, secure for her many wins. She seems to have surprisingly good width in front."*

Helmut Freiburg (Germany): *"The chest is deep and wide. The shoulders are close to the chest, and front angulation is straight."*

HINDQUARTERS

Dorothea Gruenerwald (USA): *"Strong, well-muscled rear; strong, straight hocks. This bitch rates second of the three bitches."*

Andrew Brace (UK): *"This bitch's hindquarters is my third area of concern. Some judges would love them, but is that great turn of stifle really typical for the breed? In my estimation, she is rather over-angulated, and I would expect her to show a lack of significant drive when moving away."*

Helmut Freiburg (Germany): *"The back-end is very well-muscled."*

ROTTWEILER C
Bitch (3 years old)

HEAD STUDY

Dorothea Gruenerwald (USA): *"This bitch has a typical, feminine head, with expressive, almond-shaped eyes, although she lacks fill under the eyes. She has small, well-set ears, and her skull is well-developed."*

Andrew Brace (UK): *"This bitch is obviously not a 'sudden impact' bitch, but she has lots of type about her. I like her eye shape and the strength of her muzzle, and she is clean-lipped, though there could be more work under the eye."*

Helmut Freiburg (Germany): *"This bitch has a very good head, with a slightly narrow foreface. The cheekbones are not filled in enough. The lips are dark and the eyes are brown. The ears are small, and correctly set, although they are not carried quite flat enough."*

PROFILE

Dorothea Gruenerwald (USA): *"This bitch has good boning, and a pleasing profile. She has a strong topline, and a good forechest. Her markings are good. She needs a little more angulation front and rear. She has a good depth of chest. Her rear feet appear to toe out."*

Andrew Brace (UK): *"Although I find this bitch's head quite pleasing, the profile suggests that there could be a little more break in the stop for perfection. Even though the profile shows her stretched out behind, you can see that she is moderately angulated. She has good bone, and at three years of age is obviously coming to her mature best."*

Helmut Freiburg (Germany): *"This bitch is medium-sized with good bone. She has a strong neck, and a strong, straight back. The coat is correct, with clearly defined markings."*

FOREQUARTERS

Dorothea Gruenerwald (USA): *"I like this bitch's alert expression. She has a strong front, and good markings. The pigmentation is dark on the lips and flews."*

Andrew Brace (UK): *"Her basic balance and construction are good, she has a well-developed forechest and ample width all through. Her colour and markings are very good."*

Helmut Freiburg (Germany): *"A deep chest, with broad shoulders lying close to the chest. The front is a little too straight."*

HINDQUARTERS

Dorothea Gruenerwald (USA): *"This bitch has a strong, well-muscled rear, matching a mature body. I would place her first of the three bitches."*

Andrew Brace (UK): *"In this rear shot, the bitch seems to be standing a little wider than the ideal. I would expect her to move quite well, with good reach and drive, but I would be interested to see how tight her elbows are when coming on. On her overall merit, she would be my first choice in the bitches."*

Helmut Freiburg (Germany): *"Well-muscled back-end. Rear angulation is a little too straight."*

ROTTWEILER D
Dog (2 years old)

HEAD STUDY

Dorothea Gruenerwald (USA): *"This Rottweiler has a typical male head, with dark, almond-shaped eyes. The ears are small and well-set. Pigmentation on the gums and lips is dark. Good expression."*

Andrew Brace (UK): *"This is one that the 'head hunter' may go for, as this shot of his expression is most appealing. Good markings. "*

Helmut Freiburg (Germany): *"This Rottweiler has a powerful head, with a short, strong forface. He has dark flews and dark gums. The eyes are brown, and the ears are small and well carried."*

PROFILE

Dorothea Gruenerwald (USA): *"Good boning on a substantial male body. He has moderate front and rear angulation. I think the shoulders are over-developed, and he is long in body. The topline could be better."*

Andrew Brace (UK): *"What bothers me with this dog is his lack of sharpness in outline. His topline also seems rather broken down."*

Hemut Freiburg (Germany): *"A very good neck. The topline dips slightly. The coat is correct. The overall impression is of a medium-sized dog with good bone."*

FOREQUARTERS

Dorothea Gruenerwald (USA): *"Straight, strong front. The markings on the chest not well-defined. The dog is still young and needs to mature."*

Andrew Brace (UK): *"Judging from the forehand construction, it looks to me as if, coming on, this male may well pin badly."*

Helmut Freiburg (Germany): *"A well-formed chest with sloping shoulders. The coat is good but the markings are not clearly defined on the legs. The front feet turn out slightly."*

HINDQUARTERS

Dorothea Gruenerwald (USA): *"This male has a strong rear, and straight hocks. The view from the rear shows his uneven topline. He would be my third choice of the three males."*

Andrew Brace (UK): *"I am unhappy with the narrowness, which is apparent when the dog is viewed from the rear. Given that he is just two years old, he may well fill out, but if you compare the rear view of his hindquarters with those of Rottweiler F – a male of the same age – you will see immediately that he is far less well-developed and lacks the 'hammy' quarters and overall girth. In his defence, he is nicely marked and his expression will always win him admirers! He would be my third-placed male."*

Helmut Freiburg (Germany): *"Well-muscled hindquarters, with straight angulation."*

ROTTWEILER E
Dog (4 years old)

HEAD STUDY

Dorothea Gruenerwald (USA): *"A typical, male head, with dark, almond-shaped eyes. His ears not set close to the head. He has a kind expression. Dark pigment on the gums and lips."*

Andrew Brace (UK): *"This photograph depicts a less alert dog than Rottweiler F. The dog is panting and 'sagging' rather. Nonetheless, it is a judge's job to get inside a dog and sort out what good breed points he has to offer. His head seems very pleasing front-on, with expressive eyes and good definition.*

Helmut Freiburg (Germany): *"This dog has a strong head, with a short, strong foreface. The eyes are brown, and the lips and gums are dark. The mouth corner is slightly open. Medium-sized, well-carried ears."*

PROFILE

Dorothea Gruenerwald (USA): *"This male has heavy boning, but he needs more front and rear angulation. The topline could be better. The muzzle/skull proportion is incorrect, as the muzzle is too short."*

Andrew Brace (UK): *"This male is four years old, and he is obviously more mature in body than the other males, who are both aged two years old. He seems to have good rib, but he is a touch longer than '9 to 10'. The profile suggests that maybe the skull profile is a little flat, and muzzle a little short."*

Helmut Freiburg (Germany): *"This male is medium-sized, with good bone. Soft back, and the croup is a little long. Correct coat, with clearly defined markings."*

FOREQUARTERS

Dorothea Gruenerwald (USA): *"A male with a strong, straight front. He is more of the 'old-fashioned' Rottweiler type, seen twenty years ago."*

Andrew Brace (UK): *"He is well-developed in forechest and has excellent bone, but my eye asks if he could not use just a hint more height of foreleg to complete his balance? This shot suggests that he is a little loaded in shoulder, but he does have plenty of width in front."*

Helmut Freiburg (Germany): *The neck has prominent loose, throat skin. The chest is deep, with broad shoulders fitting close to the chest. The front feet are turned out."*

HINDQUARTERS

Dorothea Gruenerwald (USA): *"This male has a strong, well-muscled rear, with strong, straight hocks. Again, he reminds me of Rottweilers we saw in the 1970s (US), which were more muscular in the rear, and more blocky overall. I would place him second among the males. "*

Andrew Brace (UK): *"The profile does not flatter the dog's hindquarters as he seems to be standing under himself, whereas the rear view indicates good development and maximum angulation. He is particularly well marked, and his tail-set and croup, are strictly speaking more 'correct' than those of Rottweiler F. I would imagine that this dog moves with power and has a very free and roomy stride. On the strength of the photographs, he would be my second choice male but I could well imagine gaiting them several times around the ring and maybe placing him over Dog F, should he prove superior in movement."*

Helmut Freiburg (Germany): *"The back-end is well-muscled. Angulation is a little too straight."*

ROTTWEILER F
Dog (2 years old)

HEAD STUDY

Dorothea Gruenerwald (USA): *"A typical male head, with dark, almond-shaped eyes. The ears are well carried, and the markings good. The lower eyelids are a little loose. No pigment on the lower right eyelid."*

Andrew Brace (UK): *"This dog is immediately at an advantage in this 'competition' because his photograph shows him totally alert and very 'together', so the first task is to establish whether or not this smartness results from his being simply a 'flat catcher', or whether he has type and quality in its own right. His head is masculine and yet has a look of quality, for forehead is nicely arched and he has a good muzzle line. The rather loose lips do create a slightly "bully" expression which is not to his advantage, and this is emphasised with a little too much throat (cleverly disguised by the position of the leash in the photos showing Profile and Forequarters!) His eye shape seems acceptable, but perhaps the eye could actually be a touch darker in colour and tighter-rimmed. The head is quite adequate, I feel, yet not classical."*

Helmut Freiburg (Germany): *" A strong head with a short foreface. The cheek bone is not completely filled in. The eyes are brown; the eyelids at the bottom are a little open. Slightly loose head skin."*

PROFILE

Dorothea Gruenerwald (USA): *"Good boning, but this dog needs a little more front and rear angulation. He is rather throaty with loose flews. He has a good depth of chest."*

Andrew Brace (UK): *"The overall impression – the vital ingredient in judging dogs well – is one of good proportions. At two years of age, it is assumed that this dog still has some way to go to reach full maturity, particularly in body as he seems to lack a little depth all through."*

Helmut Freiburg (Germany): *"This male is medium-sized with good bone. He has a strong neck and a straight back. he has a good coat, although it is a little long in the neck."*

FOREQUARTERS

Dorothea Gruenerwald (USA): *"This dog has a very imposing, alert expression, and a strong, straight front. His markings are very nice. While the profile shot shows the chest reaching to the elbows, the front view seems to show that his forechest has not fully matured."*

Andrew Brace (UK): *"My main reservation is that this dog is perhaps a little upright in shoulder and his forechest could be better developed. On seeing this dog stacked at the outset of a class, I would be wanting to study his side gait, as I would be suspicious that he would probably lack extension in front. His topline seems hard enough."*

Helmut Freiburg (Germany): *"The chest is very well formed with shoulders close to the chest. Correct, straight front. The throat skin is a little loose."*

Photography by
Carol Ann Johnson

HINDQUARTERS

Dorothea Gruenerwald (USA): *"A strong, well-muscled rear, with strong, straight hocks. Balanced front to rear from the top view. I would put this male in first place, ahead of the two other males."*

Andrew Brace (UK): *"Nicely developed hindquarters with excellent musculation. It could be argued that his stifles border on the straight, but as I said earlier, I would not find this as offensive as excessive over-angulation. From the rear, he appears to have good spring of rib. The dog's breeching on the hindquarters comes a little high, and certainly extends well above the hock, but this is a cosmetic failing which should be seen in perspective. The overall picture has a look of quality, and, for me, this dog would hold my interest more than the other two males. As far as picture-judging is concerned, this dog also displays the ingredient which no Breed Standard ever mentions, yet every dog judge longs for – 'charisma'."*

Helmut Freiburg (Germany): *"Back-end very well-muscled correct, hind angulation. Markings are clearly defined, although the brown under the tail seems to be a little pale."*

Chapter Twelve

GENETICS AND THE ROTTWEILER

INTRODUCTION

As with many breeds the Rottweiler is claimed to have an ancient ancestry. It is said that it traces back to war dogs brought over by the Roman Legions in the first two centuries BC, and since about 74BC it has been associated with the town of Rottweil in southern Germany. It is true that present-day dogs have descended in some way from ancient dogs, but in strict breed terms modern breeds can only trace back their ancestry for some 150 years and prior to that it is a matter of conjecture as to what went into the breeds.

Whatever its ancestry, the breeders of Rottweilers have over the years and especially in this current century sought to produce a specific kind of dog. The extent to which this has been achieved has depended upon the genes available within the breed. All breeds of dog carry 39 pairs of chromosomes within the nuclei of the cells which make up a dog's body. These chromosomes are thread-like structures on which are situated the genes or units of inheritance. The number of genes is not known but is likely to be at least 100,000 and may be two or three times this number.

Many of the features seen in dogs are inherited in the sense of being controlled, wholly or in part, by the genes which are present in that dog. This not only covers undesirable defects but virtues. Most aspects of type, construction, function, reproduction and behaviour will have some genetic involvement and thus are subject to control by the genetic make-up of the dog.

With many thousands of genes the number of combinations is legion and no two dogs are going to be alike in genetic make-up unless one is dealing with the rare event (in dog terms) of identical twins. However, because man and nature have been selecting dogs over the centuries, dogs within a breed will have a very large number of genes that are identical in all animals of that breed. If two Rottweilers are mated the resultant offspring will be recognisable as Rottweilers and this comes about because many of the genes in the breed are common to every Rottweiler. Some genes are, of course, common to other breeds, but two Rottweilers, even if only distantly related, will have more genes in common than would a Rottweiler and, say, a Dobermann. Nevertheless, as an example, the gene which causes the colour pattern of the Rottweiler is the same gene as that causing the colour pattern of the Dobermann.

Breeders are constantly seeking to "improve" their animals which they assess by comparison with the Standard of the breed. This is a document drawn up by early breeders and variously modified over the years, which purports to be a blueprint of what the breed should look and behave like. The extent to which breeders can modify appearance and behaviour will depend upon the genes which are present in the breed and the way in which they are inherited.

CHROMOSOMES AND GENES

The 39 pairs of chromosomes in the dog vary in size and shape but each member of any pair stems from each parent. Thus one chromosome of every pair comes from the father and one of each pair from the mother. This is achieved by the way in which reproductive cells (ova and sperm) are produced. A complex process called meiosis allows the ova and sperm to contain only one member of each of the chromosome pairs. Thus a normal cell in the body contains 78 chromosomes in 39 matching (homologous) pairs while sperm and ova contain only 39 chromosomes, one of each homologous set.

When the 39 chromosomes of the sperm meet up with the 39 chromosomes of the ovum at fertilisation the net result is a cell containing the 78 chromosomes in 39 homologous pairs. By a process called mitosis the cell divides and multiplies in such a way that from a single cell there is produced something as complex as a dog, in the cells of which are the 78 chromosomes which remain identical to those with which the sperm and ovum started.

A gene is a particular part of a particular chromosome and this location is called a locus. The gene which causes the familiar colour pattern in the Rottweiler is located at a particular locus on a specific chromosome and will always be found at that locus in the breed, as it will in the Dobermann or other tan pointed breed. Because there are two chromosomes to a pair at any locus a dog must carry two of every gene. At a great many loci only one version of a gene exists so it appears in duplicate and it will be identical in every Rottweiler in the world.

At other loci, alternative versions of the gene may occur and these alternatives are called alleles. At any locus a dog can have two of these alleles but not three. It can have two that are alike and thus the dog is said to be homozygous for this feature or it can have two different versions in which case it can be said to be heterozygous. Any Rottweiler will be homozygous for a great number of genes and that will be true of every Rottweiler. Thus a breeder cannot influence these genes by anything he does other than by crossbreeding. However, a breeder can influence genes at which alternatives exist. Here he can increase or decrease the frequency of specific genes and thus modify the genetic make-up of his own dogs and of the breed.

GENE ACTION

Genes are usually given a letter to symbolise them. Convention suggests that these letters are either upper or lower case and if several versions exist small suffixes are attached. The S series of colour inheritance has the alleles:

S solid colour no white
s^i irish spotting (white blaze, chest, feet and collar) e.g. Rough Collie
s^p piebald spotting (white markings irregularly over body) e.g. Cocker Spaniel
s^w extreme white (pure white or with odd patch) e.g. Bull Terrier.

Although very early Rottweilers used to have some white markings – probably irish spotting – selection against white has led to the virtual disappearance of white markings in the breed and virtually every Rottweiler is SS in genetic make-up. White markings can be seen on chest and toes in young puppies but these often disappear and are minor modifiers of the gene S, not versions of the other alleles. This is an example of breeders over a long period selecting towards a specific goal and changing the frequency of alleles within the breed.

Genes can be either dominant or recessive. The S allele is dominant in that it can work even if only present on one chromosome whereas a recessive allele must be present twice (i.e. on both chromosomes) to work. In the S series the order of dominance is as given, so that S is dominant to s^i which is dominant to s^p and that dominant to s^w. For a white dog with say a black eye patch to be found, that dog would have to carry both of the last recessive and be $s^w s^w$. This is common in Bull Terriers but the s^w allele is not found in Rottweilers.

A classic recessive allele is long coat. The Rottweiler is a short-coated dog and most

Rottweilers would be LL in coat type, i.e. they carry two short-coated alleles and CANNOT give rise to long-coated progeny. However, some Rottweilers are Ll and thus carry the long coat allele recessively. Such Ll dogs are just as short-coated as LL dogs, but if two Ll animals are mated together they could give rise to ll progeny which would be long-coated.

In an Ll x Ll mating one would expect 75 per cent short coats to 25 per cent long coats but that ratio will only apply over large numbers, not necessarily individual litters. In reality the ratio is really a 1:2:1 ratio in that the Ll x Ll mating should give rise to 25 per cent LL, 50 per cent Ll and 25 per cent ll animals (again over large numbers).

The fact that a short-coated Rottweiler gives rise to only short coats when mated to a short-coated mate is not proof that both are free of long coat. If we mated Ll to LL then clearly ll could not occur because for ll to occur *both* parents must carry ll. Even an Ll x Ll mating might, by chance, give rise to only LL and Ll progeny and thus one would not be aware that the parents were long coat carriers. Long coats will only arise from Ll x Ll, Ll x ll or ll x ll matings, and since the last two of these require one parent to be long-coated and such dogs are rarely used, the commonest way for long coats to crop up in the breed is the mating of two (Ll) carriers. If long coats do occur in a litter then BOTH parents MUST carry the long coat allele.

The example given above applies to all recessive alleles. It is, however, important to appreciate that all genes do not act in this dominant/recessive way. In some cases we have no dominance, in that the AA, Aa and aa versions are all distinct. Thus AA may show the full extent of a condition, Aa may show an intermediate stage and aa the lowest extent. Alternatives are shown in Table 1. Genotype refers to the genetic make-up of the dog and phenotype to what we see.

GENE ACTION
(Body of table shows phenotypic expression)

Genotype	Complete dominance	Incomplete dominance	No dominance
AA	Fullest extent of expression	Fullest extent of expression	Fullest extent of expression
Aa	Fullest extent of expression	Not quite fullest expression	Intermediate extent of expression
aa	Lowest extent of expression	Lowest extent of expression	Lowest extent of expression

Sometimes the expression of a gene at one locus interferes with the expression of a gene at another. Rottweiler colour is caused by the presence of the black and tan extension pattern which is an allele designated a^t. This gene is just one of a series called the agouti series. In many breeds other genes of the agouti series exist like saddle marking, sable and solid colour, but in Rottweilers selection has been for this black with tan points pattern. However, for this pattern to express itself as black and tan the gene D must be present at another locus at least once. So also must be the gene B. Most Rottweilers will be a a DD BB, but in the Dobermann which has the same pattern as the Rottweiler the alleles d and b also exist. The black and tan Dobermann must be a^t a^t D- B- where the - indicates that the second version is unimportant. This is the same as the Rottweiler. However, Dobermanns that are a^t a^t D- bb will be red and tan; those which are a^t a^t dd B- will be blue and tan, and those which are a^t a^t dd bb will be fawn and tan. The basic pattern is not changed by the D/d or B/b series but the body colour is. It is believed that d and b do not exist in the Rottweiler, but if they did this kind of effect could occur and is termed epistatic.

SEX INHERITANCE AND SEX-LINKED TRAITS

Although it was stated that dogs have 39 pairs of chromosomes with each member of a pair resembling the other, a modification must now be made. In females one pair is very large and in males one pair is made up of a similar large chromosome with a very small one. These are the sex chromosomes and traditionally the female ones are termed XX and the male XY. When ova and sperm are being produced all ova carry one X chromosome but sperm carry either an X or a Y. Depending upon which sperm fertilises the egg, the sex of the puppy is determined. Sex is thus determined by the sire and by chance.

It is obvious from this that any genes carried on the Y chromosome can be passed from father to all his sons but not to daughters, whereas factors on the X chromosome can be passed from father to all daughters but not to sons. In reality the Y chromosome does not appear to carry anything important beyond determining the sex. However, several features are carried on the X chromosome including haemophilia A and Duchenne muscular dystrophy.

Haemophilia A is a recessive trait given the gene designation h, while the normal clotting symbol is H. Females can thus be HH (normal), Hh (carriers but seemingly normal) or hh (haemophiliacs). In contrast, because the Y chromosome is virtually inert and designated O, the males can only be either HO (normal) or hO (haemophiliacs). There is no such thing as a carrier male.

Most haemophiliac males result from a mating of HO to Hh. If that hO haemophiliac male is bred from he is likely to mate HH bitches and will thus give rise to 100 per cent normal HO sons, but all his daughters will be carriers (Hh) and thus repeat the cycle. To get affected bitches one has to mate an affected male to a carrier female, and this is highly unlikely, so affected females will be very rare indeed.

POLYGENIC TRAITS

Many traits in the dog are not clear and distinct in the way that long or short coats are distinct. Many traits show considerable very minor variations. Thus wither height will vary over several centimetres and will also vary over a different range in males as compared to females. Most constructional features of head, shoulder, hind angulation, body length, chest depth, etc. vary in like manner. In other words, these traits vary in degree, not in kind.

Most of these traits, which are, after all, more important than simple aesthetic features like coat type or eye colour, vary in the shape of a normal curve. Thus we see few animals at the extremes and most around the centre, with a gradual decline from the centre towards the extremes. This normal curve pattern is typical of a genetic condition that is polygenic, i.e. controlled by many genes. It is also true of traits that are influenced not only by genes but by the environment. Environment in this context relates to external influences like nutrition, exercise, management, etc. A long-coated dog is still long-coated no matter how he is fed or reared, but a dog that is genetically 65cm tall is only going to make that height if he is given the right nutritional opportunities to get there.

The variation we see in these polygenic characters is made up of genetic variation and environmental variation. The extent of each will vary with the trait. Some traits will be largely genetic and only a small degree environmental and others will be the reverse. The genetic component can be further subdivided into that which can be transmitted to the next generation (termed additive variation) and that which depends upon combinations of genes and thus cannot be readily transmitted (termed non-additive). The proportion of the total variation which is of

All dedicated breeders seek to improve their stock, which they assess by comparison with the Bred Standard.

Photo courtesy: ADRK.

additive genetic type is called the heritability of the character and this can be expressed as a percentage. The higher this value is the easier it will be to select dogs to pass on their qualities.

Let us take litter size, which may be around 7 pups in this breed but which will vary from 1 to around 16 or 17. This character is very much under genetic control but it is largely of the non-additive (gene combination) type. If, therefore, we have a bitch that always had large litters, say averaging 12 pups, we will not necessarily get large litters from her daughters because the heritability of litter size is only about 10 per cent. If we breed from a bitch averaging 12 pups, that is 5 pups above the average of the breed at 7, then only 10 per cent of this superiority will be transmitted and we might get a litter size of 7.5 pups which is probably not going to be noticed. In contrast, wither height may be as much as 50 per cent heritable, and of any superiority in height selected in the parents half will pass to the next generation. It is thus much easier to select breeds to get larger (or smaller) in stature than it is to get them to give bigger litters.

The problem in dogs is that not many of these polygenic traits have been scientifically studied and thus, unlike the situation in farm livestock, we know little about heritabilities. However, some conformational features are likely intermediate to high (30 per cent upwards) and fertility features low (under 20 per cent). Behaviour is also inherited in part, even though it can be modified by training and socialisation. Fear, for example, can be about 50 per cent heritable, and something like total hip score (see later) can in this breed have a heritability of about 40 per cent.

In polygenic traits progress comes from breeding from the best. Clearly we may differ about what is the best but in simple terms if we wanted Rottweilers to get larger we would have to breed from the tallest dogs (and bitches) around. If we wanted to improve hind angulation we would have to breed from the best angulated dogs, and so on. The higher the heritability the greater the chance of success.

Dog breeding is made hard by having so many objectives and it is important to realise that the more traits you want to improve the harder it will be to do this. As a result trivial features should not be given high importance, but rather breeders should concentrate on those aspects that are crucial to the dog and its place in society.

SOME DEFECTS AND OTHER FEATURES IN THE ROTTWEILER

CRYPTORCHIDISM

The failure of testicles to descend is seen in all breeds though more commonly in dwarf and brachycephalic breeds. Total absence of testicles (anorchia) is very rare as is monorchia (presence of only one testicle). Most defective dogs have two testicles but either both have failed to descend into the scrotum (bilateral cryptorchidism) or one has failed to descend (unilateral cryptorchidism). Bilateral cases are sterile as sperm cannot be produced in the body cavity. Unilateral cases can be fertile but fertility is reduced over that of normal dogs.

Retained testicles have a greater chance of becoming cancerous than descended testicles but the risk is not enormous. In the Rottweiler it is likely that the incidence will not exceed 4 per cent of males but that is not a proven fact as data are not readily available.

The condition is likely to be inherited in a polygenic way and selection against affected males is highly desirable.

ENTROPION

Entropion results when the eyelid turns inwards causing the lashes to irritate the pupil. The condition is seen in fairly early life and appears to be inherited, though scientific proof of this is not readily found. The mode of inheritance is likely to be complex and ideally breeders should avoid using affected stock. However, the condition can be readily recitifed by surgery, so one cannot always assume that a seemingly normal dog was always so.

HIP DYSPLASIA (HD)

Hip dysplasia results from a faulty fitting of the femoral head into the acetabulum. Known in dogs for about 60 years it is found in most breeds and particularly, though not exclusively, large breeds. It can only be identified accurately by x-ray and by having the plate read by an expert panel. Most countries have schemes set up since the late 1950s or early 1960s to assess hip status. The minimum age for submission to such a scheme is 12 months except in North America where it is 24 months.

The British scheme looks at 9 features of the hip and scores out of a total of 53 per hip so that a dog can range from 0/0 to 53/53, with higher scores being worst. At the time of writing almost 6,000 Rottweilers have been assessed in the UK with a range in score from 0 to 99 and a mean total score of just under 14 which is fairly reasonable. The same scheme is used in Australia and New Zealand, where collectively some 3,500 dogs have been read and where the range is 0 to 92 and the mean around 10.5. Figures are lower in Australasia, but this is true of most breeds and may reflect a difference in reading emphasis rather than a true difference in genetic merit.

In the USA, hips are graded by the OFA into a series of groups: Excellent, Good, Fair, Borderline, Mild, Moderate and Severe, with the first three categories receiving an OFA number indicating a pass. From February 1974 to January 1984 over 51,000 Rottweilers were examined and 22.4 per cent were dysplastic, which put the breed in 19th worst position. Some 6.2 per cent were graded excellent. By way of comparison, the German Shepherd Dog had 21.3 per cent dysplastic, but only 2.6 per cent graded excellent.

Other countries grade hips into categories and in Europe most countries use the FCI scheme which grades hips into categories A, B, C, D and E. In some breeds only dogs from categories A and B can be bred from. It is important to have more rather than fewer grades. Certainly it is known that 7 grades, for example, is much more accurate than a two-grade (dysplastic or not) system.

The condition is inherited in a polygenic way and for British dogs the heritability of total score is about 40 per cent while for OFA data from the USA it is around 25 per cent. Other factors such as nutrition, exercise, sex, age and oestrus status (in bitches) can influence the overall result, though inheritance is the largest single factor.

It is imperative that breeders assess as many dogs of their breeding as they can and particularly that they should not breed from any animal that has not been hip assessed. One should clearly try to breed from the best hips possible, but there should be a consideration of other characters since breeding Rottweilers is not merely about breeding a good set of hips. Clearly poor grades/high scores put a dog beyond the pale as far as breeding is concerned, but a dog with a score say of 8/9 but of outstanding character/type is a better bet than a 0/0 dog of poor character/type. Breeders should try to get all stock that they sell hip-graded in order to understand the consequences of their breeding programme. When progeny test data become available, as they are for UK/Australasian dogs, then breeders should attempt to concentrate on sires and dams that are producing well, not merely on animals that grade well.

OSTEOCHONDRITIS DISSECANS (OCD)

In simple terms OCD is a faulty growth of bone connected with the process of cartilage becoming calcified. This condition can be seen in the shoulder, elbow, stifle and hock and is generally harder to deal with as one goes along this list. Fortunately most OCD occurs in shoulder and elbow. Elbow problems can involve Ununited Anconeal Process (UAP) or Fragmented Coronoid Process (FCP).

At one time it was believed that OCD was exclusively a feature of nutrition, usually associated with excessive use of calcium. While this is still true, in part, there is increasing evidence that inheritance is involved. In some breeds the heritability of elbow dysplasia, as this condition is sometimes erroneously called, is put at 40-60 per cent.

An elbow scheme has been set up internationally but is not much used in Britain outside the Bernese Mountain Dog breed. In the USA the OFA have examined over 1200 Rottweilers which are graded into 0, 1, 2 or 3 categories. As with other breeds there is more OCD in the elbows of males than of females and the Rottweiler ranks very high with over a third of females and almost half of males being placed in the categories 1 to 3. Clearly in the USA there is a distinct problem in this breed, and it is probable that if examination were to be made OCD would be found in other countries.

OCD in the elbow usually starts around 4-5 months of age with intermittent lameness being a common symptom. In view of the high inheritance factor breeders should instigate testing and try to breed only from 0/0 elbows or those which do not go above 1/1. They should certainly discard from breeding animals carrying 3 on any elbow and ideally all those that are 2/2.

Chapter Thirteen

BREEDING ROTTWEILERS

GUIDELINES FOR BREEDING
Breeding a litter of Rottweilers is a major undertaking, and should not be considered unless the would-be breeder can devote time, energy and money to the project.

TIME – because rearing a litter will take at least eight weeks, and maybe twice as long if the puppies do not sell easily. It requires a 24-hours a day commitment and is not something to do before 9 a.m. and after 5 p.m. sandwiched around a work schedule.

ENERGY – because rearing a litter requires physical effort, sleepless nights and constant vigilance.

MONEY – because rearing a litter costs the earth! Recently I took my courage in both hands and costed out a litter of twelve puppies reared to eight weeks of age. To my horror, it came to over £1,000 (US$1600) including stud fee, inoculations, food, vet's bills, supplements etc. I still haven't told my husband!

People come out with all sorts of reasons for wanting to breed:

Reason: Their bitch *needs* a litter – the vet says she is a lovely specimen and it will do her good.
Answer: No bitch *needs* a litter, and unless the vet is an experienced breeder/judge, he/she cannot know how good a specimen of the breed the bitch is. It might be a healthy dog, but that does not distinguish it from a cross-breed as far as correctness of type is concerned. No bitch will feel deprived of a valuable life experience if she does not have a litter – we are talking about canines here, not people.

Reason: Everyone (including the vet) thinks their male Rottweiler should be used at stud, and it will be good for him to mate a bitch.
Answer: See above! And once he has been used at stud, he will probably become more aggressive and more dominant. What he has never had, he will not miss!

Reason: We need the money – we know puppies fetch a good price.
Answer: Commendably honest, but forget it. The 'profit margin' is so small that it really isn't worth the effort, and if all the pups aren't sold quickly, it will cost a fortune to rear them.

The only constructive reason for breeding has to be a belief in the quality of your own stock, and a conviction that the breed can only benefit as a result of their propagation. To produce sound, typey puppies that are as good as, and preferably better than, their parents should be the dream of everyone who breeds dogs, be they novices or experienced old hands.

Being an expert geneticist does not necessarily mean that you will breed better stock. The majority of successful breeders have no in-depth knowledge of genetics, and have to rely on other ways of producing stock which possesses the required temperament, character, constitution, conformation, type and quality. The sire and dam of a litter should ideally be chosen to complement each other, to improve on each other's weak points and to fix and strengthen their good points. All this should be decided not merely on appearance (phenotype), but also on breeding (genotype) and progeny.

The ability to recite pedigrees parrot-fashion is of absolutely no value unless the breeder knows the virtues and faults of the animals concerned, and only close examination of progeny will show whether these faults and virtues are likely to be inherited. Using animals simply because they have a lot of red ink (naming Champions) on their pedigrees is not the ideal way to embark on a breeding programme.

Establishing a successful breeding programme is an on-going struggle, and it is only possible here to outline certain peremptory principles covering three distinct courses of action.

1. THE OUTCROSS The animals must be totally unrelated within four generations. This method will reveal the dominant characteristics which can then be reinforced by line-breeding or in-breeding. If the bloodlines in a kennel are closely bred, then outcrossing is a way of introducing new bloodlines. Great care must be taken not to breed faults which are common to both lines. This method will almost certainly produce variations of type within a litter as well as a degree of individual excellence.

2. IN-BREEDING This is a powerful tool, and in the hands of the ignorant a dangerous one for any breed. If applied to unsuitable stock by breeders with little knowledge of the bloodlines concerned, *it can cause disastrous results*. For experienced and knowledgeable breeders who can recognise problems and are prepared to neuter and/or cull, this method can be used to successfully establish and perpetuate a line. In-breeding is based on the breeding of close relatives: parent-child, brother-sister, grandparent-grandchild etc., and can quickly establish type, but it can also establish faults just as easily as virtues and is not to be used indiscriminately.

3. LINE-BREEDING This is generally accepted as a breeding which has at least one common ancestor in the third generation. It is an attempt to keep progeny closely related to a particular ancestor of exceptional merit. The excellence of this ancestor should be unquestionable, as line-breeding to a mediocre specimen is unlikely to produce satisfactory results. The progeny of the common ancestor/s should show that they are prepotent in passing on desirable characteristics and devoid of any serious faults. This is a popular method for breeders and although, strictly speaking, it requires the same qualities as for in-breeding, it is not burdened with the same degree of disapprobation from both the lay public and the media.

CHOOSING BREEDING STOCK
Most breeders have their own ideas as to what is important within the framework of the Breed Standard and, cliched though it may be, "one man's meat is another man's poison." Yet there should still be basic requirements underlying the choice of both dogs and bitches for breeding purposes.

a) TYPE – the animals should both look essentially like Rottweilers (this is not as fatuous as it seems!) and comply with the Standard as closely as possible, certainly with its most fundamental aspects.
b) TEMPERAMENT – they should have correct and equable temperaments.
c) CONFORMATION – care should be taken that animals with bad conformational faults are not used in a breeding programme.
d) SOUNDNESS – of structure, character, movement and health are imperative.

When you are planning to breed a litter it is essential to choose good representatives of the breed, which are sound in temperament and conformation, and will fit in with a structured breeding programme.

Photo: Steve Nash.

RIGHT: *Ch. Upend Gallant Theodoric (left) and his son, Ch. Poirot Romulus.*
The results of careful selection are clear to see.

Photo courtesy: Barbara Butler.

BELOW: *Four Ebonstern Champions bred in the USA: Ch. Ebonstern Ivan v d Liebe, Ch. Ebonstern Yanta v Muquaw. Ch. Ebonstern Daari of Histiles and Ch. Ebonstern Olympus v d Liebe.*

Photo courtesy: Dorothea Gruenerwald.

e) HIP X-RAYS – all potential breeding stock should be X-rayed for hip dysplasia. This can be done from the age of twelve months after which the resulting plates are submitted to the relevant screening body for scoring.

Both dogs and bitches should be clean, wormed, inoculated, generally healthy, well fed and physically fit. Bitches should be at least two years old before being mated. For experienced breeders this may appear blindingly obvious, but for the novice it is all essential detail that can all too easily be overlooked.

Choosing the best male for a bitch can often cause disagreement amongst the long-established breeders. For those new to the breed, it is important to attend shows, club meetings, seminars etc. to try and develop an eye for good and bad points. Talk to as many experienced breeders as possible. Find out the strengths and weaknesses of the potential brood bitch. Read all the books available about Rottweilers. Above all, try to avoid using "the dog down the road" simply for convenience, because the use of a mediocre dog – for whatever reason, be it price or expediency – is unpardonable.

Conversely, just because a dog is a top winner in the show ring does not mean that he is a suitable mate for every bitch. It does, however, mean that there is a good chance of seeing some of his progeny from a wide variety of bitches. Successful and well-known kennels often have dogs standing at stud that may well offer the safest choice for the novice breeder, together with help and advice from people who have spent many years learning about the breed. The perfect dog, or bitch, has yet to be born, so each mating is the result of some degree of compromise. It should be stressed that the mating of extremes in the hopes that the relevant faults will average out is incorrect. Mating an over-angulated bitch to a dog which is straight behind will not produce a litter of puppies with ideal angulation. Moderation must be practised, and the owner of a bitch must not expect miracles from a stud dog.

Having decided on a stud dog, the bitch's owner should contact the owner of the chosen dog and discuss the proposed mating. Most stud dog owners will want to see the bitch, her pedigree and her X-ray results before committing their male to the mating. They will also discuss price and any conditions of the stud service.

MATING

Nature, left to its own devices, would ordain that primitive bitches in their wild state would probably only have one season annually, which would coincide with litters being born in the spring – a time of sun, warmth and plentiful food supply. Domestication of the dog has resulted in most bitches having a season approximately every six months. There are, of course, exceptions to this generalisation. However, this does not mean that a bitch should be bred from at every season. One litter in a twelve-month period is quite sufficient for any bitch to cope with.

When the bitch comes into season, it is normally heralded by frequent passing of urine, and a great deal of licking. The vulva will swell slightly and a mucous discharge will occur which then becomes blood-stained. It is useful to wipe the bitch with a tissue every day when the season is expected. This way the breeder will have certain knowledge of the onset of the season in order to make a rough calculation as to when oestrus will occur. The start of season is the time to contact the stud dog owner again, so that they will know roughly when to expect the bitch to arrive for mating. Keep the bitch away from any males, and never leave her alone in the garden – male dogs from miles around will be attracted by the scent, and would find even the highest garden wall little obstacle. A mis-mating would be most undesirable. Now is the time to worm the bitch prior to mating.

Most bitches are in season for about three weeks; during the second week the season is usually at its height and that is when the bitch should be ready for mating. There are no infallible rules for gauging the height of oestrus. Theory has it that the discharge will change from bloody to straw-coloured and the vulva will become much enlarged and soft, but this is not always the case. However, at about the eleventh day the bitch will show signs of readiness. When approached by another bitch, or a male, or when 'tickled' above the vulva, she will twitch her tail to one side and present her rear end in an obvious manner. This is the time to get her to the stud dog.

The experienced stud dog owner will know exactly what to do and will direct the mating accordingly. It is usual for both animals to wear a stout leather collar and for them to be introduced somewhere quiet, secure, covered and away from the eyes of interested spectators! There will usually be a playful 'courting' session, during which it is advisable to stand clear – two Rottweilers in foreplay mode are heavy and frisky, and no respecters of human legs and feet! This activity will stimulate the bitch if she is ready for mating and she will show evident enjoyment when the dog licks her. If the bitch snaps at the dog it may be that she is not ready, or merely just plain nervous in the case of a maiden bitch.

When the dog mounts the bitch, her owner should stand in front of her, holding her collar firmly to prevent any turning or snapping. The stud dog owner will judge the bitch's readiness to accept the dog and, if all goes according to plan, the dog will quickly penetrate the bitch, soon effecting a 'tie' with his penis swelling inside her. If the bitch struggles, sits down, or tries to snap at the dog, then it is likely that she is not ready for mating and needs to return either the next day or in forty-eight hours to try again. If she shows all the outward signs of being ready for mating, but persists in trying to snap at the dog, then it is advisable to muzzle her until she settles down during the mating. Many bitches will 'cry' or 'moan' when the dog is swelling inside them, but they must be held steady and not be allowed to struggle or they could do irreparable harm to the dogs, and to themselves.

Even when the timing is right, the bitch will sometimes try to sit down when the dog mounts her. This is when helpers are essential! An assistant should kneel beside the bitch and support her with one hand under her stomach, with the other hand holding a hind leg so that she cannot swing her hindquarters away from the dog. Once the dog has mounted the bitch, his owner will often guide him into position. Penetration is often signalled by a wild 'treading' of the dog's hind legs and forceful heaves of his hindquarters. At this stage his owner will often stand behind the male, holding him in position while bending over and clasping the bitch's flanks to hold both animals upright and fairly still. This plays havoc with human spines as Rottweilers are not lightweight dogs!

When the dog decides to 'turn', he will start to dismount to one side of the bitch. If the animals are securely 'tied' at this stage, then they can stand for a few minutes side by side. Some dogs prefer to spend the entire 'tie' in this position, where dog and bitch can lick and nuzzle each other's ears and faces. If they are not properly tied, this is the stage at which the dog will slip out of the bitch in an erect condition. He will then need to be left alone until he has recovered and several hours need to elapse before he can try again.

Assuming a successful 'tie', the dog's hind legs can be gently lifted over the bitch's back so that the animals are turned around, facing in opposite directions. Most stud dog owners then spend anything from five minutes to an hour with their arms clasped around both sets of hind legs in order to prevent the dogs moving about, which can cause discomfort and possible injury. The bitch's muscles are holding the dog inside her and he cannot move away until she releases him. When she does, the dog will want to lick himself, and the bitch needs to be put back in her owner's car or in a holding kennel until departure time.

Sometimes, if there is a great size disparity between the dog and the bitch, it will be necessary to raise one of them so that mating can occur more easily. Thick coconut matting, or squares of carpet, are useful, as these will provide a non-slip foothold.

Having successfully completed the mating, the stud dog owner should complete Kennel Club registration forms, along with a receipt for the stud fee and written (preferably) arrangements to cover the eventuality of the bitch failing to conceive. The usual agreement is that the bitch will be offered a free return mating on her next season.

Many breeders like to return the following day, or two days later, following the initial mating in order to feel sure that they have covered the time of oestrus completely. The sperm will live for at least twenty-four hours inside the bitch. Some stud dog owners are prepared to board the bitch for several days and effect several matings. These are arrangements which need to be discussed beforehand, but it should always be remembered that, strictly speaking, the stud fee covers just one mating with no obligation to give further or repeat services. You pay for the mating, and not for puppies.

CARE OF THE IN-WHELP BITCH

Once the bitch has been mated, keep her away from other males for a few days in case a mismating should occur. Then it is just a case of being patient for the next few weeks! Keep the bitch on an ordinary diet and normal exercise; nothing needs to change at this stage. The gestation period is sixty-three days, and for the first thirty of these there are very few outward signs of pregnancy. Some bitches become very quiet and loving; others do not alter at all. It is possible to have the bitch scanned (*not* X-rayed) at thirty days after the last mating, and this should show immediately if she is in whelp.

By the end of the fifth week, it will be fairly obvious that the bitch is in whelp; her ribcage will look bigger, her 'waistline' thicker, and her teats will have become enlarged. She will also probably be hungry all the time. At this stage she should be on a high-protein diet with extra calcium added. Some breeders add raspberry-leaf tablets around this time; they are a traditional herbal tonic for the uterus and are said to encourage natural cleansing when the bitch whelps.

Between six and seven weeks, the amount of food can be increased by about twenty-five per cent, and split into two or three meals daily. It is important not to let the bitch get too fat because this can cause whelping difficulties. Let her exercise normally until the eighth week when a couple of short walks daily will probably suffice and keep ample muscle tone to help with an easy whelping.

At seven weeks it is necessary to get the whelping box situated in a quiet room where the bitch is to whelp. If the breeder has a custom-built whelping room, so much the better. The bitch should now be encouraged to spend time in this environment so that she can begin to feel at home there.

An outside whelping kennel can prove difficult from the breeder's point of view as it makes it difficult to maintain constant supervision when the bitch whelps and, unless it is large enough, there will be little or no room for a chair and/or camp bed! It is desirable to stay with the bitch when she begins the whelping process as it can reassure her, and the breeder will be able to monitor the progress of both the bitch and her new-born pups. Should an emergency situation arise the breeder will immediately be aware of it, and be able to deal with it effectively, either alone or by calling the vet.

The whelping box itself needs to be approximately 4 feet square with three sides standing 18 inches high. The fourth side will ideally consist of two pieces, each 9 inches high. This means that when only one piece is present, the bitch can easily step in and out of the box. Later on, when the pups become active, the second piece can be put into position. A 'pig rail' can be placed inside the box to help prevent the bitch from accidentally squashing the pups. This can be fixed at a height of 6 inches and about the same distance from the sides of the box; wooden broom handles actually make excellent 'pig rails'! My current whelping box is made of extra strong plywood and has seen some eight years' service! After each litter it is scrubbed and bleached, and the same thing happens again when it is brought out for the next litter.

Heat is essential for newborn pups and should be provided by an overhead heater. I use an infra-red pig lamp which is suspended over the whelping box so that it can be adjusted for height as necessary. Dull emitter heat lamps are ideal and have the added benefit of not being able to shatter should they receive a knock.

Newspaper is a must for whelping – most breeders use tons of it and have family and friends collecting it all year round! It absorbs fluids, can be disposed of easily and digs up into a beautiful nest when the bitch starts to make her whelping bed. Once the box has a thick layer of newspaper over the base, a piece of fleecy bedding material can be placed on top, covering about half the floor area. This fluffy, waterproof-backed bedding is used in hospitals and nursing homes because of its ability to allow moisture through, while the top stays warm and dry. It is invaluable as a cosy bed for bitch and nursing puppies. Several pieces are necessary, as a clean piece will need to be used every day once the puppies arrive.

During the last week of pregnancy, it is not unusual for the bitch to try and dig her own nest in the garden, or to try and burrow under a shed – this is nothing to worry about, as it is merely instinct at work. The bitch should be taken back to her whelping box and settled down with a couple of biscuits, so that she can think of it as 'home'.

WHELPING

As the sixty-third day draws closer, it is as well to inform the vet that a litter is imminent, although hopefully he will not be needed. Rottweiler bitches tend to whelp easily, especially if kept lean and well muscled, and the pups are relatively small when born, even though their subsequent growth rate is phenomenal.

It is advisable to assemble all the items which may be necessary during whelping. These include:

1. A large cardboard box
2. A hot-water bottle
3. A pair of scissors with rounded ends
4. A jug with disinfectant solution for scissors
5. A number of old clean towels
6. Newspapers
7. Paper and pencil – for noting birth-times and sex of the puppies
8. Small pieces of bedding for use in the cardboard box.

The bitch may be punctual with her whelping, but it is not unusual for the pups to arrive three or four days early or late. It is really a case of waiting for the signs to know that things are stirring! About twenty-four hours before whelping, the bitch's temperature will drop a degree or more from her normal 101 degrees Fahrenheit (38 degrees Centigrade). She will tear up the newspaper in the whelping box for several days beforehand. Rottweiler bitches rarely go off their food and will often eat within hours of the birth. The bitch will become generally restless, panting, digging up her bed and apparently unable to settle. If she goes outside to relieve herself, it is best to go with her as she may make a bolt for some dark outdoor 'nest' which she may have been preparing.

Often bitches will lick themselves, stare at their hindquarters, circle around and get extremely agitated. The expression in the bitch's eyes becomes very inward-focused, and she does not notice anything except her own physical exertions. When the panting becomes really heavy, the bitch will have muscle tremors and begin to push quite strongly. She will have been experiencing contractions for some time, but now it becomes outwardly obvious.

Once she starts to push hard, the puppy should not take long to arrive. The first sign is usually a gush of fluid as the water bag bursts, followed by the pup itself. As it arrives, it will generally still be encased in the foetal membrane which has to be broken quickly to allow the puppy to breathe. The umbilical cord will still be connected to the placenta which may come away with the puppy or wait until the next contraction. I prefer to cut the cord myself, using the sterilised scissors, thereby releasing the placenta in order that the bitch can eat it. This eating of the afterbirths is perfectly natural behaviour and does the bitch no actual harm, other than causing loose black bowel movements, but it is best to limit her to the first three or four, and then clear up the rest manually.

Often the bitch is so interested in cleaning up after herself that the puppy can benefit from the breeder's attention. Using one of the clean towels, the puppy can be wiped and presented to the bitch who will lick and sniff her new offspring. At this stage I like to put the puppy in the cardboard box, on a hot-water bottle which is covered with a piece of bedding and placed under the heat lamp. This ensures that the puppy will quickly dry off and stay warm while its siblings arrive. The bitch can continue with the whelping and can see and nuzzle her newborn puppy.

Puppies frequently arrive in the breech position, with the hind feet appearing first. This can be a more awkward delivery, and it is advisable to grasp the puppy gently with a piece of towel and with each contraction ease the pup downwards and inwards towards the bitch's legs. *Never* try and pull the pup straight out.

If the bag has broken in the birth canal, then the puppy may have inhaled some fluid and this has to be cleared from the lungs as quickly as possible. I have a Swedish friend who, in such an instance, covers the pup's nose and mouth with her own mouth and sucks out the fluid – which she then spits out! I have never had the urge to try this, but swinging the puppy in an arc seems to be fairly successful! Support the puppy, head down, in the palm of one hand, cover with the other hand and, raising both arms above the head, swing them gently down, ending up between the knees. Repeat this several times to remove the fluid from the puppy's lungs. Wipe the pup's nose and mouth to remove the fluid and place it in the warm cardboard box. Any pup which is slow to get going needs to be gently rubbed with a warm towel until its breathing has been stimulated and the pup is wriggling around.

Maiden bitches are often agitated by the birth of the first few puppies, but with some praise and reassurance they soon realise that all is well and they are being extremely good. I prefer to be with my bitches constantly while they are whelping, regardless of time or other commitments. It is the best way of averting potential problems and recognising an emergency. Also, the bitch seems to enjoy knowing that someone is there.

There is no hard and fast rule about the length of time involved in whelping. The bitch will go at her own pace and should not be interfered with unless there is a problem. It would be very unwise to allow a bitch to push and strain for more than an hour with no result. The vet should be called immediately as there could be a puppy blocking the birth canal and a caesarean section might be necessary. If contractions stop and the bitch is still obviously full of pups, then again the vet should be consulted as uterine inertia might be the problem, and the bitch will need an injection of oxytocin to stimulate uterine contractions. Never be apprehensive about calling your vet at any hour of the day or night.

Some pups arrive within minutes of each other – others can have half-an-hour or an hour in between. I had one bitch that whelped fourteen pups in three hours, which was a fairly hectic pace. Another bitch took seven hours to produce five pups – so the breeder just has to be patient. Counting the afterbirths and making a note of the time of delivery and the sex of the puppies is also a good idea. During the whelping the bitch can be offered a drink of milk and honey.

Chapter Fourteen

REARING A LITTER

BIRTH TO WEANING

Once the pups have been born, the whelping box cleaned, and fresh paper and bedding put down, the bitch can be settled down with her pups snuggled up to her. At this stage she will relax and doze, stirring occasionally to nose her pups and lick them. This licking is very necessary as it encourages the pups to urinate and defecate, and stimulates them to feed. Most bitches will eat the pups' faeces and seem to accept this as a normal part of their maternal function. However, there are some bitches for whom this activity does not come altogether naturally, and I've found that applying a small amount of ointment to the anal area of the puppies will encourage the bitch to lick them. This ointment is designed for human mothers with sore or cracked nipples from breast feeding and is available at any chemist shop.

After whelping the bitch should be given a feed of honey, warm milk and a beaten egg, and then kept on a light diet for the first twenty-four hours. This can consist of milky foods, cereal, scrambled eggs, or something of that kind, four times a day. Thereafter she can be put back on a solid high-protein diet – much to her obvious delight! Rottweiler bitches can produce large litters, twelve pups being quite common, and feeding all those mouths can be quite a draining process for the bitch. She must not only maintain and restore her own body tissues, but must produce enough milk for her fast-growing pups.

A high-protein diet is essential and can be achieved either by feeding meat, fish, eggs and milk with a good-quality mixer, or by using one of the many complete foods that are now available. I always feed tripe as well. The bitch will need four or five meals a day and can hardly be fed too much at this stage. Clean drinking water must always be available. She must also receive an adequate supply of calcium; again, there are many products available, and you can ask your vet for advice. These can be fed as tidbits, in the correct quantity; because they are so palatable the dogs love them.

The bitch must be encouraged to go outside and relieve herself several times a day; the most maternally-minded will be loath to leave their pups and might need to be put on a lead. It is quite normal for the bitch to have loose motions, often black in colour, but this is only the result of eating the afterbirths, which are very rich in iron.

Let your vet check the bitch over within twenty-four hours of the birth to make sure there are no retained puppies or placentas. The vet will also give a 'cleansing' injection to bring away any remaining waste products in the uterus. If the bitch retains anything she will quickly run a high temperature and develop a fever, leading to loss of milk and possibly death. So, a veterinary check-up is the best option for all concerned! The vet can also give the pups a quick examination for malformations such as cleft palates.

During the first week, the bitch needs a peaceful environment away from the hurly-burly of family life. Many bitches are disturbed by strangers near the whelping box and are prepared to

REARING A LITTER
Photographer STEVE NASH followed the progress of a Rottweiler litter from soon after whelping, when the puppies were just eight days old until they were eight weeks old and ready to go to their new homes.
The litter bred by Mel Matthews (Ronmal) out of her bitch
Ronmal The Country Wench and sired by Ch. Pendley Winston.

Ronmal The Country Wench with her nine-day-old litter, composed of two bitches and six dogs. This was her third litter, and as an experienced mother, she was calm and competent when dealing with her puppies.

The males are identified with different shades of blue ribbon. At this stage, the eyes have not yet opened.

The bitches are identified with different shades of pink ribbon. Tails were docked when the puppies were three days old.

guard their puppies zealously. It is best not to invite the entire neighbourhood in to view the new arrivals! This also goes for small children and their numerous friends to whom puppies are a natural source of delight. The bitch can become distressed and panicky, and this is neither necessary nor desirable. Fairly constant supervision is required during the early days to make sure that all is well in the whelping box. I make a habit of sleeping on a camp-bed in the whelping quarters for the first three or four nights.

BOTTLE FEEDING

Sometimes, with a large litter, the pups need supplementary feeding in order to help the bitch. If the bitch has had a caesarean section she can lose her milk for several days, in which case allow the pups to continue suckling, as this will encourage the milk to reappear, but supplement them with a bottle.

Over the years I have had one bitch who produced no milk at all for her first two litters, and then produced gallons for her third litter; and another bitch who totally rejected her litter of twelve at birth! These three litters were bottle-fed from birth without the loss of a single puppy. I have found that the easiest method is to use a baby's feeding bottle with the smallest hole in the teat, and a proprietary bitch milk-replacer. In an emergency two parts evaporated milk to one part warm water, plus a drop of honey, will keep the pups going until you obtain a milk substitute. There are a number of suitable brands on the market. Cow's milk is totally unsuitable and should not be used. The following table illustrates the difference in composition between the milk of various mammals:

	Protein	Fat	Lactose	Total solids	Energy K/Cal/100g.
Cow	3.5%	3.7%	4.9%	12.7%	66
Goat	3.6%	4.2%	4.3%	13.0%	68
Pig	5.2%	4.5%	3.2%	16.0%	73
Dog	8.5%	9.6%	3.5%	21.6%	130

It can be clearly seen that there is twice as much energy (for growth) in the bitch's milk than the cow's. A puppy fed on cow's milk would need double the quantity that it would of its mother's milk to provide its calorie requirements. This would entail ingesting three times the quantity of lactose – resulting in severe digestive upset with watery diarrhoea.

Bottle feeding is time-consuming and exhausting as it needs to be done every two hours, day and night, for the first ten days. After that it can be three-hourly until the pups open their eyes and can begin the weaning process. Not a job for the faint-hearted! It is also unfortunate for the pups if they are unable to receive the colostrum, or first milk, from the bitch, which provides them with maternal immunity.

ECLAMPSIA

Eclampsia can be a problem, and it is imperative that the symptoms can be recognised. This is a condition caused by lack of calcium in the blood and it may occur a few days after whelping or, more usually, towards the end of the lactation period when large quantities of calcium have been passed with the milk. The symptoms are stiffness of the hindlegs and shaking and jerky movements, which can be followed by convulsions if the vet isn't called quickly. An injection of calcium is usually sufficient to restore the bitch to full health very speedily. I have only experienced eclampsia twice in my bitches and on both occasions it was immediately after whelping – within half an hour. I find it useful to keep the bitch on her feet, massaging her all over to keep her stimulated until the vet arrives to inject her.

GENERAL SUPERVISION

Warmth is the single most important factor after food. An infra-red lamp is most widely used and provide an ideal source of heat. The use of calor-gas or paraffin heaters with a live flame and attendant fumes and condensation would not seem to be a sensible option.

Daily disinfecting of the whelping box followed by fresh paper and clean bedding provides a basis of good animal husbandry and hygiene.

If a bitch seems to be pushing a pup away and it is cold, feeble and noisy, there is a strong chance that something is wrong with it. The bitch is rarely mistaken and invariably that puppy will die, even though veterinary help is sought. Very occasionally it is possible to pull a rejected sickly pup through and I will always make the effort. Some of these pups have gone on to a long, happy and healthy life; others have died or been euthanased.

DOCKING AND DEWCLAWS

Docking and removal of dewclaws generally takes place on the third day. In the UK, since January 1993, it has been illegal for any layperson to dock pups' tails; this procedure can only be performed by a veterinary surgeon now. Prior to that date it was quite normal for breeders to dock tails using the rubber band method which caused no distress, loss of blood or trauma, and required no stitches. Vets invariably cut the tail off, which although quick, would appear to cause pain to the puppy. However, in order to keep a traditionally docked breed as precisely that, it is necessary to find a vet who is prepared to dock tails. In some countries, such as the Scandinavian countries, docking is no longer permitted.

The Standard requires that hind dewclaws be removed. Continental fashion prefers front dewclaws to remain, but in Britain and the United States they are usually removed. The vet will remove dewclaws, but the lay-person is still permitted to perform this simple procedure. It requires an assistant, sterilised scissors, potassium permanganate crystals (fine) and some cotton wool balls. After cutting through at the base of the dewclaw simply apply the crystals on damp cotton wool to seal the wound. Do ensure that the bitch is well out of earshot as the pups will wriggle and squeak momentarily.

TRIMMING NAILS

A weekly task for the first four to five weeks is the trimming of the puppies' nails. They should be carefully clipped with nail scissors to take off the sharp spiky ends. The nails, if left untrimmed, can cause considerable discomfort to the bitch as her teats will get scratched when the puppies are feeding. After this period, when the pups are starting to run about outside, their nails will wear down and stay short providing they have a concrete surface to move about on.

DEVELOPMENT

The pups' eyes generally begin to open from the tenth day onwards, at the same time as their ears begin to unseal. By the sixteenth day they can usually see and hear, and they can easily be frightened by sudden movement or loud noises. At the same time they are beginning to get up on all four legs and take wobbly steps, instead of dragging themselves around the whelping box with their front legs. This is also the time when they start to relieve bladder and bowels on the newspaper instead of fouling the bedding 'nest'.

WEANING TO EIGHT WEEKS

FEEDING REGIMES

If the litter is large, it is advisable to begin weaning as soon as the pups' eyes are open. A small litter can stay exclusively on the bitch for another few days. Every breeder has their own belief

The puppies are now seventeen days old. Their eyes have opened, and their ears are developed, although hearing does not become acute until five weeks of age.

There is little detectable difference between a dog and bitch at this stage.

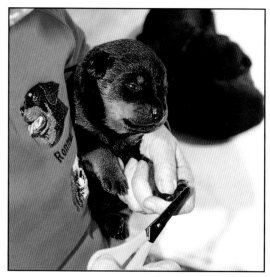

The puppies' nails must be trimmed regularly, otherwise they will hurt the dam when they are feeding.

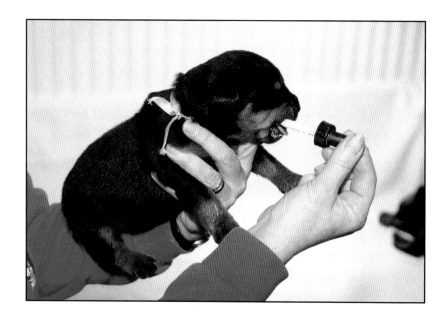

The first worming treatment: Breeder Mel Matthews uses a syringe and a liquid wormer.

At five weeks, the male is beginning to show a slightly larger head. Both puppies are showing good bone; they are bright-eyed and healthy looking, and have excellent markings.

Puppies can walk and run from four weeks, and at five weeks old the puppies are starting to explore the outside world. It is at this stage a pecking order is worked out between the littermates.

The weaning process is now under way. This type of bowl is ideal when you are feeding a litter together.

If a puppy is not putting on as much weight as its littermates, or is being pushed out of the way, it is wise to feed individually.

as to the best method of weaning, and I am no exception. For many years I have used a proprietary brand of complete puppy food, with excellent results. To start weaning, I use a small measure of the complete diet, soaked in boiling water, and when this is soggy it is mashed with a potato-masher until a porridge-like consistency is obtained.

The pups are given this in a large flat pan, with half-inch sides. Some lap it quickly and easily; others take several days to perfect the art. One meal daily is given for three days, by which time most of the pups are attracted by the smell and will lap at it heartily. Of course, they get it everywhere – but the bitch cleans them up afterwards!

Gradually the puppies are offered two, three and four pans a day, while still suckling from the bitch. By the time they are four and a half weeks old, they demolish every ounce of food in the pan. At this stage they are offered raw minced green tripe with their meals; just a small quantity to begin with, building up to a larger quantity by the time they are six weeks old. The soaking of the puppy food lessens gradually as their teeth come through and they are able to chew. At six weeks the pups have four meals a day consisting of lightly soaked puppy food and minced tripe. By now they are eating out of two or three puppy feeding dishes with raised centres, thus making sure that none of the pups misses out because of the greedier ones.

This method ensures that the pups develop a healthy attitude towards eating; it does not encourage fussy eaters to develop. It also produces firm bowel motions and little or no digestive upset. The pups grow well with firm plump bodies and strong bone. A well-covered active puppy is the ideal, not a fat Tweedledum lookalike! Excess weight will cause skeletal and muscular problems during the pups' development.

Throughout this period the bitch is allowed to be with them intermittently if she shows a strong maternal instinct – but not many bitches want to be with a litter of rowdy, boisterous six-week-old pups. Unfortunately, being with the puppies also encourages the bitch to regurgitate her food in order to feed the litter, at a time when she needs all the nutritional value it can give her in order to regain any condition she may have lost. Once the pups are weaning the bitch ceases to eat their faeces, so the breeder has a great deal of work keeping everything spotlessly clean.

There are, of course, alternative puppy weaning/feeding regimes. The traditional way is to use minced or scraped beef, baby cereal, rusks, scrambled eggs, goat's milk, rice pudding, sterilised bonemeal, etc., gradually introducing puppy meal as the pups approach five weeks old. This works wonderfully well and produces strong healthy puppies. The decision has to rest with the breeder. Whichever method is chosen, the pups should stay on four meals daily until about four months old.

Food is never left on constant offer. At mealtimes the food pans should be quickly emptied, and if there is food left uneaten it should be disposed of promptly. The quantities for the next meal can be adjusted accordingly. Clean, fresh water should be constantly available, in a heavy bowl which cannot be tipped over and thrown around.

WORMING
Worming is very important and is usually performed at three, five and seven weeks. Many puppies have worms despite the dam having been wormed before mating. Worming preparations can be obtained from all veterinary surgeons, along with advice and help if necessary. As with feeding, all breeders have their favourite products. Puppies with worms become pot-bellied, with dull coats, and do not have the bounce, bloom and obvious well-being of puppies with no worms.

THE MOTHER'S ROLE
During this stage of the puppies' development, the bitch should be spending less time with them. Once they are fully weaned at between five to six weeks she really does not want them constantly pestering her and trying to suckle. Most bitches still like to spend short periods with their

Some bitches are more maternal than other. Once the puppies are weaned, the mother will be quite happy to spend time away from the litter.

BELOW: A bitch puppy, aged seven weeks. According to breeder Mel Matthews, this litter was always very forward for its age.

BELOW: A male puppy, aged seven weeks. The members of the litter now have individual personalities.

growing brood, but mostly for play purposes, and they will often growl at offending youngsters who persist in suckling. By six weeks the pups have needle-sharp teeth which they will use without mercy on anything that takes their fancy!

The bitch's food intake can be cut down as the puppies take less milk, and by the six-week stage she will probably be back on normal rations. Some bitches lose more condition than others – they "milk off their backs", in farming parlance – in which case it is advisable to continue with extra feeds for a few weeks longer, while keeping the bitch away from the pups to discourage milk production. The bitch will shortly have a really heavy moult, which is perfectly normal after producing a litter. Daily grooming will help to remove the dead coat quickly, as will several baths. The new coat comes through quite speedily, and with her daily exercise routine restored to normal the bitch soon regains her glossy-coated figure.

GROWING INDEPENDENCE

Once the puppies are weaning it is important to get them out into the fresh air, especially if the weather is warm and sunny. After their initial apprehension at leaving familiar surroundings they will soon begin to stagger around, exploring everything. Experience suggests that it is worth investing in several sets of puppy-pen panels – not to keep the pups in a pen, but to erect around bushes, flower borders, etc.! Once they feel grass beneath their feet they tend to get excited and gallop around playing, chewing and often digging. In warm weather they can have a blanket on the lawn and will all collapse in a heap when they are tired.

It becomes more difficult with a winter litter when the weather is cold and often wet. They still need to run around and play but they must be able to return to a warm, dry, draught-free bed. Some people have an area in the house which the puppies can utilise, but as a growing litter can create mayhem indoors it is probably a good idea to invest in a puppy kennel outside. This can be fitted out with a raised bed, heat lamp, and a covered outdoor run. Stables make excellent puppy kennels, as do solid, weatherproof sheds. It is important to realise that a litter of fast-growing active puppies will make a lot of mess, in every conceivable way! The floor of their kennel should be disinfected daily and all faeces picked up immediately. Cleanliness and hygiene are important in the prevention of infection and disease.

EARLY SOCIALISATION

This is the time, as the pups grow and expand their horizons and experiences, that the breeder and family should spend vast amounts of time socialising the pups. From four weeks onwards the puppies can be encouraged to follow when called, especially to the food pan. They should become accustomed to noises such as the television, the radio, the washing machine, the vacuum cleaner, the lawn mower. Toys should be available for the pups, but commonsense is needed. Squeaky or fluffy toys will be demolished quickly and if ingested can prove hazardous. Hard rubber balls and roasted bones are ideal, as are knotted ropes and empty plastic Coke bottles. It is part of the breeder's responsibility to ensure that all puppies in a litter are out-going, friendly, inquisitive and bold; and, the decision having been taken to breed the litter, the pups must be given the best possible preparation for the outside world.

At six weeks, it is advisable to have the entire litter vaccinated against parvovirus. This can be seen as a blanket protection for the pups in case the maternal antibodies, which they receive from the bitch, are not sufficient to fight off the virus, should it be inadvertently brought onto the premises. Parvovirus is a killer, and it makes sense to protect the pups as much as possible.

FINDING HOMES

Finding suitable owners for Rottweiler puppies is an on-going process of sorting the wheat from the chaff! Pups generally go the their new homes at about eight weeks of age, by which time the

Getting used to the outside world is an essential part of good rearing. These puppies are becoming more independent and learning to evaluate new situations.

These puppies have endless curiosity and their bright, alert manner is a good indication of their general well-being – both physical and mental.

BELOW: A job well done: Ronmal The Country Wench has proved to be an excellent mother, and she appears to have passed on her sound temperament to her puppies.

prospective purchasers should have been comprehensively grilled to ensure that they can provide suitable homes. The initial approach from a puppy buyer is usually made by telephone, but the breeder should *never* conduct a sale in this manner. Many unsuitable homes can be weeded out immediately simply by asking pertinent questions. It is essential that potential owners have a house with a securely fenced garden. Someone should be home for most of the day – pups left alone for long periods get bored, lonely and destructive. Both partners (of a couple) should be equally keen to own a Rottweiler, and if there are children they should be of an age to understand that the puppy must be treated with kindness and respect – a puppy is *not* a toy. The puppy must be wanted for the correct reasons, as a family pet and companion, not as a prop to any concept of machismo, or as a "guard", nor to be given as a "surprise present".

If the enquirer can satisfy the breeder that their 'intentions are honourable' and their property suitable, then an appointment can be made to see the puppies and have further discussions. Most potential owners will happily make long journeys to visit a breeder who is prepared to consider selling them a puppy. Serious enquirers will judge the breeder's attitude and depth of concern as much as the breeder is judging them.

It is not often possible to visit the homes of prospective owners, but they should be encouraged to bring photos of house, garden, other dogs, etc. Meeting the children can be a useful guide – I firmly believe that people with badly-behaved children will rear badly-behaved dogs! The children's interaction with adult dogs and puppies can be assessed quietly and effectively.

The keen and serious potential owners may well have read books about Rottweilers and spoken to other breeders to find out as much as possible. Often an enquirer has just lost a much-loved family pet and wants a new puppy on which to lavish love and affection. Each breeder must make their own judgements as to which homes will be suitable; but they should never be afraid to send someone away empty-handed; the future welfare of the puppy is of paramount importance.

Overseas enquiries can cause many problems unless the breeder already knows someone from that particular country who can vouch for the credibility of the enquirer. Cultural differences around the world mean that varying degrees of value are placed upon animal welfare, not all of which are acceptable to the breeder's ideal. Having said that, I have sold puppies to serious devotees of the breed overseas and made good and lasting friendships. The committed Rottweiler enthusiast who wants to import a puppy generally has to pay a large price for importation.

If a potential show specimen is required then they should get top quality stock. I prefer to send show-quality export puppies at between five and six months, when they have full dentition and the pup has grown on enough to enable me to get a good idea of its future potential. This entails a great deal of time and effort, as the growing pup has to be house-trained, lead-trained, socialised, etc. before being sent to its new home. Returning to 'home' sales, once the potential owner has been vetted and accepted as a likely "good home" they return when the pups are eight weeks old. Each puppy should depart accompanied by a comprehensive diet sheet, with details of current and future feeding, inoculations, worming and do's and don'ts. Purchasers should also have a Kennel Club Registration Certificate (if these have been issued at that time), vaccination certificate and a copy of the pup's pedigree. It is also useful for new owners to be provided with a list of books about the breed, complete with ISBN references.

Breeders should provide a complete back-up service to puppy purchasers, giving help and advice when needed, and explaining that should the need arise they would wish to have the puppy back for rehoming purposes.

Not all the puppies leave the breeder at the same time, and, for whatever reason, there may be several that need individual attention for a few weeks more. This is hard work and requires much time and patience on the part of the breeder. Growing puppies become hooligans if they are not taught the rudiments of acceptable behaviour.

Chapter Fifteen

THE ROTTWEILER IN GERMANY

By Helmut Freiburg, Supervisory Judge of the ADRK

The Allgermeiner Deutscher Rottweiler Klub (ARDK) is a member of the VDH (the German equivalent of the Kennel Club) and, thus, also a member of the FCI. Currently the ARDK has sixteen specialist breed judges for the Rottweiler breed. The VDH also has all-rounder judges of FCI Group 2, who are permitted to judge Rottweilers.

JUDGING QUALIFICATIONS

The breed judges fulfil a very important task with regard to dogs. The existence and further development of pedigree dog breeding, and the public reputation of the 'Verband für das Deutsche Hundewesen e.v.' (VDH) and its member associations, depend on the practical abilities of the judge, their sense of responsibility and their exemplary conduct in all areas of cynology and in their private lives. The judges can only fulfil their responsibilities if they have considerable expertise, possess high intellectual and personal values, and are independent in every way.

To the exhibitors and the public, the breed judge represents the 'Rassehunde-Zuchtverein' (Pedigree dog breeding association), the VDH, and the 'Federation Cynologique Internationale' (FCI). The judge must bear this in mind at all times, adhering to the expected standards, both in his behaviour and with regard to his appearance.

BECOMING A SPECIALIST BREED JUDGE IN THE ADRK

In accordance with the judge regulations of the ADRK and the VDH breed judge rules of 7.3.92, applicants must have the following qualifications to be accepted as apprentice judges:

1. The applicant must apply via the district group (BG) and the regional group (LG). The regional group has to approve the application and pass it to the supervisory judge of the ADRK. The application is then published in the Club journal. Any objections must reach the supervisory judge in writing within 14 days.

2. After examining the application documentation, the judge will appoint two representatives of the relevant regional group (chairman or judge), who will set the applicant a preliminary written and oral test. The test subject will be determined by the judge in consultation with the head breed warden ('Hauptzuchtwart'), and sent to a supervisor in a sealed envelope. The envelope must not be opened until the day of the test in the presence of the applicant. The two representatives will provide a report with assessment of the test.

3. The documents, with report, must be sealed and sent to the supervisory judge as soon as possible. The supervisory judge will present all the documentation to the 'Richterehrenrat' (judges' honorary council) for further consideration.

4. An apprenticeship must be spent with a 'Körmeister' ('master' qualified to select for breeding purposes) for show or breeding suitability testing (Zuchttauglichkeitsprüfung ZTP).

In addition, the following requirements must be met:
The applicant must:
1. Be at least 25 years old and no more than 50 years.
2. Have had a kennel's name registered with the pedigree breed club for at least five years, bred three litters of the breed, and have exhibited dogs of his own breeding for at least five years.
3. Have trained at least one or more dogs in test stages SchHI ('Schutzhund I'), SchH II, SchH III, and shown the dog or dogs successfully.
4. Have been a member of the VDH Members Association for the breed for at least five years.
5. Have acted as ring secretary, ring steward or show manager at least five times in a year, and acted as show manager at least once.
6. Have taken part in the special show manager days, organised by the VDH, at least twice.
7. Acted as 'Zuchtwart' (breeding supervisor) in the BG or LG.
8. Have successfully completed the preliminary test, in accordance with para. 22 of the VDH breed judge regulations.
9. Nominate an experienced judge as sponsor, who will also supervise him throughout his training.

   The nomination as apprentice judge, or refusal of the application by the club management, must be notified to the candidate in writing. The applicant cannot ask for reasons for a refusal. After nomination as apprentice judge, the candidate must complete at least six apprenticeships under three different judges. One of the apprenticeships is for breeding suitability testing, which must be carried out with the leading breeding supervisor or supervisory judge, and one apprenticeship at a CACIB show of the VDH. All apprenticeships must be entered in the VDH register and confirmed by the instructing judge.
   It must be agreed between the supervisor, the supervisory judge and the sponsoring judge which (instructing) judge apprenticeships are to be carried out. The apprentice must describe all the dogs as if he were a judge. The reports on all the apprenticeships must be sent to the instructing judge for checking. He will confirm to the supervisory judge whether the candidate can be considered as passed or not passed, and send him the reports. This is followed by the final examination in practical, oral and written form, in accordance with paragraph 24 VDH 'Zuchtrichterordnung' (breed judge regulations).
   After the examination has been passed and all the documents have been examined, the supervisory judge presents these to the 'Richterehrenrat' (judge's honorary council) for scrutiny. After all the stated conditions have been met, the supervisory judge submits all the documents to the General Management Committee of the ADRK and proposes that the applicant is nominated as breed judge. The ADRK will then submit the application to the VDH for entry in the list of specialist breed judges, and the VDH will issue the applicant with a judge's pass. This will be presented to him by the chairman and supervisory judge of the ADRK. In addition, he will receive an ADRK judge's pass. As can be seen from the above, considerable effort and ability is required to become a breed judge. The breed judge is only bound by the Standard of the ADRK – the ADRK in Germany, being the land of origin of the Rottweiler, is responsible for the Standard. The Standard is published by the FCI No. 147 of 24.9.91 latest version. The Rottweiler belongs to the FCI Group 2 and is used as companion, guard and working dog. The motto of the ADRK is: *"Breeding for form and performance – and health."*

JUDGING TO THE STANDARD

Appointment as a judge before entry in the VDH judges list is not permitted, and the same applies to the acceptance of invitations for a judging appointment. The judge is given a strict interpretation of the Standard and he must adhere to this. He must not interpret the Standard in such a way that it might adversely affect the health of the Rottweiler. The following form gradings can be awarded by the judge:

Outstanding (V)

Very good (SG)

Good (G)

Satisfactory (Ggd)

Not satisfactory (Nggd).

In the novice classes:

Very promising (vv), Promising (vsp), Not very promising (wv).

"Outstanding" can only be awarded to a dog which comes very close to the ideal Standard of the breed, is presented in an excellent manner, exudes a harmonious, balanced nature, has 'class' and an outstanding carriage. The dog's superior characteristics with regard to his breed may camouflage slight faults, but he should have the typical characteristics of his sex.

"Very good" is only awarded to a dog which has the typical characteristics of his breed, is of balanced proportions and is in good shape. A few forgivable faults will be overlooked, but not morphological ones. This rating can only be given to a class-dog.

"Good" can be awarded to a dog which has the main characteristics of its breed, but has faults, on the condition, that these are not concealed.

"Satisfactory" will be awarded to a dog which meets the requirements of its breed, without possessing its generally known characteristics, or whose overall appearance leaves a certain amount to be desired.

"Not satisfactory" is awarded to a dog which does not meet the Standard for the type, shows definite, non-Standard behaviour or is aggressive, has a testicle fault, a tooth fault or a jaw anomaly, colour or hair faults or shows definite albino symptoms. This grading must also be awarded to the dog which displays a breed characteristic to such a small extent, that the health of the dog is jeopardised. This grading must also be given to a dog which has a severe or disqualifying fault according to the standard applicable to him. In the youth and young dog class, the highest award is "Very good". At CACIB shows the age classes are in accordance with the VDH and the FCI.

Specialist breed judges of the ADRK, who appear at shows abroad, must also judge according to the Standard. In Germany, the judge produces a report of the dog he judges. The report is dictated directly on to the typewriter. The ADRK has produced form sheets for this purpose, which enable copies to be produced. These can be handed to the exhibitor on the day of the show, with the form gradings awarded. The copies go to the main breeding supervisor, the organiser, and the judge keeps one copy. The report is divided up into:

1. Overall appearance and bone strength.
2. The temperament of the dog.
3. A description of the construction and movement.

The dog is walked around before the final judging takes place, and this serves to show its bodily shape, its condition and the dog's eagerness to walk. According to the ADRK, it is very important that this is carried out, as the Rottweiler has great endurance and must always be shown in excellent bodily shape.

It is the function of the judge to ensure that the dog, that comes closest to the Standard, is well-presented and in a excellent condition, will be awarded first place. The breed judge must include in his report the good points of the Rottweiler presented to him, and the faults.

At the annual Judges Meeting of the ARDK, which the breed judges must attend, subjects are discussed which are of interest, and give guidelines for the following year.

Faults, which are found increasingly among the dogs shown and deviate from the standard, must be observed carefully by the judge and taken into consideration when making the evaluation and grading. All breeding judges of the ADRK are also entitled to carry out breeding suitability tests (ZTP).

BREEDING ROTTWEILERS IN GERMANY
By Willi Hedtke, Chief Breed Warden of the ADRK

LEARNED OR INHERITED

Every breeder is familiar with the view that learned characteristics are not inherited, only disposition is inherited. There are also scientists, who say that this view is not a law – merely a rule, to which there are exceptions. We cannot examine here who is right, because it would have to be determined very precisely, what characteristics and to which organs, learning can be applied. Nobody maintains that all learned characteristics are inherited – all characteristics are not subject to the law of Mendel. In the breeding sense, there are no learned working dog constructions and no definite learned temperament. If both are present, we can only conclude that the necessary pre-disposition was inherited and inherent. With proper breeding and training, they are then developed to perfection. Where there is nothing, however, there is nothing to be developed. It follows from this, that 'developed' is not the same as 'learned'. This applies to all bodily, physiological and temperamental characteristics.

SELECTING BREEDING STOCK

Rottweilers brought to be examined for their suitability for breeding are at least 18 months old on the day of the test. They have left their youth behind, and their life is beginning in earnest. Their traits are more or less set. When we consider that the Rottweiler accepted for breeding will be used until the end of its breeding years, it becomes understandable that the requirements of the test relating to temperament can only be minimum requirements. What is inherited cannot be taken back. The breeding association has to accept this for better or for worse. Selection from these dogs at a 'Körung' (selection for breeding suitability) cannot repair any damage. Today, breeding is still based on dogs which have passed a valid breeding suitability test. The aim must be to improve this basis! For some critics of the selection for breeding rules, a Rottweiler has only fulfilled the qualification for selection for breeding, when he has succeeded in a task.

A question of great importance for the breeding association is the definition of 'gun-shy', and of sensitivity to touch, which is described as 'stick-shy'. This trait is widely considered to be incurable and is easily inherited. Research, so far, has shown that over-sensitivity to touch and to bangs is related to sex. Dogs tend to be under-sensitive more often, while bitches tend to be over-sensitive more often. These observations also correspond with general experience.

The problem of dogs that lack the ability to take stress cannot be removed from the world by holding long discussions about the stock to be used. No breed judge will permit a dog to be whipped with excessive severity, but the whipping must be done visibly downwards, and it must hit the dog on the croup or hindquarters; which are not very sensitive parts of the body. A courageous drover dog will not be particularly upset by this test and will soon forget it.

When the dog's temperaments is being tested, the breed judge does not expect the assistant to show himself to be a tough, fearless man. The assistant's task is to enable a temperament assessment to be made as objectively as possible. The dog has no chance against the protected assistant. The purpose of the selection for breeding is to find the best dogs from those dogs that are suitable for breeding.

The decision of the 'Körmeister' (selector) is, and always has been, final! It is valid, when all necessary documentation has reached the 'Zuchtbuchamt' (Stud book office or breeding registration office), the selection paper has been signed by the 'Hauptzuchtwart' (principal breeding warden), and the selection for suitability for breeding has been published by the ADRK.

Anyone involved in breeding Rottweilers, must observe every requirement related to breeding. The 'Körmeister' must make a considered decision. A decision, which is not taken properly, endangers breeding and the dog's performance – matters of considerable concern to the club.

BASIC PRINCIPLES FOR BREEDING OF THE ADRK

The organisation began in Heidelberg in 1905, and the foundation stock was brought together there. On January 13th 1907, the first and oldest German Rottweiler Club was founded in Heidelberg. This was the start of the not so simple task of registration in the first 'Zuchtbuch' (Stud Book).

The male dogs which count as the progenitors of the breed are: Russ vom Brückenbuckel DRK No. 1, whelped July 1904, and Champion Ralph vom Neckar, DRK-Nr. 2, whelped October 1906.

CURRENT BREEDING REGULATIONS:

Only registered Rottweilers can be used for breeding, which have passed a breeding suitability test (ZTP). When paired, one of the breeding partners must have a 'Ausbildungskennzeichen' (training qualification similar to Champion Certificate (CC). The label SchH.A. does not count as 'Ausbildungskennzeichen' for breeding regulation purposes.

There is a minimum age for breeding stock of 20 months for bitches and 24 months for dogs at the time of the mating act. The ADRK must record inherited defects they become aware of in dogs submitted to them, in order that these may be kept under observation and controlled. There is a breeding advisory service available to the ADRK, which can consult and advise on the control of genetic defects.

In 1968 the ADRK started X-ray examinations of Rottweilers for hip joint dysplasia (HD). It was found that a very high percentage of the X-rayed dogs had HD. It was decided unanimously by the members at the advisory council meeting, to eliminate Rottweilers with HD, using X-ray examinations. In order not to place too much stress on the breeding programme, the selection procedure was tightened up over the period of a year. It was shown clearly that to eliminate HD, it was necessary to make a careful selection of the breeding partner, and a high measure of patience over many years was needed to obtain the current HD status.

The X-ray findings obtained by the EDV provide clear evidence, but it is still not yet good enough for the top breeders. An application to the advisory council not to allow Rottweilers with slight HD (HD +) to be used for breeding, may be decided. The contention that breeding HD-free dogs creates weak-natured Rottweilers, is still to be proven. We must remember that the same argument was used when breeding measures were taken against loss of teeth and to eliminate entropion, in 1950. These problems were relatively easy to solve compared to HD.

The fact is that when inherited faults, which considerably impair movement, are bred, no healthy dogs can be obtained. The success or lack of success of eliminating HD by breeding measures depends on the measures, which the management of the ADRK decides on, based on confirmed knowledge and on the determination with which the agreed measures are pushed through and controlled.

Professor Dr K. Loeffler of the University of Hohenheim, who has written about German dogs and has given lectures for many years, is a committed scientist with regard to these problems. The members of the central evaluation centre for HD are invited by his institute every year. They exchange information and report on new findings, with the aim of promoting the breeding of

212 THE ULTIMATE ROTTWEILER

healthy dogs. All dog owners and handlers, especially pedigree breeding associations, are very grateful for this personal support.

The ADRK carries out a 'Köring' (selection for breeding suitability) in the Spring and Autumn of each year on forty Rottweilers. This means bitches can take part too – if there was only one date, they might not be able to attend due to being in season. A more up-to-date breeding suitability report sheet and selection form has been designed. Thus, the word 'Wesen', in 'Trieb-Aktionsverhalten' (Nature in draft action) has been changed. Words such as: courage, fighting drive, guarding drive and toughness have been replaced by: pleasure in taking part, calming capacity, ability to take stress, and willingness to be led on the lead. In addition, for the guard dog section, (handling behaviour) has been substituted.

In the last two years, a change in the head, and receding of the bone strength, especially with bitches, has been noted at breeding suitability tests 'Körungen' and breed shows. For this reason, head form, cheek bone setting, bone strength, and general temperament have been included in the breeding-selection reports. These criteria will be examined by the EDV and evaluated.

The dentition of the Rottweiler is tested for completeness. Dogs with missing teeth will be excluded from breeding and extra teeth will be re-written as: value neutral. There will be an exception if a dog, when first inspected, was registered as having all its teeth – then he can still be EZA selected after loosing a tooth.

BREED SHOW

After each show, the ADRK and the 'Hauptzuchtwart' (chief breeding warden) will receive a completed catalogue with the show assessments. It is then determined whether any possible inherited faults have shown up. These dogs will be noted by the EDV, and declared unsuitable for breeding in the Stud book. It will also be shown whether the same assessments were given at other shows, as some Rottweilers may have been entered at several shows.

The current, valid breeding show regulations, and the judges decree of the Association for German Dogs e.v. (VDH) are published in 'Unser Rottweiler'. This is superior to the ADRK breeding show regulations, and is binding, with the exception of the following points:

The following classes apply for ADRK special breed shows:
Puppy class: from 6- 9 months
Novice class: from 9 -12 months
Junior class: from 12-18 months
Young dog class: from 18-24 months
Open class: from 24 months
Working dog class: from 24 months with 'Ausbildungskennzeichen' (with training trials completed).

CHAMPION CLASS:
ADRK – Club Champion
VDH –European Champion
VDH – German Champion
International Champion.

In the age group up to 24 months, the highest grading is "very good"
Honorary class
Pair class
Breed group
Late breed group – all VDH requirements.

Awarding titles and 'Anwartschaften' (Champion Certificates (CC).

   The VDH can organise or permit at least one Federal Breed champion show, and one European Breed Show to be organised. Location, date and organisers are decided by the management of the VDH. The title German Federal Champion, German Federal Junior Champion, European Champion, and European junior Champion are awarded at these Breed Shows. The awarding of 'Anwartschaften' and titles is the responsibility of the breed judge. The minimum age is basically 15 months for the Champion and 9 months for the junior Champion.
   Pedigree breeding associations can, in agreement with the VDH, set the minimum age higher and impose further conditions. This does not apply for international pedigree Breed Shows. Pedigree Breeding Associations can award club-specific 'Anwartschaften' and titles at special breed shows, with the clubs using their own rules.
   The title 'German Champion', awarded by the pedigree breeding associations, can only be awarded after obtaining at least four 'Anwarschaften' under three different judges, whereby there must be at least twelve months and one day between the first and the last 'Anwartschaft'. A dog can only receive the title 'German Champion (Club)' once.
   The granting of the 'Anwartschaft' for the title 'German Champion (VDH)' is subject to the award regulations of January 1st 1972, with any subsequent amendments. These regulations are decided at the suggestion of the VDH Show Information Centre by the VDH management. The selection of dogs to be suggested for the CACIB is in accordance with the regulations of the Federation Cynologique Internationale (FCI).

THE STANDARD MODEL

1. OVERALL APPEARANCE AND TEMPERAMENT CHARACTERISTICS
a. General characteristics of the outer appearance of the breed and its particular temperament traits.
b. Size: Shoulder height in cm of dogs, bitches: weight in kg or gr of dogs, bitches.
c. Format: Ratio of shoulder height to body length.
d. Type: If the particular breed has different constitutional and breed types, these must be described in more detail. The required type must be described.
e. What the dog can be used for (with working dogs).

II. HEAD
a. Overall shape: In profile, seen from above, in proportion to the whole body, relationship between brain skull and facial skull.
b. Cranium or upper head: Upper contour in profile. Skull width (frontal eminence), frontal sulcus, parietal ledge 'Scheitelleiste', occiput 'Hinterhauptstachel'.
c. Stop: Degree of angle.
d. Muzzle: Length, depth, width, nose ridge, form and shape of lower jaw.
e. Nose: Form, Size, colour.
f. Lips: Strength, elasticity, looseness or tightness. lip angles, pigmentation.
g. Dentition: Scissor bite, pincer bite, protrusive occlusion – breed-specific.
h. Eyes: Size, colour, position, expression, setting of palpebral fissure, pigmentation of lid edges.
i. Ears: Setting, form, size.

III NECK
a. Position: Upper and lower contour.
b. Length: In relation to the body.

c. Thickness: Depth, width, muscles.
d. Skin tension: Tight, loose, dewlap formation, hair.

IV BODY
a. Overall appearance.
b. Withers: accentuation, join to neck.
c. Back: Upper contour in profile, muscles of the whole back, relation of length from chest to loins, length, width and muscles of loin part.
d. Croup: Upper contour in profile, shape, length, width and muscles.
e. Chest: Length, width, depth, rib cage, forechest (pronounced/not pronounced).
f. Stomach and flanks: Lower contour in profile, development.

V. TAIL: Docked short.

VI. FRONT LIMBS
a. Position and angulation of all limbs: In profile from the front.
b. Proportions: To whole body, different parts to one another.
c. Shoulder: Length, position, degree of muscle.
d. Upper arm: Length, position, degree of muscle.
e. Shoulder angles: Width.
f. Front foot tarsal joint: Width, thickness.
g. Front middle foot: length, width, position.
h. Front paw: Form, toe arches, toe closure, claws (pigmentation), pads.

VII REAR LIMBS
a. Position and angulation of all limbs: In profile, from the rear.
b. Proportions: To the whole body, different parts to one another.
c. Upper thigh: Length, how upright, degree of muscle.
d. Hip joint angle: Width.
e. Lower thigh: Length, position, degree of muscle, bone strength.
f. Knee joint angle: Width.
g. Ankle joint: Width, height, thickness.
h. Ankle joint angle: Width.
i. Rear middle foot: Length, width, position.
j. Rear paws: Form, toe arches, toe closure, claws (pigmentation) dew claws, pads.

VIII GAIT: Step: Trot, preferred gait.

IX. SKIN: Thick, firm, slightly elastic hair.

IX COAT: Length, hair condition, distribution, thickness, undercoat.

XI. COLOUR
a. Basic colour, particular marks or markings; permitted not permitted colours.

XII. FAULTS : Faults for the breed must be shown:
a. Serious.
b. Disqualifying.

LEADING GERMAN ROTTWEILERS
In Germany it is customary to give a full report, along with the dog's title, breeding, and any other relevant information. A number of outstanding German Rottweilers have been selected to illustrate how this system works.

BULLI V. HUNGERBUHL
ZBNr. 42465
DOB 20.08.1966
Club Champion 71 and 72.

ZTP REPORT (Suitability for Breeding Test Report)
Medium-sized powerful dog (male) with noble, thick-set head, dark eyes, small well carried ears, deeply set wide chest, tight shoulders, strong back, angulation correct, smooth trotter, (1st incisor lost through accident), full markings, scissor bite good-natured, alert, fearless, guarding and fighting drive plentiful, unaffected by shooting.

BREEDING
SIRE: Kuno v. Butzensee ZBNr. 40415
DAM: Britta v. Schlossberg ZBNr. 39075
GRANDPARENTS: Woltan v. Filstalstrand ZBNr. 37422 and Edle v. Durrbach ZBNr. 38079.
GREAT GRANDPARENTS: Castor v. Schussental ZBNr. 34476 and Bella v. Remstal ZBNr. 34197.

BULLI'S OFFSPRING
Axel v. Fusse d. Eifel ZBNr. 47829 Club Champion 75.
Astor v. Fusse d. Eifel ZBNr. 47828 Junior Best Club Champion Breed Show 74, European Champion.
Andra v. Fusse d. Eifel ZBNr. 47830 Junior Best Club Champion Breed Show 74.

KONNY V. LIEBERSBACHER HOF
ZBNr.63004
DOB 18.12.83
Club Junior Champion 85

ZTP REPORT
Large, harmonious, structure, and bone strength very good, head and neck powerful and dry, muzzle full, eyes dark brown, ears set high, very well carried, chest and forechest good, forequarters straight and well set, powerful and closed paws, back line excellent. Hindquarters very well angled and placed, well muscled. Strong root hair, beautiful, red-brown coat, free gait with long strides. Scissor bite. Self confidence, alertness, fighting drive and sturdiness high, courage and guarding drive very high. Fearlessness and temperament high, easiness to lead, suspiciousness and stimulus threshold average.

SIRE: Morro v. Steinkopf ZBNr. 57422
DAM: Isabell v. Liebersbacher Hof ZBNr. 58153
Parents of Morro: Dingo v. Schwaiger Wappen ZBNr. 51683 Int. Champion, Club Champion 80, Federal Champion 80 and 80, European Champion 82 and Esta v. Steinkopf ZBNr. 53621.
PARENTS OF ISABELL: Barry (ori) v. Waldhuck ZBNr. 47711 Performance Champion 76 and 77 and Dolli v. Liebersbacher Hof ZBNr. 47775.
KONNY'S OFFSPRING
Minka v.d. Flugschneis ZBNr. 77192 Federal Champion 93.

GOLDA V. SONNENBERG
ZBNr (Stud Book no) 63244
DOB 24.02.1984
Federal Champion 86, Club Champion 87.

Golda v. Sonnenberg: Federal Champion 86, Club Champion 87.

Photo courtesy: ADRK.

Benno v.d. Schwarzen Heide: Federal Junior Champion 87, World Champion 1990, European Champion 90.

Photo courtesy: ADRK.

Konny v. Liebersbacher Hof: Club Junior Champion 85.

Photo courtesy: ADRK.

ABOVE: Noris v. Gruntenblick: Federal Junior Champion 1990 Club Champion 90 and 91.   Photo courtesy: ADRK.

BELOW: Nemo v. Hegenbacher Landel: European Champion 89, Swiss Club Champion 90, Int. and VDH Champion.   Photo courtesy: ADRK.

ZTP REPORT
Medium size, solid, pleasing overall appearance. Powerful, beautiful head with powerful, thick-set jaws and good stop. Brown eyes, correctly carried triangular ears, pigmentation dark. Powerful, dry neck, excellent chest, very good angulation. Strong root hair with full brown, small markings. Perfect gait, tight, straight back. Scissor bite. Self confidence average. Alertness, courage, stability, fighting and guarding drive high. Unaffected by shooting.

BREEDING
SIRE: Migo v. Hurbetal ZBNr. 56903
DAM: Anja v. Sonnenberg ZBNr. 53543
PARENTS OF MIGO: Amigo v. Kressbach ZBNr. 52755 and Cora v. Hurbeta ZBNr. 49346.
PARENTS OF ANJA: Ero v. Wildberger Schloss ZBNr. 49423 and Lotte v. Sonnenberg ZBNr. 53543.

GOLDA'S OFFSPRING
Bea v.d. Teufelsbrucke ZBNr. 70957 Int Champion Federal Champion 90, 91, 93, Federal Junior Champion 88.
BEA Progeny:
Doc v.d. TeufelsbruckeZBNr. 75025 Int. Champion.
Dorele v.d. Teufelsbrucke ZBNr. 75028 Int./Dt. VDH Champion, European Champion 92, Club Champion 92 (Int/ German VDH etc.).
Falko v.d. Teufelsbrucke ZBNr. 78076 Int / Dt. VDH Champion, Club Champion 94, Austrian BSGR) + IFR - SGR 93.
Face v.d. Teufelsbrucke ZBNr. 78079 World Junior Champion 92, Club Junior Champion 92.
Graf v.d. Teufelsbrucke ZBNr. 79643 Lux. Champion, European Junior Champion 92, Federal Junior Champion 92.

BENNO V.D. SCHWARZEN HEIDE
ZBNr. 68199
DOB. 15.05.86
Federal Junior Champion 87, World Champion 1990, European champion 90.

ZTP REPORT
Medium size substantial, well built, powerful head and well formed, eyes 2b, muzzle (jaws) short, good stop, lips dark, gums slightly lighter, ear slightly folded, carried close, light throat skin, very good forechest, right depth, shoulders well placed, straight forequarters, neck short and powerful, back line very good, hindquarters powerful, well angulated, root hair, rust-brown, clear markings, smooth and free movement, long strides, left not stepping through completely, scissor bite. Self confidence, alertness, robustness high, fighting and guarding drive very high. Unaffected by shooting.

BREEDING
SIRE: Santo v. Schwaiger Wappen ZBNr. 62052 World Champion 86
DAM: Zecke v. Schwaiger Wappen ZBNr. 68603 European Champion 89 and 90
Parents of Santo: Dingo v. Schwaiger Wappen ZBNr. 51683 Int. Champion, Club Champion 80 Federal Champion 80 and 81 European Champion 82 and Itta v. Zimmerplat ZBNr. 54711 Int. Champion, World Champion 81, Club Champion 82.
PARENTS OF ZECKE: Hassan v. Konigsgarten ZBNr. 56895 Club Champion 85 and Itta v. Zimmerplatz ZBNr. 54711 Int. Champion, World Champion 81, Club Champion 82.
Grandfather of Dingo and Hassan Ives Eulenspiege ZBNr. 48232.

NEMO V. HEGENBACHER LANDEL
ZBNr. 68989
DOB 05.09.86
European Champion 89, Swiss Club Champion 90 Int. and VDH Champion.

ZTP REPORT
Large, with very good bone strength, ears well carried, eye colour 2b, marking ("Brand") good in colour, slightly less marked at chest, interspersed with black at the metacarpals. Very good pigmentation. Powerful paws, solid topline. The hindquarters are well muscled with sufficiently good angulation. Flowing and powerful in movement. Teeth complete. Self confidence and alertness high. Courage and guarding drive very high. Fighting drive and stability high. Fearlessness high, temperament high, ease to being led, suspiciousness, and stimulus threshold average.

BREEDING
SIRE: Duuk v. de. Nedermolen NL ZBNr. A0039 Int and Nl Champion, Winner 81, Nl Club Champion 82, 83, 84
DAM: Ria v. Echterdingen ZBNr. 63126 Federal Champion 85
PARENTS OF DUUK: Axel v. de. Nedermolen NL ZBNr. 780446 and Nuschka v. Rodehof ZBNr. 51983.
PARENTS OF RIA: Casar v. Hegenbacher Landel ZBNr. 56422 and Olgar v. Echterdingen ZBNr. 58980 USA Club champion, USRC Champion.

NORIS V. GRUNTENBLICK
ZBNr. 73857
DOB 03.12.88
Federal Junior Champion 1990, Club Champion 90 and 91.

ZTP REPORT
Large, strong bones, outstanding type, very good head, correct, medium heavy ears. Eye colour 2b, dark mouth pigmentation. Correct root hair. Deep brown markings, slightly less defined at the chest. Correct chest depth and width. Correct shoulders. Forehand set and angled correctly. Straight back line, correct angulation at rear hand. Flowing and free movement. Scissor bite. Self confidence, alertness and robustness high. Courage, fighting and guarding drive very high. Unaffected by shooting.

BREEDING
SIRE: Falko v. Gruntenblick ZBNr. 62273
DAM: Addi v. Herrenholz ZBNr. 66908
PARENTS OF FALKO: Kei v. Tengen ZBNr. 52412 and Bea v.d. Hembachbrucke ZBNr. 56263 European Champion 1984.
PARENTS OF ADDI: Harras v. Sternbogen ZBNr. 60136 and Face v. Gruntentenblick ZBNr. 62226 Federal Champion 1987.

NORIS'S OFFSPRING
Konan v. Hennekamp ZBNr. 83257, Club Junior Champion 1994.
Jana v.d. Bleichsteasse ZBNr. 83037, Club Junior Champion 1994.

Chapter Sixteen

THE ROTTWEILER IN THE UK

INFLUENTIAL BRITISH BLOODLINES

CHESARA
This first selection of influential bloodlines is due to the inspiration of Judy and Larry Elsden of the famous Chesara kennel. They changed the face of the Rottweiler by turning him into a smart, short-backed, show dog, with a stunning outline and a strong clean head. In the UK, this is now known as the 'Chesara type', and I would say that this bloodline is behind every successful Rottweiler kennel in the UK.

In 1965 the Elsdens imported Ch. Chesara Dark Luther, who sired four Champions. The Elsdens were aware that there were improvements to be made in the British Rottweiler, and so they went to Sweden where, in 1967, they imported (in Larry Elsden's own words) "a medium-sized, short, strong-backed, dog with good topline, short croup, with correct tail set, neat, well-placed ears, a dry head of correct proportions, with a very appealing expression". This dog was the famous Ch. Chesara Akilles. He sired ten Champions, and was instrumental in evolving the breed as we now know it today.

The next step was the importation of litter brother and sister, Torro and Tara Triomfator from Chesara. Tara was the dam of Top Stud Dog 1981, 1982, Chesara Dark Herod. Herod was not the most glamorous of dogs, but he served as a good template who certainly proved his worth as a sire. Torro sired Ch. Chesara Dark Roisterer (sire of Ch. Pendley Goldfinch). Herod mated a Roisterer daughter which produced Ch. Chesara Dark Charles.

Ch. Chesara Dark Charles: Top Stud Dog All Breeds 1983. This Rottweiler, bred by Judy and Larry Elsden, had a huge impact on the development of the modern Rottweiler.

Photo: Diane Pearce.

CH. CHESARA DARK CHARLES
Critique by Judge Ann Evans-Wallet (Poirot).   Limit Dog (10)
1. Elsdens' Chesara Dark Charles.
"Handsome male with a decided style about him. Medium size, beautifully balanced, plenty of bone and substance. Attractive masculine head, dark eyes, strong, well-arched neck, excellent topline and quarters, which he uses to advantage. Was happy to award his second CC and also BOB (a popular win judging by the applause)."
Charles was the product of line-breeding to carefully selected stock. He passed on all of the qualities of his ancestry to his progeny throughout successive generations. He was the ultimate in 'breed type'. He received the great accolade of Top Stud Dog All Breeds, 1983, which meant that he had produced more Challenge Certificate winners than any other stud dog in any other breed. This record still stands today! He continued to stay on top by being Top Stud in 1984 and 1985. Not only did he sire five Champions, he also left a legacy which can be seen in today's modern pedigrees, with the successful kennels line-breeding to Charles.

CH. CAPRIDO MINSTREL AT POTTERSPRIDE
Critique by Judge Terry McHaffie.   Open dog (6).
1. Slade's Ch. Caprido Minstrel of Potterspride.
"I was surprised to have been afforded the privilege of submitting this dog to examination, he has been criticised for his ring behaviour, no one present today could not say that the dog did not behave correctly, nor did I expect to handle him as required. He was subjected to the fullest inspection, and I was unduly impressed by the dog's style, utter male arrogance, yet under handler control, he is surely the best male being shown today. Correct size, has substance, yet not overdone anywhere. His head has strength and true type. I would prefer a cleaner neck. Correct shoulder placement, level strong and well-muscled back, correct rear angulation, broad thighs, very well-muscled, correct brisket proportions and, in consequence, he moved with very good drive, full use of stifle and hock, a most worthy Champion CC."

Critique by Judge Barbara Butler (Upend).   Open Dog (3)
1. Slade's Ch. Caprido Minstrel Of Potterspride CC & BOB.
"I have always liked this dog, totally male, arrogant bearing, beautiful head, full correct mouth, lovely neck and shoulders, correct topline and proportions of height to length, powerful driving movement, disappointed that he did not go ON to the Group!"
  Minstrel was bred by Mrs Dot Skinner. He had a reputation due to his anti-social behaviour, but he was an asset to the breed in being an 'Improver' , producing extremely low hip scores, to a large variation, of bitches from different bloodlines. He was Top Rottweiler in 1983 and the third generation of Top Stud Dog 1986, making a record of grandfather through to grandson, dominating the breed for six years of successful producers, and the fifth generation of 0:0 hip scores. Minstrel produced four top-producing sons: Ch. Upend Gallant Theodoric, Owner/Breeder Barbara Butler; His Masters Voice at Potterspride, Breeder Mrs R. Pool, Owner Mr and Mrs Smith; Pendley Jacob of Charledene, Breeders Mrs and Miss Yates, Owner Mrs L Dene; Ch. Potterspride Pure & Free, Breeder/Owner Mrs Vi Slade.

UPEND
Barbara Butler is most certainly an all-round dog person, having bred Champions in several different breeds, and has both shown and worked her dogs. She has bred four Champions, and her satellite kennel, Amatol, bred two Champions for Chris and Hazel Cully.
CH. UPEND GALLANT THEODORIC
Critique by Judge Joyce Summers (Nygra). Open Dog (15)

1. Butler's Upend Gallant Theodoric CC & BOB.
"A lovely dog, I judged last year when a youngster, has developed into a well-balanced, strong-boned, first-class dog. Really good head, dark eyes, well-set ears, good front, strong, short back, excellent hindquarters, tight feet, movement was, again, without flashiness but true and sound, putting his feet exactly where they should be, a dog who could obviously work all day. I hope that it won't be long before he gets his well deserved third." Theo produced five Champions and six Champion grandchildren. He will always be remembered for being a fine ambassador of the breed. With his owner, he can still be seen raising money for Rottweiler Welfare, either pulling a cart or wearing a harness with a collection box on either side. A dog with a superb character!

This extremely successful Upend line was a combination of Minstrel bred to a Ch. Ausscott Hasso Vom Marchenwald daughter, Upend Gay Jenny CDEX. Her mother was a daughter of the great Ch. Chesara Akilles.

CH. AUSSCOTT HASSO V. MARCHENWALD
Hasso was imported by the late Gordon McNeil when he returned from the forces in Germany. This Rottweiler was by Int. Ch. Elko Vom Kastanienbaum out of Cora V Reichernbachle. He sired six Champions and four Champion grandchildren.

Ch. Ausscott Covergirl was later exported to Canada gaining her title in two countries. She was mated to her father and produced Mrs Butler's Ch. Ausscot Franzell From Upend.

CH. UPEND GALLANT YNIS
Critique by Elina Haapaniemi.   Open Dog (16)
1 Culley's Upend Gallant Ynis of Amatol.
"Certainly one of the most exciting Rottweilers I have judged. So full of breed type and everything about him oozing Rottweiler Dog! Very alert, and very much on his toes. Beautiful head and expression, well-made and super move. I was happy to hand him the ticket, and even more pleased when I learned that it was his third. BOB on the referee, Mr Michael Quinney's, decision. Looked good in the Group, where he was short-listed."

Ynis indeed inherited his grandfather's (Minstrel's) ring presence! He produced three Champions. However, he later became the subject of a litigation, due to his owners' marriage break-up, and was not used at stud until the dispute was solved. He was then nine years old, so the dog's producing capabilities were never put to the test.

Ynis produced three Champion males: Ch. Abucadra Firewood, Ch. Tabias Aardvant Gallant and Ch. Amatol Double Dictata – none of which have yet made their mark as a stud dog. Hasso also produced Mrs H. Wilson's Ch. Gbos Gaytimes, bred by Gladys Ogilvy Shepard, who held the bitch breed record for CCs, with a total of fourteen – a record which stood for ten years.

PANEVORS
Owned by Mr and Mrs Hammond, breeder of four Champions. The Hammonds are probably best known as the founders of the Northern Rottweiler Club and Northern Rottweiler Rescue. In their days of showing, they produced from their Bulli daughter Gamegards Zenith of Panevor (ex Ch. Ausscott Hasso) two Champions from one litter. Ch. Panevors Proud Kinsman produced Ch. Panevors Proud Chicasaw, owned by the Godwins, and Kinsman's sister Ch. Kamille produced the Andersons' Ch. Panevors Proud Marksman of Jarot.

The Andersons bred their Kinsman daughter to a Chesara Dark Herod ex Kamille son, and this line-bred mating produced Jarot the Hooligan. He was never shown, but I remember seeing him as a youngster. He was quite a plain-headed dog, but behind the collar emerged a superbly constructed male. He was bred to a Ch. Upend Theodoric daughter and produced the Crufts BOB winner Ch. Crown Prince of Gallah, bred by Mr Tomny. Hooligan was also bred to the Pillings'

Coroline Cascade (sister to the breed record holder Ch. Rudi Anton Balli – 28CCs) and produced a second Champion, Ch. Rjans Country Sunshine.

ROSTOCK
Breeder of two Champions. I have to mention this kennel, as there has been a great deal of confusion as to the 'real' breeder of the next batch of Minstrel progeny, due to the fact that breeder Rosemary Pool did not own a KC affix at the time of producing her first litter. The foundation bitch was Poirot Katrina (Poirot The Ferryman ex Ch. Poirot Edwina), bred by Ann Evans Wallet. One of the stars from this litter were Mrs Pool's own Ch. Molly Moppet From Rostock. She was a beautiful bitch of superb breed type, who won a total of seven CCs. She was bred her half-brother, Ch. Potterspride Pure & Free, and produced one CC winner, Rostock Fancy Freida, who, when exported to Jamaica became a Champion, and on her arrival produced a good litter to Pinches' Ch. Cuidado The Ladies Man.

   Molly Moppet was not the most fertile of bitches and failed to produce after her second litter. Her owner tried her with several different dogs but to no avail – a great shame, considering the producing capabilities of her littermates! P. Katrina was mated to Ch. Rottsann Golden Venture and produced the Wrights' Rostock Duty Free. She was only bred once, by Stuart and Debbie Wright, and the sire was Ch. Potterspride Pure & Free. She produced a good-sized litter, and three pups were to hit the show ring. At this point, when the progeny were under twelve months old, the owners suffered a marriage break-up. The dogs were sold, apart from the dog pup, who was going through his 'legs and wings' at this time. The dam, R. Duty Free, was spayed and put into a pet home, as Debbie Wright decided she would give up showing completely. Stuart Wright, a complete novice, kept Sergeant, the puppy dog, who took him all of the way to the top. Ch. Carrilana Sergent Pepper took Reserve Best in Show at the Wales Championship Show in 1994. The litter sister, C. Love Me Do, was also a CC winner. S., another bitch from Rosemary Pool's breeding was to bite the dust!

AYLESHAM BEAUTY AT POTTERSPRIDE
Another top winning bitch, a sister to Molly. She was also mated by her owner, Vi Slade, to her own Ch. Potterspride Pure & Free, and produced Mrs Spence's Ch. Potterspride Amazing Alice At Nibthwait. In fact, both the breeders Vi and Bob Slade (Potterspride) thought this bitch was so outstanding that they both gave her a CC!

FERNWOOD
MODESTY BLAZE AT FERNWOOD
The Fernwood kennel, breeder of three Champions, owned the next two littermates. Modesty Blaze was shown as a youngster and was awarded a Reserve CC. She was bred to Ch. Yorlanders Solid Gold and produced one CC winner, Fernwood Bewitched. She was bred to her uncle, a His Masters Voice son, Ch. Fernwood Enforcer. This resulted in the Fernwood 'F' litter, producing Debbie Rowell's top winner, Ch. Fernwood Fallon, and brother, Irish Ch. Fernwood Firecracker, who is still awaiting his UK title.

   His Masters Voice has produced five Champions, two to the Smiths' own foundation bitch, Pleasley Princess, a Poirot The Ferryman great grand-daughter. Ch. Fernwood Arrabella, Top Brood bitch 1993 and 1994, was from the repeat mating with Ch. Fernwood Enforcer (father of F. Fallon).

HIS MASTERS VOICE AT POTTERSPRIDE
Critique by Barry Clark (Dortmund).
Smiths' His Master Voice at Potterspride.

ABOVE: Ch. Rudi Anton Bali: Top winning Rottweiler of all time, with a tally of 28 CCs. He was the first Rottweiler to win BIS at a Championship Show. Owned by Mr and Mrs T.A. Woodward.
Photo: Anne Roslin-Williams.

ABOVE: Ch. Upend Gallant Theodoric: Sire of five Champions and six Grand Champions. Owned and bred by Barbara Butler.
Photo courtesy: Barbara Butle

BELOW: Ch. Carpido Minstrel at Potterspride: Sire of four top-producing sons. Owned by Vi Slade.
Photo courtesy: Vi Slade.

BELOW: Ch. Potterspride Pure & Free: Top Rottweiler 1989, and sire of four Champions to date Owned and bred by Vi Slade.
Photo courtesy Vi Slad

ABOVE: Ch. Kensix Clingel At Panelma, owned by Pat and Maggie Bryant.
Photo courtesy: Pat and Maggie Bryant.

ABOVE: Ch. Fantasa Red Riding Hood: Top Dog 1991, a member of the record breaking 'Red litter'.
Photo courtesy: Liz Dunhill.

BELOW: Liz Dunhill and her Fantasa Rottweilers.

Photo: John Hartley.

"He is another favourite of mine. Classic Rottweiler head, good width between ears. Strong muzzle, small ears and darkest of eyes, correct mouth pigment, good reach of neck, but is carrying a little spare flesh over the shoulders which otherwise spoils a lovely neck and shoulder line. Firm back and croup, plenty of substance. Tan could be a little darker. Very true front and rear movement. Excellent overall angulation, seems to be coming back to his true form – well handled." Mike and Maureen Smith did not buy this dog from breeder Mrs Pool, but from Vi Slade, who had purchased three puppies from the same litter, of which two were males. She kept the brother, The Magician's Apprentice At Potterspride, and sold H.M.V. to the Smiths. Unfortunately, Magicians Apprentice was never a producer like his brother. H.M.V. produced two Champions in one litter for the Debrinks "Hoys": Astral Taurus and Astral Libra, and a first Champion for the Andrews in Ch. Kewmanor Golden Marksman, who was out of a Rottsann bitch. There are more H.M.V. progeny waiting in the wings, so who can predict the sum total of Champions!

POTTERSPRIDE
Vi Slade, breeder of three Champions, was the owner of Ch. Caprido Minstrel Of Potterspride. Her foundation bitch was a Ch. Gamegards Bulli vd. Waldachquelle daughter. Her most productive daughter was sold to the Shaws, who was Potterspride Bronze Angel ex Ch. Minstrel. She produced a litter of three Champions. One of these was Vi's own Ch. Rich Bitch of Potterspride, a top winning bitch of her time and the other two being Ch. McGuire Esquire, owned by the Blundens, and Ch. Glint of Gold at Ereland, owned by Jane Christiensen

CH. POTTERSPRIDE PURE & FREE
Breeder/owner Mrs Vi Slade.
Critique by Elina Haapaniemi.   Limit dog 23,
1. Slade's Potterspride Pure & Free.
"Medium-sized dog, powerfully built, excellent strong bone. I was taken with his head qualities and he was an excellent showman. Again an energetic, purposeful mover. Won the Reserve CC in excellent company."
   This dog has produced four Champions, with more of today's progeny awaiting their titles.

PENDLEY
Breeder of four Champions.
Pendley breeding is behind most of today's successful kennels. The line goes back to a Ch. Akilles grandson, Ch. Borgvaale Lion City River of Ritonshay, bred by Pat Lanz. The Pendley affix is owned by Mrs June and Miss Joanne Yates. Joanne is a police dog handler, and spent most of her childhood years after school, working in the kennels of Pat Lanz, learning all about the love of her life, Rottweilers. The Pendley foundation bitch was, of course, from Mrs Lanz's breeding – Ch. Nedraw Black Sunshine, bred by Fred Warden from Ireland. Lion City River and his litter sister Borgvaale Venus were respectively bred to Borgvaale Sea Witch and Torro Triomfator from Chesara. Venus produced Ch. Chesara Dark Roisterer (bred by Joan Adams) and Lion City threw Ch. Nedraw Black Sunshine. These two dogs were bred and produced the famous Pendley Bird litter of Ch. Pendley Goldfinch, owned by Trevor and Teresa Killick of Travillon Rotts; Pendley Peregrine, owned by Chris and Norma Window (Hanbar Rotts), and Joanne's favourite bitch, Pendley Skylark, who is behind all of today's Pendley winners. A repeat mating produced Pendley Sunshione Boy.

PENDLEY JACOB OF CHARLEDANE
Owned by Lesley Dene.
This dog, a Minstrel son, was shown very lightly, but as a youngster was always consistently

placed. His owner who was not really interested in the show scene and, suffering from a great many personal problems, never really had the incentive to show the dog. Jacob was not used a great deal at stud either. I was eventually allowed to use the dog on Regal Romance – after a thorough cross-examination! I was pleased that I persevered, as the mating produced Top Bitch Ch. Fantasa Clockwork Orange, whose progeny are winning well in the show ring.

The first Jacob son to hit the high spots was Ch. Ulsan Lord Of The Forest At Torvager. His litter sister, Ulsan the Mambo Sun, was not a Champion, although, in my opinion, she should have been. This pair, bred by Paul Jones, were both excellent animals. Jacob produced in his few litters such quality that it is a shame that more people did not persist and take advantage of his breeding. I have used him again, with excellent results.

He was mated to a Ch. Pendley Jasmin daughter, an uncle/niece mating, and produced Ch. Pendley Winston.

CH. PENDLEY WINSTON
Critique by Liz Dunhill, Fantasa.   Post Grad Dog
1. Yates' Pendley Winston.
"All I have to say is that this dog gives me 'goose bumps' every time I see him. Super clean, sharp outline, presenting masculinity with elegance. Superb chiselled head of excellent balance, clean and dry. Dark almond eye giving tranquil expression. Excellent flat upper skull, good ear set, well-filled foreface and cheeks. Deep muzzle of correct proportions, excellent bite and pigment. Good reach of neck, tight and clean, well laid shoulder, excellent bone and feet. Topline held like a board, both standing and moving; well angulated rear. An extremely well-muscled dog in super coat, his side gait is exceptional with ground covering scopy movement, he still has much more to come, his only fault in my opinion is that I do not own him! Pleased to award him his first CC." Ch. Pendley Winston is still in his infancy as a stud dog but, in my opinion, he will be the father of many Champions. Many of today's current winners are by Winston; his first litter was to my own Ch. Fantasa Red Riding Hood, which produced Top Sire 1994 and Top Rottweiler 1994, BIS Richmond 1994 Ch. Fantasa Ultra Violet. Winston is the product of line-breeding to Pendley Skylark, sister to Ch. Pendley Goldfinch, combining Minstrel to a Ch. Chesara Dark Roisterer daughter.

CH. PENDLEY GOLDFINCH
Owned by the Killicks.
Critique by Jane Bloom, Janbicca.   Open Dog 19.
1 Killick's Ch. Pendley Goldfinch
"Lovely head, well-shaped, medium-brown eyes, giving calm expression, ears neat and well set on. Moving on his toes and giving all to his handler. Beautiful movement fore and aft, a pleasure to watch, going round a worthy Champion. I was pleased to see him head the Group CC & BOB." The sire of nine Champions and ten champion grandchildren.

YORLANDER
Breeder of two Champions.
CH. CHESARA DARK HUNTERS DAWN FROM YORLANDER
Along with the German import, Ida Von Der Mouth From Yorlander, this bitch was the foundation of the Yorlander kennel, owned by Kath Hindley.
Critique of Hunters Dawn by Bill Bromley, Heranmine.   Open Bitch (5)
1 Hindley's Ch. Chesara Dark Hunters Dawn From Yorlander.
"What more can I say about this worthy Champion that has not already been said? I saw this bitch when she was four months old and predicted a great future, and she has not let me down. Credit

due to the owners for the dedicated way that they have campaigned her. She is an outstanding bitch, full of quality, with the most delightful head and expressive eyes. Good ears and correct bite, firm topline, and very good tail set. Good front, moved well, BOB."

She was bred to Chesara Dark Herod and produced Tim and Jenny Dunhill's top winning bitch, Ch. Yorlanders Grecian Girl At Vormund. Unfortunately, she had parvovirus as a puppy and never conceived a litter. When Hunters Dawn was bred to Goldfinch, a new top stud was to emerge in the form of Ch. Yorlanders Solid Gold.

CH. YORLANDERS SOLID GOLD
Owner/breeder Kath Hindley
'Bruce' was Top Sire and Top Rottweiler 1987. Like his father, Goldfinch, he inherited superb movement.
Critique by Carl Johnson, Dicarl.   Open Dog (12).
1 Hindley's Yorlanders Solid Gold.
"Sired by Goldfinch, at four years old, this dog is fully mature and looked really great, his profile and outline nothing more than stunning. From any angle the dog is built well, benefit of a clever and experienced handler, who knows just how to present him, he drove around the ring with forward reach and hind drive. CC & BOB. I must comment on Ch. Pendley Goldfinch, who was really the star of the day. You know that, as an outsider, I couldn't have known the breeding of the stock in front of me. During the writing of this critique, looking up the breeding of the winners, I have been very satisfied to see that I did judge to type.

"I do know that Goldfinch is no longer with us, so feel I can pay some tribute to him as a sire without it being misconstrued, WHAT A DOG!"

Solid Gold, when was mated to a 'Strolling Player' ex Ida Von Der Mouth daughter, produced Top Rottweiler 1988 Ch. Romanmoor Adam for breeders Mr and Mrs Thompson. He also produced the Top Rottweiler for 1992, Ch. Fantasa Crimson Cavalier, a Ch. Regal Romance son. Ch. Solid Gold produced a total of four Champions and three Champion grandchildren.

CAPRIDO STROLLING PLAYER FROM CHESARA
Bred by Dot Skinner, owned by Judy and Larry Elsden.
James Minstrel's litter brother was shown as a youngster. He was a very well put together dog with a splendid character, masculine head, and super movement. The only reason he did not aspire to dizzy heights was that he was small. However, they say that good things come in small packages, and James certainly came up with the goods as a stud dog. He was not as extensively used as his brother, but he produced four Champions and three Champion grandchildren. His most famous son, bred by Anita Witmarsh and owned by Trina Flowers, was Ch. Svedala The Scandinavian. This dog was Best in Show at Leeds Championship Show 1994, his mother being a Bulli daughter. He produced Ch. Rottsann Forever Amber when mated to top Rottweiler Ch. Rottsann Golden Vision.

WARRIMEAD
Marie Ward's Chesara Dark Lana (Ch. Chesara Dark Julia ex Herod) made an excellent foundation for this kennel, and when bred to Strolling Player produced Ch. Dark Lana's Lass of Chesara and Ch. and Ir. Ch. Warrimead Heaven Knows Its Bellicose. When bred to Jagen Blue Andante she produced Ch. Warrimead Vienna for Stewart Hitchin. Ch Lanas Lass was bred to Ch. Romanmoor Adam and produced Ch. Warrimead Black Guard, making a total of four Champions for this kennel.

As I highlight more leading kennels it becomes apparent that success has often been based on a combination of the previous bloodlines mentioned, and those of Ch. Gamegards Bulli v.d. Waldachquelle.

CH. GAMEGARDS BULLI V.D. WALDACHQUELLE

Imported by Joan Blackmore from Germany, he was by Ch. Bulli v. Hungerbuhl Sch2, ex Anka v. Reichenbachle. In the words of Mary McPhail (Blackforest): "He came to England, and he was to prove enormously influential in the development of the breed. He was medium-sized, powerfully built, with a broad and attractive head; qualities he passed on to a high proportion of his many offspring, for he was extensively used at stud." He sired six Champions.

POIROT

Ann Evans Wallet of the Poirot kennel bred from the Bulli daughter, Jentris Nicolina Belle. Like Herod, not a star of the ring, but, again, a good template, being behind some of the best of the Poirot breeding, which graces nearly every successful kennel's pedigrees!

CH. POIROT CAMILLA

When this bitch was bred to Ch. Gbos Goshawk, she produced the famous Poirot 'F' litter:-
Poirot Francesca at Herberger, producer of Ch. Herberger Touch of Brilliance at Vanhirsh, **Poirot the Ferryman**, sire of three Champions, and four Champion grandchildren, and **Poirot Fantasa.**

ROTTSANN

Poirot Fantasa, bred by Ann Evans Wallet and owned by Carol Brady, was the foundation bitch of the Rottsann kennel, breeder of nine Champions. A most beautiful bitch with, a strong but feminine head, ultra clean outline. She was campaigned to one CC with BOB.

She was bred to the Elsdens' Chesara Dark Herod, with remarkable results – the famous Classic litter, which contained three Champions:-
Ch. Rottsann Classic Gold and **Ch. Rottsann Classic Crusader at Vormund,** owned by Tim and Jenny Dunhill. Classic Gold produced three Champions and two Champion grandchildren.
Ch. Rottsann Classic Centurian, who came from a pet home and ended up in the ownership of Bill Bromley (Heranmine). He won the Working Group at Crufts in 1983. Producer of three Champions and two Champion grandchildren.

Rottsann Classic Lines won one CC and was BIS at the Midland Rottweiler Championship Show. When mated to Goldfinch she produced the famous three Champion litter – the 'Golden litter', previously mentioned.

Rottsann Classic Cicero, who will always be known as Arthur Brady's own dog, came from the same home as Centurian. Shown very lightly, he was not extensively used at stud. But he produced one Champion, Edwina Johnson's Ch. The Astronomer.

Rottsann Classic Cascade, 1 CC, was bred once by Dennis Harding and, unfortunately, she died not long after producing her only litter to Ch. Poirot Led Zeppelin.

Rottsann Classic Crystal, the mother of Ch. Rottsann Regal Romance, was the foundation bitch of my own Fantasa kennel.

FANTASA

Breeder of eleven Champions
CH. ROTTSANN REGAL ROMANCE
Breeder Carol Brady, owner Liz Dunhill.
Critique by Elizabeth Harrap, Amafair.   Limit bitch (17)
"Rottsann Regal Romance was the star of the show, a beautiful bitch, just what I was looking for.

Medium-sized, lovely feminine head, dark eye and alert expression, good front, feet and neck, strong firm body, well-muscled and angulated quarters, level topline retained on the move, free flowing movement, has that extra sparkle and never stopped showing for a minute, very well handled – I just loved her! Delighted to award her the CC, her second, with full agreement with my co-judge BIS."

She has a remarkable record, producing eight Champions and three Champion grandchildren. She holds the record of being the only Rottweiler Bitch to have won BIS at three different Breed Club Championship Shows, and, most importantly, she was Top Brood Bitch *All Breeds* 1990, Top Working Brood in 1991, and in 1992 took the award of Top Brood Bitch *All Breeds* for the second time! Her father, Jagen Blue Andante, owned and bred by Pat and Les Price, was a very successful showman attaining top puppy. Due to a tragic accident, his show career ended, but he produced three Champions. He was sired by Ch. Janbicca The Superman, owned and bred by Jane Bloom, a Bulli son.

Regal Romance produced two Champions to Goldfinch in her first litter, Ch. Fantasa Scarlet Pimpernell and Ch. F. S. O'Harah. The second litter, to Poirot Wham, produced the record breaking 'Red litter' of four Champions: Ch. F. Shades of Red (owner Duffy), Ch. & Irish Ch. F. Simply Red (owner McEwan), Ch. F. Red Hot Lover (owner Baker), and Top Dog of 1991 Ch. Fantasa Red Riding Hood, also the mother of Ch. Fantasa Ultra Violet, Top Dog of 1994.

In her third litter to Ch. Yorlanders Solid Gold, Regal Romance produced Irish Ch. Fantasa Crimson Cardinal (owner McEwan), Ch. Fantasa Crimson Cavalier, Top Rottweiler 1992. His sister, Fantasa Crimson Cupid, was mated to Ch. Poirot Wham and produced the Top Bitch 1994 Glarvey's Ch. Fantasa Green Emerald, BOB Crufts 1994, and Trinidad Ch. Fantasa Green Peace.

Regal Romance was mated to Pendley Jacob of Charledene for her fourth litter, and the result was Ch. Fantasa Clockwork Orange Top Bitch 1992. The least successful litter was to Solid Gold's full brother, Yorlanders Jackobowski, out of a repeat mating. This produced a litter of males which were consistent winners, but there were no real stars – which disproves the myth that so long as the pedigree is the same you will get the same. In reality, all individuals in one litter or from a repeat mating will produce differently to their littermates.

POIROT THE FERRYMAN
Sire of two Champions, Grandsire of six Champions.
When you write about Ferryman, you find yourself writing about Ch. Poirot Edwina, as the success behind numerous Champions of today has evolved from the combination of the Edwina-Ferryman mating. We can go back to the Poirot 'K' litter of Katrina Karia, on which Rostock and Fernwood based their breeding, or the 'J' litter which Anne (Poirot) has successfully used in her own breeding programme. Ferryman was mated to a sister of Ch. Chesara Dark Charles, Vanhirsh Dark Secret, owned by Jane and Michael Heath of the Vanhirsh kennel, and produced two Champions in one litter for the Debrinka kennel. When mated to the Ferryman grandson, His Masters Voice At Potterspride (previously mentioned), Poirot Franchesca Ferryman's litter sister produced two Champion grandsons, Ch. Vanhirsh Black Brilliance (out of Charles' sister) and Ch. Vanhirsh April Lord, Top Rottweiler 1986. Ferryman's other Ch. daughter was bred by the Brennons' Ch. Breckley High Fidelity, owned by Jane Cristienson. This Poirot 'F' litter may not have been Champions themselves, but I do feel some of them should have been, particularly Poirot Fantasia and Ferryman. However, they have left behind a legacy which continues to breed on.

CH. POIROT WHAM
Critique by Judge Barry Clark (Dortmund).   Junior Dog (27):
1. Wallet's Poirot Wham
"Beautifully proportioned, possibly the best front of any exhibit today, classic head of correct

proportions, neat small ears, dark eye, lovely shoulder line to good depth of chest, strong topline, plenty of substance without looking coarse. Correct tan and coat texture, good rear angulation, which gave him the most effortless and true movement front and rear. Would like to have seen more sparkle, but well-handled. Reserve Best Dog and also this win gave him his Junior Warrant."

This dog was never a showman, but he was a worthy Champion; Anne longed for the overcast, rainy day when 'George' would be at his best! He was a regally bred dog. His mother, Poirot Jocana (a Charles daughter) produced Ch. Poirot Pickwick, a Crufts BOB winner, a line-bred Camilla son. When this bitch was bred to Chesara Dary Harry, son of Caprido Strolling Player of Chesara out of the most beautiful grandmother of Charles, Ch. Chesara Dark Julia – today, highly rated among breeders as possibly the epitome of Chesara females.

Unfortunately, Julia was a difficult bitch to breed, but she most certainly left a legacy in her son Harry and through Wham, another record-producing Top Stud Dog of 1991, 1992, 1993, 1994, proving how prolific the Charles line is today! Wham produced five Champions, with more today awaiting their titles. Wham produced the famous Fantasa 'Red litter', which still holds the record for the most Champions in one litter, with four gaining their titles, and Fantasa Red Alert winning 2 CCs and BOB at Crufts. This dog was retired before winning his third CC – so, perhaps, it could have been five Champions in the litter! The litter included the father of the breed record holding bitch CC winner, Ch. Fantasa White Gold, owned by the Monk family, and so ably handled to 22 CCs by Marie Monk, the father of Top Rottweiler 1991, F. Red Riding Hood, and her son (his grandson) Top Rottweiler 1994 Ch. F. Ultra Violet, and Top Bitch 1994, owned by John Glarvey, who was also BOB Crufts 1994.

He produced Ch. Romanmoor Pageant for Mr and Mrs Thompson, with Ch. Fantasa Shades of Red producing several young and up-and-coming stars for Mavis Duffy's Wannonas kennel. He also has several other CC winners. We will have to wait and see how many Champions he ultimately produces.

His father, Chesara Dark Harry, who was joint Top Puppy, would have made more of a mark on the breed if the Elsdens had not suffered the immense tragedy of having Harry and kennelmate, Chesara Dark Clare, stolen! Despite a search which was even featured on national TV, the two dogs were never recovered. The breed suffered a great loss. Harry only mated a few bitches before he disappeared. He was another great dog from the Chesara stable. Indeed, he could have been the next Chesara Top stud dog.

CUIDADO

Another kennel that bred along the same Chesara-Bulli mix was Kate Pinches of Cuidado, which produced five Champions. Kate owned the Charles daughter Cuidado Cloud Cuckoo, who, when bred to the Bulli grandson Ch. Fryans Advocator, produced a litter of three Champions: Ch. Cuidado My Girl (owned by the Sprungs), Ch. Am. Ch. Cuidado Je Taime (who won BOB at Crufts at six months of age and then had a very successful career in the USA), and Ch. Cuidado The Ladies Man, whose daughter, C. Dizzy Miss Lizzy is awaiting her title. The product of line-breeding, a Ch. C. Je Taime grandson to a Ch. C. My Girl daughter produced Ch. Bewize Imagination, bred by Barbara Morris and owned by her sister, Bev.

Kate also has the Jentris Nicolina Bell daughter ex Poirot Brigadier, Poirot Delila of Cuidado. She was bred to Poirot The Ferryman and produced Ch. and Ir. Ch. Cuidado The Dandy – another example of line-breeding. C. Cloud Cuckoo was bred to Ch. Upend Gallant Theodoric and produced Am. Ch. Cuidado Marathon Man. He was bred to a Ch. Minstrel ex Cuidado Double Agent of Adoram daughter, Adoram Violet. This mating produced Kate's top winning bitch Ch. Keyhole of Cuidado (bred by Mrs Jones). This bitch was line-bred back to Ch. Cuidado The Ladies Man and produced Ch. Dizzy Miss Lizzy. Tragically, Keyhole Kate died at the age of four

– a great loss to the breed. Her grandson, the Ch. Fantasa Ultra Violet son, Cuidado Another Hero was Top Puppy in 1994, and litter sister, C. Simply The Best took a Puppy Group at Championship Show level. Cuidado breeding is also behind the Amicus kennel, owned by Elaine and Dennis Caine.

AMICUS
Breeder of three Champions
CH. ANNIE GET YOUR GUN OF AMICUS
This bitch by Ch. Rottsann Classic Centurian ex Cuidado Private Eye (a Poirot Brigadier daughter) was the foundation for the Amicus kennel. When line-bred to Ch. Rottsann Golden Venture, she produced Ch. Amicus Othello, owned by Mrs Brawn. He, in turn, when bred to Cuidado Threes a Crowd of Amicus (Ch. Rottsann Classic Centurian ex Cuidado My Funny Valentine, Advocator daughter) produced Ch. Amicus Charisma. When Ch. Annie Get Your Gun was bred to Ch. Yorlanders Solid Gold she produced Ch. Amicus Calypso.

CH. POIROT EDWINA
Another fine representative from the Poirot stable, she was a Crufts BOB winner in her own right, and left behind a dynasty when bred to the Nicolina Bell grandson, Poirot The Ferryman. This Edwina/Ferryman mating is behind The Poirot 'K' litter, which produced Poirot Karia. When she was bred to the Camilla grandson, Ch. Rottsann Classic Crusader of Vormund, she produced Ch. Karias Volcanic Eruption. Eruption in turn produced one Champion son in Mr Mycock's Ch. Rowtaire Black Knight. He was totally line-bred, his mother being a Classic Centurian Ch. Edwina daughter. To date, this dog has never been used at stud. The other combination of Edwina/Ferryman was litter sister Poirot Katrina, the foundation bitch of Rosemary Pool's Rostock kennel.

JAGEN
Breeders of nine Champions, Les and Pat Price's foundation bitch Kenstaff Jaega produced three Champions from a total of eighteen puppies. From her litter to Peter and Joyce Radley's Danish import, Ch. Castor of Intissari (Int. Ch. Farro v.h. Brantpark Sch 2 ex Danish Ch. Ursula PH AK) she produced Ch. Jagen Dust My Blues. Brother, Ch. Jagen Mister, an ultra-typical Castor son, was the first Rottweiler to win a round of the Pedigree Chum Champions Stakes. He was also a Group winner, and Top Rottweiler 1980. When Kenstaff Jaega was bred to Poirot Brigadier, she produced Ch. Jagen Asterix.

   The next producing bitch came in the guise of a Jaega daughter, Jagen Midnite Blue. She was bred to a Bulli son, Ch. Janbicca the Superman. This mating produced Ch. Jagen Blue Aria, mother of Ch. Ir. Ch. Jagen Blue Chicago Bear, owned by Billy McCallum from Northern Ireland. This mating was the other way round to Ch. Rottsann Regal Romance, one of three Champions produced by Jagen Blue Andante – the other being Ch. Lara Vorfelder Beauty of Lloydale and Barbara Butler's Ch. Upend Gay Quilla. J.B. Andante was a top winning puppy of his time, and most certainly would have become the second Champion for Midnite Blue, but tragedy struck when Andante nearly lost his hind leg and was retired from the show ring.

   Les and Pat felt that the British gene pool was limited and so decided to import stock from Germany. These bitches were integrated into the Jagen breeding programme in order to give some new blood. The fruits of these breedings are now beginning to emerge.

PANELMA
This is another Ch. Charles story. Pat and Maggie Bryant's bitch, Panelma The Special Lady (of Borgvaale breeding) when bred to Ch. Chesara Dark Charles produced another good litter

including Ch. Panelma The Highwayman, the winner of 10 CCs. When mated to a German import, he produced the Bryants' Ch. Kensix Clingel At Panelma.

When Ch. Panelma The Adventurer was bred to Ch. Poirot Edwina, he produced Ch. Poirot Quizical, and my favourite, Panelma The Pirate, who so tragically died at a young age, and would most certainly would have become a Champion.

POIROT BRIGADIER

Last but not least comes Poirot Brigadier – again all roads leading to Rome! Brigadier is the sire of three Champions and four Champion grandchildren. He is the father of: Ch. Poirot Camilla, Ch. Linguards Jupitor (father of Potterspride Bronze Angel, dam of three Champions), Cuidado Private Eye (sire of Ch. Cuidado Annie Get Your Gun Of Amicus), Linguards Jacquiline (mother of Ch. and Can. Ch. Auscott Covergirl and Ch. Ausscott Donnerstag Desera), Poirot Delilah of Cuidado (who produced Ch. & Ir Ch. Cuidado The Dandy), and Taroh Tamarind (who produced Ch. Toroh Rowina at Gibos) bred by Helen Wilson, owned by Gladys Ogilvy Shepherd.

Another top winning Ch. Camilla son was Brenda Toe's Ch. Poirot Led Zepplin. He was the son of the Chesara bred Janivicjs Alexis. 'Harvey' won well, but failed to produce a Champion son. His son Oliria Harveys Mean Machine, owned and bred by the Monk family, attained two CCs, and produced a Champion son, Ch. Rottsann Soldier Blue of Oleria, when mated to Carol Brady's top winning bitch, the Goldfinch daughter, Ch. Rottsann Golden Vision. Led Zepplin's litter sister, Poirot Leonora, owned by the Riches, was mated to the Reserve in Group at Crufts, Ch. Janbicca The Superman son, Ch. Isala The Saxon – himself Reserve Group winner at Crufts. The result was the Group winning bitch, Ch. Rockanor Royal Adventure. Her litter sister, Rockanor Royal Amber, when mated to Ch. Upend Gallant Theodoric produced the Greys' Ch. Farnmoor Apach Soo at Blackgrange – a truly beautiful bitch of superb breed type and balance.

MAKING THE CHOICE

While compiling these profiles of leading dogs, I have tried to include most of the kennels of influence *today*, some of whose true potential is yet to be felt upon the breed. Current breeders of great success today may pull out of the breed tomorrow for whatever reason. The breeders of yesteryear have left a solid foundation for us to follow. Like all countries, our gene pool is becoming very tight, and I feel that progress is to be found with those who dare to venture to foreign climes. I have given some prime examples of British breeding at its best. For the more analytical, it is interesting to see which kennels have chosen the correct combination of breedings which have made them and their 'satellite' kennels successful. There are also those kennels who have made a good start in their breeding careers, and have failed to proliferate the line left to them by their breeders. You can be given the best bloodlines in the world, but if you fail to understand the basics of dog breeding, you will never progress!

Chapter Seventeen

THE ROTTWEILER IN NORTH AMERICA

DEVELOPMENT OF THE BREED

Harras, Erno, Bengo, Dux, Fetz, Falk, Axel, Quelle, Afra and Priska were household names among the handful of US Rottweiler owners and breeders in the mid-sixties to the seventies. These were the stud dogs and brood bitches who helped set the phenotype and genotype of the American-bred Rottweilers. We shall always owe a debt of gratitude to those early American breeders (Rodsdens, Panamint, and Freeger, to mention a few) for their foresight in bringing such dominant stock to the United States. Even thirty-five years later, an in-depth examination of most pedigrees can be traced back to these important dogs and bitches.

The Rottweiler was virtually unknown in the United States until after World War Two. Returning soldiers brought back a few dogs for companions. Very few owners were breeding or exhibiting. As late as 1958, The American Kennel Club registered only 58 Rottweilers. By contrast, over 104,000 were registered in 1993. This period of development of the Rottweiler, the late sixties through to the seventies, was of major significance, and the effects are still seen today. Scattered across the country from coast to coast at that time were small breeders. For many, it was the golden age of Rottweilers. The strengths and weaknesses of the German bloodlines gradually became evident. We were all in a learning mode, all trying to breed good dogs. There was a sincere love of the breed and concern for its well-being on the part of every owner. There was little monetary consideration, for how could one sell puppies if nobody knew what a Rottweiler was?

Continuing through the eighties, the Kastanienbaum, Steinkopf, Brabantpark and Schwaiger Wappen bloodlines were exported to the US, along with some Swedish and English dogs to expand and strengthen the gene pool. Some breeders followed a definite generational line-breeding programme; others outcrossed to the then currently winning stud dogs. The importation of primarily German and Dutch stud dogs and bitches continues to this day.

With the breed's increased popularity during the 1980-1990 period, greater emphasis was placed on the Rottweiler as a "working dog". This prompted more owners to train their dogs in all phases of obedience: a title before the registered name signified "beauty"; a title after the registered name signified "working ability".

Another important factor which influenced many bloodlines was the adoption by some regional/local clubs of a mandatory Code of Ethics. The Code of Ethics (with variations between clubs) was devised primarily to set out guidelines for breeding practices. Great emphasis was placed on the dog or bitch being HD-Free (Hip Dysplasia Free) prior to breeding. The Orthopedic Foundation of America (OFA) was designated as the central agency for evaluating X-rays of dogs over two years of age. After several revisions in methodology, gradings of normal hips were designated as Excellent, Good and Fair. A permanent OFA number was then assigned to each dog after the age of two. A rating of Borderline or Dysplastic meant the dog should not be bred. The services of the OFA have been expanded in recent years to include certification of elbows.

The Code of Ethics also covered numerous other criteria, such as not breeding a dog or bitch with any disqualifying faults, not selling puppies without a sales contract and, obviously, not breeding before two years of age. Any member of a COE club is subject to censure and/or suspension from the club if there is a proven violation of the Code of Ethics brought to the attention of the club's Grievance Committee. Peer pressure thus became a tool which affected many breeding programmes.

EVALUATING THE ROTTWEILER

In the limited space available, it is impossible to give a full and fair representation of the important dogs, bloodlines or kennels in North America. The geographical area is so large, and definitions of success can depend on the criteria by which dogs and kennels are being judged. Therefore, after giving considerable thought to this project, I decided to present some of the Top Producers in the Breed, according to The American Rottweiler Club's Annual Production Awards (May, 1994). The statistics speak for themselves. In 1985, Catherine Thompson, a charter member of The American Rottweiler Club, initiated the following criteria for dogs and bitches:

"These awards are open to all Rottweilers, living or dead, that have distinguished themselves by their American titled offspring. As production points accumulate, the individual sire or dam may receive the next higher award.

   "To be eligible for any award, a Rottweiler must meet the following four (4) requirements:
1. have produced at least one (1) AKC Champion of Record
2. have produced at least one (1) advanced obedience titled dog (CDX, TDX, or SchH 1)
3. have produced at least three (3) titled offspring
4. have met the point requirements."

BRONZE PRODUCTION AWARD: Males 25 points, Females 15 points.
SILVER PRODUCTION AWARD: Males 50 points, Females 30 points.
GOLD PRODUCTION AWARD: Males 75 points, Females 45 points.

Production Points are calculated as follows:

AKC Champion	3 points
AKC CD	1 point
AKC CDX	2 points (3 points total, CD & CDX)
AKC UD	3 points (6 points total, CD & CDX & UD)
AKC OTCH	3 points (9 points total, CD & CDX & UD & OTCH)
AKC TD	2 points
AKC TDX	2 points (3 points total, TD & TDX)
SchH I	1 point
SchH II	2 points (4 points total, I & II)
SchH III	2 points (6 points total, I & II & III)
FH	2 points

The emphasis on Obedience titles is obvious. Without an advanced obedience title earned by an offspring, the dog or bitch cannot become a Bronze, Silver or Gold Production Winner. Unfortunately, there are many outstanding Rottweilers with outstanding bloodlines, with exceptional Champion offspring, who have not earned an advanced obedience title and who are not included in this chapter.

The most perfectly created Rottweiler can only become "great" if he or she produces well, and the resultant offspring are developed to their full potential and then shown in both the conformation and Obedience ring. It must be emphasized that without the dedication of the breeder, the owner, the handler, and the trainer, who together work hundreds, even thousands, of hours with the dogs from puppyhood to and through adulthood, there would be no reason for awards. As of May, 1994 there were 41 gold sires and dams, 64 silver sires and dams and 144 bronze sires and dams.

As previously mentioned, this system began in 1985 but covers dogs and bitches going back to the seventies. All owners of Gold and Silver sires and dams were contacted (many individuals owned or had owned more than one of the above). The scope of the "interview by mail" covered both imported and American-bred dogs. Each owner or breeder/owner was furnished a list of possible subjects to address.

I requested a pedigree review of the dog/bitch, i.e. of their sire, dam, grandsire or granddam. If the owner was the breeder of the dog or the bitch, I wanted to know how many generations back their bloodlines extended. I wanted to know what the owner felt were his/her dog's major contributions to the breed in the United States. What were its strengths and, conversely, its weaknesses? Were these attributes passed on to its progeny? Were the first generation progeny stronger or weaker than succeeding generations? If the dog or the bitch was an import, I wanted to know the primary consideration for acquiring the dog or the bitch. The same questions relating to strengths, weaknesses, and the ability to pass on these traits to its progeny were to be covered.

Finally, besides conformation qualities and working ability, I asked for a discussion of temperament and character contributions. These were only suggestions, but gave the interviewees some guidelines to follow. Unfortunately, many who were contacted did not or could not respond, but I am indebted to those who did.

My independent source material was primarily the *ARC Rottweiler Pictorials*. During my tenure as President of The American Rottweiler Club (1975-77), I initiated the first of several *Rottweiler Pictorials* which, periodically, have been updated through 1992. The *Fifth Rottweiler Pictorial* contains pictures and three-generation pedigrees on over 500 dogs and provides an historical record of Rottweilers in the United States. The *Fourth and Fifth Pictorials* are still available and should be in every owner/breeder's library. The combined accomplishments of the breeder, the owner, and the dogs themselves are reflected in each of the following commentaries, which are presented chronologically. (A Key to Abbreviations is available at the end of the chapter.)

GOLD SIRES AND DAMS

CH IGOR VON SCHAUER
Gold Sire – ARC System
Whelped: August 22nd 1970
Sire: CH Ferdinand von Dachsweil
Dam: CH Erika von Schauer
His record: 24 CH; 1 OTCH; 5 CD; 1 TD; 1 SchH 1
Breeders: Merle and Robert Schauer
Owner/handler: Katherine C. Hewitt

Igor's grandsire, CH Jaro vom Schleidenplatz, a German import, was the first Rottweiler to receive a Group 1 in the US and placed in the Group ring when Rottweilers were virtually unknown in the US (ranking 75th or below in AKC registrations then, as compared to No.2 in 1993 registrations). His granddam, Follow Me's Michelle, was a granddaughter of both BS CH Harras von Sofienbusch and BS Blitz von Schloss Westerwinkel.

Igor's sire, CH Ferdinand von Dachsweil, was the first Rottweiler in the US to win five Specialty shows. At the age of two, Ferdy was Best of Opposite Sex at Colonial Rottweiler Club Specialty (East Coast), and for the next three years he was awarded Best of Breed at the same Specialty show, 1966-68. He also won Best of Breed at Medallion Rottweiler Club (Midwest) and Best of Breed at Golden State Rottweiler Club (West Coast). He was then retired.

Igor's dam, CH Erika von Schauer, was Merle Schauer's first generation breeding. To quote Frederick Berger's critique of Erika given at a show in Baltimore, MD, "This could be the ideal bitch for the breed...." Igor Von Schauer was second generation breeding. According to Merle Schauer, "His excellent temperament and neat personality won many friends to the breed." As Muriel Freeman said of him: "Igor had an outstanding and successful career as a stud dog on the East Coast, producing many excellent phenotypes out of bitches of various lines – the acid test of a stud dog's quality."

His major contribution was that he was able to reproduce himself in his offspring. Igor produced progeny who were "intelligent, workable and beautiful"..."and many were HD free offspring." He also produced both Gold and Silver Sires and Dams. For example, Igor's daughter, CH V Gailingen's Welkerhaus CIA, CD (a Gold Producer), became the foundation bitch for Rita Welker (Welkerhaus Kennels) in North Carolina. Pat-Hickman Clark (Northwinds Kennels) used Igor twice for her I and K litters, which resulted in ten Champions out of Northwind's Danka. A/C CH Northwinds Kaiser of Mallam was owner-handled by Jessica Nichols to the top of the ratings in the United States and became a Silver Sire. Kaiser was a top Rottweiler in Canada in 1978; 4th in the United States in 1980; and top Owner-Handled in 1981. His sister, CH Northwinds Kriemhild CD, finished her championship with three 5-point majors. In 1982, the top dog in Canada was A/C/Ber CH Northwinds Ingo TT. An Igor grandson was used in the AKC Video of the Visualization of the Standard. In addition, the first Rottweiler Obedience Trial Champion (OTCH) was an Igor daughter, Mondberg's Donamire V Beier. Her brother, Dain, was an A/C CH A/Ber CD. Another Igor son, A/C CH Phaedra's Amax of Sunnyside, was No.1 in the States in 1978 and an early stud dog of Marcia Tucker in Florida. A Producer of Merit was CH Susan V Anderson, an Igor daughter owned by Radio Ranch who produced many Champions for them in the early eighties. A/C CH Powsell's Sherman V Schauer was sold to Venezuela to continue his career there.

Merle Schauer wrote: "Considering how few times he was bred...and seeing third and fourth generations from him, he really had a great influence on many fine Rottweilers from Florida to eastern Canada. As I looked through *The American Rottweiler Club's Fourth Pictorial,* I was quite amazed to see the number of dogs that had Igor in their background – and even more amazed to see how the physical resemblance was still very obvious."

All breeders know just how difficult it is and how very important it is to place the right puppy with the right owner. In Merle Schauer's estimation, Katherine Hewitt, Igor's owner, gave Igor the opportunity to live up to his potential. And live up to it, Igor certainly did!

A/C/BDA/MEX/INT CH JACK VOM EMSTAL. A/C CD. PC. SchH 1 – RO 861
Gold Sire – ARC System
Whelped: April 6th 1972
Sire: BS Ferro Von Der Lowenau, SchH II
Dam: BSG Dolli vom Schloss Ickern, SchH I
His record: 17 CH; 3 CDX; 14 CD; 2 TD
Breeder: Karl-Heinz Daut
Owners: Stephen and Charlotte Johnson (Frolic'n Acres)

Jack vom Emstal was born in Germany in 1972, and was from Kor und Leistung breeding. His

*Ch. Igor Von Schauer,
pictured in 1975.*

*Photo courtesy:
Dorothea Gruenerwald.*

sire was BS Ferro von der Lowenau, SchH II; his dam BSG Dolli vom Schloss Ickern, SchH I. He was shown in Germany under almost every well-known judge and "was always V-rated." During his brief German career, he earned his SchH I, his Ztp, 3 CACIBs and a VDH. In 1975 he was sold to Stephen and Charlotte Johnson. According to Mrs Johnson: "Jack was willing to attempt any new challenge. He proved this to his new owners by adapting to his new home, the American life-style, and by completing his AKC championship with four majors."

Former ADRK head breed judge Paul Shafer critiqued Jack as: "Very beautiful, powerful, compact, noble male correctly built, correct size and in very good condition. He is well behaved, attentive and lively. A very beautiful, noble head with dark eyes and a small well-carried ear. Powerful neckline, deep wide chest. The shoulders are tight, the back level and strong, the angulation very good. Feet are nice and tight, good pasterns. Beautiful smooth trotter, beautiful, proper markings. Scissor bite."

It seems that many American judges agreed with this critique, as did many of those who saw him in the conformation ring. In addition to his American championship, he placed in Group, and earned Obedience titles and championships in four other countries as well as an International (FCI) Championship – all of which were completed while he was owned and handled by the Johnsons. As Mrs Johnson remarked: "Had Jack been actively campaigned with a professional handler instead of staying at home as a friend....he [most likely] would have accrued a much more impressive national standing. Nevertheless, Jack was ranked nationally in the United States; in 1979 at age seven, he ranked No.2 in Canada; and the following year he ranked No.1 in Canada."

Mrs Johnson noted that Jack and Panamint Nobel v Falkenberg, his housemate, won Best Brace in Show three times in two different countries – the first time such a feat was accomplished by two male Rottweilers. Jack, his daughter and two grandsons won Best Team in Show at the Golden Gate K.C., another first for Rottweilers of common ownership.

His owners stated that: "Along with his outstanding conformation, Jack contributed well-balanced, powerful movement. He also passed on to his offspring a blending of intelligence, trainability and courage. His lineage is sought after by working and conformation enthusiasts alike."

CH KOKAS K'S DEGEN VON BURGA CD TD – RO 562
Gold Sire – ARC System
Whelped: April 4th 1973
Sire: CH Lyn-Mar Acres Arras V Kinta (Gold Sire)
Dam: Burga V Isarstrand
His record: 21 CH; 4 UD; 1 CDX; 5 CD; 1 TD
Breeders: Shirley Huntington and Olive Andrews
Owners: Mary and Dorothy Stringer (Hidden Meadow)

CH Kokas K's Degen Von Burga CD, TD, was sired by CH Lyn-Mar Acres Arras V Kinta, another son of CH Ferdinand von Dachsweil. His dam, Burga V Isarstrand was a German import.

Although Degen was the runt of a lively litter of thirteen, he was a dominant puppy that developed into a strong and handsome pet for the Stringer family. When he was a year old, a trusted horse vet recommended castrating him....to keep him from wandering. However, Margaret Walton, breeder/owner of his sire, felt he was a nice dog and encouraged the Stringers to get Felicia Luburich to show him. When Felicia saw him, she said: "Oh, he'll finish." He did. In fact, he finished his AKC Championship on the Florida circuit in 1975, almost three months short of his second birthday. Subsequently, he earned his CD and two legs towards a CDX (in two attempts) and a TD.

"CH Kokas K's Degen Von Burga CD, TD, was a robust, athletic dog, 25 1/2 inches tall and weighed 120 pounds. He had a strong head with medium-small ears; almond shaped, medium brown eyes; and markings of a deep rust color. His chest was broad and deep with well-sprung ribs and his body was compact. His expression was alert and intelligent, and he was of an adaptable and self-assured nature. He was also wet through the throat area with slightly open flews, and he needed more turn of stifle. These characteristics were also inherited by his offspring, and, as a prepotent sire, it was easy to spot his progeny. "Of those that were radiographed, a large percentage were issued OFA numbers. There were generally no major debilitating health problems from his line. Incidence of missing teeth was seen in four litters that he sired. As his record shows, Degen possessed a great deal of self-confidence, was highly trainable, exhibited a protective instinct, had a high degree of tolerance, was good-natured, and as such evidenced the many attributes of a desirable companion. He is the only ARC Producer of Merit currently recorded as having produced four AKC Utility titled offspring. This, the Stringers believe, "in addition to the dedication of enthusiastic owners, is a reflection of the willing spirit and sound body that he generally reproduced."

In assessing Degen's contributions to the breed as a sire, the Stringers concluded that Degen's strengths "included the ability to pass on correct Rottweiler type according to the Standard, good temperament, correct character, and overall physical as well as mental soundness."

From his first litter, in 1976 when he was almost three years old, to his last one at nine years of age, in May 1982, Degen sired a total of 35 litters, some 230 registered puppies. The first generation progeny included 21 CH, 4 UD, 1 TD, 1 CDX, and 5 CD. In addition, two Degen daughters, CH Rojas A Gumbo File UD, and Windtara Von Liebotschaner, achieved the status of ARC Bronze Dam. A grandson, CH Razdy's Akemo Grande CD is an ARC Silver Sire and is "reminiscent in type and structure of his grandsire, although overall drier in appearance," said the Stringers. When not performing in the conformation or Obedience rings, Degen was a member of K-9 Capers, regularly visiting nursing homes, attending county fair demonstrations, and competing on a scent-hurdle team. He received a club Journeyman I award for hours and miles logged backpacking in New Jersey forests.

Author's note: Dorothy Stringer served on the Board of the American Rottweiler Club for several years and is now a retired school teacher.

Ch. Anka Von Gailingen.

Photo courtesy: Dorothea Gruenerwald.

CH ANKA VON GAILINGEN – RO-522
Gold Dam – ARC System
January 18th 1973-1982
Sire: CH Dux vom Hungerbuhl, SchH I (Gold Sire)
Dam: CH Natascha vom Hohenreissach CD
Her record: 10 CH; 2 UD; 1 CDX; 5 CD; 2 TD
Breeder/Owner: Catherine M. Thompson (Von Gailingen)

Catherine Thompson's first litter in 1973 was sired by CH Dux vom Hungerbuhl SchH I, who was bred to her CH Natascha von Hohenreissach CD. This was the first generation of Von Gailingen Rottweilers, which produced CH Anka von Gailingen. Seventy-five per cent of the dogs in the pedigree were German imports. Anka was bred only four times to three different studs of the same sire line, a CH Ferdinand von Dachsweil son and two of his grandsons. Her record speaks volumes. She was the *Kennel Review*'s Top Producing Rottweiler bitch in 1977 when five of her pups finished their championships in one year. Three of Anka's sons were used at stud, though not widely, and all three produced titled offspring. One of her daughters, CH Von Gailingen's Welkerhaus Cia CD, became an ARC Gold Dam.

Breeder-owner, Catherine Thompson commented that: "Anka's pups generally had substantial bodies and bone, good front and rear angulation with strong backs. They also could have high-set, fly-away ears, be very dominant, and somewhat hyperactive. She was bred away from the latter traits. However, offspring from the second generation (CH Srigo's Zarras v Kurtz X CH Anka von Gailingen) did not produce as well as their dam, "perhaps through poor stud choices or just bad luck."

The third generation, Von Gailingen's Lofty Ideals CD, (CH Arras vom Hasenkamp X A/C CH Von Gailingen's Dassie Did It, UDT, Can. CD), produced only one litter before her untimely death at two and a half years of age. She was bred to a CH Von Gailingen's Chancellor son and produced 2 CH, 2 UDTX, 1 CDX, 2 CD, and 1 TD to become an ARC Silver Dam.

A Von Gailingen fourth generation dog, V-rated, A/C CH Von Gailingen's Matinee Idol,

UDTX, Can. CDX, AgI, HIC (CH The Fuhrer of Adamwald X Von Gailingen's Lofty Ideals, CD), is "all a breeder could ask for," Mrs. Thompson wrote, "....linebred, being a double Anka great grandson, handsome, typey, sound, and a very willing worker." Mrs Thompson commented further: "Rudi [a shortened call name for Rudolph Valentino] throws consistent litters with his short, strong back, substantial body and bone, good feet, excellent movement, short, broad muzzles and, most importantly, his confident, willing temperament. He has winning offspring in Canada, South America, Australia and the United States."

Author's note: Catherine Thompson is an AKC licensed Obedience judge (thru UD), and currently approved to judge Rottweilers and Dobermans. Her assignments have taken her to Canada, Jamaica, Hawaii, New Zealand and Australia.

CH WELKERHAUS' ROMMEL UD – RO-759-T
Gold Sire – ARC System
Whelped: July 13th 1974
Sire: Circle ML's Aster
Dam: Wonnemund
His record: 17 CH; 2 CDX; 19 CD; 1 TD
Breeder: Richard Werder
Owner: Rita Welker (Welkerhaus Knls)

Rommel was bred to less than twelve bitches during his entire lifetime. Of these, two contributed significantly to the total number of champions he sired: CH V Gailingen's Welkerhaus Cia, CD, an ARC Gold Dam bred by Catherine Thompson and owned by Rita Welker, and Concord's Special Edition, an ARC Bronze Dam bred and owned by Susan Porter. The Rommel X Cia breeding was repeated three times. The third breeding was by far the most successful, with the entire litter of six X-raying OFA Good or Excellent. Mrs Welker noted that one bitch, Welkerhaus' In Diamonds CDX, TD became an ARC Bronze Dam.

The breeding of Rommel to Concord's Special Edition was also successful, producing seven champions and five Obedience titled offspring. A bitch from this litter, CH Concord's Abend AM Ravenstal CDX also became an ARC Bronze Dam. "Raven" went Best of Opposite Sex from the Veteran Bitch class at the ARC Regional Specialty in Knoxville, TN in 1987.

Mrs Welker felt that the major contributions from these breedings were good temperaments and OFA hip ratings. "As far as the Welkerhaus lines are concerned, I feel that Rommel's direct offspring came up with a large number of OFA Good to Excellent, but his grandchildren had an even better average." For example, a grandson, Welkerhaus' In Search O' Lurch CD received an OFA Excellent, and in turn his two sons, Welkerhaus' Nicholas, CD and Welkerhaus Lurch's Legacy, out of different dams, also were OFA Excellent. "It is rare to see so many Excellents from the same kennel." All three males are owned by Rita Welker.

Mrs Welker also had some interesting comments about temperament in her bloodlines. "I wonder if close line-breeding with certain crosses has caused some of the stubbornness which has not been evident with other crosses that I have bred. One particular cross had a very heavy dominance of some well-known German ancestry." She went on to say that perhaps Rommel had spoiled her, since by the time he was two years of age he had earned the titles of CH, CD, CDX and UD, all in a twelve-month time frame. And Rommel was her first Rottweiler!

She continued: "...I have found that, as a general rule, it is easier to train a male versus a female....I have almost always gotten better scores with my males than with my females." But, she stressed, there is always an exception either way. Currently she is training a young two-year-old male, who is the "most stubborn" Rottweiler she has ever attempted to train. "My goal is to put a CD on him, which will be a great feat."

Mrs Welker commented further: "I feel Welkerhaus has improved the breed by breeding for good hips, larger bone, good movement and good temperament. I feel the one thing I need to improve on is the eye (both shape and color). This is being accomplished, but it is taking longer than expected....I am finding it easier to correct eye color than shape."

Mrs Welker noted that after eighteen years of breeding, Welkerhaus is still producing the same type Rottweiler as when it started in 1974. Her breeding programme has concentrated primarily on structure, soundness and intelligence.

Special notes: "....regardless of a dog's potential, without all the hard work of bringing the dog into the ring (be it Obedience or conformation), this dog will never be fully recognized; therefore, it is extremely important to place these "cute" puppies in proper homes. If Rommel's children had not gone to the right homes, he wouldn't have had the distinction of being a GOLD SIRE, regardless of his ability to reproduce good dogs."

A/C CH DONNAJ VT YANKEE OF PAULUS CDX TT – RO-964-T
Gold Sire – ARC System
April 4th 1975-1983
Sire: CH Axel vom Schwanenschlag (Silver Sire)
Dam: CH Amsel von Andan CD (Silver Dam)
His record: 43 CH; 2 UD; 1 CDX; 31 CD; 2 TD
(from a total of 51 litters over a 7-year period)
Sire of 1 Silver & 2 Bronze Sires; 1 Silver & 5 Bronze Dams;
Best in Show – 1979
Breeder: Pauline Rakowski (von Paulus)
Owner: Jan Marshall (Donnaj)

Yankee's maternal grandsire, A/C CH Rodsden's Kato v Donnaj CDX, TD, was Jan Marshall's first Rottweiler. Of the nine litters sired by Kato, two were out of Mrs Anna Tilghman's Ehrenwache's Andernach and produced six Champions. Mrs Marshall wrote: "I considered CH Amsel von Andan CD, owned by Pauline Rakowski, to be the best offspring of Kato. The "A" and "B" von Andan litters carried the excellent genes of Gold Sire CH Rodsden's Kluge v d Harque, CD, (Kato's sire) and Ehrenwache's grandsire (Kluge's sire), BS CH Harras vom Sofienbusch SchH I. Rodsden's importing of Harras was of immense importance to our breed."

Mrs Marshall first spotted Yankee's sire, CH Axel vom Schwanenschlag (Silver Sire), "a very impressive German import," in Baltimore soon after he had been imported into the United States. His sire was Furst v d Villa Daheim SchH 1 and his dam was Cora vom Grevingsberg. He finished quickly and soon was used at stud. Like his sire, Yankee also had an impressive record – even more so. He won four Specialty Best of Breeds, including the first American Rottweiler Club's National Specialty at eight years of age. Yankee was the sixth all-breed Best-in-Show winner (his grandsire, Kato, being the first). Yankee also had twenty-four Group placings, including six Group I's.

Besides being an impressive conformation dog, "Yankee was dominant in passing on his topline, his flowing sound gait and his charismatic personality. Judges told me they could recognize his offspring across the country from these traits." According to his owner, "Yank produced his best offspring when bred to compact bitches with good bone and substance and 'boxy' heads with good fill." He is behind many successful show dogs and kennels through his sons and daughters. In the United States, his offspring won 8 Best-in-Shows; 1 Best-in-Show in Canada and 1 Best-in-Show in Venezuela. He also sired 5 US Group winners and 14 Group placers.

ABOVE: Welkerhaus' Rommel UD at two years, pictured in 1976.

BELOW: Welkerhaus' In Search O' Lurch CD, pictured at six years of age.

Photos courtesy: Dorothea Gruenerwald.

TOP: Ch. Kokas K's Degen Von Burga CD, TD

ABOVE: Ch. Donnaj Vt Yankee of Paulus CDX: Group I, August 1979, pictured at four years of age.

Photos courtesy: Dorothea Gruenerwald.

Reflecting upon this impressive Rottweiler, Mrs. Marshall recalls that: "Yank loved life, people, dog shows and Obedience training! He was sensible, adaptable, loved to please, and was protective when called for. Altogether, a joy to live with. Since I showed him ninety per cent of the time, I was privileged to have Yankee as my constant companion. Yankee was a once-in-a-lifetime dog."

Author's note: Jan Marshall is another of our breeder-judges. She has taught Obedience and is a delegate to the American Kennel Club.

CH RODSDEN'S BRUIN V HUNGERBUHL CDX – RO-1189
Gold Sire – ARC System
Whelped: March 19th 1976
Sire: CH Dux vom Hungerbuhl SchH I (Gold Sire)
Dam: CH Rodsden's Frolich Burga CD, TD (Bronze Dam)
His record: 51 CH; 2 UD; 4 CDX; 27 CD; 8 TD; 3 TDX
Best in Show – 1979 (3); 1980 (2); 1981 (2)
Winner of Kato Bowl – 1979, 1980, 1981
Breeder/owners: Jeffrey and Geraldine Kittner (Kerztenlicht)

"Bruin" was out of the first litter bred by the Kittners. His sire was CH Dux v Hungerbuhl SchH I, a German import, and himself a Gold Sire. It is interesting to note the preponderance of German bloodlines in his dam's pedigree, including grandsire CH Max von der Hobertsburg; great-grandsire Caro vom Kupferdach and great-great-grandsires CH Erno v Wellesweiler, Fetz vom Oelberg, Int. CH & BS CH Harras vom Sofienbusch SchH I, and CH Bengo vom Westfalenpark CD. Max, Erno, Fetz, Harras and Bengo, all top German bloodlines, were exported to the US during the mid-sixties and early seventies.

His owners describe his strengths as a sire as "producing size, substance, head type, topline and outline, clean movement with a lot of reach and drive. He was very good in producing good hips. Coloring could have been better. His weak points were eye shape and size of markings."

Bruin's contribution as a stud dog, the Kittners feel, was basically the same as his sire's, except that Bruin could produce size and substance. They note that Dux produced best when bred to bitches who could produce size and substance without relying on the sire for help with these two aspects. Bruin's sisters also were "great" producers, who produced very well "with most any male they were bred to."

Bruin's greatest strength, however, was in passing on his temperament to his offspring. "He was not only a great dog to live with, but had a sheer willingness to work. His attitude and presence were part of what made him such a great show dog," commented the Kittners.

Bruin was the winner of the Kato Bowl for three consecutive years. This award, in memory of CH Rodsden's Kato v Donnaj CDX, TD is given to the dog earning the most points accumulated in group competition, as determined by *Kennel Review* magazine.

Mr and Mrs Kittner acknowledge their success was due in large part to the help of others such as "...Joan Klem, Pat and Martha-Jo Rademacher and Jane Wiedel, to mention a few." And, of course, Bruin's career would not have been so successful without his handlers and friends, Brian and Cindy Meyer.

KS/INT CH/ CH MIRKO VOM STEINKOPF CDX SchH III FH IPO CDX – RO-5239T
Gold Sire – ARC System
November 9th 1980-October 1988
Sire: KS/BS/ES/INT CH Dingo v Schwaiger Wappen SchH III

Dam: Esta vom Steinkopf, SchH I
His record: 24 CH; 3 UD; 6 CDX; 24 CD; 1 TD; 1 TDX; 1 SchH II
Breeder: Reinhold Salzmann (Steinkopf)
Owners: Dr and Mrs Richard Wayburn (Waxel)

Mrs Wayburn wrote: "We purchased our first Rottweiler nineteen years ago. Over the years, we had Champion bitches and dogs, Obedience title holders, seven litters – all loved and delightful house companions. But one, Mirko vom Steinkopf, made a lasting contribution to us and our breed."

Mrs Wayburn recalls that she had seen Mirko at the 1982 Klubsieger Show in Germany and thought that he showed great promise. During the following year the Wayburns lost their Champion dog; therefore Mrs Wayburn returned to Germany to look for a young dog. None could compare to Mirko in her eyes.

A series of unbelievable events then took place. With Mrs Wayburn watching, Mirko became the 1983 Klubsieger. He had already earned his SchH III, IPO III and FH, and was HD Free. These accomplishments were all prior to his third birthday. The Wayburns were able to purchase Mirko and he came to the United States and adapted immediately to his new life and Mrs Wayburn's "southern German" accent. "We started showing him in November and he completed his American Championship undefeated. He OFA'd Good." The Wayburns started 'specialing' him (showing him as a new Champion) in January 1985. "I travelled with him and while his handler showed him in conformation, Mirko and I completed his CD and CDX."

Mirko won Best of Breed at the Colonial Rottweiler Club Specialty in 1985 under breeder-judge, Mrs Muriel Freeman, and later that day won Best-in-Show at Bucks Co. KC, defeating three thousand all-breed dogs. "The IFR Congress was held in the United States that year, and we were so pleased that the Germans could see their Klubsieger win here." He was the No.1 Rottweiler in the United States in 1985. He quickly completed his International championship (Puerto Rican CH, South American CH, Champion of the Americas, Dominican Republic Champion, where he was again judged Best-in-Show.

In 1986, Mirko again won Best of Breed at the Colonial Rottweiler Club Specialty under breeder-judge Mrs Marcia Tucker, and repeated his Best-in-Show at Bucks County KC, defeating 3200 all-breed dogs. "Mirko will go down in history as the ONLY Rottweiler to win a Specialty *and* an all-breed show in one day...." In 1986, he won the Stud Dog Class at the Medallion Rottweiler Club Specialty. He has 3 all-breed Best-in-Shows, 8 Group I, 5 Group II, 1 Group III, and 2 Group IV.

It is worthy to note here that Mirko, a SchH III German import, possessed the versatility and stability to become a therapy dog. While traveling with Mirko, Mrs Wayburn had read a great deal about dogs being used in children's hospitals and nursing homes. "We felt that with Mirko's sensitivity and love of people, he would be an ideal therapy dog." After four months of training, he was on to another challenge – that of a Registered Therapy Dog.

Mirko was used at stud very selectively – a total of only twenty-five times during his five years in the United States. The Wayburns commented that "Mirko had a magnificent head, with the proper fill under his eyes and the driest neck we had ever seen. He lives on in the temperament he passed on to his offspring."

Mirko having sired 24 Champions and 35 Obedience-titled offspring, the Wayburns are most proud of his children and grandchildren who possess his character and his working ability as therapy dogs, the same work Mirko performed until the week before he died at eight years of age. Naturally, a Mirko son, "J.R." (Seren's Image of Mirko), owned by the Wayburns, is following in his father's footsteps. In 1992 "J.R." was presented with the American Rottweiler Club's first Mirko Award "in recognition of exceptional volunteer services."

A Mirko son, BIS CH Weissenburg's Lucifer Roxer CD, was rated ARC No.5 Dog in 1991. A Mirko daughter, A/C CH Weissenburg's Mizchief-Maker CD, at almost nine years of age, is still working towards the one last leg of her CDX. Both Roxer and Mizchief were out of A/C CH Weissenburg's Don't-U-Dare.

CH MERRYMOORE'S IMP VON DOROW TT – RO-4816
Gold Dam – ARC System
June 22nd 1981-1989
Sire: Merrymoore's VIP
Dam: Tasha von Huntshof
Her record: 8 CH; 1 UD; 2 CDX; 6 CD; 1 TDX
Breeder: Jack A. Hunt
Owner: Nancy C. Estes (Von Dorow)

CH Merrymoore's Imp von Dorow, foundation bitch for von Dorow Kennels, was a stud fee puppy bred by Jack A. Hunt and purchased from Merrymoore Kennels in 1981. Imp took her first major her second time in the Open class by going Best of Opposite Sex over three champion bitches, including the then #1 Bitch in the US. She was "specialed" on a very limited basis after obtaining her Championship and was ranked No.5 Bitch in 1984 and No.9 Bitch in 1985 (ARC system). Besides qualifying for the ARC Gold Dam, Imp is a member of the Medallion Rottweiler Club's Hall of Fame.

Imp was bred three times to two different dogs, and produced 22 offspring. In November 1984 Imp was bred to A/C CH Tulake's Apollo, RO-3044-T (ARC Silver Sire). In the "A" litter of nine puppies, five survived. One male, CH Agitato von Dorow, was the only puppy to go to a show home. Two show quality bitches ended up in pet homes and were never shown. Of the five surviving offspring, one was OFA Excellent (Agitato) and two were OFA Good. Two were X-rayed, but the X-rays were never submitted to OFA.

In January 1986, Imp was bred to A/C CH Rodsdens Berte V Zederwald CDX (ARC Gold Sire). Berte won Best in Specialty Show at the 1985 Medallion Rottweiler Club Specialty. The "B" litter produced ten puppies, of which nine survived. Of this litter, there were: 5 CH, 1 UD, 1 TD, 1 CDX and 3 CD. The OFA ratings were: 3 Excellent, 3 Good, 1 Fair and 1 Mild. One pet bitch was never X-rayed. In December 1986, the Berte-Imp breeding was repeated, with eight puppies in the "C" litter. From this litter, there were: 2 CH, 1 CDX and 3 CD get, with 2 OFA Excellent and 6 Good. One CH/CD dog is also a Paws Across Texas Therapy Dog.

Two of Imp's get were Grand Prize Futurity Winners at the Medallion Rottweiler Club Specialty: CH Black Orpheus von Dorow in 1987 and Cataline von Dorow in 1988. In 1992, a grandson of Imp, CH Andrecas Aramis von der Mond CD, was Grand Prize Futurity Winner at Medallion Rottweiler Club Specialty. To date, six of her grandchildren have their CD title, one is a CH, and three are pointed. Her great-grandchildren just began showing in 1993. One has 2 Best of Breeds from the 6-9 month Puppy class and 2 Best of Breeds and a Group III from the 9-12 month Puppy class.

According to Nancy Estes: "The majority of Imp's offspring had good hips, toplines, length of neck and heads. Imp also consistently produced stable temperaments with many of her get inheriting her 'showy' and 'up' personality. Despite her aversion to Obedience (poor training – my fault!), Imp's get were good Obedience dogs."

Imp's sons were either very limitedly advertised at stud or not advertised at all. Only eight have been used, on a very limited basis. Of Imp's eleven daughters, only five were bred, none more than twice. Imp died at the age of 7 1/2 years of lymphosarcoma.

Ch. Rodsden's Bruin V Hungerbuhl CDX:
Best-in-Show, Packerland K.C.
Photo: Ralph Karlen.

Ch. Mirko Vom Steinkopf: BIS Colonial
Rottweiler Club.
Photo courtesy: Dorothea Gruenerwald.

MRC 1988 – 1st in Stud Dog Class: Ch. Mirko Vom Steinkopf, Ch. Wittz Rad and Weissenburg's Turbo.
Booth Photography.

Belg. Schon. Ch. Grave Kapenborgh CD,
SCHHI.
Photo courtesy: Dorothea Gruenerwald.

Ch. Merrymoore's Imp Von Dorow TT:
Best of Breed.
Photo courtesy: Dorothea Gruenerwald.

BELG. SCHON. CH GRAVE KAPENBORGH CD SCHH I – RO-8229-T
Gold Sire – ARC System
June 1982-February 1992
Sire: Int. CH Ulli vom Kastanienbaum SchH III, FH
Dam: Donja Kapenborgh
His record: 19 CH; 2 UD; 3 CDX; 3 TD; 1 SchH I
Breeder: Jan Vandereyken
Owners: Hildegard and Franz Mikoleit (Vom Sonnenhaus)

Grave was imported by Hildegard Mikoleit as an adult dog. His sire, Int. CH Ulli vom Kastanienbaum, SchH III, and his dam, Donja Kapenborgh, came from well-known German and Belgian bloodlines. Mrs Mikoleit had previously imported several Kastanienbaum dogs, which had proved to be successful producers for her long-time breeding programme.

Am/Mex/CH Wotan vom Kastanienbaum, a German import owned by the Mikoleits, was the sire of Vom Sonnenhaus Tanja von Vera CD. "Tanja" was selectively bred to Grave producing among others, BISS CH Vom Sonnenhaus Krugerrand CD TT (Silver sire). BIS BISS CH Imago's Midnight Cruiser CD came from a litter sired by Grave out of CH Trollegens Tressida. Can. BISS CH Chukuni's Shining Auricle was yet another Grave offspring.

Mrs Mikoleit's breeding programme has been primarily line-breeding on the Kastanienbaum bloodlines. "To sum it all up, line breed for the true temperament, soundness, correct conformation and working. He [Grave] has left behind strength in topline, movement, good temperament and the working aspect."

As Mrs Mikoleit concluded: "This is a wonderful breed. I'm very proud to be part of the betterment of the breed with the help of Wotan and Grave and the line-bred dogs in their pedigrees which made it all possible."

A/C/M/CH QUICK VON SIEGERHAUS A/C CDX SchH I TT TDI – RO-8521T
Gold Sire – ARC System
July 15th 1983-August 1993
Sire: CH Birch Hill's Hasso Manteufel CDX, TD (Silver Sire)
Dam: CH Meid von Siegerhaus
His record: 21 CH; 8 CDX; 24 CD; 1 TD; 1 SchH I
Breeder/Owners: Thom and Carol Woodward (Von Siegerhaus)

There is a predominance of imported German and Dutch bloodlines behind Quick: his sire was CH Birch Hill's Hasso Manteufel CDX, TD (Silver Sire); his grandsire, BIS CH Rodsden's Bruin V Hungerbuhl, CDX (Gold Sire); and his great-grandsires, CH Dux vom Hungbuhl (Gold Sire) and CH Falco vh Brabantpark (Gold Sire). The Woodwards bred his dam, CH Meid von Siegerhaus, sired by A/M CH Wotan vom Kastanienbaum (Bronze Sire) X CH Kyna vom Odenwald CD (Silver Dam).

After completing his Championship, Quick was campaigned extensively as a "Special" for three years, 1988-1990. In 1990, he was *Kennel Review*'s No.1 Sire. He received the *Dog World* Award of Canine Distinction, and was always rated in the Top Ten while in competition.

A brief ADRK Breed Survey by Chief Judge and Kormeister Helmut Freiberg, made in 1985 describes Quick as follows:

General impression: Medium size, well built with strong bones.
Character: Alert, manageable.
Conformation: Strong head with good teeth. Medium brown eyes. Ears are set and carried

Ch. Quick Von Siegerhaus, pictured while earning his International Championship in Mexico.
Photo: Mitchell.

correctly. Strong neck. Chest very well developed. Forearm straight. Strong feet. Back straight with strong muscled thighs. Correct coat with brown markings. Gums and inner lips dark. Scissor bite.

According to his owners: "Quick passed on to his progeny short backs, good fronts and toplines, and good side gait. His true strength was his personality which was also in evidence in his get. He was pre-potent for passing on good hips, with many of his offspring having received OFA Excellents."

BIS Select A/C CH GOLDEICHE ARA VON BRADER A/C CD – RO-12987
Gold Sire – ARC System
April 5th 1985-May 27th 1994
Sire: CH Eiko Vom Schwaiger Wappen CDX, SchH III (German import/Gold Sire)
Dam: CH Rodsden's Hella V Forstwald, TD
His record: 30 CH; 1 UD; 3 CDX; 32 CD; 3 TD; 2 TDX
Best in Show – 1988 (2); 1989 (1)
Best in Specialty Show – 1987 (1); 1988 (2); 1989 (1)
Breeder: Barbara Grisell/Frank Brader (Goldeiche/von Brader)
Owners: Dale and Karen Innocenti (Darak)

Ara's pedigree is most enviable. He was the son of the renowned German import, CH Eiko Vom Schwaiger Wappen CDX, SchH III (OFA Good), who had been bred to CH Rodsden's Hella V Forstwald TD (OFA Good). This means Ara goes back to such foundation dogs as Igor Vom Kastanienbaum SchH III, FH; Int. CH Anka Vom Lohauserholtz SchH III, FH; CH Rodsden's Roma V Brabant; and Int. CH Bulli Vom Hungerbuhl SchH II.

His owners proudly state that "If Ara could be described in three words, they would have to be 'balance, topline and movement'. When Ara was in the conformation ring, he made his presence known. He was a balanced Rottweiler, medium sized with correct proportions.... with effortless eye-catching movement. Standing still, Ara's topline exemplified the Standard, but more importantly, when he moved, his topline was 'flawless'. He possessed the topline that the breed lacks." Looking at Ara's pedigree, one sees "true" working temperament coupled with "excellent Rottweiler type". That is what Ara possessed and what he produced in the first and second generations. A large percentage of his sons and daughters possess "his intelligent expression, dark eyes, model topline and great working temperament."

Although Ara was bred minimally during his life, he produced over 30 American Champions and over 40 get with working titles, plus many more titled dogs in Canada. Ara has many Specialty winning progeny, plus several advanced working titled offspring.

Ara was shown exclusively during his show career by his then novice owner/handler, Dale Innocenti. Together, they won three all-breed Best-in-Shows and four Specialties, including one in Canada. His Canadian Championship, Canadian CD, and Canadian Specialty win were acquired in a SINGLE weekend. Ara was No.1 owner-handled Rottweiler all systems in 1988 and 1989, and he was #2 Rottweiler all systems in 1989 as well. He is an ARC Gold Sire, Colonial Rottweiler Club Gold Achievement Award Winner, and a Member of the Medallion Rottweiler Club Hall of Fame.

Ara lived just nine years, and during that time he was, besides being an excellent show and working dog and producer, the "cherished companion of Dale and Karen Innocenti and their two children. He was a perfect housedog and playmate as well as faithful protector throughout his life...Ara did all that was asked of him because he was a Rottweiler through and through."

Because of these qualities, his owners feel blessed to have had Ara in their lives even for so short a time and "are grateful to the Lord for such a special friend."

BIS BISS CH NELSON van het BRABANTPARK – RO 15579
Gold Sire – ARC System
Whelped: April 1st 1985
Sire: Simba vh Brabantpark
Dam: Golda vh Brabantpark
His record: 35 CH; 2 CDX; 11 CD; 4 TD; Best in Show (see below); Best in Specialty Show: (see below)
Winner of Kato Bowl: 1988; 1989; 1990
Breeder: Mej. A. Huyskens – Holland (vh Brabantpark)
Owners: Clara Hurley/Michael S. Grossman (Powderhorn/Wencrest Rottweilers, Inc.)

"Nelson" was imported from Holland by Clara Hurley and Michael Grossman, who stated that "our primary consideration for his acquisition was to incorporate him into our breeding program and, thus, continue with the lines which have been so successful for us."

Nelson's outstanding record includes: 5 Best-in-Shows; a Best in Rottweiler Specialty; 48 Group Firsts, 45 Group Seconds, 36 Group Thirds, 30 Group Fourths and 222 Best of Breeds. Nelson was No.1 Rottweiler in the United States for 1989 and 1990. According to his owners: "The show career of Nelson was outstanding by any measure. He defeated more Rottweilers than any other Rottweiler in the history of the breed in any country!"

Nelson's main strengths, which, according to Mrs Hurley, have been passed on consistently to his progeny, are: true Rottweiler type, dark eyes, good bites, correct and well-carried ears, overall substance and heavy bone. He is strong for straight fronts, prominent forechests, short backs and broad-level toplines, moderate angulation, "beautiful coloring", and working ability.

"In our opinion, Nelson has changed the face of the breed in the US and Canada. The temperament and character of the Nelson progeny are outstanding. They are wonderful family dogs, as well as show and working dogs, and excellent ambassadors for the breed," wrote Mrs Hurley. Five of his sons have been awarded Best in Show. One of his sons recently was entered automatically into MRC's Hall of Fame as the first Rottweiler to achieve the American Kennel Club's Herding Dog degree.

"All of the above characteristics are present in equal strength in his first generation and succeeding generations of progeny ... an enviable record for a stud dog. Nelson is a truly prepotent stud dog in that he is able to pass on these qualities to his progeny from line breedings as well as from total outcrosses."

SILVER SIRES AND DAMS

PANAMINT DAGNA VON DER EICHEN CD – RO-245
Silver Dam – ARC System
February 26th 1969-January 25th 1982
Sire: CH Panamint Storm
Dam: CH Datmar v Kupferdach
Her record: 5 CH; 3 CDX; 7 CD; 1 TD
Breeder: Barbara Hoard (Panamint)
Owner: Judith Hassed (von Arktos)

"Von Arktos" Rottweilers is a small breeding kennel established in 1972, which was founded entirely on the offspring of Panamint Dagna von der Eichen. Dagna was the great-granddaughter of Int. CH Harras v Sofienbusch SchH I, who is in the pedigrees of both her sire and dam. BS Dora vom Burgtobel, SchH I was the maternal great-granddam of Harras.

Mrs Hassed's primary objective was to conserve the desirable qualities of Bundesseigerin Dora von Burgtobel SchH I (1952) and to produce a group of Rottweilers which would reliably reproduce this type. Dora's breed survey described her "as being of noble appearance and very alert". CH Apache von Arktos, Winners Dog at Colorado Springs, Colorado and a third generation Von Arktos, is typical of the dog she has chosen to breed.

According to Mrs Hassed, Von Arktos Rottweilers are noted for consistent temperament: they are friendly when introduced, enjoy obedience training and are stalwart guards. They like children and adapt well to kind and intelligent training. "In appearance they resemble the old-style Rottweiler, blocky in head and body, with efficient trotting gait, and the physique to pull a loaded cart. These are all qualities listed in all descriptions of the ideal Rottweiler, and I believe present in mine because of the close breeding to Dora von Burgtobel SchH I."

Mrs Hassed noted that all dogs used for breeding have been screened for hip problems, eye disease, and any other necessary physical problems that have become apparent in the breed. Only Rottweilers who can pass all these tests are used for breeding. "I have never had one of my puppies develop functional dysplasia which has caused discomfort to the dog. My dogs tend to live longer than the norm for the breed, with fewer health problems during their lifetimes. I now have two who are over eleven, one of whom will soon be thirteen. I believe this is due to the concentration of old bloodlines which still demonstrate the vitality the breed used to have."

The Von Arktos bloodline has consistently performed in both Obedience and conformation competition during the last twenty-two years. Mrs Hassed stated that "with the exception of one bitch, all the breeding stock has either been titled by the American Kennel Club or been designated Producers of Merit by The American Rottweiler Club."

Ranger von Arktos CD, CGC, UKC-CDX, the most recent titleholder, will be the sire of the litters now in the planning stage. He is in training for his Utility title. "He is also an example of the correct type and temperament, being very sociable, but an excellent guard." His titles have been achieved with consistent scores in the mid-190s, with many class placements and High Scoring Rottweiler awards. Mrs Hassed comments that she will be breeding her sixth generation, the first outcross breeding done since the founding of her bloodline. Future litters, now in the planning stage, will carry crosses to the original bloodlines as she has been able to acquire two line-bred outcross bitches to use with Ranger. She fully expects to continue to produce puppies "who will display the proper temperament and structure, and who carry the pedigree to reproduce this type, until the next century. This project has been extremely gratifying to me, and also to the fortunate few who own one of my puppies."

EBONSTERN BRYT PROMIS V HELLER – RO 479T
Silver Dam – ARC System
Whelped: April 4th 1972
Sire: CH Rodsden's Hardecanute Brandy
Dam: Heidi's Molzberg Hella, CD
Her record: 8 CH; 1 UD; 4 CD; 1 TDX; 1 SchH II; 1 FH
Breeder/Owner: Cheryl Wheeler

"From the very beginning, it has been my strong conviction that it is the *bitch* that must form the foundation of a breeding program in order to establish the consistency from generation to generation that we all seek," writes Cheryl Wheeler.

Her foundation bitch, 'Hella', produced a total of 16 puppies, who earned 13 conformation and/or Obedience titles, with several others pointed. Most of her offspring exemplified her type "...a powerful, muscular, agile Rottweiler with good movement, a compact body and a strong head."

Ch. Nelson V H Brabantpark: Best-in-Show, Colorado Springs K.C.
Photo: Wayne Cott.

Ch. Apache Von Arktos: Winners Dog, pictured at 15 months of age.
Photo: Wayne Cott.

Bis Select A/C Ch. Goldeiche Ara Von Brader - MRC 1991 Speciality: First in Stud Dog Class, aged six years, with offspring: A/C Ch. Goldeiche Ara Von Brader, Ch. Tri-Lee's Drummer Boy, and Ch. Tri-Lee's Down The Road TD.
Booth Photography.

Ch. Gatstuberget's Hilma Honoris.
Photo courtesy: Dorothea Gruenerwald.

Ebonstern Bryt Promis V Heller.
Photo courtesy: Dorothea Gruenerwald.

With one of Hella's daughters, Ebonstern Bryt Promis V Heller, ("Missie"), Cheryl Wheeler chose to take her breeding program into the next generation. "With Missie's offspring my co-owners and I have continued this strong unbroken line of bitches who consistently produce the quality and type we are seeking."

Missie had 19 puppies; among them they earned 25 titles, including 3 who were owner-handled Group placers, and several who were multiple Best of Breed winners and nationally ranked. Several others had points toward championships and legs toward obedience titles. All 18 who were X-rayed passed OFA. "The most important fact, however, is that Missie's children were endowed with that same elusive 'produce-ability' that she had. Using a strong line-breeding program, we have developed the ability to preserve the qualities that we admired in Missie, on into the sixth generation."

Real strength came, however, when Missie was bred to her half-brother, A/C CH Ebonstern Cabo V Klahnerhof. The puppies from the "O v d Liebe" litter produced some of the best, both in the conformation ring and as producers of the type and quality desired by Ebonstern, and carried her breeding program forward into the third generation, with their offspring earning over 50 AKC or CKC Obedience and conformation titles. Many were multi-BOB winners, Group placers and nationally ranked.

The Missie/Cabo offspring (grandchildren) provided the next generation. "This combination, with Missie appearing three times in five generations, has produced some of our most consistent and typey dogs....including our most recent multi-BOB winning, Group placing and nationally ranked breeder/owner/handled Rottweiler bitch, A/C CH Ebonstern Brava V D Liebe."

According to Cheryl Wheeler: "the strengths flowing forward from Missie to Ebonstern's current generation include: strong topline, muscular well placed neck, prominent prosternum and correct front assembly, powerful hindquarters, smooth movement, strong heads, as well as substance and bone, without coarseness and sloppiness ... what always set the Missie kids and her succeeding generations apart from all others would have to be that intelligent, sensible, sound character. Quick to defend and protect, but slow to anger or over-react. The weakness, depending upon your point of view, could be the solid, easy-going temperament. Many exhibitors and judges appear to admire the more high-strung and nervous 'high energy' dogs because they often seem more 'impressive' in the show ring.

"What endeared Missie to those of us who knew and loved her was her outlook on life. She clearly believed her purpose on earth was to love, take care of, and teach those around her...human and canine alike. It was for this reason that all of Missie children are named with 'Y.D. Lieben'. She was, and is still today, much 'Beloved'."

CH GATSTUBERGET'S HILMA HONORIS CDX – RO-2100T
Silver Dam – ARC System
Whelped April 12th 1978
Sire: CH Trollegen's Fable (Gold Sire)
Dam: CH Gatstuberget Asa V Kleinholz CD (Bronze Dam)
Her record: 6 CH; 3 CDX; 2 CD; 1 TD
Breeder: Margareta McIntyre (Gatstuberget)
Owners: Margareta McIntyre & Janna & Marjorie Morgan (Evrmor)

Hilma's sire, CH Trollegen's Fable, was a son of CH Dux vom Hungerbuhl SchH I. Other well-known German imports show up in the second and third generation. Her dam, CH Gatstuberget Asa V Kleinholz, CD, had numerous German and Dutch imports in her pedigree, including: Dutch CH/Am CH/Lux Sieger Falco V H Brabantpark (Gold Sire); CH Falk vom Kursaal SchH I (Bronze Sire); CH Afra vom Hasenacker CD, SchH I; CH Nick vom Silahopp (Silver Sire); and

Ch. Razdy's Akemo-Grande CD.
Photo courtesy: Dorothea Gruenerwald.

Ch. Rodsden's Heika V Forstwald CD, VB, TT.
Photo courtesy: Dorothea Gruenerwald.

Ch. Pomac's
Lexa P Vanlare
CD, HIC: Best
of Breed, 1982.

Photo courtesy:
Dorothea
Gruenerwald.

Ch. Sophe Von Bergenhof: Best of Breed –
Bonneville Basin K.C.
Photo courtesy: Dorothea Gruenerwald.

Ch. Vom Sonnenhaus Krugerrand: Best of
Breed – Kachina K.C.
Photo: Missy Yuhl.

Circe vom Gertrudenhof CD. Two of her littermates were Champion and Obedience titled, and a third was an ARC Bronze Dam. According to Mrs Morgan: "Hilma's fine topline, front and rear were among the attributes passed on to her offspring. They all loved to please, as she did." She was very athletic. This quality was passed on, as demonstrated by the CDX titles earned by her three sons from the "O" litter: CH Gatstuberget Ono of Evrmor CDX, TD; CH Gatstuberget Onyx of Evrmor CDX, Can. CD; and Gatstuberget Omni of Evrmor CDX. For those offspring that have been bred, six Champions have been produced, proving that "type" seems to have been passed on to a succeeding generation. There are several more that have all majors and need only single points to finish. Mrs Morgan recalls: "The best way to remember Hilma was the sentiment from all of her puppy owners: 'This is the best dog I have ever owned'."

CH RODSDEN'S HEIKA V FORSTWALD CD, VB, TT – RO-4323
Silver Dam – ARC System
January 28th 1981-January 13th 1985
Sire: CH Rodsden's Kane V Forstwald, CD (Gold Sire)
Dam: CH Rodsden's Roma V Brabant
Her record: 6 CH; 2 CDX; 6 CD; 1 SchH II
6 Can. CH; 4 Can. CD; 2 Can. CDX; 1 Can. TD;
8 BH; 1 SchH III; 2 SchH I
Breeder: Richard Rademacher (Rodsdens)
Owners: Linda P. and William Michels (Lindenwood)

Heika was sired by CH Rodsden's Kane V Forstwald CD, a great-grandson of BS/INT CH/CH Harras Vom Sofienbusch SchH I. Kane went Best of Breed under Mrs. Muriel Freeman at the Colonial Rottweiler Club Specialty in 1981, and later that year took Best of Breed at Medallion Rottweiler Club Specialty. Her dam was CH Rodsden's Roma V Brabant. The Kane-Roma breedings were noted for producing litters with very good hip ratings.

  Heika was bred three times: twice to CH Gasto Vom Liebersbacherhof CDX, TD, SchH I, and once to CH Mirko vom Steinkopf CDX, SchH III, FH. Both Gasto and Mirko were German imports. Heika is the dam of the ARC National Specialty Select CH Windwalker's Ada Y Mirko, SchH I, BH, and of Can. CH Rodsden's Lindenwood Lamia A/C CDX, VB (ARC Bronze Dam). She is the grand-dam of CH Nordike Aluger V Lindenwood, who went Best of Breed at the Medallion Rottweiler Club Specialty and the ARC Region III Specialty, Best of Opposite Sex at the ARC Region I Specialty, and Winners Dog at the ARC Region I Specialty. She is also the grand-dam of CH Big Timber's Baron CD, Winners Dog at the ARC Region III Specialty. According to Linda Michels: "All of her puppies were very similar in type, but *very* different in size." Remarkably, four of her first litter of six puppies have celebrated their eleventh birthday. *Author's note: Behind Heika's impressive pedigree are 3 Gold Sires; 1 Silver Sire; 1 Bronze Sire; 1 Gold Dam; and 2 Silver Dams. There is obvious depth in both Dutch and German bloodlines.*

CH POMAC'S LEXA P VANLARE CD, HIC – RO-7269
Silver Dam – ARC System
Whelped: December 31st 1982
Sire: CH Radio Ranch's Axel V Notara (Gold Sire)
Dam: CH Hallmark's 'The Sting'
Her record: 8 CH; 1 UD; 2 CD
Breeder: P. & O. McDonald (Pomac)
Owners: Greg Benkiser and L. Benkiser-Gach (Vanlare)
"Having seen some of the progeny from the first litters of CH Hallmark's 'The Sting' (call name

Jody), we were very excited when a breeding was planned between 'Jody' and CH Radio Ranch's Axel V Notara, who was well on his way towards becoming an all-time Top Producer," wrote Lauri Benkiser-Gach. There were two bitches in the litter: one a smaller, more clearly marked, tighter-footed bitch, and her larger-eared, bigger-bodied sister. "We chose the more typey, stocky, larger bitch who closely resembled her mother and have never regretted that decision. Lexa, 'Axel' spelled backwards...turned out to be a superb bitch, both in competition and as a producer of quality Rottweilers."

Lexa stood 25 inches at the withers and weighed 120 pounds, when fully mature. Despite her size, she was very well proportioned, with a superb topline and forechest. Lauri Gach recalled that the day she finished her AKC Championship, she was in whelp with 11 puppies, weighing some 135 pounds, and the judge was unaware of her delicate condition! As anticipated, she was a little long in the ear and somewhat long and narrow in the muzzle, and had weak pasterns and feet. "She was somewhat over-angulated front and rear, which actually resulted in excellent movement, as she was so well balanced. Not only strong in body, Lexa was also a very "alpha" personality who, while level-headed and even-tempered, would let you know when she didn't agree with you." Based on her genotype and phenotype, more compact males with stronger heads and better fronts, who came from good working backgrounds, were sought as sires. Lexa was bred 4 times (a total of 27 puppies) and produced 8 CH, 1 UD and 4 CD titled get, along with various other American and International titled offspring.

Her first two breedings were outcrosses, with the overall quality of puppies good, but with desirable traits mixed with inadequacies. Her breeding to CH Birch Hill's Quincy CD, TD, the more successful of the outcrosses, produced 4 AKC CH, 1 CKC CH, 1 PRKC CH, 1 States KC CH, 1 UD, 2 CD, 1 CKC CD and 3 HIC, as well as 1 OFA Excellent and 5 OFA Good (2 were never OFA'd). Lexa's last two litters were line breedings to CH Arinov's Mikhail Zum Vanlare. These puppies were more consistent in type, with the bitches looking like Lexa and the dogs very much like Micky, according to Lexa's owners. Out of the Quincy litter came the next generation bitch, V-1 rated Vanlare's Kimchi HIC. "Kimmy is very similar to Lexa in type, although she is smaller. Her head is blockier and she has an exceptional front with strong pasterns and tight feet. Unlike Lexa, she lacks forechest and is more moderately angulated, but with good balance, she also exhibits correct movement. While even-tempered, she, too, has a strong personality – a trait to be found in the majority of Lexa's offspring."

Kimmy was bred four times and produced 27 puppies, all outcross breedings. "We saw more of Lexa's faults in this generation than in any of Lexa's puppies, although the overall quality of the puppies is better with more breed type. Many are well on their way towards making Kimmy a seventh generation Top Producer." Two bitches out of Kimmy were kept, with plans to eventually line-breed [rather than outcross] them in order to strengthen type and to refine their overall quality. Kimmy's breeder-owners state that: "By continuing to look only at dogs with good pedigrees and proven working temperaments, we hope to achieve our objectives."

Author's note: CH Radio Ranch's Axel von Notara's pedigree includes a Gold Sire, a Gold Dam and a Silver Sire. CH Hallmark's The Sting has two Silver Sires behind her.

CH RAZDY'S AKEMO-GRANDE CD – RO-8329
Silver Sire – ARC System
Whelped: June 4th 1983
Sire: CH Cortina's Brute Force
Dam: CH Cedar Knolls Alexis (Bronze Dam)
His record: 16 CH; 1 CDX; 10 CD
Breeder: Judith Uggiano (Razdy)
Owner: Dorothy Smith & Judith Uggiano (Akemo/Razdy)

Akemo's sire, CH Cortina's Brute Force, was a medium-sized, powerfully built male, with a good topline, dark almond eyes, tiny triangular ears which were set well on his head, although the right would rose (fold) backwards when he got excited. According to his owner, "he was people suspicious, but with good confidence – outgoing when it suited him. Tough, but fair. A talker." Akemo's dam, CH Cedar Knolls Alexis, was a larger-sized bitch with large ears correctly placed on head and a broad square backskull, good topline, moderately angulated, good, straight front with tight feet and a nice sleek coat. Her owner recalls that "....she was people friendly, had excellent guarding ability, was very pushy and dominant....fearless, trained well, fair and not quick to judge situations unjustly, very alert and aware of everything that went on around her. Razzle had a larger vocabulary than most children". She became a Bronze Producer after only two litters.

In assessing Akemo's strengths, the owners describe him as possessing a strong topline; short, cobby body; robust; low station to the ground; good bottom line; "beautiful" classic square head; nice tight feet; almond eyes; correct coat with "lovely" mahogany color; correct "courageous" Rottweiler temperament and correct phenotype and genotype. His weaknesses, according to his owner, were that he was "Sometimes a bit too stubborn and Alpha, strong-willed for a modern day American house pet." He sometimes produced offspring that were "a bit too throaty for my taste." Akemo (call name "Bronson") produced very tough in temperament. Dorothy Smith further described him as "...an avid talker who always got the last word in, even for a cookie!"

He took time to assess the situation fairly, never expecting anyone to instruct him how to react. He was extremely sensitive to the tone of voice used or emotions displayed, whether sad or happy. Mrs Smith noted that..."His character was noble but very whimsical, never failing at eight or nine years of age to grab a dish towel or roll of paper towels and run through the house with it in his mouth". All of the above characteristics were definitely passed on to his progeny.

Mrs Smith feels "...his grandchildren and great-grandchildren are just as strong in phenotype, (but a bit milder in temperament), and a lot more tolerant and patient. He lives on in his get. By the end of this year [1994], we hope he will become a Gold Production sire." CH Razdy's Akemo Grande CD, ATTS, CGC "was the type of an animal that once you had the pleasure of meeting him, you would always have a lasting impression of him in your mind."

Author's note: Not surprising, Akemo's paternal grandsire was CH Kokas K's Degen Von Burga CD, TD, and his maternal granddam was a German import, CH Frauke vom Haus Schottroy.

Select 1 CH SOPHE VON BERGENHOF CDX CGC – RO 15681EL54-T
Silver Dam – ARC System
Whelped 18th September 1985
Sire: Select BIS CH Rhomark's Axel V Lerchenfeld UDT (Silver Sire)
Dam: Zimmer's Heidi V Kriegerhof
Her record: 7 CH; 2 CDX; 2 CD; 3 TD
Breeder: J.& S. Caruso & J. Zimmer (Kriegerhof/Zimmer)
Owner: Joan Harrison (Bergenhof)

Sophe's sire was BIS Select CH Rhomark's Axel V Lerchenfeld UDT, ARC Silver Sire. Behind Axel are one Gold and two Bronze Sires. Her dam was Zimmer's Heidi V Kriegerhof, a daughter of CH Rocky V Anderson, ARC Bronze Sire, and granddaughter of CH Radio Ranch's Axel V Notara, ARC Gold Sire – all three generations representing American-bred dogs and bitches.

Sophe, purchased "as a seven-week-old show prospect", was to become the foundation bitch at Bergenhof Kennels and at a young age was a serious competitor in the conformation ring. Her successful show career included Best of Opposite Sex at the 1988 ARC National Specialty and a place in the ARC Top Ten Bitches. Her first litter was sired by the Dutch import, BIS/BISS

Nelson von het Brabantpark (ARC Gold Sire). This litter produced six American champions, among them Best-in-Show CH Bergenhof's BB LeRoy Brown. The remaining five littermates all earned numerous obedience and tracking degrees. According to Joan Harrison, "The combination of Nelson's Dutch and German lines and Sophe's American lines had certainly proven to be a nick!" The Nelson-Sophe breeding was repeated in 1989, producing Group placing CH Iron Chancellor V Bergenhof and Bergenhof's Bruni V Braun, a major-pointed bitch, who won the Open bitch class at the 1993 ARC National Specialty.

Sophe's third litter was sired by V-1 BISS CH Von Der Hess Braxx V Ryatti in 1991. Braxx is a grandson of CH Eiko V Schwaiger Wappen, a German import through his sire's side, and on his dam's side a grandson of BIS Dut/Bel/Am CH Oscar VH Brabantpark. From this litter came Bergenhof's Reba of X-Bar-R, CD, a major-pointed bitch who is also pursuing the CDX title.

In 1992 Sophe was bred to BISS CH Cannon River Independence CD. Independence is from the American bloodlines developed by Rodsden's and Ebonstern. This was her fourth litter, the "D" litter. Bergenhof's Drifter, CD is now working towards his CDX, and several other littermates are winning their conformation classes in Specialty events.

Sophe's "E" and final litter was sired by BIS/BISS CH Von Der Lors Braxx Nelson CGC. Braxx, a son of BIS CH Nelson VH Brabantpark which again combines Dutch and German bloodlines. From this breeding came Bergenhof's Ebony Sierra TD (at eight months of age) and AKC pointed. Her littermates are also promising youngsters. Joan Harrison noted in evaluating Sophe's progeny: "I consistently see good fronts and strong rears, clean coming and going according to many professional handlers and judges, fluid side gait, nice heads and the intelligence and working attitude needed for the tasks the Rottweiler was bred to do." Sophe tied for ARC Top Producing Bitch in 1990 and again in 1992, and is listed in the Medallion Rottweiler Club Hall of Fame. "Today, at age nine, she is active and healthy and shares her home with CH Bergenhof's Gunther V Nelson CD, TD and Bergenhof's Ebony Sierra TD."

BISS/SELECT CH VOM SONNENHAUS KRUGERRAND CD –RO-14802. CERF #RO-462
Silver Sire – ARC System
Whelped: October 26th 1985-April 28th 1994
Sire: Belg. Schon CH Grave Kapenborgh CD, SchH I (Gold Sire)
Dam: Vom Sonnenhaus Tanja von Vera CD
His record: 12 CH; 2 CDX; 8 CD
Breeder: Franz & Hildegard Mikoleit (Vom Sonnenhaus)
Owner: Joanne & Richard Cochran (Rrand)

Krugerrand was sired by CH Grave Kapenborgh, CD, SchH I, a German dog imported by Mrs Mikoleit, who was then bred to her Vom Sonnenhaus Tanja von Vera CD. The pedigrees of both sire and dam carry the impressive bloodlines of Int. CH Ulli vom Kastanienbaum SchH III, FH; Am/Mex CH Wotan vom Kastanienbaum; and Int. CH Benno vom Allgauer Tor SchH III, FH.

"Krugerrand was an exceptional dog in many ways." He finished his championship at seventeen months of age, and in limited showing won numerous Best of Breeds and Group placements. His wins at the American Rottweiler Club National Specialties include: 1988 Select, 1989 Best of Breed, 1990 Select. He went Best of Breed in 1990 and 1991 at the ARC Region VI Specialties. According to Mrs Cochran: "He was V-rated at the 1990 Club Sieger Show in Las Vegas, Nevada and tested very high for Schutzhund work, but we did not pursue it." He received his CD title, owner-handled, after only six months of training with scores of 187, 191 and 194$\frac{1}{2}$.

Besides his "beautiful" conformation, Krugerrand possessed a very sound "Alpha" temperament, and was a good working dog. His owner noted that "His strengths were a very strong, straight topline, black eyes, and mouth. The mouth had pink marbling in later years. His eyes were beautiful, but a little on the round side. I see many of Krugerrand's qualities in his children and grandchildren: the nice toplines, movement and his beautiful head. Of course, the beauty comes from the magical combination of the male and bitch," noted Mrs. Cochran.

Krugerrand passed on in April of 1994. "Although we had much too short a time with him, we are very thankful and blessed to have had such a wonderful, loving and devoted companion. His memory will live on in his progeny."

SUMMARY

The bloodlines discussed here are only a fraction of those which have contributed to the success of the Rottweiler breed in the United States during the past 35-40 years. While the "greats" of the past are, in most cases, off the five-generation pedigrees, they live on genetically. We now have the "greats" of the present to carry the breed forward. In researching this project, it was extremely interesting for me to note the commonality of pedigrees among these particular dogs and bitches. The following is an appropriate quotation from an article written in 1965 by Dr Edward Montgomery (noted breeder of Bull Terriers, Cattle and Thoroughbred horses, as well as an AKC approved judge of all Terrier breeds), taken from the October 7, 1994 issue of *Dog News*.

"All breeds of dogs which exist today are the result of the blood of the greats and near-greats of that breed. Improvement in a breed comes only through a dog or a bitch or both which are ahead of their time, which cast future events from their shadows, which have in their genetic and physical make-up the transmittable inheritance to improve themselves. There are many specimens in every breed relatively free from faults. These are all bred too frequently and thus compound their ordinariness and low quality. On the other hand, the striking stud or the exceptional bitch which teem with type, though full of faults, will produce better than themselves.

"To retain and possibly improve the type, quality and conformation in a few of the progeny is the aim of a breeding. Then, if you lose a few of the faults in these same progeny, you have bred a most successful litter, even a great one."

KEY TO ABBREVIATIONS

A/C: American and Canadian
CH: Champion
OTCH: Obedience Trial Champion (In the United States, a title won after the Utility Dog degree. In Canada equal to a Utility Dog Title.)
CD: Companion Dog
CDX: Companion Dog Excellent
UD: Utility Dog
TD: Tracking Dog
TDX: Tracking Dog Excellent
PC: Mexican Companion Dog
TT: Temperament tested by American Temperament Test Association
BS: Bundessieger
BSG: Bundessiegerin

KS: Klubsieger
WS: World Sieger
ES: Europasieger
SchH: Schutzhund
FH: Fartenhund (Tracking)
AD: Endurance Test
VB: Traffic Sure Companion
WD, WB: Winners Dog, Winners Bitch
BW: Best of Winners
BOB: Best of Breed
BOS: Best of Opposite Sex
BISS: Best in Specialty Show
AGI: 1st Level Agility
HIC: Herding Instinct Certificate
TDI: Therapy Dog International

Chapter Eighteen

THE ROTTWEILER WORLDWIDE

The Rottweiler has spread from its German homeland, and has now achieved worldwide popularity. Types may vary from country to country, but the essential Rottweiler character, which has made the breed so highly-prized, remains unmistakable. In some countries, the Rottweiler is a relatively recent import and the breed is still in the early stages of establishing itself. Elsewhere, the Rottweiler has achieved a national identity, drawing on a wide gene-pool within its adopted home. Both the show and the working side of the Rottweiler have been developed, and it is interesting to see how the versatile Rottweiler has adapted to the different demands made on it, both in terms of work and in adapting to widely varying climates. From the frozen terrain of Finland to the lush, tropical climate of Singapore, the Rottweiler has triumphed to become one of the world's most popular breeds.

AUSTRALIA
By Helen Read

EARLY HISTORY
Doug Mummery (Heatherglen) was the first person to attempt to import a Rottweiler into Australia. However, the dog, called Balthazar, imported from the UK, died in transit to Australia in 1959. So it was not until August 1962 that the first Rottweilers arrived in Australia. These dogs belonged to an Englishman, Roy Smith, who bred Rottweilers in the UK with the Rintelna prefix. Roy emigrated to Australia, bringing with him a Rottweiler male, named Rintelna the Dragoon, and a bitch, named Rintelna the Chatelaine.

The pair were mated, and a litter was born in quarantine in Perth. Only one buyer could be found for this new breed, and that was Mr De Jong of Adelaide. He took a bitch, called Rintelna the Empress, with him to Adelaide, and the rest of the litter had to be destroyed. Dragoon and Chatelaine were mated again, and two dogs and two bitches were produced in July 1963. One bitch was donated to Guide Dogs and the other, Rintelna the Fatale, was purchased by Doug Mummery. Fatale was later bred to Doug's British import, Pilgrimsway Loko, who arrived in Australia in 1963. Both the original imports died of cancer in 1967.

Marthleen Balthazar, a son of Loki and the Empress, was the first Obedience-titled Rottweiler in Australia. He gained conformation Championship, plus Companion Dog and Companion Dog Excellent titles.

ESTABLISHING THE BREED
From this point onwards, many imports arrived in Australia and the breed became firmly established. Breed Clubs were set up, with the Victoria Club leading the way in 1971, followed by New South Wales and South Australia in 1976, Western Australia in 1986, and Northern

ABOVE: Aust. Ch. Stromhall Picka Pack: A Specialty and Royal Show winner, who has produced Specialty and Royal Show winning offspring. Owned by Sue Bashford.   Photo courtesy: Sue Bashford.

ABOVE: Aust. Ch. Ormslee Proud Impudence (left),Top Show Bitch in Victoria 1988, and Aust. Ch. Ormslee Proud Herald CDX, TD, AD. Owned by Helen Read .

Photo courtesy: Helen Read.

LEFT: Aust. Ch. Jaegersieger Alpha CDX, BH, owned by John and Val Leigh of the Dreistleigh kennel.   Photo courtesy: John and Val Leigh.

BELOW: Beau Ormslee Maxamilian, owned by John and Angie Stoneham.
Photo courtesy: John and Angie Stoneham.

Territory in 1987. The NT club has since folded, and two new clubs have been formed – one in NSW (Northern Districts Rottweiler Club, 1987), and another in ACT in 1991. A National Rottweiler Council was formed in 1988.

THE CURRENT SCENE

Rottweilers are now very popular in Australia, with the population growth following world trends, which show ever-increasing numbers. The rapid increase in numbers has caused concern in Australia, as it has elsewhere in the world. Fortunately, breed clubs are well organised in each state, and they are working hard to educate the public and to maintain the correct calm, stable temperament of the Rottweiler. In Australia, as elsewhere, the Rottweiler is valued as the epitome of the perfect companion dog – hence the popularity of the breed.

As well as being much-loved family pets, the Rottweiler is used in various working competitions, and the success in these fields shows the tremendous versatility of the breed.

Because of the distance between Europe and Australia, the Rottweiler Clubs make a point of inviting specialist conformation and working judges to assess the breed. The FCI Breed Standard, from the Rottweiler's country of origin, is used in Australia. The leading breeders include John and Val Leigh (Dreistleigh), who have had great success with Ch. Jaegersieger Alpha CDX, BH and Winn von der Grurmanscheide BH, Sch II, AD, Zpt (imp. Germany); Sue Bashford (Sanmar) whose most famous dog is Ch. Stromhall Picka Pack, a Specialty and Royal Show winner who has gone on to produce Specialty and Royal Show winners, and Helen Read (Ormslee), who breeds for the show ring and for Obedience, most notably with Dual Ch. Auslese Bold Gammon – Australia's first dual-titled Rottweiler. The overall quality of the Rottweiler in Australia is good, with many top-class dogs. Imports come into Australia from all over the world, bringing in fresh bloodlines, and the import of semen from top dogs in other countries also helps to ensure the continuing health of the breed in Australia.

NEW ZEALAND
By Alison Franks

EARLY HISTORY
The first Rottweiler to be registered with the New Zealand Kennel Club was Auslese Montrachet (imp. Australia) who was whelped in March 1970. He was soon followed by Asgardweiler Winston (imp. Australia), whelped in November 1971, who became the first New Zealand Champion. The next Australian imports were Auslese Lafite and Auslese Echezeaux, bringing the total number of Rottweilers in New Zealand to four!

The first bitch to be imported from the UK was NZ Ch. Attila Bathsheba, who was imported in whelp to Upend Gallant Alf, and the resulting litter was probably the first born in New Zealand. Ch. Korobeit Hero, who gained his title in 1976, was rated the pick of the litter. He was an outstanding mover, but was light in build. Heatherglen Hebe (imp. Australia) gained her title at the same time, but she was outstanding in quality. Her maternal grandsire was Attila Ajax, and she went on to produce Champion offspring, sired by Ch. Korobeit Hero, whose maternal grandsire was Attila Astrid. Among their progeny was Ch. Blairgowie Bayla Lugossi, the first Rottweiler to gain CDX and UDX titles in New Zealand.

Kerugal Black Cleo (imp. Australia) was also mated to Hero, and in the resulting litter was Overlander Helga, who became the foundation for Jim and Sheena Ferguson's Firgorran kennels. When Helga was mated to Alf Church's import, Grossheim Igor, they produced Ch. Great Valour of Firgorran, sire of New Zealand's first Grand Champion Rottweiler, Gr. Ch. Salvo of Firgorran.

An increasing number of imports followed in the next few years, mostly from Australia, but bringing German and British bloodlines into the country.

THE CURRENT SCENE
There are now three Rottweiler breed clubs in New Zealand: The Rottweiler Club, Auckland, the Central Rottweiler Club, Wellington, and the South Island Rottweiler Club, Christchurch. The Central Rottweiler Club, formed in 1984, has Championship status, and also caters for Obedience and Agility competitors. The South Island Rottweiler Cub was recognised by the NZKC in 1987, and in 1992 it was granted Champion status. Obedience training is a significant part of the club's activities. Leading Rottweiler breeders include Maggie and Andy Murray (Murradale), Errol Tooth (Geshundheit), Logan and Jill Linton (Linden Grange), Leonard Ferns (Pantheon), Alison Franks (Sanduka), Maxene Kauri (Rothgar), and the von Sahne kennel.

SINGAPORE
By Tony Ong

EARLY HISTORY
The Rottweiler was not known in Singapore until the late 1970s when the first Rottweiler was imported from Australia. The breed soon grew in popularity and imports from the UK, Germany, the Netherlands and Australia followed. To begin with it was in its role as guard dog that the Rottweiler was most prized, but the breed soon became an attraction at dog shows and, with German Shepherd Dogs, was making up one-fifth of entries at the Singapore All Breed championship shows. Rottweiler imports and litter registrations increased throughout the eighties, while, at the same time, the number of Dobermanns dwindled. The breed spread to other South-East Asian nations, such as Malaysia, Indonesia and Thailand.

THE CURRENT SCENE
There are three leading kennels breeding Rottweilers at the present time: Lismore, Willieko and Lisking. Alex Chua (Lismore) phased out his kennel of German Shepherd Dogs to concentrate on breeding Rottweilers. He started his line with a Champion called Rupert from the Brabantsia line in Australia, who he imported in 1983. Rupert achieved some success in the show ring, and his most successful litter was from a mating to an Australian dam, Ch. Kuhnheit Frau Sigrid, owned by the Willieko kennel. However, it was the importation of two German Rottweilers in the early 1990s – Esta von Lenthe and Dago von Lenthe – that was to be the turning point for this kennel. William Koh (Willieko) imported Kuhnheit Frau Sigrid from Australia in 1986. She did well in the show ring, and was mated to Brabantsia Rupert in 1989. A bitch from this litter, Willieko Frau Rupertrid Beddy was acquired by Tony Ong (Lisking), and William Koh kept Willieko Frau Rupertrid Betty. Both bitches shone at shows, and Betty became a Champion in 1992. Tony Ong's Lisking kennel was formed in 1990, and Willieko Frau Rupertrid Beddy was quick to make her mark on the show scene. In 1991 she was mated to the English dog, Hanbar Fedor, which resulted in a litter of nine puppies. Five of them were shown in Singapore and achieved good ratings. The pick of the litter was Lisking Gene Autry, who achieved Best in Show status. There are many Rottweiler owners and breeders in Singapore who are not registered with the Singapore Kennel Club, and many Rottweiler puppies are imported without registration papers, filling the demand created by those who want to keep the Rottweiler as a guard. However, Rottweiler entries average around 25 at most Championship shows, second only to the GSD.

SOUTH AFRICA
By Denyse Tutt

EARLY HISTORY
The first Rottweilers were reported in South West Africa in 1914, arriving with the German

RIGHT: NZ Ch. Linden Grange Bridermei (Kauri Lodge Dark Czar – Brantberg Sugar Bear): Best in Show at the Central Rottweiler Club Specialty Championship Show 1990. Owned by Errol Tooth of the Geshundheit kennel.
Photo courtesy: Errol Tooth.

NZ Ch. Sanduka Frankly Speaking: A fine representative of Alison Franks' Sanduka kennel.
Photo courtesy: Alison Franks.

NZ Ch. Rothgar Pickerty Witch: Specialty Reserve Best in Show winner. Owned and bred by Maxene Kauri of the Rothgar kennel.

RIGHT: Ch. Esta von Lenthe, pictured in Bishan Park, Singapore. Owned by Alex Chua of the Lisemore kennel. *Photo courtesy: Alex Chua.*

BELOW: Representatives of William Koh's Willieko kennel – all four Rottweilers were whelped in Singapore. *Photo courtesy: William Koh.*

ABOVE: S.A. Ch. Bezville Carmen and S.A. Ch. Bezville Cajan:
This brother and sister have both been awarded eight 'V'
gradings under ADRK specialist judges.

RIGHT: S.A. Ch. Jimy von der Ruine Scharfeneck of Tankerville
(Lesko von der Karl Adolf Ranch – Esta von der Ruine
Scharfeneck. Owned by Pam and Dudley Bennet of the
Tankerville kennel.   Photo courtesy: Pam and Dudley Bennet.

ABOVE: S.A. Ch. St. Tuttston Lando (Lenlee
Phantom – St Truidens Samantha of St.
Tuttston). Bred and owned by Denyse Tutt of
the St. Tuttson kennel.

LEFT: S.A. St. Tuttson Raine (Ch. Jagen Blue
Ragged Robin of Sheidal – Ch. St. Tuttson
Jenna). Bred and owned by Denyse Tutt of the
St. Tuttson kennel.

Photos courtesy: Denyse Tutt.

settlers of that era. However, it was not until 1934 that the first three Rottweilers were registered with the Kennel Union of South Africa. They were owned by the South African Police, and were listed as Beauty (Arras v Riebland – Blanka v Pfalzgau), her litter sister Bella, and Minnar (Arras v Riebland). The South African Defence Force also had Rottweilers from an early date. They are still incorporated into their programmes today, although the German Shepherd Dog has taken over to a certain extent.

The early South African Rottweilers had a good background of Dutch, English and German bloodlines. Links with the UK were strengthened with the adoption of the British Rottweiler Breed Standard, which was adhered to for many years. However, in 1987 it was decided to follow the 'mother' country (Germany), and the FCI was officially adopted in 1987.

From the sixties onwards, the number of Rottweiler imports steadily increased, often accompanied by their owners. Stella Gawthop (Binjum) arrived in 1963 with her bitch Dada of Mallion. Jan Cornelius (Arcadia) arrived in the late sixties with Chesara Dark Zorro, and later imported a number of Chesara bitches from Judy and Larry Elsden's UK kennel. Imports also came from the Vom Gromerstein kennel in the Netherlands. In 1973 Maud Wait arrived with Lenlee Phantom. Unfortunately, he sired only one litter of puppies in South Africa, and that was from a mating to St Truidens Samantha of St. Tuttson, owned by Denyse Tutt (St. Tuttson). The litter was outstanding and included the famous Ch. Tuttston Lando.

ESTABLISHING THE BREED
From these early beginnings, the Rottweiler steadily increased in popularity until it became the second highest registered breed in South Africa. Registrations reached their highest point of 4581 in 1983. They have since dropped to around the 1500 mark. Breed clubs were formed, and there are now seven Rottweiler breed clubs in South Africa: the Rottweiler Working and Breeding Association of Transvaal, the Natal Rottweiler Association, the Rottweiler Club of Eastern Transvaal, the Meridian Rottweiler League, the Rottweiler Club of Eastern Province, and the Genesis Rottweiler Club.

THE CURRENT SCENE
The best-known kennels breeding Rottweilers include Binjum (1959), Arcadia (1968), Betasso (1970), St. Tuttson (1971), Von Sophias (1972), Tankerville (1976). Kennels registered within the last decade include: Sheidal, Bezville, Teversal, Engelberg, Madleycott, Amjade, Gelert, Mipret, Joybo, Arakdale, vom Paladin and Romaniwil.

The most influential sire in South Africa is provably Mr and Mrs David Lower's imported male, Ch. Jagen Blue Ragged Robin of Sheidal, bred in the UK by Les Price. The top-winning male is Ch. Von Sophias Bulli, bred by Sophie Langen. His wins include: over 100 BOBs, 60 Group 1st placings, numerous BIS placings, and KUSA National Dog 1989-1991. He has produced many Champions, and is still in strong demand as a sire.

On the working side, Rottweilers compete in Obedience, Classic Working Trials, International Working Trials (LWT), the Swedish Aptitude Test, Carting and Dog Jumping. The Rottweiler National Council is hoping to introduce the 'Beleighthunde' Family Dog (FD) test for Rottweilers in the near future.

ZIMBABWE
By Cyndy Ordman

EARLY HISTORY
The first Rottweiler in Zimbabwe was imported from South Africa in 1973 by Mrs Billie Adams of the Essexvale kennel. Rutah of Essexvale was the first Rottweiler to be exhibited and to gain

Rotterburg von Lugerburg IPO II, CDEX, TDIEX, Class C Obedience. Owned and trained by Cyndy Ordman in Zimbabwe.
Photo courtesy: Cyndy Ordman.

Ch. Valentine Cruzeiro IOP I, Class B Obedience. Owned and trained by Graham Rees in Zimbabwe.
Photo: Barry H.

Ch. Mardorn Bandit with owner Marie Cramond of the Marant kennel. This is one of the most successful Rottweilers in the breed ring in Zimbabwe with 14 CCs, 14 Best of Breed, and two Best in Show wins.
Photo courtesy: Marie Cramond.

Six-month-old litter brothers, bred by Marie Cramond of the Marant kennel.
Photo Barry H.

Championship status. In 1981 Mr and Mrs Dave Pell purchased three-year-old Ch. Essexvale Gina from Mrs Adams, and she became the first Rottweiler to win a Best in Show award, judged by R. Norris from Australia.

In 1989 the Rottweiler Association of Zimbabwe (RAZ) had a membership of 52, and was granted affiliation to the Zimbabwe Kennel Club. The KC is affiliated to the FCI, and Rottweilers are judged by the FCI Breed Standard. From 1986 to 1989 Rottweiler registrations averaged 200 a year; they then started to drop dramatically, due to the adverse publicity the breed received. From 1991 to 1993 registrations averaged 55 a year.

THE CURRENT SCENE
Membership of RAZ is now 142, and the club invited specialist Rottweiler judges to officiate at its annual Championship show. There are now a number of leading Rottweiler breeders who are working hard to improve the standard and quality of Rottweilers in Zimbabwe, and this has resulted in some high-quality imports from South Africa.

Influential breeders include: Marjory McGhee (Mardorn), Marie Cramond (Marant), Nigel Sligh (Burgoyne), and Andreas Livaditakis (Labatse). Cyndy Ordman (von Lugerburg) has concentrated on the working side of the Rottweiler, and her Rottweilers compete in all working disciplines throughout Zimbabwe. Graham Rees and Gerry Webster have also trained some highly successful Rottweilers in the working disciplines.

FINLAND
By Katriina Vuorinen

EARLY HISTORY
Rottweilers were registered in Finland as early as 1920. The first recorded Rottweiler was a bitch called Lutzi av Medestein, bred by Lieutenant A. Winge and owned by Mrs L. Winge. She was sired by Nero av Aso out of Gyllis-Lutzi. The first recorded male was Hammarby's Puck (King av Aso – Dolly av Medestein), who was born on March 1st 1923. He was owned by Sea Captain Gustaf Apelgren. The first Rottweiler litter was born in Finland in 1933. Sired by Lindhagas Gero, the dam was Lindhagas Bella, owned by Mrs Moen Ullberg of the Kiikkuniemen prefix.

The Finnish Rottweiler Club was founded in April 1946. To begin with, it was a breed club in own right, but a sub-division of a bigger working dog club. By the end of 1946 the club had 33 members, who owned a total of 26 Rottweilers.

ESTABLISHING THE BREED
As the breed began to grow in numbers in Finland, vom Heidemmoor emerged as the most important and influential kennel. The prefix was given to Maria and Olavi Pasanen in 1949. In 1945 a Rottweiler bitch, Sonnbos Happy (Tell Vonden Hackerbruecke – Nizy) was imported from Sweden in whelp to Ch. Raj. The Rottweilers from the resulting litter included Belzebub and Barry, who were to form the foundation of the kennel's breeding programme.

In the sixties the number of Rottweiler kennels gradually increased. They included: vom Feuerwald, von Birkenweiler, Joukonheimon, Attalos, Negusheim, von Heidesse, Katajiston, Kaisukan, Katweilers, Finnweilers, Vahvan-Tassun and Onnimannin. The majority of these kennels are still going strong today.

Initially, nearly all the Rottweilers were imported from Sweden. The founding of the SRY-FRF marked an important starting point for breeding in Finland. Breeders had to overcome early difficulties, particularly lack of knowledge regarding the pedigrees of their dogs, and possible faults and weaknesses in imported lines.

LEFT: Vahvan-Tassun Chiquitax, pictured as an adult in Finland.

Photo: Monica Anderson-Anttila.

BELOW: Finnish Show and Working Ch. Aiken Alfa (Loytovuoren Santeri – Yornilan Hellu) bred by P. Marin-Matikainen, owned by Tumo Vanhatalo.

Photo courtesy: Katriina Vuorinen.

RIGHT: Finnish Working Ch. Honkala Faarao (Finnweilers Xerkses – Honkala Nerita) bred by Arja Aaltonen, owned by Paula Haggman and Jorma Reinila.   Photo: Jorma Reinila.

BELOW: Minzenhof Yazz (Vahvan-Tassun Yki – Minzenhof Royce) bred by Maijaliisa Rainesto, owned by Katja Hammar and Mika Reini-kainen.   Photo courtesy: Katriina Vuorinen.

THE CURRENT SCENE

Breeding is still on a small scale in Finland, with the majority of kennels keeping a couple of bitches living with the family. A number of kennels, formed in the last few years have achieved considerable success. They include: Minzenhof, Ukko-Pekan, Muskett, Fold's Face and Weiferin.

The Finnish Rottweiler Club has grown as the popularity of the Rottweiler has become more widespread. There are now over 3,000 members; there are nine sub-divisions of the parent club, plus three independent Rottweiler clubs that organise training for Working Trials. The breed has proved very successful in this field, and is also highly valued as a rescue dog. Obedience training plays an important part in Finland, as the Rottweiler is very much a dog who lives at home with the family and children.

Registrations of Rottweiler puppies have grown dramatically, going from 674 in 1989 to over 1,000 in 1993. Imported puppies, which totalled 43 in 1993, came mostly from Estonia, with some from Germany. Finnish breeders produced 200 litters in 1993, and 45 per cent were born of foreign parents or of a parent of foreign origin. To date, tail-docking is still allowed in Finland, although there have been moves to make this practice illegal.

Chapter Nineteen

HEALTH CARE

This chapter sets out to give some simple advice on maintaining the health of your Rottweiler. It is not exhaustive and cannot be so. However, it does give guidance in recognising that your dog is fit and well or conversely in recognising poor health.

Like it or not, Rottweilers tend to have a "be careful" reputation with veterinarians because of the few which are not well-mannered in the surgery. The Rottweiler is a strong and imposing dog, and good socialisation and training are an essential requisite. Alongside this it would be sensible to ensure your dog is comfortable with strangers and tolerant of having feet examined and claws clipped, and ears, eyes and teeth examined, and is not nervous about people handling their hindquarters. Therefore the first part of this chapter deals with grooming and hygiene, as this is the basis of trouble-free visits to the surgery. It is also the way you will notice when something is amiss, for if you groom your dog regularly you will notice subtle changes which indicate that your dog is not in the best of health. It is generally very obvious when your dog is feeling *acutely* ill, but sometimes illness is less obvious in the early phases. Subtle changes will be noticed by the person who examines their dog regularly, and early recognition of problems gives every chance of cure. Maintaining a healthy dog means you will need a veterinary surgeon, so choose one you get on with and one who is comfortable with Rottweilers. Veterinary services are not cheap either, so consider some form of health insurance to be certain that the best veterinary care is available to your dog.

GENERAL GROOMING AND HYGIENE
Rottweilers are not difficult dogs when it comes to grooming. Their relatively short coats benefit from a daily brush and comb, especially when they are shedding (or moulting). Grooming is also an ideal time to check that your dog is in good condition, and it is a demonstration to your dog that being handled can be pleasurable and fun.

Start grooming your Rottweiler as a puppy by lightly brushing with a soft brush to ensure he/she grows up accepting this process as routine and normal. Also get others to groom your dog; it does wonders for your dog's future temperament and socialisation. Of course, be gentle and kind, as rough handling can have a detrimental effect too!

As you brush your dog, look at the condition of the skin and coat; note areas of coat thinness or alopecia. Is there any evidence of parasites and, of course, any signs of swelling or tumours? When you become accustomed to looking regularly at the normal dog you will more rapidly notice anything abnormal. As part of the grooming process, check your dog's ears, eyes and teeth and do not forget the rear end either!

EYES: These should be clear, bright and alert. Eyes are the windows of the body and you will see through them how your dog is feeling. In ill health eyes lose their lustre and you will gain the strong impression that all is not well. Eyes also suffer their own specific diseases, so any signs of abnormal redness or discharge should receive veterinary attention. Both eyes should appear the same, so non-uniformity of the eyes should attract concern.

EARS: A sore ear is probably one of the most irritating conditions a dog can have, and an irritated Rottweiler can certainly be a problem. So preventing ear problems is a sensible activity. Cleaning ears is a routine job that anyone can do, but do not prod and poke the ear canal beyond what you can see. Clean the ears with an ear bud after applying suitable ear drops to dislodge any wax. Your vet can supply and advise on suitable ear cleaning preparations.

The external ear canal runs downwards and inwards from the exterior, and when using ear drops you will need to massage the base of the ear to ensure the drops reach the bottom of the ear canal. This massage will also help to dislodge any wax or debris too. The area to massage is around two inches (5cms) below the opening of the ear, just about where the ear tip falls on the face. If you have doubts about this, ask your vet for guidance. Ear cleaning should not be too frequent or too vigorous. Fortnightly should be often enough.

TEETH: Dental care has become much more of an issue over recent years. There are now canine toothpastes which can be used to regularly clean your Rottweiler's teeth. Be careful in young puppies, as they may have sore gums when they change their teeth, so as a general rule teeth cleaning only needs to be done once your dog has permanent teeth. However, if you wait until then to start examining and cleaning teeth you may find your dog is reluctant to co-operate. So start checking the teeth and mouth in young puppies.

Start gentle brushing at around four to five months of age, avoiding obviously sore areas where teeth are erupting, and remember to clean all the teeth, not just the front ones. The benefits will be stronger, healthier teeth and sweeter breath. This is a good time to look for dental problems, any signs of which are for veterinary attention, especially if the teeth have any tartar on them and need cleaning with more than a brush. Young puppies will lose their milk (deciduous) teeth and grow permanent teeth between four and seven months of age and occasionally the milk teeth are reluctant to dislodge. These persistent juvenile teeth can cause problems for the new permanent teeth and push them out of line. Watch for these problems and ask for help if they occur.

NAILS: Keep nails short, as over-grown nails can be liable to breakage or may cause toe injuries. Cutting nails is an art and ask for advice if you have never done it before. If you cut too short you will draw blood and it will hurt the dog – not a very good experience for all concerned. No doubt you will occasionally cut too short (we all do!) and a styptic pencil or some potassium permanganate is useful for stopping the nail tip bleeding.

Use good "guillotine-like" clippers – and for Rottweilers they need to be good and strong. Take only the tip and cut the nail horizontally not vertically. Use a nail file if you want to go further. When the foot is on the ground the cut edge should be horizontal to the ground.

Nails do sometimes get split or broken and these will often bleed and be very painful. If the broken nail can be cut off, do so; but if it is really painful for your dog he may need veterinary help. If it is left it will take a long time to heal and your dog will be quite lame.

Examination of the feet of a dog gives a good indication of fitness. Tight, well knuckled feet indicate fitness, whereas flat, splayed feet indicate the opposite.

VACCINATIONS

There are several diseases in dogs for which there are vaccines available. Generally these diseases have serious consequences for dogs and are also difficult to treat. Therefore it is sensible to immunise our companions to ensure they do not suffer these infections. Your veterinarian can advise you of the recommended timing of these vaccinations, but generally they commence with a course of two injections, the first given between eight to twelve weeks of age and the second two to four weeks later. Sometimes a third vaccine is recommended in Rottweilers for parvovirus, to ensure immunity to this specific disease (see discussion on parvovirus below).

After the initial puppy course it is generally recommended that annual booster vaccinations are also given to ensure life-long immunity. In time, vaccine technology may mean this is unnecessary for some of the classic canine diseases but at the moment the use of annual boosters is the best advice that can be given. The diseases against which we commonly vaccinate deserve some discussion, if only to justify the need for vaccination. They are the following:

DISTEMPER: This is a viral disease of dogs which is thankfully now seen only sporadically in most of the western countries today, although outbreaks do still occur in urban communities from time to time. The virus is related to the measles virus and like measles can afflict the brain. Initially the infection causes a mild illness, the best description being that the animal is off colour for a few days. The virus infects nearly all tissues, including the brain, the invasion of which causes nervous symptoms such as fits and paralysis or spasms and twitching. There is no reliable cure once this stage has been reached. The chronic disease is unpleasant for owner and dog, and euthanasia is often the only sensible option.

The vaccines used today are live vaccines which are highly effective in inducing immunity to the disease. Occasionally the disease is seen in country areas where there is unlikely to be a regular challenge from natural infection and where owners have allowed immunity to wane due to inadequate vaccine boosters. It can be very sad to lose an old friend to this preventable disease.

Distemper is a disease of the dog family and can infect relatives to the dog, and also those of mink and raccoons (e.g. the fox and other wild dogs, the ferret, the skunk and coati-mundi).

HEPATITIS: This is another viral disease which comes in principally two forms and is spread by *apparently* normal but infected dogs. It is now seen only sporadically, thanks mainly to vaccination programmes. The disease invariably causes death or severe debility principally due to the liver damage inflicted by the virus, although the virus is capable of damaging a whole variety of organs. Essentially the virus destroys the liver cells and this interferes with many body functions but most dramatically with blood clotting. So haemorrhages are a common symptom. Despite the best medical attention, cases of viral hepatitis often fail to survive. Fortunately the modified live vaccines, which are available, are excellent and therefore highly protective.

LEPTOSPIROSIS: This is a bacterial disease which uses the rat as its main vector. Infection damages liver and kidney principally but also affects heart muscle and the bowel. Acute infection is highly damaging to most major organs. The liver is capable of regenerating damaged cells whereas the kidney is not. Therefore kidney damage is permanent and kidney failure is a very serious consequence of this disease. Vaccines are reasonably effective and yearly boosters are *strongly recommended.* Vaccination prevents the disease in its worst forms, but the fact that many dogs suffer from chronic kidney disease later in life suggests that we are not wholly successful in combating leptospirosis in dogs using vaccines. Therefore as the disease is carried by rats, rodent control is essential. In particular, be sure dogs drink clean fresh water and that rats cannot contaminate water dishes. As a bacterial infection leptospirosis can be treated with antibiotics but it is preferable to maintain immunity as the first line of defence.

PARVOVIRUS: This is another viral disease of dogs. However, unlike the previous viruses which rely on direct animal contact, parvoviruses can be brought home on clothing or shoes. Parvoviruses survive for long periods in the environment and thus can infect dogs long after outbreaks seem to have finished. The virus attacks the bowel causing intense and profuse sickness and diarrhoea. Dehydration is the real killer in this disease and even in those dogs which survive recovery is prolonged and may never be absolute.

Parvovirus is a relatively new disease, appearing simultaneously in several countries in 1978. At first it ravaged the dog population, but rapid vaccine development has now limited its incidence and its effects. However, parvovirus should never be underestimated and it still kills puppies in significant numbers. Rottweilers seem to be particularly at risk from parvovirus. Although research has shown that vaccines are effective in producing immunity, it is a fact that Rottweilers do seem to die more frequently from parvovirus than most other breeds. The reason, for the moment, is uncertain; perhaps it is because the Rottweiler has some inherent weakness in its ability to combat the disease? We just do not know.

It was speculated at one time that some Rottweilers did not respond to the vaccine given at eight to twelve weeks of age, but it has been since shown that Rottweiler pups show no difference to other breeds in their response to vaccination at this age. However, because of this theory many vets will recommend that a Rottweiler is not taken away from home until it receives a third dose of vaccine at eighteen weeks of age. Yet to do this will interfere with the socialisation of young puppies, which is essential between eight and eighteen weeks of age.

Such advice makes a difficult decision for the puppy owner. Do you go against your vet's advice and decide to take the risk of this disease in the interests of achieving adequate socialisation of young puppies? Hopefully, by attending training classes consisting of only vaccinated dogs this risk is minimised and socialisation can proceed with safety.

RABIES: This is a viral disease that is transmissible to all mammals including man. This disease is a horror, invading the nervous system and causing intense character changes followed by seizures, paralysis and death. The major criminal in the spread of rabies is thought to be the fox in Europe and the raccoon in the United States, although any feral carnivore is able to transmit the disease. As the character changes involved in this disease mean the affected animal may wander into populated areas this is a real threat to domestic animals and man.

Historically, vaccines were painful to administer and not reliable, but now there are very much improved vaccines available to control the spread of disease. In particular an oral vaccine is being used in western Europe, in bait, to prevent the spread of the disease in the fox population, with apparently good success. In those countries which have lived with rabies there is far less inherent fear of the disease than in those who have never experienced it as an endemic disease. However, it is a virus disease that needs to be controlled because of its fatal and horrific implications for man. To do this some countries have a compulsory rabies vaccination policy (e.g. USA, Germany) and others, such as the UK, which are free of the disease tend to favour a quarantine policy to control the disease. The rabies vaccine is then used only in dogs for export.

KENNEL COUGH: This is a syndrome caused by a cocktail of infectious agents and there are vaccines available for immunising dogs against the principal viruses and bacteria involved in the kennel cough syndrome. Spread principally through direct contact, it is boarding kennels and dog shows that are often incriminated for spreading this disease. This infection is not so life threatening as the others we have discussed. There is popular disagreement about how effective the vaccines are in the practical sense, but nevertheless many boarding kennel owners prefer dogs to have been immunised against the disease prior to spending time in kennels.

It is usually initiated by a virus which causes inflammation of the major airways to the lungs, the dog coughs and is lethargic for a few days. Secondary infection with bacteria can prolong the disease for several weeks and, left untreated, it can cause significant damage to the respiratory system. Afflicted dogs will cough for several weeks and may be carriers of the disease agents during that time. So do consult your vet for treatment.

In my experieince, recovered dogs are subsequently immune or at least suffer the disease more lightly on later occasions. Kennel cough can be treated satisfactorily in the vast majority of cases, providing the problem is referred to your veterinary surgeon promptly.

SUMMARY

Thanks to effective vaccines, dogs do not commonly die of the diseases discussed above in the western world, and so it is easy to become complacent about the situation when so little disease is seen. Yet all the diseases described have very serious implications for dogs. This alone is sufficient justification for immunisation to continue.

PARASITES

When you own a dog you can be sure that you will need to pay some attention to parasites. Most people regard the presence of parasites with some considerable horror, which is understandable but unrealistic. All dogs will carry parasites from time to time. The secret is to know which ones are a significant problem, and how to rid your pet of the infestation and prevent it recurring.

Let us start with the parasites which you may find on the skin and coat of your Rottweiler.

EXTERNAL PARASITES

FLEAS: Most mammals have a type of flea which likes to infest them, and the dog is no different. However, the flea is not overly selective and dog fleas will bite and feed on other mammals including man, and similarly the dog will occasionally and temporarily harbour fleas from other animals (e.g. cats, rabbits and hedgehogs). These temporary visitors are also likely to try human skin as a food supply as well. The only real way to identify these fleas is to ask a parasitologist or veterinarian to identify them, but experience shows that when dog fleas are on their preferred host (i.e. the dog) they are not easy to see unless present in large numbers! So if you do see a flea on your dog it is usually a "foreign" flea, which it has picked up from another mammal, and which is more likely to be seen on the outer coat. (A survey in the UK in 1994 showed that most fleas on dogs were in fact cat fleas!) Traditionally, fleas are a summer-time menace, but central heating in homes has ensured that the flea is now an all-year-round problem, surviving the winter happily in the carpets and crevices of the house. Fleas only live part-time on the dog, to feed and lay eggs. The eggs and the immature larvae they produce and the adult fleas all can and do survive for many months off the dog quite naturally. Additionally, adult fleas can live for many months without feeding. So treating a dog for fleas is only part of the exercise when infestation is found. We also need to treat the house or kennel too. Vacuum cleaning helps and washing bedding or burning old bedding is essential. Finally, environmental sprays and fumigants are now readily available from veterinarians.

For the dog there are a variety of treatments and preventatives. Shampoos and washes containing insecticides are commonplace for treating infestations. There are also aerosol sprays for treatment and long-term control. More recent preparations allow just a few drops of product to be applied to the back of the neck giving several weeks of effective prevention. Other control measures include impregnated flea collars, and now there are also oral compounds available which mean flea treatments can be given by mouth or in the food. Your vet is the best person to ask for advice if you have a problem but all of these methods will work if used correctly. Just remember these are all potent compounds, so use them as directed by the label.

How do you know your dog has fleas? Some dogs are allergic to flea bites, which can cause scratching and sore patches on the skin. Fleas also leave "flea dirts" in the coat which are dried digested blood excreted by the fleas. A fine comb will also drag live fleas out of the coat so they can be seen. Most people discover fleas accidentally while grooming or petting their dog or when they are bitten themselves.

Fleas can also act as vectors for the tapeworm Dipylidium caninum. The immature tapeworm infects the flea and upsets its behaviour and this allows the dog to consume the flea whilst licking itself and thus the tapeworm infects the dog (see below for more information on tapeworms). So this is another good reason to keep fleas to a minimum.

LICE: These are not so common in dogs, but they do occur. They live their whole life on the dog; even their eggs are glued to the hairs. Therefore lice are more easily eradicated using similar products to those used for fleas.

TICKS: These are usually sheep or cattle ticks which will attach themselves very strongly to the skin to suck blood. They are unsightly and often can be, at first, mistaken for small growths or tumours. Ticks can be difficult to remove without leaving the head of the tick embedded in the skin. This can cause a small abscess to form. There are several home remedies ranging from burning the tick with a lighted cigarette (one I would not recommend for your health and the dog's safety) to soaking in alcohol. Also many flea sprays work quite well too. However, if you are in doubt, let your vet remove the ticks for you. The most worrying thing with ticks is their ability to transmit disease and in particular Lyme Disease (a bacterial infection).

Ticks are most likely to be picked up during countryside walks in areas where cattle and sheep graze, so always inspect your dog's skin for these parasites after a day in the country.

MANGE: There are several types of mange, all caused by different mange mites. Hopefully, you will never see the principal types of mange, namely sarcoptic and demodectic.

SARCOPTIC MANGE: This disease is caused by the mange mite Sarcoptes scabeii which lives in burrows in the surface of the skin. Characteristically, it is seen in puppies and young dogs, causing crusty areas on the ears and face or on the forelegs. This needs veterinary advice and there are medications which can help rid the dog of sarcoptic mange. However, very heavy infestations can become untreatable.

DEMODECTIC MANGE: This disease can be more serious. Demodex mites live in the hair roots and can be found in many normal dogs. However, some dogs have an apparent reduced immunity to this mite and the infection can then develop. It is often seen repeatedly in certain individual dogs when they are stressed or ill for other reasons. Infection gives bald areas almost anywhere and they can appear quite insignificant at first. It may start as a small bald patch and spread quite rapidly. Historically, it has proven quite difficult to treat demodex, especially when the infestation is generalised over large areas of the body. Some of the newer antiparasitic products can clear the infection, but it often recurs, probably because of the link with poor immunity. As it does seem related to an immune system deficiency, demodex tends to be familial (i.e. seen in related dogs). Therefore as a general rule it is not advisable to breed from afflicted individuals.

EAR MITES: Ear canker, as it is often known, can be caused initially by ear mites, normally caught from an infected cat. The inflamed ear often gets infected with bacteria and other organisms and sets up the classic "canker" situation. Treatment with suitable ear drops at an early stage will usually rectify the situation. Of course, veterinary advice should be taken. Ear infections will be generally prevented by routine cleaning of the ears.

MOVING DANDRUFF: So called because the dander, when brushed out of the coat and observed closely, appears to move, due to the presence of mites in the debris. This mite causes very few symptoms in most dogs except for a scurfy coat. Occasionally it may become so profuse the dog scratches or licks excessively, producing a sore bald patch on the skin. Often overlooked as a parasite it is often called the rabbit fur mite because this is one of its hosts. It can be easily removed by bathing in suitable antiparasitic shampoos, but it can also be difficult to eradicate from a kennel of affected dogs.

INTERNAL PARASITES
Roundworms and tapeworms are the principal internal parasites which infect dogs. As a general rule the roundworms are capable of causing far more damage to the dog than tapeworms, which are considered to be very efficient parasites living off their host without causing very much effect at all. However, they are both unsightly, and we would rather our dogs did not have them. But, like all parasites, it is a fact of life that the Rottweiler you own will harbour a few worms.

Every puppy is born infected with the roundworm Toxocara canis. This is an important parasite, as the young larvae of the worm are a small, but highly publicised, risk to human health. Whatever the variety of worm, it is best to assume your dog is carrying them. Therefore routine regular treatment is to be recommended. Your vet can advise you of specific local problems with worms and recommend suitable worming regimes, but generally worm your Rottweiler at least twice per year and preferably every three months. Use recommended compounds and be sure the wormer you use will kill parasites effectively. Not all products available are effective against roundworms and tapeworms, and some species of worms require very special drugs.

ROUNDWORMS: Toxocara canis is probably the most well-known roundworm to infest dogs. It is present in the tissues of *all* dogs as dormant immature worms (larvae). In late pregnancy these migrate to the uterus to infect foetal puppies before they are born! Therefore *all* puppies start life infected with these worms and after three weeks start to contaminate their play area with thousands of eggs in their faeces. The problem is that these eggs will produce larval worms which can infect humans as well as dogs. Simple hygiene, like washing your hands before eating, would largely prevent this risk but, children particularly, can be a little lax in such personal hygiene. The larval worms swallowed in this way have on rare occasions found their way to the eye and been confused with a particularly nasty form of cancer. So press stories about worms causing blindness are the result, and consequently, dogs get bad publicity.

So regular worming treatments are essential to allay fears of this risk to human health. In fact regular worming of puppies, every three weeks, with *effective* worming products can minimise this risk most efficiently. It is also possible to reduce the prenatal infection of puppies using long-term treatments for the bitch in late pregnancy. It must be stressed that the risk of Toxocara worms causing problems in humans is greatly exaggerated, but we as dog owners must ensure we regularly worm our dogs and so reduce this risk to as close to zero as possible.

HEARTWORM: There are many types of roundworm found in dogs but most live in the bowel to reproduce. The routine treatments recommended in this chapter for adult dogs will control most of the common roundworms. However, the heartworm is an exception.

This parasite lives in the heart (actually inside the right-hand chamber of the heart) and the major artery to the lungs. Heartworms can cause significant problems to the dog, the symptoms being confused with other heart diseases. It is found worldwide but tends to be found in specific areas, usually rural communities, where snails (the intermediate host) are found. Once infection is established in an area it is difficult to control. However, there are modern wormers which are effective treatments and routine use in affected areas is advocated.

TAPEWORMS: These are relatively harmless parasites in the dog, but some of these parasites have dire consequences for the intermediate host and sometimes this can be man. They can be recognised in dogs by the appearance of white or cream-coloured tapeworm segments in the faeces or occasionally stuck to the coat around the anus. These may appear as flat "worms" which can be seen to move or as "rice grains". Infection is obtained from eating raw infected offal or, as in the case of Dipylidium caninum, by consuming infected fleas which act as intermediate hosts. Feeding raw offal is a risk and so strict adherence to cooked meats and/or prepared commercial foods should prevent infection, except for D. caninum which is transmitted through the agency of the flea. Routine treatments with suitable products, however, will keep such tapeworm infestations under control.

AVOIDING ACCIDENTS

So far, we have discussed diseases, but what about accidents and injuries? Obviously we cannot avoid all such events but we can try to prevent the common incidents from happening.

PUPPIES: Eight-week-old puppies are fond of chewing. However, they are occasionally electrocuted by chewing through a trailing power flex, a source of great attraction for youngsters.

Be careful to ensure that toys are robust enough to stand chewing. Swallowed pieces of plastic or rubber can cause problems in the stomach or bowel. Keep pups out of the kitchen when cooking. Falling over a sleeping puppy or spilling a hot pan of soup over it will potentially damage human and Rottweiler alike. Be careful of stairs; use gates or doors to stop puppies falling down them. Ground-level swimming pools and ponds are also a danger to inquisitive pups. They often swim instinctively but, if they cannot get out, they tire and drown!

ADULTS: Adults occasionally suffer the same accidents as puppies. However, they are also exposed to a different set of risks. Travelling in cars is best done in a cage, or behind a strong dog guard. This is not cruel; it is commonsense. In an accident your dog is safer in a cage, less likely to jump out of the car, and less likely to hurtle towards the front if you stop suddenly. A cage could save your dog's life and yours! When playing "catch and fetch", use a ball which cannot get stuck in the throat. This does happen, and a choking dog is very frightening and the results can be deadly. Throwing sticks can be dangerous too; chose a solid one and be careful. Never assume your dog is obedient near a road; always use a lead.

POISONS: A special word about poisons: your house and garden are full of potential poisons for dogs and they cannot read labels. Be careful with weedkillers and slug bait. Know which of your plants are toxic. Beware of rat and mouse poisons. Your dog will eat all these things with gusto, and many of them have no antidote.

GENERAL COMMENTS ON HEALTH

How should you react when your dog is sick? Should you call the vet immediately? Can you do things yourself? The answer will largely depend on your experience, but below are a few general tips and suggestions. Remember, though, if you are unsure it will never do harm to ask for advice!

VOMITING AND DIARRHOEA: Dogs do tend to eat first and worry about what it was afterwards. So it is not surprising that occasionally an upset stomach is the result. Therefore a single instance of vomiting or a loose stool should not necessarily send you rushing to the vet, especially if the dog otherwise appears well. Withholding food for twenty-fours hours, allowing only small quantities of water to drink and then feeding white meat and rice will often correct minor gastric upsets. However, if your dog is obviously ill or if diarrhoea or vomiting persist, seek help.

LAMENESS: Rottweilers do have a breed tendency for joint problems but this is not always going to be the cause of lameness. Always check the foot on the lame leg; often a thorn in the pad or a cut pad may be the problem. Check the nails for damage too.

EXERCISE: Your Rottweiler will need exercise to keep fit, but do not work hard on fitness until the dog is mature. For the first twelve to eighteen months the amount of exercise needs to be strictly controlled.

THE FACTS OF LIFE
Boys and girls were thankfully made different and there are a few things to be said about this difference and the on-going health of your Rottweiler.

BITCHES: Heats or seasons will start at seven to twelve months of age, and bitches generally come into season at five to six monthly intervals. If you are not a breeder you will need to think about neutering, as this will be raised by your veterinarian. There are advantages to spaying but there are some disadvantages too. Spaying will mean no accidental pregnancy, but if this is likely to happen you may not have chosen the right breed, or you should improve on your dog management. Another advantage of spaying, as far as the owner of the bitch is concerned, is that bitches lose quite a lot of blood during heat; not significant for the bitch but it can be messy in the house. Spaying obviously stops this. Neutered bitches also suffer less from cancers of the mammary gland and cannot get pyometra (an infection of the uterus).

MALES: Male aggression can be reduced in castrates, but this can also be controlled with hormone treatment. Additionally, castrates do not get prostate trouble in older life. However, castration does not guarantee good behaviour and is no substitute for effective training. There may be other factors not included here, but do not decide this issue quickly. Take advice from breeders as well as your veterinarian before taking this extremely final step.

THE ELDERLY DOG
Rottweilers should reach ages of at least nine or ten years. However, in later life they will slow up and they need slightly more attention at this time. The following examples are given to help the owners of older dogs cope with their companion's declining abilities. The Rottweiler is a strong, powerful dog, and it is a pity if a dog becomes suspect in temperament because we humans have failed to cater for declining faculties in our friend and companion.

EYESIGHT: A Rottweiler's eyesight can fail for a variety of reasons. For example, cataracts can occur and the increasing opacity of the lenses diminishes sight. Such impairment of vision can mean the dog becomes unsettled when the familiar pattern of furniture is changed or the garden is rearranged. They may become more nervous of approaching people if they are not sure who it is. Fortunately a dog uses its senses of hearing and smell more than we do and these often compensate for defective vision, but make sure you and your family and friends know how to approach your dog if it loses its sight. Speak to the dog before you approach it in order to allay fears, and also ensure that the dog is not going to stumble over a casually discarded garden rake, or some other item.

HEARING DEFECTS: Loss of hearing ability is probably more serious to a dog than sight defects. Being surprised by a human patting you on the head as you are sleeping is shock enough, but often sight and smell do not give quick enough reassurance to the dog in these situations and then accidents happen. A deaf dog will no longer obey verbal commands – so be sensitive to this and be more careful when out in public areas.

URINARY INCONTINENCE: This is a problem more often seen in bitches. It can be due to poor kidney function or other ageing changes which have changed the ability of the bitch to control her bladder. Restricting water late at night may help, but be sure this is advisable in the case of medical conditions. Be sure to give your bitch every opportunity to pass urine last thing before retiring, to help as much as possible. There are also some good products which help incontinence in bitches which your vet can prescribe, so do not be frightened to discuss incontinence problems with your practitioner.

EXERCISE TOLERANCE: As bodies age and hearts become less efficient, fitness declines and the dog takes less exercise. Joints in large dogs, like the Rottweiler, tend to degenerate too, adding to the general reduction in the dog's willingness to take part in physical activity.

Obesity does not help this and feeding practices should change to adapt for falling exercise levels so that excessive weight does not further aggravate the situation. Also, check with your veterinarian why your Rottweiler is less active. Joint pain can be alleviated and heart function can be improved, and now products exist which will generally improve your dog's circulation and health. The simple message is, pay more attention to elderly dogs to ensure they are not suffering unnecessary pain or limitation to their life, and help them live active lives right up to the end.

Chapter Twenty

BREED ASSOCIATED DISEASES

There are a number of diseases which are commonly seen in the Rottweiler which deserve to be discussed individually. These diseases are possibly inherited as genetic traits but because the evidence of inheritance is circumstantial in many instances, it is more accurate to refer to these diseases as 'breed associated'. However, in each case, where possible, the evidence for a genetic cause of the disease is discussed.

OSTEOCHONDRITITIS DISSECANS
Osteochondritis Dissecans (OCD) is a defect in articular cartilage (which is the cartilage which lines the bone surfaces of a joint) and is classically seen as a defect in the shoulder joint and more recently, with increasing frequency, in the elbow. It has also been diagnosed as affecting the stifle and hock joints. OCD manifests as a thickened area of cartilage on the joint surface which cracks and eventually the area will lift up as a flap of cartilage on the surface of the joint. The bone under this cartilage flap will be inflamed and eroded. In time this cartilage flap may detach and the lesion will then heal spontaneously, but whilst the flap is in place the joint will be painful and lameness will result. However, many cases are often left undiagnosed for some months or years because the lameness can be intermittent, which often persuades owners and their veterinary surgeons that the problem is improving.

ELBOW DISEASE
In the Rottweiler the commonest joint affected is the elbow joint where the term OCD is not strictly correct in all cases, especially where the defect is not in the joint cartilage but in surrounding areas of ossification in the bone. There has, therefore, been some discussion about the correct terminology for 'osteochondrosis' of the elbow joint and, although 'Elbow Dysplasia' has found some advocates, the general term being used internationally is 'Elbow Disease'. However, forgetting the arguments around this issue of terminology, we are left with the fact that diseases of the Rottweiler elbow are probably the most worrying problem in the breed.

DIAGNOSIS: Elbow disease is characterised by lameness in the affected forelimb. This is usually first noticed in puppies between four and nine months of age and examination reveals pain in the elbow joint. The condition is often bilateral and so lameness may appear in both forelegs over time. The affected dog may even appear to be relatively sound occasionally where the pain in both elbows is equal! However, close examination will reveal that the elbows are restricted in their normal range of use and length of stride will be shortened. There is a strong sex bias, with the incidence in males being significantly more than in females. Radiographs may show changes in the bones of the joint which can lead the radiologists to confirm the diagnosis, but this is not always an obvious defect to see on an X-ray and very often surgery is the only way to confirm or refute the presence of disease. In fact, there are four conditions which can cause

Elbow Disease in Rottweilers and in some cases two or more conditions will co-exist in the same elbow. The classic OCD lesion, described earlier, is one of the possible causes of Elbow Disease. The other three possibilities are all defects in the cartilage surrounding 'centres of ossification'. When the elbow develops in the foetus it grows from a number of 'centres of ossification'. Each of these islands of developing bone is surrounded by cartilage, and their growth and fusion form the eventual structure of elbow joint anatomy. Sometimes the normal process of ossification (which slowly replaces the cartilage with bone) does not work and then parts of the elbow joint do not fuse properly with the rest of the bone. These bone fragments can eventually break away from the major bones and the result is loose fragments of bone and an unstable joint. Ultimately, left alone, there may be some healing and resolution, but the inflammation that the instability causes results in osteoarthritis and this can lead to further pain, to lameness and certainly to a reduction in the range of movement for the joint.

SURGICAL REPAIR: If Elbow Disease is diagnosed at an early stage, before major arthritic change has occurred, surgery can be expected to be reasonably successful. Surgery to remove the flap of cartilage from cases of OCD and fragments of cartilage which may be present in the joint will produce good responses. Where there is failed fusion of 'ossification centres', removal of the fragments causing inflammatory response or fixation of larger fragments with surgical screws to stabilise the joint can produce an improvement in around 75 per cent of cases. However, the extent of the improvement will depend on the amount of damage and inflammation which has already occurred, and on the amount of stability that surgery can impart to the joint.

In summary, surgery can be useful in cases diagnosed early and it can be expected to produce a good response in around 70-80 per cent of these cases. However, a good response does not mean a perfect cure and some residual lameness is to be expected. In chronic cases where changes in the bone are already strongly evident on X-ray, surgery is very much less likely to improve the situation.

CAUSES: It is not clear why this disease complex of the elbows afflicts Rottweilers. There are other breeds which can be affected and these are all large breeds (e.g. Retrievers and the Bernese Mountain Dog), so it would seem to be a problem associated with large size. It has been suggested that an excess of dietary calcium is to be blamed and others say vitamin C plays a part in the process. The question that everyone wants answered is the role of hereditary factors and, to date, there is no proof to support a genetic link, but it has to be said it is suspected by many. If there is a genetic link it is not likely to be a simple and highly predictable situation.

PREVENTION: The lameness induced by this disease complex is clearly not compatible with a full and healthy life. It is a problem that starts in puppyhood and with long-term consequences which logically require something to be done to prevent it occurring, if at all possible. Despite the doubt surrounding the mode of inheritance of Elbow Disease, it is advisable not to breed from an affected dog. While it may not be an inherited defect, it is at least likely that an affected dog has characteristics which pre-dispose the dog to suffering from Elbow Disease, and therefore in the absence of better advice or knowledge, it would be foolish to propagate these characteristics further. *It is possible to diagnose overt cases of Elbow Disease using X-rays, and thus assist breeders to avoid breeding from affected dogs.* Radiography would need to be used for screening for affected elbows, as some dogs do not show serious clinical signs until they are several years old, or where the disease is bilateral symptoms may be masked, or the extent of the disease may be slight so that lameness is not even noticed. Therefore it has been suggested that an internationally accepted health scheme be devised which makes the use of radiographic screening of mature dogs to assist breeders in selecting suitable breeding stock that has a very low incidence of the disease. This screening would grade the changes seen in elbows and identify those Rottweilers that would be suitable for breeding.

OTHER FACTORS: There is also sufficient evidence to suggest that the calcium/phosporus balance in the diet may play a part in the disease process. It has been said that it is the major factor, but it would be foolish to ignore the potential genetic causes in favour of a dietary theory. However, such theories on diet do justify paying attention to the amount of dietary supplementation given to young growing Rottweilers. It is common practice in large breeds to supplement calcium in the belief that this will help the development of strong bones. This supplementation can disrupt the balance between calcium and phosphorus, which is essential for bone growth. It would, therefore, be reasonable for owners to avoid excessive and unbalanced supplementation of diets. If in doubt, the advice of a veterinarian or nutritionist should be sought.

In addition, weight and exercise will certainly play a part in the severity of the disease and excessive exercise of very young dogs should be avoided. In fact, all exercise should be strictly controlled in Rottweilers until they are eighteen months to two years of age. Clearly, excess weight will also influence the future integrity of the joints and if there is a case for ensuring weight is not excessive, the Rottweiler qualifies for attention in this regard.

OCD OF OTHER JOINTS: As stated previously, OCD can affect several joints and the shoulder, stifle and hock joints of Rottweilers have been reported as affected with OCD. As with the elbow, early diagnosis and surgery carry the best hope of a satisfactory resolution to the problem. Probably the shoulder joint carries the best chance of full recovery and even in untreated cases, some can improve remarkably on six weeks of rest. However, generally, surgery is to be recommended for cases of OCD of the shoulder. As with elbow disease, the condition is often bilateral,which can confuse the early recognition of the problem.

Hocks and stifles respond slightly less well to surgery on average, but this still remains the best option. Fortunately, cases involving hocks and stifles are still relatively rare.

HIP DYSPLASIA (HD)

Hip Dysplasia is an inherited disease of the hip joints; it usually affects both hips to a similar degree and causes variable amounts of lameness. It is probably *not* the most significant disease in Rottweilers despite its high public profile. Hip Dysplasia is also, potentially, the most misunderstood disease in dogs today! It does have a significant genetic basis. It is thought to be inherited through the agency of several genes (polygenic), which makes its predictability very difficult. In plain language this means that using parents with good hips is more likely to produce offspring with good hips, but it is not necessarily a guaranteed process! As the problem does have a high profile within the world of dogs and with the veterinary profession, it is pertinent to discuss it at some length.

DIAGNOSIS : The normal hip joint is described as a ball and socket joint. The ball is formed by the head of the femur (or thigh bone) and the socket by a depression in the pelvis called the acetabulum. The joint is intended to be a snug fit, and rotation of the 'ball' within the socket permits a wide freedom of movement of the hip and therefore of the hind-limb.

Hip Dysplasia describes a condition whereby the 'ball' is no longer a snug fit in the socket and the joint is loose or lax. This laxity permits the 'ball' to wear upon the edge of the socket and the joint reacts to this with inflammation and thickening of the surrounding tissues. In time, more bone is laid down around the socket in an attempt to deepen the acetabulum and improve function, and the abnormal wear on the 'ball' tends to remodel its shape. The end result is arthritis and deformation of the joint. Clearly the laxity is capable of many degrees of variance –

from very lax, where the joint is effectively permanently dislocated, to slightly lax, where there is little change to normal function. Logically, there is a range of changes in joint structure which relate to the amount of laxity, but the relationship of lameness to the extent of dysplasia is not so easy to predict. It would be reasonable to expect that the worst affected dogs would exhibit the most lameness, but this is not necessarily the case.

Remodelling of the hip is an attempt by the body to stabilise the defective joint. Other external factors (e.g. body weight, diet and exercise) play a part in the remodelling of the hip, and so each affected dog will react uniquely to the laxity in its hips, and, because of this, dogs may or may not exhibit lameness. As puppies, affected dogs can have discomfort in rising or sitting, whereas older dogs may exhibit changes in their hind gait or movement. Yet none of these symptoms is reliable in assessing the magnitude of the problem; they only draw attention to its possible existence. Therefore, the only reasonably reliable measurement of Hip Dysplasia is obtained by radiographing young adults over one year of age. Some workers have argued that young puppies, on manual examination, can be diagnosed as dysplastic at a few months old, but there is sufficient disagreement between this system and subsequent radiography to cast doubt on physical examination ever becoming a realistic method of assessment.

We are left, therefore, with the radiographic process, which, because of the need to position the patient accurately and on its back, requires a general anaesthetic to achieve satisfactory results and to remove undue risk to the radiographic staff. Understandably, some owners are wary of anaesthesia and its small element of risk, and this fact alone probably prevents many dogs being screened for Hip Dysplasia.

TREATMENT: The fundamental instability of the joint cannot be reversed. However, some veterinarians claim that removing a small muscle (pectineus) on the inside of the thigh will improve the function of the hip, and reduce pain and secondary arthritic changes. In severely affected animals hip replacement surgery has been performed, but for the vast majority the treatment is symptomatic. Anti-inflammatory drugs will help with the control of any pain, and yet it should be remembered that the vast majority of dysplastic dogs show very little evidence of pain. Therefore, treatment is often limited to maintenance of a sensible body weight which will not aggravate the condition, and *regular, controlled* exercise to ensure that mobility is maintained. There are many working dogs which are good examples of how well a dysplastic dog can perform.

CONTROL SCHEMES: The control of hip dysplasia is made difficult by the fact that its inheritance involves several genes and that expression of the disease, as visible radiographic clinical signs, depends upon a combination of genetic and environmental factors. The environmental factors involved are probably body weight, growth rate and possibly level of exercise, but we should not lose sight of the fact that even if we were able to provide the optimum environment for pups, we would not have removed the underlying genetic cause of Hip Dysplasia. Therefore, it has to be accepted that breeding '*normal*' dogs together is more likely to yield long-term benefits in the control of Hip Dysplasia than environmental changes. It bears repeating that Hip Dysplasia has a polygenic nature and that '*normal*' dogs can produce normal and abnormal hips in their offspring, although the odds are in favour of '*normality*'. The converse situation is also true; '*normal*' offspring can result from '*abnormal*' dogs. This type of odds assessment sits uncomfortably in the minds of most breeders, probably because it is not a straightforward answer. So, control methods have tended, quite rightly, to focus on the radiographic assessment of hips and this data has been used to select breeding stock which is '*normal*'. Before we consider the use of the italics on the word 'normal', let us briefly consider the use of scoring or grading systems used to evaluate hips using radiography. Many countries have grading systems but they are not necessarily compatible with each other.

The USA has a system run by the Orthopaedic Foundation for Animals (OFA); in the UK it is the British Veterinary Association and the Kennel Club who administer a Hip Dysplasia health scheme; in Europe the FCI has made good efforts to standardise Hip Dysplasia assessments across mainland Europe; and schemes also exist in Australia and New Zealand. All the schemes supply data on the hip conformation of dogs assessed, but it is recognised that progress has been slow in improving hip scores overall.

CRUCIATE LIGAMENT RUPTURE

The stifle joint (the equivalent hind-limb joint to the human knee) is held together by a number of ligaments and muscles. As the hind-limb is chiefly used to propel the dog forwards, it is not surprising that the stifle joint is under strain and that, occasionally, rupture of ligaments can occur. The cruciate ligaments are found in the centre of the joint and are so named because they cross over each other as they keep the two sides of the joint together. They perform the function of stabilising the joint during movement.

Rupture of one or both ligaments can occur, but it is usually the anterior (cranial) cruciate ligament which is most frequently damaged. The result is an unstable stifle joint. This instability permits the lower joint surface, on the top of the shin bone (tibia), to move forward when stress is placed on the knee. Such instability produces inflammation in the joint and the joint thickens as a result. In the longer term, if nothing is done, the inflammation turns to fibrosis and arthritis. The joint may stabilise to a degree. However, lameness will continue, albeit at a reduced level.

Cruciate rupture is caused by trauma; a fast turn or any action placing strain on one stifle can cause it. The dog will be acutely lame afterwards and, if left untreated, will slowly start to use the leg over a period of weeks or months. Lameness, therefore, is a persistent feature. Cruciate rupture can happen at any age or to any dog, but it is seen most frequently in the larger breeds whose stifles are under the greatest strain. Unfortunately, it frequently follows that the other stifle is also subsequently damaged, as the dog favours the originally affected leg, thus placing extra strain on the uninjured limb.

There are a variety of surgical methods available to treat this condition, most of which utilise a ligament implant, usually a strip of skin or tendon, inserted through or around the joint. The technical details are largely irrelevant in this book, but the surgery should be considered a major operation. Results can be expected to be good where little arthritic change has occurred, and if the joint is satisfactorily stabilised by the surgery. In many cases some residual lameness should be expected due to chronic arthritis developing in response to the injury.

The Rottweiler is prone to rupturing cruciate ligaments and some have speculated it may have an hereditary basis. However, no concrete proof is available. It is clear that excessive weight and lack of fitness may play a part in the incidence of this condition.

BONE TUMOURS

Osteosarcomas are one of the most malignant cancers that veterinarians have to deal with. In terms of incidence, osteosarcomas are more commonly seen in large breeds of dog and the Rottweiler is one of the breeds affected. They are commonly found in the long bones of the fore and hind legs. They are an aggressive and destructive cancer which can be painful once advanced, especially where pathological fractures occur as the tumour weakens the bone structure of the limb. The affected dog will initially show mild lameness and a swelling, usually close to a shoulder or stifle joint. The growth and invasion of the tumour is rapid, and most affected dogs will die, or be destroyed on humane grounds, within six months of diagnosis.

Treatment of osteosarcomas has been attempted by amputating the affected limb. However, because this tumour is highly malignant, cells from the tumour will rapidly spread to other tissues in the body and usually in advance of any surgery. Secondary tumours will rapidly develop in the rest of the body, even after amputation has removed the primary growth. Modern treatments with chemotherapy have been claimed to be effective in some cases, but controversy exists over the potential cost and morality of such treatment. For the average case the outlook is very bleak, and euthanasia is probably the most likely outcome.

The fact that Rottweilers are strongly represented in numbers of dogs suffering this cancer can lead to suspicions of genetic involvement, but none has been proven to date. Rapidly growing dogs, like the large breeds, are thought to be more at risk from tumours of this type.

EYE DISEASES
The Rottweiler is not commonly a breed which is considered to suffer from eye disease, but there have been a number of reported cases of Entropion and Retinal Dysplasia. These are the principal eye conditions, but isolated reports from around the world indicate there have been cases of Inherited Cataract, Micropthalmia (small eyes) and Progressive Retinal Atrophy (PRA). However, as these latter diseases are apparently rare in the Rottweiler they are not covered in this chapter.

ENTROPION
There is evidence to suggest that in some breeds Entropion is an inherited defect of the eyelids. It manifests itself as an in-turning of the eyelids so that the eyelashes tend to abrade the surface of the eye. The resulting inflammation and irritation often cause the dog to squint, which further intensifies the problem. Some cases can be induced by a conjunctivitis, but generally the incidence of Entropion is indicative of poor eye conformation.
SURGERY: A relatively simple surgical operation will correct the defect, but if the afflicted dog is subsequently used to breed from, it is highly likely that the defect will be seen in some of the offspring. Therefore, it is advised that affected dogs are not used for stud or brood purposes.
PREVENTION: Selecting dogs for breeding with good eye conformation will help prevent this problem. Dogs with drooping lower eyelids or small eyes, which lead to loose eyelids, are thought to encourage a predisposition to Entropion.

RETINAL DYSPLASIA
The retina of the eye is the lining of cells inside the eyeball which are sensitive to light. In other words, it is the layer of the eye that permits vision. Retinal Dysplasia manifests itself as detached areas of retina, which interfere with vision. Detachment will mean blindness, and the condition can also be associated with cataract formation. It is considered to be inherited. An autosomal recessive gene is suspected, which basically means that a dog can be apparently normal but a carrier of the condition. However, as the Rottweiler tends to suffer from the multifocal form, this assumption may not be accurate. Retinal Dysplasia normally causes blindness in puppies, but the multifocal form can be diagnosed later in life. Therefore the consequences are more serious for breeding animals which have already produced litters. Blindness is a serious consequence, and any occurrence of Retinal Dysplasia should result in the culling of affected puppies and removal of the parents from breeding programmes. Many countries have eye examination schemes, and use should be made of these where eye problems are seen. Generally, the Rottweiler has good eyes, but vigilance must be maintained to ensure this track record is maintained.

DEMODECTIC MANGE
In some parts of Europe Demodectic Mange seems to be prevalent in some breed lines. Further information on this disease is available in the chapter on health, and there it is stated that Demodex is frequently associated with a poor immune response, and this condition is often found in offspring from affected bitches. It is advisable not to breed from affected dogs.